# SIMPLE FLAVOURS

*Geoff Slattery*

# SIMPLE FLAVOURS

*Australian Home Cooking*

THE TEXT PUBLISHING COMPANY
MELBOURNE AUSTRALIA

The Text Publishing Company Pty Ltd
220 Clarendon Street
East Melbourne Victoria 3002
Australia

First published 1991
Reprinted 1991, 1992

Edited by Jane Angus
Illustrations by
Katerina Plastaras and Chong Weng-Ho
Designed by Chong Weng-Ho
Recipes tested by Sally Cuthbertson
Printed and bound at Griffin Press, Adelaide
Typeset by the Text Media Group, Melbourne

National Library of Australia Cataloguing-in-Publication data:
Slattery, Geoff.
Simple flavours: Australian home cooking

Includes index.
ISBN 1 86372 202 5

1. Cookery, Australian.
I. Title
641.5994

# THANKS

THE FAMILY: Forget cooking for a moment. Without my wife, Sally, there would be nothing. An aimless youth suddenly crystallised when she entered my life. And then came Andrew, Kate and Sarah. This book is put together entirely for them. It is of family, by family, for family — as is cooking.

NOW TO FOOD AND COOKING. It was Sally who first led the way. Then we worked together, then I led, and she led, all the way up the mountain. In the end we stand together, criticising each other, fighting over who cleans up at the end. She once put a theory before me which makes me laugh, and makes her shudder whenever I repeat it in public — and you can't get more public than this: 'People who don't like food and cooking couldn't like sex.'

COOKS AND CUSTOMERS: Chris Philip, Gail Halsall, Lesley Russell, Gerald Douglas, John Flack, Janine Ballantyne, Maria Wray, Denis Lucey, John Moran and John Hurlston

THE PROFESSIONALS: Walter Bourke and Iain Hewitson

THE LOOK OF THE BOOK: Chong Weng-Ho

THE WINE NOTES: My close friend and brother-in-law Hugh Cuthbertson, Education Manager at Mildara and independent wine-maker. The best wine to drink with food is the one you have in your cupboard, but if you seriously need to choose wine to match a special meal, then follow Hugh's advice.

THE RADIO: Doug Aiton put me on air sight unheard, and has been putting up with my 'wisdom' and biases ever since. I don't think there would be this book without him, and his faithful and wonderful ABC audience.

AND ... My mother and father, who instilled in me the values of loyalty, respect, commitment and selflessness, with varying degrees of success. This book is dedicated to them. I only wish my father could be here to see it.

# CONTENTS

# FOREWORD

Where do you begin to describe Geoff Slattery and his constant, occasionally frenzied search for perfection? A former sports editor whose greatest joy after deadline was to munch happily on a clove of garlic? A writer who can weave into a story about couscous a sporting snapshot of modern life. A father, food critic and former restaurateur who tasted the perfect fruit cake at a local fête and launched a city-wide manhunt in search of its anonymous creator?

His guises might be varied, but all are inspired by the same spirit, and all of them appear in this, his first book. Michael Leunig, celebrated cartoonist and poet, who has worked with Geoff at the *Age* and the *Sunday Age* and whose works hung in Slattery's restaurant, describes his long-time colleague as 'an ANZAC of the table. There is a courage about his work. If there be a mythology to the Australian character, then Geoff has it. It is not crude and patriotic, it is a robust joy that he brings into his food. He is not stifled by his education; he brings it outside into the Australian sunshine.'

Where did he begin? Not many of his colleagues know that Geoff Slattery began his working life, at seventeen, in a Melbourne accountant's office. However, this attempt at an ordered professional life was shortlived. A year later, in 1971, he entered newspapers, joining *Truth* as a racing cadet journalist.

Geoff became a sports writer for the *Australian* in 1977, before crossing to the *Age* in 1979. At the *Age* he enjoyed a distinguished four-year tenure as a sportswriter and columnist, winning the National Press Club's major sports feature writing award in 1981 for a story on Jack 'Captain Blood' Dyer.

I was a junior sportswriter at the other end of town with the Melbourne *Herald* when, in 1983, a colleague hung up his hotline and announced with some mirth that 'Slatts' had quit the *Age* to open up a sandwich shop in King Street. How wrong the messenger was, and how wrong we were to laugh.

But we weren't the only ones.

'He was buying meat from my butcher', recalls Iain Hewitson, perhaps the most successful restaurant entrepreneur in his field. 'I didn't know him but my butcher told me about this sportswriter from the *Age* who was opening up this restaurant. I said: "Well, he'll last about three minutes." We all said it. But it was a very brave thing to do, done in sheer ignorance, of course, and Geoff was very pugnacious. His restaurant was very good and Geoff became a sort of jack-of-all-trades in the kitchen and the dining room, with no experience, and we all stopped sneering.'

There were others from the turbulent world of AFL football who regretted his departure.

'He was the best Australian Rules football writer in Australia,' says one of the sport's most enduring gurus, Graeme Richmond.

Journalistic colleagues, of course, still enjoy a laugh at Geoff's eccentricities. Peter Smark, senior columnist for the Fairfax Group, between chortles, has this to say:

'I think Geoff was very upset that only about four episodes of Fawlty Towers were ever made. So he was determined to carry on the tradition. The unknown factor about eating at Slattery's was not the standard of the food, which was always excellent, but the state of the liver of the proprietor. If he was in a bad mood he would abuse more customers per square metre than Basil Fawlty.'

My memories, from a brief tenure as a Saturday night waitress at Slattery's, are a little different. Geoff controlled his ship totally; he toiled, he tasted, he listened, he gave orders, he thought, he read and he wrote — but he never yelled. In the restaurant, as in the sports department, teamwork was all.

Not that he ever stopped writing in those restaurant days.

'He wrote a very good article about his first night at the restaurant,' says Iain Hewitson, 'and the ice-cream, which he had made so often at home, which didn't set. It's happened to all of us of course, but he's one of the few who wasn't too embarrassed to admit it. I respect him a lot more as a food critic for that reason.'

'He was the first person to say to me: "Go out and read something, and learn from it"' says leading Australian chef Greg Brown. 'He is an academic chef. He is tireless in his reading, and if there's an obscure chef doing something new in Italy, he'll know about it. Geoff's about the only food critic you can trust to transfer his views to the plate. We disagree on a whole range of issues, but he backs up all his arguments with examples and he executes those examples.'

'He proceeds from a position of goodwill,' says Stephanie Alexander, the renowned food writer and restaurateur. 'He really wants to have a good time and he never sets out to be harsh and funny like some critics. I've been on the wrong side of his reviews, but I'm comfortable with that because I believe he is fair. I don't mind having a disagreement with him — and we've had a few over the years — because he is intelligent. And if he tastes something he likes, he is very generous in his praise.'

This is a view shared by the sports writers who worked under Geoff Slattery at the now departed Melbourne *Herald* —the pages of which he transformed when he was sports editor between 1987 and 1989 (and he still ran the restaurant for his first year in the job) — and the *Sunday Age*, whose nationally acclaimed sports section he created in 1989 and guided for its first twelve months.

Although his food columns and restaurant reviews continue to grace the *Sunday Age*, Geoff again departed full-time newspaper work in the middle of 1990 to establish a publishing company, The Text Media Group. While this book is largely a collection of his recipes published in the *Herald* and the *Sunday Age* between 1987 and 1991, some readers may recognise the philosophies he expounds weekly on Doug Aiton's high-rating radio program on the ABC's 3LO in Melbourne.

'Geoff Slattery', says Doug, 'is a long, lean, anxious peasant (and I mean that in the nicest sense of the word) who came on my 3LO program to talk about food and now gets more mail than I do. His approach to food is basic and earthy and tough. His approach to radio is bewildered and terrified. His impact is magical.'

*Caroline Wilson, June 1991*

# Fun First, Second, Third

For most of us, cooking is not about recipes, or routines, it's about what's in the fridge, or what's cheap, or what's growing in the garden. Recipes, I have noticed, are for special occasions, or for those things which need fine detail to make them work. For me, that is more likely to be for baking or desserts.

This is not a book about fine detail. It's a book about discovering flavours, simply. It's about the constant joy of surprise in the kitchen. There are two kitchens in the world, one a drab, sad, quiet monument to pragmatism; the other a bubbling, aromatic cauldron of desire, spontaneity, and familial joy. This book is in praise of the latter.

This is, for those who haven't experienced that, the sort of fun you have during adolescence when you discover that there's more to the world than football, or basketball, or comics or swimming, or mum and dad. Life in my kitchen is about constant discovery with fun and joy as key ingredients. It's messy, in its physical, but ordered in its mental. So, you can have a kitchen with ingredients all over the bench yet neatly arranged in your head. I wouldn't recommend it. It is a sort of illness I have yet been unable to deal with, so I look on it, unwisely, as a virtue. If I didn't, I'd be dead.

If you ever have the opportunity to watch a really special, classy, professional chef in action, you will notice a couple of things immediately. He/she is impossibly well organised. Everything is pigeon-holed to be grabbed routinely, blindfolded, under the most intense pressure, and — and this is the most important item in any cook's repertoire, the only lesson you must not dismiss, no matter how poor your aspirations are — the pro is incredibly cool. You sense that nothing is a worry, nothing can go wrong. If the observer senses things are getting out of hand, such negativity never enters the head of the pro. There is always another way. Or, heaven forbid, if it is a disaster, then it can be done again. Nothing's lost, except time, valuable time.

There's another lesson about cooking which has

nothing to do with routine, or technical skills, or the ability to whisk egg whites while standing on your head. It's about tasting, tasting, tasting. Don't ever assume anything. Never assume the raspberries you bought today will be the same as those you bought yesterday; never go into a recipe blindly without tasting first, if possible; and never add an ingredient you've not met before without tasting it, or learning about it and its idiosyncrasies.

How else will you really know what a quince will add to a recipe, if you haven't puckered up your lips at its acidity and wondered how something so grainy could be worth looking at? How can you be bothered with all the de-seeding required for a cumquat marmalade if you have never bitten into a cumquat and resiled at its initial sharpness before swooning at its brilliant middle sweetness? How can you serve a sauce if you haven't put your finger into it and tasted it for all its flavour levels in its bare, unaccompanied state?

And finally, when you must do something blind, go back to your roots, and think of those wonderful after-school days when you dashed into the kitchen, raided the bread bin, and then wondered what you would have between the slices. *That's* what cooking is all about: familiar flavours combined with a little style and a compromise when something is missing.

So don't get cross if something is not where it should be. Just think back to those times when there wasn't any peanut butter left in the cupboard. Remember? First the disappointment, then the positive change of heart: to the vegemite, or cheese, or lettuce, or jam. Do the same now, and finish off your preparation with a gin. You'll wonder what all the fuss was about.

*Geoff Slattery, May 1991*

# SOME KITCHEN 'RULES'

he best thing I did in the early days of cooking was to learn to make perfect pastry cream. I learned something else as well: always read new recipes right through before trying them on.

It was the usual story. I was halfway through a first-time attempt at making the pastry cream when the phone rang. The cream was bubbling and I was stirring furiously. What to do? I glanced at the instructions: 'Boil for one minute.' So I left it to boil and answered the phone. It was an old mate. We exchanged a few one-liners and I returned to the battle to find my labours stuck to the bottom of the saucepan. It took a week to clean. I cursed and swore, naturally blaming the fool who wrote the book.

Then I looked again. 'Boil for a minute.' There it was. Aaaah, but there was more on the next line: 'stirring constantly so the mixture does not stick.' The moral to the story: read all the instructions before you start something new. And never answer the phone during the delicate moments of your life.

My kitchen rules are amended daily. Try these on for size.

1 **Try anything in the microwave just to see what happens.** Since the first day I bought one, I went at this routine with a gusto and have achieved marvellous results with jam, sauce, pumpkin, eggplant, polenta and more.

Take jam. Before the microwave, I had considered jam making the sackcloth and ashes job of the kitchen. Not any more. It is simply a matter of thinking of something that will make nice jam, tossing it into the microwave, adding some sugar, and dancing. Give it a try.

2 **No matter what a recipe says, taste before you deliver.** This is the sign of a cook who cares. Taste, taste, taste. This dictum is especially important with seasonal fruits like gooseberries, like apples all through the year, like mangoes, pears, plums, apricots. And always taste before serving sauces or creams. Your tongue is a far better barometer than the lines in the recipe before you.

3 **Think seasonal.** The benefits extend from the plate to the pocket. So, if your latest glossy cook book or magazine asks for red capsicums, and it's

July, think of something different. Don't decide what's for that special dinner before you think about what's fresh. So, for instance, if it's February, forget about asparagus for another year and start practising tomato recipes. Pull out all your apple pie specials and go for broke. And whenever you see something new, try it, unless it's a pomegranate. They look lovely, taste awful.

4 **Don't be adventurous when it's dinner-party time.** Cook the dishes you cook best and think about dishes you can prepare well ahead. Nobody enjoys a host who spends most of the time in the kitchen.

5 **Whenever you see a recipe you like, and decide to cook it, don't cook it from the book.** Sit down at the table and write down the details yourself, in the style in which you cook. Think it through, list the ingredients in the blocks in which they come in the recipe, and then get yourself organised. Make it part of your life to get all your ingredients weighed and in bowls, and all your necessary equipment in front of you, before you light a jet or chop a chive. In this case, do as I say, not as I do.

6 **You obviously don't need any machines other than tender hands and well-muscled forearms, but then you don't need a swimsuit to have fun at the beach either.** I have more machines than you would find in Myer but these represent more my need for the latest gadget than a group of 'I'd die without it' whizzers and woofers. There are a few things you must have if you really want to create marvels. A microwave is not a toy for heating coffee, it's an extra pair of hands in the kitchen. Mine is a cheapie, at 500 watts, and is more than suitable. I bought a cheapie because I didn't have a clue what it could do, and neither did anyone else at the time. If then was now, I'd go for a large, full-powered number. A whizzer is a food processor with guts — you can't leave your lounge chair without one; a Kenwood or Kitchen-Aid food mixer means you can have bread every day; an ice cream machine is a luxury which I can't do without; an extra coffee grinder is a must for creating fresh, simply put together spice mixes; a sugar thermometer is needed to ensure perfectly smooth custards; and a knife you love.

7 **Perfect at least one recipe in the next twelve months.** It doesn't sound much, but think about it. When I say perfect it, I mean know it backwards, know how to do it away from home, know how to do it with any peripheral ingredient missing, know how to do it in a state of drink and, most importantly, know how to vary it, so that from something simple comes something original, wonderful, yours. Try these recipes on for starters: custard, pasta, bread, risotto, steak, stews and cakes.

8 **Don't be lazy in the kitchen.** Everything you cook is special, so don't take any short cuts. It's fine to compromise — from compromise comes surprise, and from surprise comes creativity. But compromise is considered strategy; laziness is not.

9 **When things have gone really wrong, don't send good money after bad in an effort to redeem the impossible.** If you burn the bottom of the jam pan, take good note of the reasons that it happened. But don't waste time believing the burned flavour won't go through the entire batch. It will. Forget it, but never burn your jam again.

10 **Create a hearty repartee with your favourite butcher and fishmonger; better still, set up accounts with them.** Then you'll be encouraged to shop there regularly, and you'll know that you are getting the best produce in the shop and the best service. And ask them for special favours. They spend most of their lives doing the same old thing, day in, day out. Ask them to stuff, or roll, or twist, or fillet, or hang, and they'll be more than happy to do it for you, their special customer. And make sure you pay your account on time.

11 **Be a wise buyer.** If the fish is cheap, you can be sure it's fresh and running; know every which way with the cheap cuts of meat, and become expert at them. Remarkably, the cheaper the cut, the bolder the flavour. Learn well the more-meals-per-dollar routine — thus roasts begat bones begat stocks begat soups begat joy.

12 **You will note that chillies are very much part of my cooking.** This is because of their marvellous talent for bringing out the essence of any sauce, particularly stocks and sauces based on tomatoes. Food would be dull without freshly ground pepper; so too without chilli. You *can* leave it out if you wish, if you must.

13 **Never be shy when it comes to asking for special recipes.** In the kitchen, it is as delicious to give as to receive. This applies equally to restaurants as to friends. In my experience, restaurateurs are delighted to be asked. It is, I guess, the ultimate approval of their cooking.

14 **While I'm on this, and without getting gruesome, don't let your old family favourites go to the grave.** I received a lovely letter from a typical grandmother who was collecting her favourite recipes and putting them in a special book for her grandchildren — she wanted to make sure that her recipes didn't disappear with her. Maintain your family traditions.

15 **And never forget the title of this book: Simple Flavours.** Cooking is all about simple steps, followed with various amounts of regimented routine, aimed at bringing out essential flavours. Simple Flavours.

# PASTA, RISOTTO AND OTHER YUMMIES

Pasta has been around for thousands of years; so has rice, so has couscous, so has polenta. Yet when you introduce them into conversation and describe how you made them yourself, you are immediately accorded some form of celebrity status.

Italian restaurants still paint 'home-made pasta' on their windows as though it's as unique as a sighting of the Tasmanian tiger, and people still think of pasta and risotto dishes as desperately tough to prepare and requiring large reservoirs of knowledge and experience. It should not be so. Pasta and grains and all the opportunities they proffer for simple yet classy eating should be as much part of our understanding as the 3Rs.

Perhaps this is starting to be the case. I think I was well past the voting age before I had tasted my first bowl of pasta. Such was life in Australia for the baby boomers. But it has all changed in the heady days since baby boomers became baby makers. My children, all born in the middle of the eighties, now speak fluently when it comes to pasta. And the middle one, whose eating habits are a pay-back from the Lord for my own obtuseness when young, now has two all-time favourite dishes:

(i) 'noodies', which may well have been her first words, closely followed by 'more' as in 'more noodies';

(ii) Parmigiano Reggiano, which in the language of a two-, three-, and now four-year-old has become 'parjano rejano'.

Of course she took ages to like the one mixed with the other. Now noodies are not noodies without pajarno rejano. I can't get cross with her. I was 12 before I tasted the wonders of baked pumpkin, on the way to 30 when I made my first pasta dish, and 35 before risotto became more important than the latest sports scores.

Now I like to think of pasta and risotto in the same way as sandwiches. They are carriers of fun in food — carriers of glorious, extra special flavours, or of flavours that are just hanging about, as in sitting around in the fridge waiting to be loved.

Treat these staples well, and you'll never regret it.

## WHAT YOU'LL NEED

1 A simple pasta machine, as has been hanging about Italian kitchens since Marco Polo was in short pants. This is a bright, stainless-steel affair, which looks like an old-time washing machine from the days when we used to run white-as-white shirts through the high rollers. If you are fair dinkum about pasta you must have one of these machines. They are very cheap and last for what seems like forever. And don't think it will mean pasta won't appear as often on your table. The reverse is true.

If you are lazy, and can't be bothered making your own pasta, find a good dried version. You can buy fresh pasta from speciality shops, but for the effort it takes, it is very expensive.

2 A herb garden or, at the worst, a pot plant at the back door or on the window sill dedicated to growing herbs. Any pasta dish will get a boost with the addition of a handful of herbs picked seconds earlier. For those of you with little patience, like me, the most reliable perennials are rosemary, thyme, oregano and tarragon. Of course, you must make room for basil every spring.

3 Flair. Pasta and rice work with anything in the fridge, as long as you are prepared to try it. Remember one basic rule: never drown the pasta, risotto, couscous or polenta in sauce; just let the sauce hold the strands or nooks or twists or grains, and keep it simple.

4 An occasional windfall of cash, so you can go out and buy a few kilos of Parmigiano Reggiano. I have referred to this wonder all through the book as Parmesan, so you won't think you have to spend freely to enjoy simple food. Parmigiano Reggiano is the hard, cow's milk cheese which comes to us courtesy of centuries of traditional cheese making in Parma, north-central Italy. It is so beautiful, words fail me, but because it takes several years to reach peak maturity — there are younger versions available which are like young wines: still lovely, but short of their top — it can get pretty pricey. Try it now and then as a treat, but do as the Italians do, and go for the Grano Padano as your standby daily grating cheese. Each of these cheeses has its name stamped on the rind, so don't be conned by the unscrupulous. And don't consider Parmigiano Reggiano to be merely a grating cheese — that's a little like calling cricket a ball game. Try it with pears, try it with raspberries. And whenever a melting cheese is called for, try Raclette, the famous Swiss cheese, now made in commercial quantities at Wodonga on the Victoria – New South Wales border.

5 Chillies are not usually found in much modern Italian cooking. You'll find it in my versions because I like it for what it does best — enhancing the flavour of its master. Chilli does not have to mean fiery; consider it more like salt and pepper, an enhancer and underliner of the main event.

6 Tinned tomatoes are essential for the pasta cupboard, so you can always know there is a sauce waiting to be cooked, no matter what's not in the fridge. I don't usually recommend tinned products, but tinned tomatoes, with no added sugar or

salt, are just as good as your own bottled version when it comes to making sauce, and they're very cheap. Just open the tin, squash them up with a strong fork, add a bit of salt, and a chilli, and put them in the microwave. You'll have a powerful, thick sauce in half an hour.

7 Several packets of different pasta shapes, so, as with the tomatoes, there's always a meal around. Shapes are not a return to childhood fantasies — they are great for holding thick sauces, and hiding surprises, and they keep the kids happy in their grumpiest moments. Try something like orecchiette — little ears — with clams or chopped olives. You'll never know what might turn up, where. And always have farfalle around; there's a lovely wit in these little butterflies, or bow-ties.

8 Make sure you've got a solid supply of full-flavoured virgin olive oil. It can help turn the mundane into the magnificent with a few swishes here and there. It is also a must to kick-start the risotto, and it doesn't have to be wildly expensive. Treat your reserves of olive oil like wine: some for quaffing, some for extra special occasions.

9 Arborio rice is the signature of risotto. It's plumper than most rice and gives a wonderful excess of starch to the risotto pot. In the best of Arborio rice, that starch tastes marvellous, and adds a certain extra thickness to the finished dish. Arborio rice, produced in the Po Valley of northern Italy, absorbs liquid very well, and, strange as it may seem, is rather handsome in its final glory. I couldn't live without it.

10 A heavy-bottomed stock pot with a bit of size is probably essential in any kitchen, but you absolutely can't do without it when cooking rice or pasta. It will ensure a minimum of sticking.

11 A microwave is my left and right hand, for fun and efficiency. It will turn polenta on its ear in minutes, and tomatoes into glorious, thick sauces while you are downing sherry in the easy chair. It's also pretty good at re-heating pasta and risotto.

12 Bacon imparts a very special flavour to most things it is mixed with. How can you resist the aroma when somebody wakes early and starts cooking bacon? There are different qualities of bacon available, although the commercial variety is much better than many things made in bulk. If your butcher makes his own, all the better. Support him, even if the price is a little outside your budget.

## THE RECIPES

♥
## A SIMPLE PASTA: TAGLIATELLE IN A BACON CREAM SAUCE

You approach restaurants with extraordinary naivety. The day we opened our one and only eating house we had two pasta dishes on the menu. We made the pasta in the early hours of the morning we opened, just after we had finished hand-churning the ice cream. Husband and wife, not long married and still wide-eyed and in love, we looked at the huge mounds of pasta we had cut out with a little, very cheap machine, then at each other, and said simultaneously: 'There is no way we will run out of pasta.'

Remarkably, there was a capacity crowd on opening day, and we had sold out of pasta before half the orders had made it to the kitchen. What a day that was. If any of the customers came back after that opening shambles, they deserve, they have, our undying respect. I suppose every opening day is the same, whether you have expertise or not. Think about new newspapers — have you ever seen a first edition newspaper that was not filled with mistakes, and riddled with poor judgements? I know I haven't. Restaurants or newspapers, you always forget something, or expect something to work better than it has been made to work, or rely on somebody who doesn't turn up, or run out of pasta!

Home-made pasta is like home-made bread: each really needs no assistance, but in each case, if you add ingredients to brilliantly fresh pasta or bread, those add-ons don't have to be all that flash. Bread and butter and cheese — beautiful. Pasta and butter and cheese and black pepper — beautiful. So mix together all the simple things in the kitchen, toss them with some pasta, and you will have a wonder. And never forget that once you start fiddling with your own pasta, you'll never need a recipe book again. Just open the fridge door and try anything. Anything.

♥   ♥   ♥   ♥   ♥

### THE PASTA

6 eggs

6 cups plain flour

salt

a little olive oil

### THE SAUCE

250g bacon, sliced into 2-cm cubes

150ml cream

a little water

50g butter

salt

black pepper

chives for the finale

fresh herbs

*Chives are fantastic, but anything seasonal is just fine.*

some chopped nuts, just a few to provide a surprising crunch

*Hazelnuts are great, but almonds, cashews or walnuts will all be terrific.*

Parmesan cheese for grating

1 In a bowl, make a well in the flour and mix in the eggs, salt and oil. Work together with a fork until it all comes together. You might need another egg or a little more flour, depending on the moisture in the eggs, or the air, or the

flour. The dough will not be sticky when it is right.

2 Knead a little. You don't have to knead too much, so don't be discouraged — the machine will do most of the work for you. In fact, I find kneading a most enjoyable pastime: there is something special about feeling the dough come together, arriving at that special sheen that says it is just right.

3 Feed the dough through the pasta machine, moving it through one thickness at a time, until you get to the machine's finest setting (no. 6). You can, of course, do this on a bench with a rolling pin. 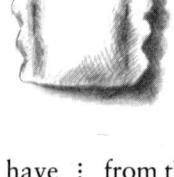 Umpteen millions of Italians have been doing just that for centuries. It does take a little more labour, and a lot more time, and few of us have much of that these days. Hang the dough to dry a little (over the back of a chair if you like), as it will make it easier to cut. But don't let it dry out completely. It needs some moisture to get through the rollers.

4 Cut the pasta into whichever shape you prefer; the wide cutters are for tagliatelle, the narrow for *capelli d'angeli*, a delicious picture translated as angel's hair. It is best to trim the pasta into manageable lengths — about 30 cm is a good starting point. Toss the cut pieces with a little flour to stop any sticking, and leave in 'nests' on a wire rack.

5 Heat a little bit of oil in a frying pan until it is very hot. Add the bacon, working it around the pan with a wooden spoon until it is cooked and quite crisp, but not dry.

Alternatively, cook the bacon in the microwave — it's much easier. Just set the bacon on a sheet of absorbent paper and cook on high for about 60 seconds. But watch it. It cooks very quickly and can become as dry as an old boot.

6 Turn down the heat, add the cream, and cook gently, infusing the cream with the rich flavour of the bacon. Allow it to bubble away and thicken, but keep an eye on it. You don't want it to get too thick. Add some water when the cream looks like fading away. Keep tasting. When the cream flavour has gone and the richness of the bacon has come through, take the sauce from the heat and whisk in the butter. Add salt and pepper to taste.

7 Cook the pasta. It needs a large pot of boiling salted water. Home-made pasta will cook very quickly. If you make it yourself, it should not be cooked *al dente*. It should not be limp, nor firm. It should not be chewy. If you taste it all through the cooking, you will note its changes. If the pasta is yours, and a little dry, it will take a couple of minutes. If it is very fresh, it will take about half that time. If you've never cooked it before, just keep tasting. You will know when it is done. If you reckon it's right, and nothing else is ready, don't despair. Just drain the pasta and cool it quickly under cold water. Re-heat it in boiling water when you are ready. This is always a good idea during big occasions, like dinner parties for bosses, etc. It gives you more time to be good company, and less time to worry. Otherwise, it should go

straight from its cooking pot into the sauce.

8 Toss the pasta through the sauce, letting it cling to it, and serve with finely chopped herbs, the nuts and Parmesan for grating.

WINE ✤ *Italian red — stick to a good maker like Antinori. Most of the reds from Coonawarra have the balance for this dish — Rouge Homme, Wynns, Hollicks, Mildara or Bowen Estate.*

♥

## PASTA WITH SMOKED SALMON IN A SMOKY SAUCE

S moked fish makes a delightful companion for pasta, for the same reasons as bacon does. It imparts an intense, smoky flavour to its carrier, the cream, and some delicious chunky bits to float through the pasta. The way to go is to use one set of chunks to flavour the cream, and a new, uncooked set to provide freshness at the end. Smoked trout, the rainbow variety, tends to be flakier than the superior salmon or ocean trout, but there is an advantage — it's also many multiples cheaper. Use the cheapie to flavour the sauce, the costly version to add style and freshness to the plate.

♥   ♥   ♥   ♥   ♥

150 ml cream

1 cup fish stock, flavoured with aromatic vegetables

the flesh from half a smoked trout to flavour the sauce
*Remove the flesh from the bones, taking care there are no bones attached.*

zest of 1 lemon

50 g butter

salt

black pepper

a shaped pasta, like farfalle — little butterflies, or little bow-ties, depending on your imagination

1 cup shelled peas

bunch of chives, chopped finely

several slices of smoked salmon
*Allow 1 slice, cut into slivers, per person.*

1 Cook the cream with the stock, gently, mixing the one through the other. Add the smoked trout and lemon zest, and continue cooking for about 10 minutes, on a low heat, until the sauce is bubbling and much thickened. You might need to add a little more stock or water if it is getting too thick. Taste and season with salt and black pepper. Strain, discarding the trout chunks, and set the sauce aside.

2 Cook the pasta until just done, adding the peas towards the end of the cooking.

3 Gently warm through the sauce, whisking the butter into it. Toss the pasta and peas through the sauce, working most of the chives through, and place the smoked salmon strips on top. Sprinkle with the extra chives.

WINE ✤ *Smoked trout calls for a good bottle of chilled white. Rhine riesling or chardonnay will do the trick.*

~ 17 ~

♥
## BAKED NOODLES IN A BACON, LEEK AND WALNUT SAUCE

I have read a lot about Italian cooking, eaten a lot of Italian cooking, here and there and at home. And I can't help but feel that Italians love their food, but cook without much spontaneity, preferring the tried and true, almost to the stage of admonishment if certain procedures are not followed. Gualtiero Marchesi, that much-lauded three-star chef from Milan, took a hardly radical, but different look at some old and tried pasta dishes, and the establishment said of him: 'Lovely restaurant, but it's really French, isn't it?' What he had done was to take traditional cooking into a classy restaurant, and smoothed out the rough edges. To me, this represents the greatness of cooking — maintaining tradition and flavour, while giving the lot a new vigour.

The reactionaries don't agree. Their view is that the cuisine of long-established, usually peasant, cultures has been passed down from generation to generation — and don't you dare meddle with it.

We, down under, on the other hand, can do what we like with cooking from all cultures. It's not ours; we can twist it and turn it any way we like. Which is something of an advantage when the kids pester you and grapple with you and drive you crazy with requests for pasta, day in day out, then refuse to eat it. Don't shrug your shoulders — turn a potential waste into something glorious.

The beauty of this dish is that you can make it up in advance, and re-heat it whenever you like. It's great for breakfast, for a dinner party or for a party of hundreds. I don't know where the chilli came from. Doesn't seem too Italian to me.

♥ ♥ ♥ ♥ ♥

**300 g dried pasta**
*Use anything you like. I prefer those with a bit of shape, like orecchiette — little ears. I always use dried pasta for shapes — not for any hankering for childhood lost, but because of their rare talent for gripping hold of a sauce.*

**1 onion, chopped finely**

**1 clove garlic, chopped roughly**

**1–2 leeks, chopped finely**

**1 chilli, chopped roughly**

**4 slices bacon, fat removed, chopped finely**

**125 ml cream**

**salt**

**dozen walnuts, cut into quarters**

**1 cup grated Provolone**

**1/2 cup fresh herbs — thyme, oregano, parsley**
*Use whatever you like, or have. Chives would be terrific. If you haven't any of these, plant some for next time.*

**black pepper**

**1 teaspoon freshly ground nutmeg**

**1 cup grated Parmesan for the cook, more for the table**

1 Cook the pasta until just done. Stop the cooking under cold running water, drain well, and set aside. This presumes you have no pasta left over from frustrated children.

2 Gently cook the onion, garlic, leeks and chilli in a little bit of oil until they soften.

3 Fry the bacon gently, stirring about the pan, and add the cream and salt. Cook over a low heat until the cream is cooked and has taken in the flavour of the bacon. Add the leeks, onions, garlic and chilli mix.

4 Mix the pasta, bacon- and onion-flavoured cream, walnuts and Provolone together. Add the herbs, nutmeg and black pepper.

5 Grease a baking tray and add the pasta mix so that it is just about level with the top of the tray.

6 Spread the pasta with half the Parmesan and cover with aluminium foil. (You can prepare to this stage and leave until later if you wish.) Cook in a 200°C oven for about 15 minutes until the mixture is well and truly cooked through. Sprinkle the rest of the cheese on top and return to the oven, uncovered, for a few minutes, or place under a hot grill for 30 seconds, until the cheese melts.

7 Serve at the table, with some freshly grated Parmesan and roughly chopped herbs on the side.

WINE ♣ *A chardonnay with some acid backbone would go well — say a Hardys out of Padthaway, the top of the line Eileen Hardy if you can push your pocket. Others to try: Jamiesons Run chardonnay or Seppelt Black Label.*

♥
## PASTA WITH A SAUCE FROM THE GARDEN

The garden is such a fantastic inspiration, summer or winter, hot or cold, I wonder why we bother with recipes. Kick the mint and the air is filled with mint sauce, and roast lamb is a natural to follow. Rush into the kitchen and cook it.

Fondle the rosemary and all those delicious oils are released: aaah, can't you just imagine a little fish, or vegetables, with a thickly flavoured rosemary cream sauce? Or a little tomato and soy, given guts with rosemary. Or sage, flavouring the stuffing of roasted veal. How about thyme with duck livers? Oh, and peppermint ice cream: is there any better with chocolate?

There's more to this. Tarragon can turn a tired old chook into a thing of beauty, and there is never ultimate cooking happiness until it's late summer and you can afford to throw basil left, right and centre. And it's not always the obvious or the most fragrant of herbs that will do the trick — I always have to go out and buy large leeks for stocks and the like, as we always pick ours from the garden when young and juicy, to eat like chives; and beans, with their flowers still attached, and tiny zucchini. It's not very much fun being a vegetable in our garden.

You want just a little pasta with this dish. It is not a dish of pasta with a few vegetables tossed about, it is a tiny entrée/appetiser based on fresh, vigorous vegetables, supported by pasta. It's the sort of dish the best restaurants will give you. Pasta like this should be a 'kiss 'em lightly' triumph. Too many cooks drown pasta, and risotto too, in rich sauces. Don't do it. Touch the pasta, touch the grains. Kiss 'em lightly.

♥ ♥ ♥ ♥ ♥

### ½ dozen spears of asparagus
*Use only the tender spears and keep the stems for tomorrow.*

### ½ dozen leeks, as thin as you can find them
*Cut three-quarters into bite-size pieces, the rest chop finely. If you're buying for this, 1 thick leek, sliced into julienne shapes will do the job.*

### a little silver beet — stalks to be cooked first, then greens
*Spinach is fine, but silver beet has something extra going for it. Guts, I think it's called. And it's usually much cheaper.*

### ½ clove garlic

### 100 ml cream

### couple of sprigs of rosemary

### salt

### black pepper

### handful of fresh tagliatelle per person

### 50 g butter

### some chives, chopped

### Parmesan for grating

1 Steam the asparagus, leek pieces and silver beet until just done — 6–8 minutes. I prefer the asparagus to be tender to the knife, but less than crisp. Refresh under cold water, drain, and set aside.

2 Steam the silver beet greens, and allow to cool. Squeeze out any excess moisture. Chop roughly and toss in with the other vegetables.

3 Soften the chopped leeks and the garlic in a little olive oil, on a

gentle heat. Add the cream and bring to the boil gently, adding the rosemary when the cream is just warm. With a wooden spoon, work the rosemary about the pan until the cream bubbles and thickens. Season with salt and plenty of black pepper to taste. The cream should have a rich flavour of rosemary. Cover and keep warm off the heat, leaving the rosemary in the cream. The leeks will have softened, but still have crunch.

4 Cook the pasta until just done.

5 While the pasta is cooking, re-heat the asparagus, leeks and silver beet gently in the cream. Gently, gently, whisk in the butter as you go. The idea is to re-heat slowly, allowing the juice from the vegetables to assist the sauce, not for the sauce to bubble into oblivion. Remember, a gentle dish, a tiny dish.

6 Add the hot pasta and mix through the vegetables. Serve in the middle of the plates, with the sauce just holding onto the strands of pasta and vegetables, and a little running through onto the plate. Sprinkle some chives over the top. Have some black pepper and a little thickly grated Parmesan on the side. Add plenty if you like it. I do.

WINE ✤ *This is a delicate dish. I would see it sitting nicely as an early lunch on a Sunday with a good bottle of bubbly — French or Australian. Of the Australian* méthode champenoise *I like Croser, Yellowglen Vintage, Domain Chandon or Seppelt Vintage Brut.*

♥

## ANGEL'S HAIR PASTA WITH BABY BEANS

S pecial food has as much to do with visuals as it has with expensive ingredients. I guess this is one of the reasons why so many bright young chefs have so much fun fiddling with food. The consequences have been wonderful, save a minor period of misuse, and a major attack of misjudgement by many critics. Nouvelle cuisine is gorgeous in its ultimate application, but unfortunately it became saddled with tiny portions, bright colours and weird flavours rather than perfect combinations and simple, thoughtful, attractive presentation. Attractive in the sense of bees and flowers, boys and girls.

We've been through all that, and back to hearty flavours and exotics, but cooking is far better for its excursion into simplicity and raw, unadulterated, understood flavours.

I am reminded of this every year, when the beans we grow start to do what the packets say they will, and produce large top and tail 'em beans. Well, they would if you let them. Not me. I'm out there from the first sight of subtle white flowers, poking here and there for any hint of bean as it pushes clear of the flower in search of its new life.

No patience here. When the beans have reached no more than 10 centimetres, grab them, and you have the basis of the most wonderful dish.

I reckon that's what the home garden is for. Use it for its raw, pure product. Use it as soon as you can, and you'll be pleasantly surprised.

♥   ♥   ♥   ♥   ♥

a few drops of balsamic vinegar

1/2 cup best olive oil

salt

black pepper

hefty piece of Parmesan

**a tiny amount of the thinnest pasta you can make or buy**
*There is no doubt this dish is greatly enhanced if you make your own; if you can't, go for the thinnest spaghetti, or the pasta labelled* maccheroni alla chitarra, *the regional spaghetti from the Abruzzo, east of Rome.*

50g butter, cut into rough cubes

small bunch of tarragon, leaves pulled from the stem

8 baby beans per person, preferably with a little white flower still attached

1 You will need two pots of salted boiling water.

2 Mix the vinegar and the oil, together with a little salt and black pepper, at the bottom of a middle-sized bowl. Taste for seasoning and set aside.

3 Grate the Parmesan roughly, along the broadest edge of the grater.

4 Cook the pasta. Your own shouldn't take more than 60 seconds. If you're using packet pasta, follow the instructions.

5 Drain, and toss the pasta through the butter and tarragon leaves, until the butter melts. Add the grated cheese and mix through.

Turn the pepper mill over the lot for about 8 seconds.

6 Toss the beans into the boiling water for no more than 45 seconds. Drain, and toss into the oil and vinegar mix.

7 Place the pasta delicately into the middle of an attractive plate and toss the beans every which way over the top.

WINE ✤ *This is a subtle dish — it needs a subtle, delicate wine. Try a young Rhine riesling or, if you can, a German riesling from Moselle or an Alsace riesling.*

♥

## LAMBS' KIDNEYS WITH BUTTERY NOODLES

L ambs' kidneys are at their most delicious when lambs are young and lovely; when grass is green and plentiful, the weather is warm and the lambs are pretty happy with their life, such as it is.

♥ ♥ ♥ ♥ ♥

1 kidney per person

a little milk

100g unsalted butter, cut into cubes

salt

black pepper

1 clove garlic, sliced finely

handful chopped mixed, fresh herbs — whatever is available, whatever you like

*Chop them roughly, so you don't take any of the personality or identity from the herbs.*

**fresh pasta**
*You need the richness of flavour and the tenderness of the home-made product. Try not to use dried.*

1 Cut all the green muck from the centre of the kidneys, slice into bite-size pieces and leave for half an hour in a little milk and water, to eliminate a little of the: (i) earthy, (ii) original, (iii) unpleasant, (iv) all of the above flavours, flavours which have much to do with the kidney's sole, living purpose.

2 Heat a little water (about half a cup) and whisk in the butter piece by piece. The butter mix must be fluid, but not oily. Season with salt and plenty of black pepper and add the garlic. Keep warm.

3 The kidneys cook very quickly. Heat a little oil in a heavy pan until the pan and the oil are very hot. Toss in the kidneys, making sure you do not overcrowd the pan, and work them around until they sizzle. They should be firm, only just cooked. Toss in a handful of the herbs and work them around the pan until they grip all of the kidney pieces. Set aside in the pan — off the heat — while you cook the pasta.

4 Cook the pasta briefly in plenty of boiling, salted water, until just done. It is to be eaten tender, not tough, nor *al dente*.

5 Toss the pasta through the melted garlic butter, so that all the strands are touched by the butter. Put the kidneys and attached herbs at the bottom of a soup bowl, and season with a little salt and black pepper. Cover with the pasta in the butter sauce and sprinkle with more

herbs. The pasta will cover the kidneys and the butter will seep through, mixing with them. As you eat, you'll go through pasta, garlic, butter and herbs; and the kidneys will be a pleasant surprise at the bottom of the bowl.

WINE ✤ *I like the thought of a pinot for this — you could buy French Burgundy but the mortgage is still there. Try Bannockburn, Coldstream Hills, Balgownie Estate or De Bortoli Yarra Valley.*

♥

## TAGLIATELLE WITH SUGAR PEAS IN A LEMON BUTTER SAUCE

One sure way to succeed with pasta is to return absolutely to basics, to childhood, to that frantic time after school when you'd pulled out the bread and butter and had to decide what to put on it. That first lesson of associating flavours has never left me. Later on it was bread and butter at the table, to fit the last of the beef into a sandwich, or to wipe up the sauce. During my restaurant days, dinner was often a piece of freshly baked bread, a slab of butter and a handful of sugar peas, or snow peas, cooked quickly in a roaring stock. It was nothing to add a good turn of black pepper, some herbs from a nearby bowl and a squeeze of lemon. It was delicious, and always looked forward to.

In no time, this dish, the bread replaced by some pasta, had made it to the main menu, and there it was to stay in many guises until the day the joint was sold. It's a valuable lesson: think of what you like, and keep adding to it. Soon the pasta

and lemon butter were working with prawns, and corn, and scallops, and beans. Anything which liked butter liked this dish; and anybody too.

♥ ♥ ♥ ♥ ♥

juice of 2–3 lemons

100 g unsalted butter (use unsalted, so you can season it to your needs), cut into cubes

salt

¹/₂ dozen sugar peas per person

handful of sweetcorn, cooked on the cob and sliced free (per person)

fresh pasta, made yourself

zest of 1 lemon

black pepper

fresh herbs

1 The sauce is simplicity itself. Heat the lemon juice in a saucepan and whisk in the butter, piece by piece, until it has gone from lemon juice and butter pieces into a silky smooth sauce. Add salt and taste. Set aside in a warm place. You can also do this in the microwave. Just put the butter and lemon juice in an open bowl, and cook for about a minute until the butter is just melting. Whisk until it has emulsified. You must make sure it does not get too hot, or the butter will split into its components.

2 Cook the sugar peas and corn quickly in boiling water.

3 Cook the pasta and toss it through three-quarters of the sauce. Toss the hot vegetables and lemon zest through the rest of the

sauce and add to the pasta. Serve with the sauce holding the pasta. Sprinkle with fresh herbs and several turns of the pepper grinder. That's it.

WINE ✤ *Lemon butter sauce and good Rhine riesling. Ah! The best Australian Rhines consistently come from Clare and Eden Valley in South Oz. Sure bets are: Barry, Knappstein or Petaluma from Clare or Orlando, St Helga, Krondorf or Leo Buring from Eden Valley. All these wines age beautifully.*

♥

## TAGLIATELLE WITH BLACKENED SCALLOPS

Once you've done that, you'll want to show off with it, and when you show off, it usually means you spend money. That means seafood. Prawns and scallops are just wonderful tossed through simple buttered noodles, and they take a quantum leap into glory when you douse them with spices, hit them in a red-hot pan, and watch as the kitchen fills with smoke and the seafood turns black. We picked up this sort of thing during the eighties, when Paul Prudhomme's famous blackened fish dish was racing through most restaurants across the world. That in itself is a wonderful dish, served with a little melted butter, but if you follow the same course with prawns or scallops, you'll end up writing love letters to M. Prudhomme.

♥　♥　♥　♥　♥

### THE SEASONING

4 teaspoons sweet paprika

1 teaspoon salt

$^1/_2$ teaspoon onion powder

$^1/_2$ teaspoon garlic powder

1 teaspoon cayenne pepper

1 teaspoon ground black pepper

1 dried chilli, ground to powder, or 2 teaspoons chilli powder

a little butter, melted

4 peeled prawns, or scallops for each portion

*Make sure you buy 'dry' scallops. Scallops which have been soaked in water are an insult and should be reserved for the dog.*

freshly made pasta for four

1 Mix the seasonings together in a bowl.

2 Dip the prawns or scallops in the melted butter, then into the spice mix. Make sure they are well coated.

3 Heat a dry, heavy-bottomed pan on high heat for about 5 minutes, until it is as hot as it ever will get. A drop of water should evaporate instantly.

4 Add the scallops or prawns, one at a time, easing each about the pan so it will not stick. Don't cook too many in the pan at once, and toss them or work them about with a wooden spoon until done, about 90 seconds. Make sure the prawns and scallops are just done. There is nothing worse than overcooked versions of either. Scallops seem to take a little longer than you would think. Just squeeze them. They are right when they are firm but tender.

5 Serve on the edge of freshly cooked pasta, tossed with lemon

butter sauce (see page 23), snow peas and fresh herbs.

WINE ✤ *You need a white wine with some zing to stand up to this onslaught. Sauvignon blanc will do the job. New Zealand is making some lovely styles — look for Cloudy Bay, Moreton Estate and Montana. The top Aussies are Taltarni, Eaglehawk and Katnook.*

♥

## SPAGHETTI CARBONARA

One thing to remember about great Italian cooking is that there is nothing over the top about it. No tricks of presentation — no sprigs of parsley here, nor judiciously laid leaves of chervil there — just readily available, simple flavours, cooked with gusto, spirit and plenty of love. Love for the raw ingredients, love for the tradition, love for the company.

Pasta carbonara sits exactly with this philosophy. You really have to love the ingredients, respect them and know where they have been, to serve eggs basically raw, 'cooked' only by the heat of the sauce. The only way you'll get that is at home. Restaurants have 'evolved' the sauce to such an extent, it tastes nothing like it should — it has become something like bacon with cream. Eggs? Well, there might be one, cooked, to every four or five portions.

Carbonara, at its most simple, is no more than fresh pasta — it *must* be made at your bench — tossed with raw, free-range eggs, bacon, salt and black pepper. When it is all together, a little Parmesan and fresh herbs are sprinkled on top.

Note: Raw eggs. There might be some who will blanch at that, particularly after eggs getting some poor PR over the last few years, but the fact is, the pasta, straight out of the boiling stock, will give them a fair cook-up anyway. What we are aiming for is the warm, runny version, as in poached eggs with runny yolks.

I am indebted to a marvellous cooking/history book by Julia della Croce, *Pasta Classica*, for the fine detail of carbonara. She says carbonara could refer to the generous sprinkling of coal-like (carbone) black pepper sprinkled over the dish; or it could date from a dish preferred by coal miners (carbonari). Whatever its derivation, it is at its best in spring, when the grass is still lush and green from the winter, and the food is plentiful, and the chooks are as happy as Larry.

♥   ♥   ♥   ♥   ♥

1–2 leeks, depending on their size, roots and the tough green parts chopped off, the rest chopped roughly

25 g unsalted butter, cut into cubes

30 ml cream

1 chilli, sliced finely

100 g best ham or best bacon, the bacon cooked

4 eggs — 1 per person

enough home-made pasta for four

*Of course you can use dried pasta, but in this case it is not as good as freshly made. The eggs need the extra flavour, fresh texture of the tender home-made product. Cut to fine spaghetti.*

salt

Parmesan cheese for grating

black pepper

1 Soften the leeks in the butter and cream, toss in the chilli and

ham/bacon, and cook gently until the flavour is infused. Set aside in a warm place in a warm bowl.

2 Whisk the eggs thoroughly, so the white and yolk are well blended.

3 Cook the pasta — only for 60 seconds if it's fresh — and work it through the leeks etc., until well mixed. Toss the lot into the eggs and make sure the eggs touch all of the pasta. Add salt, Parmesan and plenty of black pepper from the pepper mill. You can't use too much. If you feel like it, a few peas, or a few tips of asparagus are delicious with this dish. They may not be part of the most pure of carbonara sauces, but who cares?

WINE ❖ *Our Sunday night staple. A Coonawarra red like Jamiesons Run, or Rouge Homme claret, or, for a special Sunday night, a cabernet from Margaret River in the Wild West (Cape Mentelle and Mosswood are my favourites).*

♥

## MISTAKEN IDENTITY, OR CLAMS WITH PASTA SHAPES

Time tends to fog the minute details of visits to the great cities of the world. Thus anything that has happened to me in Paris or New York or Rome or Florence turns into one of life's greatest moments. Which means the *tagliatelle alla vongole* I took at a tiny trattoria just outside the Santa Maria Novella railway station in Florence may not really be among the finest dishes I have eaten, but my memory says it was.

When I ordered, I had no idea what I would be served. That's trust for you. I suspected something to do with wings, such is the sound association with *vongole*; when the fliers turned out to be swimmers, if clams swim, I was reminded of another time in Paris, when my little sweetbread ordered the *ris de veau*, expecting a rather hefty chunk of veal, assisted by a bowl of rice. Fortunately, the elderly, endearing *maître d'* sussed out that we were a couple of rather strange people from another world.

'Madame,' he said, in a low voice, 'you know this eez, how you say, sweetbreads?'

Well, you can't be pretty and brave as well. She turns a strange colour whenever you mention the insides of anything. She smiled a wan smile, did an about turn, and went for the *poisson du jour!*

Since the affair *di Firenze,* I have had plenty of disappointments with clams, all suffering from the same problems: grit and overcooking. There is not much you can do about the former. It really depends on where they come from. If they have been allowed to disgorge any sand or whatever while still at sea, then you can expect an extraordinary purity of flavour, as delicious as oysters, with an entirely different texture. The best I have come across came from a supplier in Burnie, on Tasmania's north coast (where else but Tasmania?).

'Why no grit?' I said to Alan Flintoff, who deals in all sorts of seafood.

They are purged, he informed me, in waters as pure as the original sea. Two weeks they hang about in baskets, disgorging themselves of any unpleasantries. They are, I was told, perfect specimens. I had eaten some by then, and was nodding away furiously down the phone in agreement.

'How did you cook them?' he asked.

'Just,' I said. 'I split them down the middle and tossed them through a warm sauce. They need to be just cooked.'

I could sense he was pretty pleased with that.

'So many people say they taste like balls of rubber,' he said. 'They always overcook them. I prefer ours raw, or barely cooked.'

Hear, hear. The mistake is tossing the closed, live clams into a steamer, or boiling water, and letting them steam inside until they are forced to open. By then they have become miniature microwave ovens, as the aductor muscles put up such a stink when invaded by heat, everything inside is slaughtered before they give up the ghost. Don't do it. Slit them apart and barely cook them.

♥  ♥  ♥  ♥  ♥

½ kg clams is enough for two, although I could probably eat a kilo on my own

1 shallot, or small onion, chopped finely

½ clove garlic, sliced finely

½ cup white wine

2 tomatoes, skinned, chopped finely

salt

1 chilli, chopped finely

a little cream, perhaps 40 ml

pasta

*I prefer to use shapes for this dish, rather than the traditional tagliatelle — the clams sometimes hide in the pasta, as if in the sea. If you make your own tagliatelle, keep the quantities small and use the pasta as a holder of the sauce, no more. The dried shapes are not as rich, and you can take more of them, without affecting the flavour, the joy of the clams.*

the freshest herbs you have, especially chives, tarragon, or chervil from the garden; or coriander

black pepper

1 Split the clams with a sharp knife over a bowl to collect any juices.

2 Heat the shallot or small onion, and the garlic, in a little olive oil until the onion softens. Add the white wine, reducing quite heavily over a high heat. Remove from the heat and add the chopped tomatoes, salt and chilli, moving it about with a spoon. When the pan stops sizzling, return to a low flame and cook gently until the tomato thickens a little.

3 Add the cream and blend with the tomato mix, cooking gently for another minute or so. Test for seasoning and set aside while you cook the pasta.

4 When the pasta is just about cooked, heat the tomato sauce to just about boiling and toss in the clams, any clam juice and the herbs. Work around off the heat with a spoon, so the sauce touches all the clams. It might help to hold a lid over the pan and invert, re-invert, and so on.

5 Drain the pasta and toss the hot pasta through the sauce.

6 Serve simply, in wide pasta bowls, and turn the pepper mill over the top of each bowl. Make sure you have plenty of napkins and finger bowls at the ready.

WINE ❖ *A nice, big, peaches-and-cream chardonnay — the Hunter and McLaren Vale make the best of these styles. Try Rosemount Show, Tyrell's, Krondorf, or Broken Wood.*

♥

## FUSILLI IN A THICK TOMATO SAUCE WITH SALAMI

I n superior times, specifically those times when running a restaurant was my life, it was not seen to be *de rigeur* to have anything to do with the dried form of pasta. Not that there was anything absolutely wrong with such a thing — more it was to do with effort being seen to be made.

If you're making your own pasta, then you are trying very hard at all levels of the show; and that, more than anything, is what should be happening in the restaurant's engine room. The home-made product is superior in most ways I can work out, but when it comes to different shapes — dried is the way to go. There's another little rule I have devised to unravel all this: when you want to taste the sauce, use shaped pasta — it certainly won't intrude; and when you want to taste a light, melt in the mouth pasta, roll your own.

There's another, frivolous, yet important reason to go for shapes like spirals, and butterflies, and little ears, and cylinders: the kids love shapes, so why not give them what they want.

♥ ♥ ♥ ♥ ♥

4 fresh tomatoes, skinned

50 ml soy sauce

sprig of rosemary

250 g tin of peeled tomatoes, preserved in their own juices

*For a long time, I was sceptical about tinned tomatoes, for illogical, superior reasons, but in the end, it is immensely practical to use tinned tomatoes when a full-on sauce is all that's needed. I keep the fresh, ripe seasonal product to eat as they are.*

salt

1 chilli, chopped finely

1 clove garlic, chopped finely

black pepper

2 zucchini, sliced finely

a little butter

pasta

*Any dried pasta with nooks and crannies to catch an unsuspecting sauce would be fine. Fusilli are long whirls, about 5 cm long.*

a little mild salami per person, cut into short slivers

Parmesan for grating

1 The tomatoes will come at you from two flanks. Those from the tin will be be cooked down hard to provide a very rich and thick sauce to toss with the pasta; the others, less cooked, imbued with a little soy sauce and rosemary, will sit at the bottom of the bowl to provide a pleasant surprise, a little more substance and texture, and a slightly different tomato flavour.

2 Prepare those to sit at the bottom of the bowl first, cooking them on top of the stove. These can be then set aside while the others are

cooking. Slice the fresh tomatoes into quarters or eighths, depending on their size, pack them closely in a saucepan, sprinkle with the soy sauce, and cook very gently with the rosemary on a low heat until the tomatoes soften, about 5 minutes. Cook gently for a couple of minutes more, then set aside, covered. The tomatoes must be firm enough to have retained their shape.

3 Chop the tinned tomatoes roughly and toss them into a glass bowl, complete with any juices. Sprinkle with a couple of teaspoons of salt, the chilli and garlic, and put them in the microwave, uncovered. Cook on high for about 25–35 minutes, depending on the power of your machine. You might need to check them every so often as there can be hot spots in microwaves. If necessary, remove and stir occasionally. The sauce is done when it is thick, but moist, and the room is filled with the aroma of tomatoes. Season with black pepper and set aside.

4 Cook the zucchini with a little butter until soft. This is done easily in the microwave. The zucchini should have softened, but not disintegrated.

5 Cook the pasta. Fusilli usually take about 15 minutes, but check as they go.

6 When the pasta is just about cooked, check the sauces for temperature and seasoning. Re-heat if necessary.

7 Arrange a little of the zucchini and a couple of pieces of the cooked, marinated tomato at the bottom of a pasta bowl. Toss the fusilli through the thick, rich tomato sauce until it has all been swallowed up. Cover with a few strips of the salami and as much grated cheese as you like.

WINE ✤ *The Rutherglen region of the north-east of Victoria is rightly renowned for its fortifieds, but it also makes good halfback-flank dry reds. Look for Bullers, Baileys, Campbells or Stanton & Killeen.*

♥

## HOT DOGS, GIVEN NEW LIFE WITH PAPPARDELLE

T he thick tomato sauce from the previous recipe has plenty of uses, especially if you don't drown the pasta with it. Just let it hold on to the ribbons or curls or whatever. I have found it particularly attractive when faced with leftover hot dogs or frankfurters after one of the kids' birthday parties. It's a common problem with 'dogs. You always get too many and wonder what to do with the leftovers. Fear not: they make for a terrific dish if tossed with pappardelle — very wide pasta, about double the width of tagliatelle. This is generally purchased, but it is very easy to make yourself.

In a way, this recipe is an up-market version of hot dogs with tomato sauce.

♥   ♥   ♥   ♥   ♥

a rich, thick tomato sauce, laced with chilli (see page 256)

small bunch of basil

a few small chunks of broccoli

some pappardelle

leftover hot dogs sliced into bite-sized pieces

*Many of these — particularly the European knackwurst or the Spanish chorizo — have been pre-cooked. If the sort you are left with have not, then cook them through.*

plenty of chives, chopped finely

black pepper

Parmesan

1 Cook the sauce, adding a handful of basil towards the end of the cooking time. Keep in a warm spot.

2 Cook the broccoli, sliced into individual flowers, while the pasta is cooking.

3 Heat through the hot dogs in a hot pan, thus replicating a barbecue grill. Set aside.

4 When the pasta is cooked, toss the sauce, hot dogs, broccoli and chives through the sauce. Serve hearty portions in deep bowls. Turn the pepper mill over the lot and sprinkle with grated Parmesan.

WINE ✤ *Australia produces the best quality, value-for-money wine in the world. There are lots of value reds for this dish. Some to try are Jacob's Creek, Seaview Cabernet Sauvignon and Church Hill Cabernet Merlot.*

♥

## SPIRALS OF PASTA WITH RED PEPPERS AND CHORIZO SAUSAGE

Red peppers are not red peppers until they have been roasted and had their blistered skins removed. Then they are as different from the unskinned version as autumn apples are from those of spring — 'fresh' from the cool store.

The roasting process concentrates the flavours marvellously, compressing what is already something pretty special into something grand, grand, grand. I guess it's the removal of excess moisture, as well as the slightly plastic skin.

Add a few slices of roasted peppers to pasta tossed with tomatoes, salami — or better, Spain's staple sausage, the chorizo — and sprinkle about some olives, and you've got something very special. There's another combination which seems to find happiness with red peppers: capers mixed with mildly salted anchovies.

♥    ♥    ♥    ♥    ♥

pasta in spirals, or some shape to hold a thick sauce

a thick tomato sauce, flavoured with chilli (see page 256)

a good amount of chorizo sausage, sliced into chunky pieces

*This is the very red, very spicy sausage of Spain, prepared pre-cooked, or preserved like salami, or ready to grill. Any of these are right for this dish, but if they have been pre-cooked, make sure they are heated through during assembly.*

2 red peppers, roasted or grilled until their skin blisters

*This is probably easiest done in a hot oven for about 25 minutes. You'll know when they are three-quarters done — that's when the kids start arriving in the kitchen asking 'What's cooking?' Allow to cool, then peel and cut them into slivers.*

several olives, seeds removed, per person

¼ cup full-flavoured virgin olive oil

black pepper

Parmesan for grating

1 Prepare the pasta and the toma-to sauce. Make sure the tomato sauce is rich, and thick enough to almost hold onto a vertical spoon.

2 When the pasta is ready, heat through the sausage, red peppers and olives in the olive oil. Sprinkle with black pepper and pour straight into the tomato sauce.

3 Toss through the pasta and serve with some Parmesan on the side.

WINE ✣ *It depends how heavy-handed you are with the chilli. I would drink a good beer with this — Cascade or Tuborg. Try a young red from the Clare district of South Australia and beside it a tall glass of chilled water (not South Australian).*

♥

## MUSHROOMS WITH PASTA; OR NOT FAR FROM TRUFFLES AS THE CROW FLIES

I f you take risks you'll learn something new every day. Often it will be something that you shouldn't have tried in the first place; occasionally you will hit on a winner.

I had been fiddling around with mushrooms, generally scorning their disappointing taste, and pronouncing to whomever wanted to listen, that their long-time attractive PR was wrong. They were over-rated, watery, over-priced; under-achievers.

What I did like about them was their blackness, that rich ebony hue of the crow that makes your eyes pop out. Classic blackness is such a delicious colour, perfect, startling,

deep. But so often mushrooms turn into an insipid brown-grey sludge when cooked.

I started thinking. Was not the flavour dependent on the amount of water in the beasts, and, if you could remove the water without drying out the mushrooms, or worse, burning them, wouldn't you end up with something very black, with a very intense flavour? Something like their very rich cousin, the truffle.

The truffle is the essence of the earth. Eating a truffle evokes an overall body sensation that is best equated with the turning of rich, damp compost. You are part of it, in smell, taste, feel and often body, slipping and sliding in thick, living mud. This is a truffle. Unfortunately, nobody I know can afford it.

What I wanted to do was to get as close as that with the 'umble mushroom. Enter the microwave. Something about the microwave allows you to cook certain things entirely in their own moisture, so that the moisture departs before anything happens to its carrier. Thus, hallelujah, it was with mushrooms.

♥   ♥   ♥   ♥   ♥

**¹/₂ kg of large capped mushrooms, gills open, and black**
*Don't even consider fooling about with the closed, white button tops. Throw them on the compost. The very best mushies for this are field mushrooms, but that's for autumn only.*

**bunch of parsley, leaves chopped very roughly, stalks tossed aside**

**¹/₂ cup thick beef stock, if you've got it — but who has these days?**
*If you haven't, the next best thing to*

*perfect beef stock is real Madeira; and if you ain't got that, go for a rich port, with plenty of body and not too much sugar. Not that either? Well any port will do. No? Then be damned, 1/4 cup water.*

salt

black pepper

**1 hot chilli, chopped finely**

*I can't imagine any richly flavoured dish surviving without the kick of chilli.*

**enough curly, squiggly, twisted pasta for two**

**1 dessertspoon of fresh thyme leaves**

*If you do nothing with this recipe, at least file away the combination of mushrooms and fresh thyme. They go together like strawberries and cream.*

**1** Cut the stalks off the mushrooms and throw them into the pot for your next stock.

**2** Lay the mushrooms out on a flat plate, not touching, and put them in the microwave. Cook on high for about 10 minutes, depending on the power of your machine, or until you can smell the rich mushroom aroma. Open the microwave and squeeze the mushrooms. They should have lost a lot of moisture and will be about half the size they started. They are done when they are *just* moist to the squeeze. They must not be bone dry, or you will have gone too far; nor still containing (relatively) large quantities of moisture. Imagine the mushrooms as a soaked washer. Then squeeze, and squeeze, and squeeze. The washer will still feel wet, yet it won't give up any more water. That's what we want with the mushrooms.

**3** Remove, and toss the getting-to-be-dried-out mushrooms into the

whizzer with the parsley, stock (or whatever), pinch of salt, several turns of black pepper and the chilli. Whizz the lot until you have a thick, black sludge, redolent of the earth. Set aside while you cook the pasta.

You might think it a little strange that you have spent so much effort removing moisture, only to put it back via the stock etc. The reason is simple: perfect beef stock and mushrooms are like two left-handed batsmen wearing helmets and batting 200 m away. You can't tell them apart. The idea is that you get a double whammy of the mushroom/stock flavour.

**4** Cook the pasta until just done, drain, and mix the sludge through until it is coating every nook and cranny. Sprinkle with the thyme and serve in white bowls. The funny thing is, this is just like pesto: you can't eat too much of it. It doesn't even need Parmesan.

WINE ✿ *What a hearty feed. You need a hearty wine — a traditional Australian shiraz with richness and warmth, like a good Hunter or McLaren Vale. Lindemans, Hardys and Rothbury Estate are good bets.*

♥

## CHEATING WITH SCALLOPS

I remember when scallops were so plentiful you would buy them in batter from your local fish'n'chippery; when they used bulldozers to get into the piles of them at the market (now they use tongs); when they were the cheapest of cheap. They were the affordable shellfish. Not any more.

Real scallops — which means scallops which have not been soaked overnight in water, thus eliminating flavour and adding free weight — are getting to the pure luxury stage, up there with crays and crabs. There is nothing exploitative about this. It's just that the abundance of the past has led to the scarcity of the present. Amid all this is the politicking of fishers vs fishers, and environmentalists vs professionals. A common argument in these aware times.

Amid all the discussion, I can't help but wonder whether the scallop is going the way of the dodo. But, with all respect to this legendary flightless bird, did it taste anything like a fresh scallop?

Nothing from the sea can match the delicacy of these strange little blobs with the red tail. Rich yet tender; flavoursome, without overwhelming; special to present, yet simple to cook. Sounds a whizz, eh? But how to accommodate all these pluses without having your bank manager on the phone?

The trick is to blend the expensive with the cheap, but delicious, so you can have the satisfaction of the bulk, but the flavour of the rich, at an affordable price.

♥   ♥   ♥   ♥   ♥

1 onion, chopped roughly

1 clove garlic, sliced finely

1–2 chillies, de-seeded, sliced finely

1/8 large pumpkin, cut into chunks, or 1/2 butternut pumpkin

bunch of chives, or fresh herbs, chopped

juice of 1 sweet orange

50g unsalted butter for the pumpkin

50ml cream

salt

black pepper

1 head of broccoli, 'flowers' cut from the stem, leaving only small, bite-size pieces (or beans, or peas, or asparagus — whatever is fresh, seasonal and thus cheap)

dried pasta shapes, whichever you have in the cupboard

*The pasta should have plenty of nooks and crannies to take and hold a thick sauce.*

250g 'dry' scallops — scallops which have not been soaked and removed of their freshness and flavour

*Run a tap over them to remove any clinging sand or whatever is left behind from King Neptune's locker. Using a paring knife, remove the hard gristle running down the back of the scallop.*

juice of 1 lemon

50g butter for the scallops

1 Soften the onions and garlic with the chillies in a little olive oil, 15–20 watchful minutes. Meanwhile, cook the pumpkin, wrapped in plastic, in the microwave until it takes easily to the knife — somewhere about 10–15 minutes, depending on how thick the pieces are. It should be firm, yet soft enough to mash with a fork.

2 Mash the pumpkin with a fork or potato masher. The pumpkin should not be puréed in a food processor. It should be done by hand to maintain its slightly 'rustic' feel. Mix in the onions–garlic–chillies, half the chives, orange juice, the butter and cream, and taste for seasoning. It will probably need a teaspoon of salt, and no pumpkin dish can take

too much black pepper. Set aside in a warm place. The mixture should be quite thick, but still pourable — just.

3 Cook the broccoli until it takes easily to the knife. Broccoli has more flavour if allowed to cook until it might seem to be overdone. Keep it slightly on a raw side when you are using broccoli with dips. Set aside. You will re-heat the pumpkin and broccoli at the death.

4 Cook the pasta, following the instructions on the packet. Heat the oven to 220°C.

5 Heat a heavy pan which can go into the oven, with a tiny amount of oil, until it is very, very hot. Toss in the scallops, without overcrowding the pan. You have to allow each scallop plenty of room to sizzle successfully. The scallops will exude their own juice as they cook. Don't be fooled into undercooking scallops. They are quite muscular little fellows and need at least a couple of minutes belting about the pan, and several more in the oven. Feel them. They should be firm, with plenty of give. Slice one as a test: they should be just done, translucent, but not pure-white in the middle. When they are done, leave them in the pan but off the heat, douse them in the lemon juice, give them a little salt and pepper, and allow the butter to melt into them.

6 Re-heat the pumpkin and broccoli as needed — they should be hot enough anyway, as all the above takes only a few minutes — and toss the pumpkin through the pasta in

the pan with the scallops. Add the broccoli and extra chives, and serve.

WINE ✤ *I like aged riesling with scallops. Winemakers unfortunately describe these wines as having a kero-like aroma. The best come from Clare or Eden Valley or central Victoria. After 4–6 years in the bottle they are a treat.*

♥

## PUMPKIN GNOCCHI, GIVEN A GRILLING

Gnocchi are now to be seen in the smart shops and flash kitchens across town. A certain irony there. What is, essentially, not much more than what my mum used to call a dumpling, a very working-class, peasant-level feed, is hitting it off in places which house Range Rovers and clipped poodles.

I can't think of anything better to be hot, unless it is *osso buco*, or fish soup, or braised ox tail, or mashed potatoes, or anything, in fact, that peasants cook. It has to be good, just think about it. If you are not too flush with the folding material, you are going to work like hell to make sure the flavours you serve up day and night, week in, week out, are pretty good.

Thus it was/is with gnocchi. A purée of a staple like potato, or pumpkin, held together with a little egg yolk, if you had a few old chooks, given body with flour and flavoured with herbs from the garden; from that comes the basis of any food you like. From a staple through to something that shows how smart you are. Thus, if you've suddenly come into some money, you can show off with gnocchi tossed in a rich, expensive sauce, flavoured with cream and mushrooms and some lobster, and, if you're really swell, truffles. If you're in the midst of a losing streak, don't lose heart, just throw the gnocchi about with a bit of ham, or butter, or cheese, or herbs.

When I'm not feeling lazy, I double-cook the gnocchi. First in boiling water, until they float, then briefly in a thick, rich, heavily flavoured sauce, allowing the gnocchi to take in all the flavours from the pan. Drain off any excess and serve sprinkled with fresh herbs, or slices of lobster or chicken or turkey, or just a handful of herbs and a grated, flavoursome, hard cheese.

When I am feeling lazy, which is the other 99.9 per cent of the time, I'll spoon all the gnocchi into an oven-proof bowl, sprinkle some olive oil and herbs about, grate some melting cheese over the top (Gruyère, Raclette, cheddar or the like), and put the lot under the grill. Once the cheese is melted, sprinkle the bowl with your best virgin olive oil, then the herbs from the garden. *This* is wow department.

♥ ♥ ♥ ♥ ♥

**1 kg of butternut pumpkin**

**2 egg yolks**

**1 teaspoon salt**

**plenty of black pepper**

**1 teaspoon nutmeg**

**freshest herbs you have, chopped roughly**

**2 teaspoons good quality virgin olive oil for the mix, as much as you like for the sauce**

**a few nuts, chopped to the size of peppercorns**
*These are optional —the use of nuts in gnocchi is hardly loyal to their peasant beginnings. Nuts add a little surprise crunch in the middle.*

**300 g sifted plain flour**

**more herbs**

**your favourite melting cheese**
*Raclette is best, Gruyère runs second, cheddar gets the bronze medal.*

**a hard grating cheese**

1 Cook the pumpkin in its skin and allow it to cool. The best way to do this is in the microwave. Put it on a plate and cook on high until the skin changes colour and is soft as a baby's botty. You can do this a day ahead. Slice away the skin. Remove the seeds, and put the pumpkin through the mouli (or a fine sieve) to purée it. If you use the end without seeds, just mash it with a fork. (The same applies with potatoes. Use floury spuds, and don't purée them in a processor.) The pumpkin could be quite moist. If it is, spread it on a plate to allow some of the moisture to evaporate. This is not absolutely necessary, but it will allow for a marginally better end result. Once the seeds and skin have been removed, you will be left with about 650 g of purée.

2 Gently mix the egg yolks, salt, black pepper, nutmeg, herbs, olive oil (and nuts) through the cooled pumpkin purée.

3 Fold in the flour in several additions, doing it gently, to keep the mix as light as you can. The gnocchi will be a long way from firm when they are ready. They have no legs of their own, and can only be patted

into shape, never kneaded. The amount of flour added depends on how much moisture there is in the potatoes or pumpkin. You will need a fair amount of flour on the chopping board to keep the gnocchi on target for the pot and not the board.

4 Break the dough into two (or three) parts. With floured hands, gently roll out the gnocchi like a long sausage, about 3 cm in diameter. Cut into pieces at about 3-cm intervals. Dust with a little flour and set on grease-proof paper.

5 Bring a large pot of water to the boil and toss in enough gnocchi to cover about three-quarters of the base. Cook at a fast boil until they float — about 2 minutes. Leave for about a minute and remove, draining well. Put them into an oven-proof bowl, allowing a layer of gnocchi per person, and drizzle some olive oil and herbs over the top. Cover with melting cheese and cook under the grill until the cheese is melted.

6 Serve as is, with grated hard cheese and more olive oil and herbs on the side.

7 If you toss the gnocchi through a sauce in a pan, do it gently, allowing the sauce to impregnate the dumplings. Serve with only the sauce which adheres to the balls. Whatever else you are serving with the gnocchi, cook separately and either toss through or serve on the side.

WINE ✤ *Almost anything goes here. In winter, try a glass of amontillado or oloroso sherry. In summer, a nice, aged Hunter semillon.*

♥
## PESTO, BY HAND

I could eat pesto until my hair turned green. It has everything that good eating should have — the freshness of the season, through the basil, the pungency of the garlic, the twists and depths of flavour of the olive oil and the Parmesan, the chunky texture of the nuts, and the romance of thousands of years and millions of hands making it, loving it.

And yet, remarkably, none of these powerful forces overcomes any of the others. Toss a spoonful around the mouth, and you should be able to taste all the players, each making its mark bit by bit. That's real quality.

I first ran into pesto in a very down-market, though highly attractive, Italian eating house, entered after a climb up rickety, dark stairs. I remember clearly the day I asked the waiter what the *pesto Genovese*, listed as a daily special, was. There was a sharp intake of breath and a rolling of eyes, together making for that wonderful moment that comes from a combination of frustration and contempt. You could tell this very Italian man thought that this Australian, all Australians, were drongos, or the Southern Italian equivalent.

'Pesto,' he said, extending to his full height, 'is a very old dish from ma country. It is made from basil, the besta cheese and virgin olive oil.' What he could well have added was this: 'What you are about to take may well affect you terminally.' It did. Life without pesto would be, well...

In Genoa, where it all began, they say, they are horrified if you use anything but a pestle and mortar to make the sauce (pesto — pestle, get it?), but in other parts of Italy they are not so strict, and use various knives and whizzers. I am not prepared to compromise. There is no doubt the version made with a pestle and mortar is wildly superior to that made in a machine, and not just because it suits my romantic nature. It is better in the same way as *Casablanca* is/was better on the silver screen than it is/was/will be on TV.

♥  ♥  ♥  ♥  ♥

**50 g pine nuts**
*You can use walnuts if you like. Some Italian food historians suggest that walnuts were in fact the original, others pine nuts. Use what's available, then choose what you like.*

**1 teaspoon salt, preferably rock salt**

**2 teaspoons black peppercorns**

**1–3 cloves peeled garlic, depending on your need for it**

**1 ½ cups best quality olive oil**
*Don't compromise here.*

**5 cups basil leaves**

**200 g Parmesan, grated**
*Of course Parmigiano Reggiano is best, but it is also very expensive. The difference between it and Grana Padano is there, but even I can cope without it here, given the price difference.*

**1** Mix the nuts, salt, peppercorns, garlic and a little of the oil, and crush them in the mortar. It's a good idea to crush the garlic with the back of a knife before you attack it with the pestle. If you haven't got a mortar, you can do all this with a kitchen hammer, but I bet you wouldn't do it twice.

**2** Add most of the basil leaves — leave a half a cup for later — a handful at a time, and work the lot together, adding a little oil here and there to assist the blending.

**3** Add the cheese, and pound it all together.

**4** Put the lot into a bowl and gradually add the rest of the oil, working the mix with a wooden spoon. Work in the rest of the basil. That's it. Don't worry about how long it lasts. It won't.

Try the following:
♥ Pesto on toast, with finely sliced tomatoes and black pepper.
♥ Steamed spinach, chopped, tossed with pesto.
♥ Boiled potatoes, drained, and immediately tossed with stacks of pesto.
♥ The loin of lamb — or the fillet of beef or chicken — stuffed or wiped with pesto, and roasted.
♥ Any vegetable- or cheese-based ravioli, tossed with pesto and given a double whammy of Parmesan, a little melted butter and black pepper.
♥ When making bread, mix pesto through the dough as you mix it; or roll it in before the last proving.
♥ Scrambled eggs, mixed generously with pesto (sigh); or boiled eggs on toast with pesto.
♥ Eggplant, sliced in half, roasted (gently) until tender, given a thick rub with pesto, and grilled.
♥ The boiled rice from a local takeaway, given a new lease on life with pesto.
♥ Anything — with pesto.

WINE ✤ *There is something about garlic and red wine — I'm sure they make Italy such a civilised place. There's lots of underlying richness in pesto that needs* some acid from a younger wine to cut through it. Don't pull out your prized bottle of twenty-year-old red. Try a young Coonawarra shiraz (it may be labelled 'Hermitage') or a cabernet from southern Victoria (Geelong, Yarra Valley, Mornington Peninsula).

♥

## GOAT'S CHEESE AND SPINACH RAVIOLI

Food machines are my favourite toys, but I do draw the line occasionally. Asparagus cookers? Forget it. Expensive steamers? What's wrong with a battered old colander? Ravioli makers? Now *that* is the limit.

There was a time when I thought you couldn't make ravioli unless you had one of those extraordinary instruments that attach somehow to the top of those extra useful, tried and trusted, hand-powered pasta machines. The ravioli extra is something like a laundry shute, as seen in forties hotel movies. Two strips of pasta approach each other from opposite sides and a highly flavoured mixture is gobbled up as the strips rush through the machine. At least that's what happens in the literature.

What really happens is that you get bored, and end up in a sticky mess, and in a tizz, and probably give up. The attachment ends up in the back of the cupboard with the jams and chutneys you bought at a fete in 1979. You know the place. There's another, simpler solution, but don't be fooled by it either. This is a tray — like an ice-block tray, with ridged squares on top, looking not unlike moulds of ravioli — a roller, and that's it. They sell like hot cakes at Christmas. You lay a sheet of pasta on the tray, easing it into the

slots, spoon in your mixture, lay another layer of pasta, roll, and pop, you have your ravioli! Forget it. Another waste of money. Why? Too few ravioli per gram of sweat, too sticky, too messy. A waste of time. There's only one advantage to the show. The tiny roller makes for a terrific first pastry roller for the kids.

It is clear why such 'machines' as these proliferate. We are so gullible, such consumers, such dreamers. Suckers. We see and love a bowl of ravioli in a flash restaurant. Next we are strolling past a food shop, and there it is, the answer to our dreams: a ravioli maker.

I have mentioned to friends that I have made ravioli. They look at you aghast, as if you had said you were best mates with Frank Sinatra. If I'd a spare ravioli machine on me, they'd have snapped it up in a flash, used it once, and offered it for sale in the local trader for a quarter of what they paid for it.

The local trader is a great place to watch as dreams explode into life's shrapnel. You see whizzers, bread makers, electric pasta machines, mixers, juice machines, coffee makers, microwaves, ice cream machines; and of course, ravioli makers. Forget the tricks. Think of ravioli as a pair of silk sheets. You slide in between and cuddle up. There's your filling. There's your ravioli.

♥ ♥ ♥ ♥ ♥

**80 g spinach, weighed after it has been cooked and wrung out of any excess moisture (about ½ bunch)**

**80 g goat's cheese, or a strongly flavoured cheddar, or Ricotta**

*Goat's cheese has taken off in the last few years, at no surprise at all to me. It has more guts per cubic millimetre than* any other cheese I know. It makes for a glorious key component of ravioli, a luscious topping on pizza for a quick but delicious lunch, and much more. Ricotta is a terrific cheese for this dish if you look at it from another flank. If you go for goat's cheese you are looking to it to provide the dominant flavour; if you use Ricotta, then the spinach provides the guts. Don't take that as a put-down of Ricotta: spinach is a really gorgeous, much under-rated vegetable. And one other thing: Ricotta is about ten times cheaper than goat's cheese.

1 chilli, chopped finely

1 clove garlic, chopped finely

juice of 1 lemon

a good pour of olive oil

a little nutmeg, grated

¹/₄ bunch of chives, chopped

salt

black pepper

1 Break up the cheese into walnut-sized pieces.

2 When the spinach is as dry as you can get it, toss it into a whizzer with the cheese, chilli, garlic, lemon juice, olive oil, nutmeg and chives, and let 'er rip. When the mix has become a purée, taste for seasoning and adjust with salt and pepper.

3 Make the pasta as usual (see page 15). Roll it out to its thinnest and place two sheets side by side. Spoon bits of mixture about 6 cm apart on one layer, moisten with a little water around the filling, put the other layer on top, and push down gently with your fingers. Slice into separate rounds, squares, whatever, and re-roll the edges. You must do this or you will have a ravioli with two different thicknesses of pasta — one covering the filling, and the two parts coming together at the edges. Cut away any excesses caused by the re-rolling and keep the extra pasta for soup, or something.

4 Bring some water to the boil and cook the ravioli for about 4–5 minutes, testing all the while. They are done when the edges are done.

5 Serve the ravioli with your favourite cream or butter sauce, or pesto, or a tomato purée given a lift with a handful of herbs. There's another ripper sauce that takes any ravioli into the glorious: a good pour of the best virgin olive oil, a vigorous turn of the pepper mill, fresh herbs, a touch of balsamic vinegar, and plenty of Parmesan. Always serve a gentle sauce with ravioli. If you have made them properly, they should provide enough flavour and fun of their own: the sauce is only for its moisture, and middle flavour.

Note: There's another rule to *knowing* whether the ravioli will work. If the mix is happy on a piece of thick, crusty, buttered bread, then it's a goer.

WINE ✤ *Light red has always sounded more like a faction of the Labor Party rather than a wine style to me. Too many of them lack complexity of flavour. The best in this style is Cab Mac — or just buy a good medium-bodied shiraz.*

## ♥
## A SEXY TALE OF SWEDES AND PASTA

This piece of writing, which was originally written for *The Sunday Age*, is reproduced here, word for word, because it makes me laugh whenever I re-read it.

I think I must be drifting into some sort of mental illness. The symptoms manifested themselves just the other day when I strolled into the local fruit shop and fell in love with the swedes.

It takes a certain mind to fall in love with vegetables, especially brown and yellow balls that look remarkably like those strange steel orbs that European men toss about in parks on sunny Sunday mornings. I used to think that swedes tasted like steel balls too, but that was in those dark days when such vegetables were force-fed to ungrateful children; like me.

I'm not like that any more, but now my past is coming back to haunt me through my children. If you ever see a cook book claiming it is full of enticing recipes for children, it's either lying or each recipe is stacked to the eyeballs with sugar. I have discovered you can serve up the same dish four nights in a row, and one of them will eat it on Monday, another on Tuesday, all will deny it on Wednesday, and on Thursday they'll sing in chorus: 'Why can't we have this more often, dad?' But ...
... What can you do when your own mother recalls such atrocities from your early, and not so early, days? Like the time, I am reminded, when I took a mouthful of swede, thinking it was potato, and spat it out all over the table. 'There, there, dear,' she said at the time. We don't deserve such mothers, do we?

Swedes don't deserve their reputation as pig feed either. They have a guts that pumpkin doesn't, a colour that turnips miss, a touch of this and a hint of that, and they are cheap now, and always will be. Which, in the end, is why I fell in love with them.

The challenge was to make them more interesting to the unbelievers. As much as my new-found lover has plenty to recommend it in its usual guises of steamed, baked, or puréed accompaniment to most roasts, it needs a little lift to make it, well, sexy.

Try this: mash it gently, confuse it with a little aggressively tasty cheese, and a little chilli, and wrap it in pasta. Naturally, it would be Swedish ravioli.

♥   ♥   ♥   ♥   ♥

**4 firm swedes**
*Forget the soft ones, they've been waiting for a lover for too long.*

**salt**

**black pepper**

**1 hot chilli, chopped finely**

**handful of fresh thyme, squeezed from the stems, for the filling, and more for the sauce**

**50g butter, and 50g more (softened) for the sauce**

**200g Parmesan, and 50g more for grating**
*You could use a milder cheese for the filling, like Ricotta, but I prefer a more aggressive flavour, somewhere between Ricotta and goat's cheese. Provolone would be fine, or an aged cheddar. You must use a Parmesan style for grating.*

1 Peel the swedes, chop them into eighths, and place them in a bowl for the microwave. Cook them on high, covered, for about 10 minutes, depending on the power of your machine, until they are tender to the knife. Drain any excess moisture and sprinkle swedes with salt, black pepper and the butter. Set aside to cool.

2 Once the swedes are cool, mix the cheese, chilli and thyme through with a fork, or your fingers, until it comes together. It should be just short of dry, with a tangible amount of moisture.

3 Place on your sheets of pasta and enclose as before. Cut into shapes you like.

4 Cook in rolling boiling water for 4–5 minutes, until the pasta is cooked and gives to the bite. Drain.

5 Toss in the softened butter, black pepper, grated Parmesan and extra thyme, until the butter has melted and attached to the ravioli. Serve more Parmesan on the side.

*WINE* ✤ *Hunter semillon is something you cannot hurry. They often take 4–6 years before they blossom. The most consistent styles are from McWilliam's and Rothbury.*

♥
## COUSCOUS, FOR SWELLS

L ife seems to run permanently on the edge. Not enough time for this, not enough time for that, too much time for not much at all. What it means, I guess, is that you've got the ball, 20 metres from goal, you can win the game with the last shot, but five opponents are about to grab you.

It's how you react to the pressure that counts.

I've done it by subscribing to couscous on a very regular basis. When all else is lost you can be sure that a shot at couscous will win the big game. It's one of those rare 'givens' which takes hardly a second to prepare, and yet has a marvellous capacity to take on board the most ordinary of guests and change them into something of great class.

Couscous, the dish, is the steamed, or infused, swollen grains of semolina, made from wheat grain. With all sorts of add-ons, it is very much part of life in North Africa, particularly in Morocco, where it can claim status as a national dish.

Not so long ago, each family would have its wheat ground to its needs at local mills; back home, the grain would be rubbed with fine flour, so that grains would separate easily when steamed. The true-to-generations form of couscous is as far away from the pace of today as the ship of the desert. In old times it was at first moistened and then rubbed between the fingers, sieved, steamed, rubbed again, steamed again, and then served. Too much for me. I'll go for the pre-cooked, packaged couscous.

The big-shot couscous meal of Morocco is couscous with seven vegetables, some of which are certain to be zucchini, eggplant and carrots, but more likely to be whatever vegetables cope with slow cooking and are still hanging around at the end of a busy week.

What I like about couscous has not a lot to do with traditional recipes put together laboriously in a couscoussier, but more to do with its great texture, and its ability to assist with other sometimes lesser flavours. In my wild butter-with-everything days, a ripper couscous was no more than piping hot grain laced with melted butter, black pepper, stacks of herbs and a creamy blue cheese. Those were the days.

♥ ♥ ♥ ♥ ♥

6 tomatoes, skinned (or 250 g tin of tomatoes)

1 hot chilli, chopped finely

salt

black pepper

250 g packet couscous

good pour of olive oil

4 eggs

the freshest grab of herbs from your garden, but you must have tarragon

a few strips of smoked salmon per person

1 teaspoon caraway seeds

Parmesan for grating

1 Cook down the tomatoes with the chilli, some salt and black pepper until they have reduced and thickened — about 25 minutes in the microwave.

2 Prepare the couscous as described on the packet: bring 250 ml of water to the boil with a little salt and olive oil. Remove from heat and stir in 250 g of the couscous grains. Allow to swell and add a good pour of your best virgin olive oil. Set aside.

3 In a wide saucepan, bring a few centimetres of water to the boil, reduce to barely a murmur, and add the eggs, one at a time. Maintain at a simmer for a minute. Put on a lid and turn down the heat for another minute, then turn off the gas. You must make sure that both parts of the white have set just firm and the yolk is undercooked.

4 Re-heat the couscous gently and mix through the tomato sauce, herbs, strips of smoked salmon and caraway seeds.

5 Serve with the egg sitting gently on top of the pile of couscous. Sprinkle with plenty of black pepper and some herbs, and have some grated Parmesan on side.

6 Pop the egg and go for your life.

WINE ♣ *Traminer is the forgotten grape of the Australian wine industry, but the good ones are still great. Try one with this dish. I like Orlando Flaxmans, Lilydale Vineyards and Tim Knappstein's from Clare.*

♥

## POLENTA, ANY WAY YOU LIKE

Polenta is one of those archetypal Italian dishes which conjures up pictures of medieval housewives — sleeves rolled up, stirring and stirring, and stirring and stirring, in front of a massive hearth. Meanwhile, the men folk are lounging at table taking drink and waiting for mum to serve lunch, or afternoon tea, or dinner, or whatever.

It had not been part of my repertoire, shying away as I do from jobs which take any great length of time. In stepped Barbara Kafka, and her marvellous book, *Microwave Gourmet*. This book, more than any other, set me on a path of creativity through the microwave. Until then I had considered it with some fair amount of disdain, probably based on distrust as much as anything.

Ms Kafka had been through similar crises, confronted them head-on, and discovered the microwave as a marvellous tool in the kitchen. Now I look on it as an extra cook in the kitchen, another pair of hands, something entirely consistent in its results. It is always able to come up with another surprise, or better still, a breakthrough.

Such is the case with polenta, the grain resulting from dried corn kernels. If you look at ten thousand Italian cook books, this is what they will tell you: 'Toss the grains gently into a stream of boiling water, and stir constantly for half to one hour.' Do it in the microwave and it costs you no time at all.

♥   ♥   ♥   ♥   ♥

³/₄ cup polenta

4 cups water

2 teaspoons salt

50g butter

black pepper

50g Parmesan, or for something really rich, your favourite blue cheese

plenty of fresh herbs

1 Mix the polenta, water and salt in a wide bowl, and cook uncovered for 6 minutes. Stir, and then cook for about the same time, until the mixture gets somewhere near what you'd call 'setting point' if you were making jam. The longer you cook the mixture, the firmer it will become.

2 It's really up to you what you add to the cooked polenta. A good starting point — and this applies to most pasta, or rice, or couscous, or polenta — is to look about and see what has a gusty flavour, but needs a carrier to take it into the big time. Start with plenty of butter, black pepper and a solidly flavoured cheese, and whip the lot together, adding the freshest herbs from your garden. That's it really. It makes for a delicious accompaniment to just about anything.

3 If you leave the polenta to cool down, it will firm up, and be not unlike bread. This is the sort of stuff that flash restaurants serve next to beef and lamb and chicken when they are going through a back-to-peasantry phase. They usually serve it grilled, drizzled with more butter, and perhaps topped with a melting cheese.

WINE ✤ *Shiraz from the mother Barossa has all the spice, oomph and honesty needed here. Try St Hallett's Old Block, Rockford's or Wolf Blass Brown Label.*

♥

## RISOTTO, THE BASICS

Before I became really keen on risotto, I had always believed it to be about long and tedious and watchful cooking. And it is. And also about richly flavoured stocks adding bite to just-crunchy rice, and it is. But, and this is an important but, it is also rice which does not need hard-working stock to make it perform at its top — not at all. It is simple rice, with rich sauces providing the necessary kick to take you and it into heaven.

What I have learned well is this: if there is anything more wonderful, at the end of 20 minutes of reasonable concentration and minimal labour and hardly any cost, then I haven't found it.

It's open to debate whether cooking is an art form or not, but it certainly needs an audience to reach its peak. I think if I were cooking for myself, I'd become a vegetarian, extend the vegetable garden, and cook a huge batch of risotto once a week. I'd re-heat it daily, adding different vegetables, herbs and spices to give it new life. I'd fry it, bake it, turn it into a soup. I'd become a world champion risotto maker, an authority, an evangelist, and change my life. I'd start a risotto restaurant, write risotto books, become a risotto consultant, make a fortune, hire somebody to cook for me, and probably never eat risotto again. That's what life's all about, isn't it?

The secret to success with risotto is to have two large, heavy-based pots, one for cooking the rice, the other for preparing and maintaining a stock at a simmer while you are making whoopee with the rice. A vegetable stock is best as the basis for anything. It needs to be made of a decent load of aromatics: plenty of carrots, plenty of celery, plenty of parsnip, a good amount of black pepper, some herbs, bay leaves, and not much more. Just do it once a week and you can keep it on top of the stove. Whatever the guide books say, risotto tastes very good if made with no more than boiling water. Don't be put off if you can't be bothered with a stock.

Ideally, you will need a full-flavoured vegetable stock to infuse the grains. Those who don't believe this should think again. What we are enjoying here is the starchy flavour of high quality rice. A simple stock to try needs 1 tin of peeled Italian (Roma) tomatoes, 2 parsnips, 1 leek, 2 carrots, 1 stick of celery, a little white wine, 4 cups water, black pepper, 1 chilli, all cooked for an hour or so gently; the stock strained and reserved, the vegetables left to accompany something dull.

♥　♥　♥　♥　♥

### THE RISOTTO

**1 medium-sized onion, chopped finely**

**1 clove garlic, chopped finely**

**1/2 cup virgin olive oil**

**2 cups Italian rice, usually labelled Arborio rice**

**plenty of stock or boiling water**

### THE GARNISH

**50 g butter**

**parsley, chopped roughly**

**plenty of Parmesan**

**1** Cook the onion and garlic gently in the olive oil, allowing it to glisten rather than fry. Keep stirring gently for a few minutes, until the onion softens.

**2** Toss in the rice and stir it around on a low heat for a couple of minutes to allow each grain to be touched by the oil.

**3** Add a ladle of boiling stock, stirring through the rice until the stock has been absorbed. Repeat about 5 more times, stirring until the rice absorbs the stock. The whole process will take about 15 or 16 minutes: you can bet on it. You can feel and see the rice getting to the cooked stage. It is obvious that it has been cooked through. Test it by feel and taste. It is much better to test it too often than to find you have a soggy, overcooked mass, or an undercooked bunch of crunchy individuals. Set aside.

4 When the risotto has reached its ideal state — it should have some pourability, but not by any sense, a liquidity — mix through the sauces you like. At its most basic, minimalist level, it works very well with no more than butter and parsley and Parmesan. And there are two other little tricks which make the basic job luxurious: a little tarragon and a splash of poppy seeds. Might sound funny, but trust me.

Try these options, before you move on:
♥ Risotto with chunky pumpkin, tarragon, chilli and Parmesan.
♥ Risotto with puréed pumpkin, flavoured with a little curry, caraway seeds and peeled, chopped tomatoes.
♥ Risotto with steamed broccoli and steamed cauliflower, cooked until quite soft, mixed with parsley and cheese.
♥ Risotto with uncooked shredded carrot and garam masala.
♥ Risotto with baked, skinned red peppers, olives and cheese.
♥ Risotto in a soup of vegetable stock from all the leftovers of the week.
♥ Risotto with a handful of podded peas, sugar peas, or beans.

♥ Risotto with steamed mussels and clams, and all sorts of herbs.
♥ Risotto with the most full-flavoured, dried mushrooms, cooked from the beginning through the rice, and tossed with thyme and Parmesan.
♥ Risotto with eggplant, tomato and zucchini, with stacks of basil and Parmesan.
♥ And for meat eaters: risotto with the meat from a slow-cooked ox tail, removed from the bone and tossed through, late. Don't forget the carrots!

♥

## MY FAVOURITE, RISOTTO WITH PUMPKIN

The microwave opened a new door to the wonders of baked pumpkin, freeing us from the agony of slicing it and the danger of skinning it. Baked in the microwave, pumpkin reduces to a marvellous melting consistency, easily, relatively quickly, and you can peel the skin away as if it is a new season's mandarin. Worked through pasta with a little cream, pepper and herbs, it makes for a quick and delicious dish. Worked similarly through risotto, it stands as the most cooked dish in my kitchen.

♥ ♥ ♥ ♥ ♥

### THE RISOTTO

1 medium-sized onion, chopped finely

1 clove garlic, chopped finely

1/2 cup virgin olive oil

2 cups Italian rice, usually labelled Arborio rice

plenty of stock or boiling water

1 butternut pumpkin

plenty of tarragon, leaves removed from the stems

a good amount of thyme

salt

black pepper

Parmesan

2 teaspoons black poppy seeds

1 Make the risotto (see page 43) and while it is going through its usual phases, have the butternut pumpkin in the microwave chuffing away. It will take about 25 minutes on high, depending on the power of your machine.

2 When the pumpkin is done, skin half of it, leaving the rest for another day, and remove the seeds. Lightly mash the pumpkin with a fork, mixing in most of the tarragon and thyme. Keep a little of the herbs for the table.

3 When the risotto is about nine-tenths done, mix the pumpkin in, stirring it so it touches as many grains as possible. Continue the cooking until the rice is done. Season, toss in the poppy seeds, and mix through.

4 Serve in large bowls, with Parmesan on the side for mixing through and herbs for sprinkling.

WINE ❧ *Imagine a cold winter's day, a big steaming bowl of pumpkin risotto in front of you. How about an Australian amontillado or oloroso sherry? Nutty, bitter–sweet, delicious. Seppelt, McWilliams, Mildara all make good sherry. Go to the top of the range.*

♥

# OLD FLAVOURS: RISOTTO WITH CAULIFLOWER

Cauliflower has made a comeback. For most of Australia's history, it was a heavily cooked holder of very thick, very rich white sauces given a final kick along with nutmeg. Nothing wrong with that, and nothing better to serve at a dinner party, especially if the guests are thirty-forty-fifty-sixty-something. There's another way to give them a hit of the memories, while offering something different, something with style. Give them risotto with cauliflower and let them add the nutmeg, grating it themselves, at the table.

♥   ♥   ♥   ♥   ♥

### THE RISOTTO

1 medium-sized onion, chopped finely

1 clove garlic, chopped finely

½ cup virgin olive oil

2 cups Italian rice, usually labelled Arborio rice

plenty of stock or boiling water

1 cauliflower, chopped into its little flowers

¼ broccoli, cut into its little flowers

plenty of Parmesan

the freshest herbs you can find

salt

black pepper

50g butter, unsalted

nutmeg, and grater or sharp knife

1 Start the risotto as usual (see page 43), cooking through a couple of additions of stock, then add the cauliflower and mix it through.

2 Continue cooking the risotto, stirring, making sure you do it gently. It's okay for most of the cauliflower to give itself to the dish, but any pieces left here and there add another dimension of texture and a different burst of flavour.

3 Cook the broccoli pieces in the microwave, covered, for a few minutes, until tender.

4 When the risotto is just about done, add the broccoli pieces and the Parmesan, and season. Complete cooking and serve, with a liberal sprinkling of fresh herbs and a good whack of butter.

5 Play an Elvis record and don't forget the nutmeg!

WINE ✚ *The other great semillon style in Australia, besides that of the Hunter, comes from the Barossa. These wines are more approachable when young and can do with some oak maturation. Basedows White Burgundy is a good example of the style. Other variations on the theme to try are Peter Lehman's and Krondorf Chablis.*

♥

## RISOTTO WITH SARDINES

This is not absolutely faithful to classical risotto making, but more a case of me seeking as many ways as possible to utilise the unique qualities of this very under-rated and always cheap fish. The difference is that you cook the fish separately, fillet it yourself at the table, and toss it through the traditionally cooked risotto. It makes for a wonderful, hands on, hands in, community dish, and that's the best part of eating anyway.

♥   ♥   ♥   ♥   ♥

1 large onion, chopped roughly

a good pour of virgin olive oil for the risotto, a little for the sardines

2 cups Arborio rice

some boiling stock on the side

2 zucchini, sliced finely into coin shapes

1 chilli, chopped finely

dozen sardines, gutted

*You can do this simply. Just pop open the belly with your fingers, rip out the guts, and clean the lot under a little running water.*

a little flour

1 carrot, grated

zest of 1 lemon

handful of fresh herbs

a little lemon juice

salt

black pepper

some Parmesan or cheddar, grated

1 On a low heat, cook the onions in the oil until they change colour, then add the rice, stirring so it is well-coated by the oil. Add a cup of boiling stock and stir until the rice has taken it in. Maintain the gentle heat all through the cooking process.

2 Add the zucchini slices and the chilli, and stir through. You can use any seasonal vegetable, or any combination of them — the idea is

not necessarily to create flavour, but variations in texture, a little flavour and some colour.

3 Repeat the addition of stock, stirring it through until the rice is just about cooked. This takes about 15–16 minutes. After about 15 minutes, test a few grains to see how cooked they have become. The rice is perfectly cooked when it is tender, but still just takes to the bite. You know you have put your teeth into it. Set aside when the rice is just a little undercooked.

4 Now the sardines. You can fillet them completely and throw the boneless fillets into the risotto at the final stages, but the filleting process would drive you crazy. Better to cook them quickly, serve them on the side, and fold them through the risotto at the table. It also provides a bit of action and peasantry at the table.

5 The best way to cook sardines is by using a wide, heavy-based, flat frying pan, of the sort made by Le Creuset. Pat the sardines dry in a paper towel and dip them in a little flour. Heat a little oil in the pan until a speck of flour sizzles. Add the sardines quickly, but one at a time, kicking them about the pan so they don't stick. When they are all sizzling furiously, the adhering flour has cooked and the base of the pan is hot, turn off the heat. Turn the sardines, cover the pan with a lid, and leave the sardines to cook in the retained heat of the pan for a minute or two.

6 Finish the risotto with a final addition of stock, and work through the grated carrot, lemon zest and fresh herbs, and serve in a bowl at the table.

7 Serve the sardines with a finger bowl. Fillet them with your fingers — the flesh will come away from the bone easily. Sprinkle the fillets with a little lemon juice and then fold them through your bowl of risotto. Season and sprinkle with the grated Parmesan if you wish.

WINE ♣ *Sardines demand white wine with character — even eccentricity. I like the wines from Western Australia with grassy, herbaceous characteristics: Houghton White Burgundy, Goundrey Sauvignon Blanc or Cullen's Semillon.*

♥

## RISOTTO FOR WHISKY LOVERS

N ow for a dish for swells, or for those who have come into luck. It seems a remarkable mix — rice and whisky and crayfish — but it works wonderfully. The whisky seems to add guts to the crayfish, while surviving on its own; and yet it doesn't affect the glories of the risotto. I pinched it from Bill Marchetti, the chef of Melbourne's most popular Italian restaurant, the Latin. Marchetti, born in Germany of German–Italian parents, first saw this combination in the middle of Italy, liked it, filed it away, and serves it occasionally — usually to rave reviews.

♥    ♥    ♥    ♥    ♥

2 onions, chopped roughly

virgin olive oil

2 cups Arborio rice

stock from the crayfish carcass, kept at a boil

You can do this with boiling water, at the worst, or vegetable stock, or fish stock.

**1 crayfish, cooked for about 5 minutes per kg, so that it is undercooked**
*Remove the flesh from the carcass.*

**³/₄ cup Johnny Walker Red Label whisky**

**salt**

**black pepper**

**Parmesan**

**plenty of herbs, particularly parsley, chopped roughly**

**1** Cook the onions gently and briefly in the olive oil, until they change colour. Add the rice and coat the grains with the oil.

**2** Add a ladle of boiling stock at a time, stirring through until absorbed. After the second addition, add a little of the crayfish chopped into smallish chunks and half the whisky, sticking your nose over the bowl so as not to waste any of that wonderful aroma. Some of the crayfish goes in early to cook down almost to disintegration, so it becomes very much part of the risotto as a powerful middle flavour. You will use somewhere between six and eight ladles, and it will take about 16 minutes until the rice is just done. It should have a pouring consistency, something like lava, and be slightly resistant to the bite.

**3** When done, fold through the remaining crayfish flesh, leg meat included, and another good shot of whisky. Season.

**4** Serve with Parmesan and sprinkle with freshly chopped herbs.

A good, cheap alternative to crayfish would be mussels, cooked and removed from their shells, and worked through the rice with a few minutes cooking to go. A not so cheap alternative would be scallops — and try them with Irish Whiskey!

WINE ✤ *This needs a chardonnay that's seen some excellent oak maturation to balance the oak flavours of the whisky. Try Mt Helen from Victoria or Tyrell's Vat 47. Or just a dram of Highland Riesling!*

♥

### LEFTOVER RISOTTO

It's getting to be a little confusing when the dish you make with the leftovers turns out to be just as attractive as its parent of the day before. But I suppose that's how the pie'n'sauce came to be.
Whenever we cook risotto, we throw enough rice into a pot to feed fifteen people, and wonder why there is so much left over — occasionally, anyway.
So if you get tired of reheating the risotto, try these balls. The truth is, they hold together so well, the potential to mix and match the contents of the fridge is just about endless. You could even, for heaven's sake, use some of those things we bring out when nobody is watching — you know, tinned tuna or tinned salmon.

♥  ♥  ♥  ♥  ♥

**1 onion, chopped finely**

**200 g Provolone, or any tasty, flavoursome cheese, grated**

**3 cups cooked risotto**

*This will make about a dozen balls. Obviously, this applies equally to any leftover rice.*

**1 egg**

**1 chilli, chopped finely**

**1 clove garlic, chopped finely**

**zest of 1 lemon**

**handful of fresh herbs: basil, mint, chives, thyme, oregano — any or all of them, chopped roughly**

**a little flour**

**juice of 1 lemon**

1 Cook the onions gently in a little olive oil until they soften. Set aside to cool.

2 Grate the cheese over the rice and add the egg. Work the mixture together with a fork until it has all come together. Add the chilli, garlic, lemon zest, onions and herbs, and mix together well.

3 Form into balls about as big as a golf ball, squeezing gently in the palm of your hand. Roll in flour and set aside.

4 Heat a small amount of oil in a pan or wok until a little flour sizzles when added. Cook the balls in batches until golden, turning as required. The cooking can be completed in the oven once the balls are brown on the outside — this way they are less likely to disintegrate. Allow to drain on paper towels, and then heat through in a 200°C oven until very hot — about 3 minutes.

5 Serve as an appetiser with a little lemon juice. That's it.

*WINE* ♣ *Get a really good Fino sherry. 'Fino' means fine. These wines are apéritifs — they make you hungry. Of the Spanish Fino, Tio Pepe is the best; Aussies are well represented by Seppelt D.P.117 and Mildara George.*

# FISH AND SHELLFISH

D on't be frightened by fish. Not so long back, you might have thought you needed to be a star in the kitchen to be able to handle the slinky creatures of the deep and not so deep. I say baaagh to that. Certainly it is not true to suggest that all fish are the same and respond to similar cooking methods, but the variations are not so great as to require volume after volume on method and counter-method.

The secret to cooking fish is to start simply and to keep it simple. Make sure that the fish you buy is fresh as fresh and that you maintain that freshness, its true flavour, its essential moisture. Never cook it earlier than the moment of service, never serve it with fruit, dismiss any ideas of serving it with meat (whoever invented surf'n'turf should be slow-cooked with chillies and garlic), and never whack it in a chicken (viz: chicken stuffed with prawns — a waste of each).

Whatever you intend to serve with fish must be looked on as a flavour enhancer. A helper, an assistant to the main event. Fish has such a subtle flavour — except for the sardine, perhaps — that it should never be overwhelmed. The Japanese method of preparing fish may well be the best way to *taste* its true flavour — raw, with a little black pepper, oil and lemon juice (although I think you have to be Japanese to enjoy its usual accompaniment, wasabi, the green fiery horseradish of Japan).

But that doesn't mean that the best way to *enjoy* fish is to munch it in its natural state. There are few things better than the flavour and texture — and never underestimate the texture — of superbly cooked fish. Cook it in a little bubbling water, with a slice or two of lemon; bake it, after dredging with flour; and how can you beat one of the oldest and simplest of dishes — fish, dredged in a little flour, hit hard in a very hot pan, turned and served with melted butter, lemon juice and pepper, all brought together in the same pan?

## WHAT YOU'LL NEED

1 A friendly relationship with your local fishmonger. You'll know how good the fishmonger is by the dullness of his eyes. The eyes of the fish should sparkle; the eyes of the supplier should be tired, on the edge of sleep. The best of the fish people are up hours before dawn and they're still going at the fall of the sun. These are your most trusted friends, picking out the freshest fish of the catch, caring for it, filleting it for you, steering you in the right direction. Most of them spend their lives doing it. They are rather special, different people, anxious to assist. So don't be afraid to ask a simple, vital question when in doubt: 'What's fresh today?'

2 A rather solid bank account. Fish are generally not cheap these days, some of that because of fashion, some of it because of the scarcity of the product. But you can get bargains if you shop wisely. The trick is to buy whatever is cheapest and most plentiful. Pretty easy to remember that. If there's plenty of it, you can be sure it's running freely and the fishers have missed out at auction. Keep an eye out for specials, and don't go to the fish shop with a list. Buy what's bright-eyed and cheap, unless you're looking at the fishmonger. And don't be afraid to ask for a close look. Sometimes the special lights in the shop can trick you.

3 Eye-brow tweezers for the sole purpose of removing pesky bones from all sorts of fish. Every time I use them I wonder how some women, and the odd man, can put themselves through such agony. And why painted eyebrows anyway? What would Bob Menzies have looked like with thinly painted brows? But, in the end, thank heavens for vanity. If somebody hadn't decided thin eye-brows were hip, we would have had to invent tweezers to pick out the tiny bones in fish.

4 A very sharp knife. You should have a sharp, heavy knife for all cooking, but you must have a knife you like for fish. It doesn't have to be a boning knife, but a flexible knife of that style will certainly help. Keep it sharp, and it will open a whole new form of cooking and showmanship for you.

5 Good organisation. There is really nothing to cooking fish. No special skills are needed, no whizzo-wacko gizmos. The organisation comes with the extras you intend to serve. Make sure they're all ready. Remember, the fish will cook in a flash.

6 Herbs, fresh from the garden. A simply steamed or poached fish, a twist of lemon and a splash of redolent herbs — the dish of a three-star chef.

7 Respect for the level of your cholesterol. Fish is such a delight on its own, without splashes of oil or butter, that it is a marvellous boon for those of us with little discipline when it comes to dieting. Just serve it as it is.

8 No respect for your cholesterol level. Fish is such a delight when tossed with melted butter, it makes a mockery of all diet disciplines. Once you've tasted it moistened with melted butter, or with a touch of hollandaise or bearnaise sauce,

you keep hankering for it. If you're sensible, you'll read point 7, then point 8, then 7, then 8 ...

9 **A heavy-based pan which can go in the oven.** The simplest way to ensure moist fish is to hit it in a hot pan for about 30 seconds, then commit the lot to the oven for a couple of minutes. Moist and tender.

10 **And be aware that cooking times for fish can vary markedly from fish to fish, from day to day.** The times listed are thereabouts — it depends on the power of your oven and the thickness of the fish. After a while, you'll know exactly when fish is done, by looking at it. In the meanwhile, check regularly, pushing your finger into the fish to test its consistency and how it changes, minute by minute. And if you are cooking in the oven, remove the fish when it is underdone: it will keep cooking in its retained heat.

## WHAT YOU DON'T NEED

1 **A microwave is a marvellous kitchen tool, and will forever hold a special place in my kitchen.** But I can't see the point in cooking fish in the microwave. Fish in the microwave means exact timing, and countdowns are not part of my cooking needs. Fantasy and flair in the beginning, sight and feel in the end. And if you tell me fish cooks quickly in the microwave — how long does it take in the oven?

2 **A fish kettle looks great as a kitchen ornament and is marvellous for that annual cook-off of the lucky catch of big snapper, but you can do without it.** Too expensive.

## THE RECIPES

♥
## RAW SARDINES AND A STORY OF LIFE

I can't go past a fish shop without grabbing a handful of sardines. Some of that has to do with the fact you can get a feed of these little lovelies for not much more than half a dollar; most of it has to do with the absolutely stupendous flavour of the bright-eyed little fellows. They are also the perfect opener for an important dinner party. They are so fiddly that nobody I know can be bothered to buy them, and that giveaway price allows you to lash out on main course: perhaps crayfish or salmon or crab.

And children love them. Not to eat — but to look at and consider and wonder. One day, when I had taken a half kilo of sardines, with the intention of filleting them and marinating them for a raw sardine salad, my son decided to help. He was going through that pre-school stage of life when he was forever wondering about death, and had questions which not even a phalanx of philosophers could have answered.

'Is the fish dead, dad?' he opened.

'Yes, of course,' I replied.

'How did it died?'

'I suppose it was caught in a fisherman's net.'

'Why?'

'So we could eat it?'

'Why?'

'Why do you think?'

'I don't know.' There was a moment's pause, and then he said: 'Probably he died because he was unhappy being a fish.'

'Probably,' I said.

I decided it was a good time to go for a walk in the garden to inspect the progress of the tomatoes. When he starts to wonder about death, it seems a good time to look at a bit of new life. The dog had been excavating the tomatoes.

'I'm going to kill that dog,' I said.

'Why?' he said.

♥   ♥   ♥   ♥   ♥

½ bunch of basil

100 g butter

½ kg sardines, bright of eye, red of gill, scales firmly in place

a good pour of virgin olive oil

juice of 2 lemons

1 clove garlic, chopped finely

tarragon, chopped

2 hot chillies

250 g asparagus

1 avocado, sliced

salt

black pepper

best bread for toast

1 Make basil butter for the toast. Snip the basil with scissors. Work the butter in your hands until it is almost creamy. Mix through the basil. Refrigerate until firm. You won't need all of it for this dish, but keep it for a sauce, or a late addition to soup.

2 It takes the dickens of time to clean and fillet the fish, they are so fiddly. I suggest you take a good chair, a plastic bag, and a roll of absorbent paper. Make sure you have some restful music playing. Perhaps something from the Baroque — or a

talkative child to keep you content, or thoughtful, or thinking. Each fish takes about 30 seconds — at a relaxed pace — to clean.

Firstly, wipe away any scales under running water, then get down to the messy business. Actually, I quite like filleting sardines. It is such an ancient ritual, unaffected by the passing of millenia. All you need is some running water, a forefinger and a thumb, and a dog to take up the refuse. They would have been doing it before Christ was preaching in the temple. They would have done it before Captain Cook claimed Botany Bay. They would have done it before Federation. And I'm still doing it. The guts can be removed easily by slicing from the sardine's waste disposal department through to its neck. Take out the guts by rubbing with your forefinger, then clean the fish under running water.

3 Once the fish is gutted, pinch behind its head with your forefinger and thumb and put pressure on the backbone. Maintaining that pressure, just pull your fingers along the backbone towards the tail. On the way through, the flesh will come clear of the bones. Break off the head and tail, and you have your first cleaned and boned sardine. Wipe the fish dry of any blood or loose scales.

4 In a bowl, toss the fillets with the olive oil, lemon juice, garlic, tarragon and chilli. The chilli is vital, even if you don't believe you can cope with raw chilli. You can. I prefer to add oil to this dish, rather than rely on soaking the fish in lemon juice or lime juice as is the way with Mexican ceviche. My view is that a long swim in lemon juice dries out the fish, toughening them up. The olive oil keeps them moist, while the citrus enhances their flavour. Leave for about half an hour. That is enough for the lemon juice and oil to do their job — a day later and the flavour remains much the same. This routine applies similarly for less fiddly fish, like snapper or flathead or bream. The fillets will be much firmer and have a less forceful flavour.

5 While the fish is marinating, cook the asparagus. Chop off the tough stems, keeping them for another day, and cook the tips in boiling salted water until just done — about 5 minutes.

6 When the asparagus is done, stop the cooking quickly in cold water and set aside.

7 If you are out to impress, remove the sardines from the marinade and splay them on a pretty plate with avocado, sprinkled with the marinade, salt and black pepper.

8 Make the toast and butter it with the basil butter.

9 Re-heat the asparagus quickly and toss it through the rest of the basil butter. Serve asparagus individually and allow everyone to pile the sardines, avocado and the asparagus on the toast.

WINE ✣ *There's the tang of citrus and oil here. You cannot go past Rhine riesling. I would serve a young Rhine — 1-3 years — or a beer.*

♥
## AND NOW, SARDINES IN THE PAN

♥ ♥ ♥ ♥ ♥

1 kg sardines, fresh as fresh

250 g tin of peeled tomatoes, with no added sugar or salt
*If it's deep summer, use fresh Romas.*

salt

few sprigs of rosemary

1–2 chillies, sliced finely

black pepper

**1** Clean the sardines by wiping away any scales under running water. Break off the head, and run your fingers down the guts, until there ain't no more guts. Clean the fish under running water and set aside on paper towels. This time there is no need to fillet the fish. Cooked sardines are simple to fillet at the table, coming away from the bone very easily, and with a minimum of fuss. You will need a finger bowl and a large napkin.

**2** Make a simple tomato sauce by cooking down the tomatoes with a little salt, the rosemary and the chillies in the microwave. Cook for 20–30 minutes, and the sauce will be luscious. Remove the rosemary and set aside.

**3** In a heavy-based fry pan, heat a little olive oil until a piece of sardine sizzles on contact. Put one or two or three sardines in the pan, kicking them around to make sure there is no danger of sticking, now or later. Add the rest slowly and work them around the pan. Move them gently so they don't break

apart, and keep piling them on top of one another. Allow them to bubble away for a few minutes in their own juices, then add the tomato sauce and black pepper. Allow to heat through until just at boiling, and remove.

**4** Serve as is on buttered toast, or tossed through fresh noodles, or with steamed rice. You can eat the fish bones and all, but that is only for people who like gnashing bones between their teeth. Probably this is the bunch which has grown up taking tinned salmon, bones and all. The better thing to do is eat them as you would in bathers on the beach — without much dignity. Pick out the sardines with your fingers and draw away the fillets from each fish. You will end up with a pile of tiny backbones on your plate, tomato-encrusted fingers and a smile on your dial.

WINE ♣ *Fried sardines or raw, still it's beer and/or a young Rhine riesling.*

♥
## SARDINES, FRIED VERY SIMPLY, WITH LEMON JUICE

**I**f there are only a few of you, and not so many sardines, they are delicious pan-fried.

**1** Put a few in a sieve and toss them in sifted flour over a plate.

**2** Heat some oil in a heavy-bottomed pan (Le Creuset pans are perfect) until a little flour thrown in fries instantly (about 190°C).

**3** Put the sardines in the pan one at a time, making sure that they sizzle instantly. Cook for about 90 seconds on one side, turn over for about 30 seconds, turn off the heat, and sprinkle with freshly chopped herbs, especially parsley.

4 Put a lid on the pan and get the rest of the meal organised. When you're ready, drain the fish on absorbent paper and serve with no more than the sprinkle of lemon or lime juice, a little salt and some black pepper.

WINE ✛ *With sardines it's got to be beer and/or a young Rhine riesling.*

## ♥
## AND FINALLY, SARDINES FROM THE MIDDLE EAST

A brilliant combination I came across in Toofey's, a delightful seafood restaurant in Melbourne, is sardines with baba ghanoush, that marvellous Middle Eastern dip of eggplant and tahini (see page 102). Just cook the sardines as above (or fry them in a light batter) and serve on a few tablespoons of baba ghanoush.

Most of the things you do with sardines can be done with whitebait. The best way to serve these tiny fish is to sift some flour over a handful of them, then toss them again in a sieve, leaving only a lightly powdered fish. Pan-fry as with the sardines, for about 60 seconds, and serve with lemon or lime juice. Eat them heads, guts and all.

Funny thing about all of the above. Most people look on sardines and whitebait as bait or burley. How sad.

WINE ✛ *A young Rhine riesling or beer is the only way to go with sardines.*

## ♥
## CRAB, FOR FUN AND FLAVOUR

You cannot be considered a really, truly, serious, fun-loving cook until you have attempted to cook a giant crab. They are so intimidating, so large, so handsome, so admirable and so wonderful to eat, so satisfying and such a joy to cook successfully.

Crabs are also, despite what you might think, desperately simple to cook well.

It's just the size that has you wondering. But do try a crab, at least once in your life. The flesh and texture are at the very top of my list of all-time greats.

Those most readily available are the King Island variety and the Queensland mud crab. You'll see them wrapped in thick bands, usually still alive, eyes darting, often at the fish market rather than the suburban fishmonger's.

If you're lucky enough to have a terrific fishmonger, make a special order of a big crab now and then.

The first job to consider when you have a crab sitting on the kitchen table is how to invade that impressive armour and get at the wonderful flesh inside. Do it the way you feel most comfortable.

There is another factor to consider — where to eat it. I have come up with three alternatives: over the kitchen sink; in the bath; or in a concreted yard, with a hose handy. Eating crab is the adult version of tossing mud pies.

Whatever you do with the crab, don't smother the flesh with sauce. It is at its best when cooked in a richly flavoured sauce, but that sauce should merely be allowed to touch the flesh, rather than overwhelm it or confuse it. Any leftover sauce should be kept aside for a luscious pasta or rice dish the next day. And don't forget to retain the shell, and any bits and pieces. A crab soup is nearly as good as the first taste of the flesh.

For two, three, four, five, or six people.

♥   ♥   ♥   ♥   ♥

1 live king crab, about 2 kg

2 onions, chopped finely

¹/₂ cup sweet wine (dry, if you haven't got it)

6 rich, ripe tomatoes, skinned, chopped roughly

2 chillies, sliced roughly

2 walnut-sized pieces of ginger, chopped roughly

2 cloves garlic, sliced finely

2 sticks of celery, chopped

2 carrots, chopped roughly

1 potato per person, peeled and cut in half

salt

3 cups water

¹/₂ cup best soy sauce

¹/₂ cup virgin olive oil

bunch of coriander, chopped roughly

black pepper

1 To kill a live crab — presuming its weapons are well tied — turn it on its back, lift its tail flap and stick a skewer through its stomach and out its eye. For the crab, that will be that.

2 Soften the onions in a little olive oil, then cover with the wine. Cook quickly, making sure the onions do not burn. When most of the wine has evaporated, and the onions have softened, add the tomatoes, chillies, ginger, garlic, celery, carrots, potatoes, salt and water, and allow to bubble away until the tomatoes have softened — about 15–20 minutes.

3 Add the soy sauce, olive oil and coriander, and simmer. The stock/sauce is ready when the potatoes are done, the water has evaporated and the sauce is thick. Season with black pepper.

4 Now to the crab. With a strong knife, tear away the carapace by sliding the knife between the top and bottom shells. Run your fingers around the inner shell and remove all the muck. You will see good flesh clinging here and there. Tear away the legs and the claws.

5 Wrap a table-cloth around your neck (nothing smaller will do) and get ready to eat. Throw the body, claws and legs into the bubbling sauce first and cover. Allow to cook for a few minutes, then take out the claws and crack them with a nutcracker. Put them back after cracking, to allow some of the stock to get into the flesh while you are eating the legs. The claws will take about 5 minutes, the legs about 4. When the claws are ready, remove and start eating. Suck out the flesh and slurp on any sauce clinging to the legs/claws. Take the potatoes from the pot and scoff them between legs. (I know, I know, it sounds like a party trick. What I am saying is suck a leg, then a potato, then a leg, etc.)

6 Don't worry too much about making mistakes. If the flesh is a little undercooked, just toss it back into the sauce and keep sucking. There will be spots of crab meat and sauce all over you, your napkin, the table and the floor.

7 When it's all over, put all the left-over vegetables and herbs and shells and leg debris into another pan and cover with a cup of white wine and 4 cups of water. Bring to the boil and allow to simmer gently. This should bubble as long as your nose can stand, until heavily flavoured. Leave overnight, then remove the shells and serve as a soup/stew with plenty of bread.

WINE ✚ *A good rich chardonnay is the go here. Don't use your best crystal, as you might have hands that are a bit crabby. The best Hunter, McLaren Vale and Yarra Valley chardonnays are perfect. Or there is, of course, XXXX.*

♥

## CROSSED CULTURES AND MAKING STOCK

The bream looked terrific. Bright of eye, red of gill, something like a dasher at a fancy party. Down the back of the shop were the real workers, the cleaners of fish.

About the cleaners stood a rather excited bunch watching the last rites of a huge carp, not dead long, but dead all the same. One day I'll learn what to do with carp, but not just yet. The audience left, head with one, bones with another, fillets with a third. Then it was my turn to watch. The filleter started to fillet, which is when I started to giggle.

The fish cleaner was bristling with knives and scissors, and a cigarette hung from the corner of his lip. He was one of these smokers with that wondrous ability to speak with the fag attached miraculously to the lower lip. The ash, lengthening slowly, somehow hangs on like grim death.

As the ash grew, the fish quickly disrobed. I was transfixed by the side-show. I had no doubt the ash would not drop and, such was the display of cleaning, I knew this was a man who had done the same job thousands of times. The fillets were separated and washed meticulously, the bones snipped into manageable pieces. He looked around and smiled, packed the fillets and bones in separate bags, and, at last, flicked the wildly extended ash into the rubbish bin. It was all I could do not to cheer.

He had made such a point of trimming the bones, and the culture of the shop was clearly to utilise absolutely every portion of the fish — I just had to take the lead and make a stock. And I did, flamboyantly, somehow imagining I had a huge cigar hanging from the corner of my gob. In went the bones, onion, white wine, carrots, fennel, galangal, coriander, chilli and the last of the bottled tomatoes from the summer just gone. Soon the room was filled with a magic aroma.

Fish fillets on to a plate, into a colander, over the steaming stock. Steamed for a few minutes. Set aside for a minute, the fish still slightly undercooked. Stock ladled into a saucepan, and a little tomato purée. A quick bubble, to bring the flavours together, a little flick with a wooden spoon. Salt, black pepper, rosemary twigs, and the fish into the pan for 30 seconds, sauce on top. To table. Eat. (The cigar in the corner of the mouth is optional.)

Leave the stock bubbling. Turn off after dinner. Allow to cool overnight. The next day, strain the sauce into a new bowl, re-heat with fresh rosemary, chilli, lemon grass and galangal root. Bring to boil. Turn off, and leave for the rest of the day. Strain, check seasonings, and serve with rice or curly pasta.

The moral of the story is simple:
Ashes to ashes,
Dust to dust,
If the steamed fish doesn't get you,
Then the stock must.

WINE ✤ *For the steamed fish: the white wines from Graves in France are produced from a blend of semillon and sauvignon blanc. I actually prefer a few Aussie wines that use this same blend — they are great fish wines. Try Tim Knappstein Fumé Blanc.*

♥

## CRAYFISH BASTED WITH BASIL BUTTER

C rayfish and champagne have a lot in common. They cost too much and their joys have as much to do with the antici-pation as the taking. I have always believed champagne tastes bet-ter in the mind than on the tongue.

It's a most clever marketing wheeze. If champagne was flat and cheap nobody would have heard of it. Whoever decided that a generally dry, mildly yeasty drink from a gen-erally dry, hardly yeasty region of France should be given life through bubbles and a high price was a mar-keting genius.

The bubbles give it that 'some-thing special' feeling and the price makes it doubly exclusive. I would much prefer to drink a top-shelf white wine than a top champagne, but there *is* nothing like champagne to lift the spirits.

And it's just the same with cray-fish. You can't beat a cray for antici-pation, but there *are* plenty of tastier fish in the sea, and most of them are cheaper as well. Crays have always been expensive because they are usually captured in rather com-plicated cages rather than pack'em in nets. One advantage crayfish has over champagne is that you can get more than one go at a live, bubbling cray — the only extra that comes from champagne is a mother and fa-ther of a hangover.

I am inclined to the view that the soup, or stew, or sauce, or whatever dish you prefer to try with a crayfish stock, is as good or better than the fish itself, but that's an argument which can only be resolved after you have attacked the fish with a gusto, and then made the stock from its extras.

At one level, cooking crayfish is the easiest job in the world — you just toss them in a pot of water, bring the lot to the boil, and cook for about 10 minutes. But if you try to assist the crustacean's flavour, to bring out some of its hidden nu-ances, then you *can* run into bother.

♥ ♥ ♥ ♥ ♥

150 g unsalted butter, softened

handful of basil leaves, cut in half
*If basil is not available, go for tarragon as second best, chives third.*

juice of 1 lime or lemon

black pepper

1 live crayfish, about 850 g

*The easiest way to kill a cray is to plunge a knife between its eyes, then split it through the middle down its length. You can send it to sleep in the freezer if you wish. Clean the carapace, saving the mustard for a soup or sauce, although long-time cray fans have been known to toss it down as soon as the cray is cut. You'll find that 850 g is a good size, as it will fit in most home pans and won't need much cooking — thus ensuring the exposed flesh does not dry out.*

1 Heat the oven to flat out.

2 With your fingers, fiddle with the butter until it softens, then mix the basil with the butter, lime juice and several turns of the pepper mill, and half fill the carapace of each crayfish half with most of the basil butter, keeping about 50 g in reserve.

3 There is nothing fancy about the cooking. Lay each half — with its shell side down — in a metal pan and cook on high heat on top of the stove for a couple of minutes. That's the easy part. The secret to cooking these babies successfully is to make sure the flesh is kept moist and just cooked — not undercooked, *just* cooked.

4 Put the lot in the oven. Every few minutes, open the oven and wipe the flesh with the reserved basil butter.

5 The cray is ready when the flesh is firm, but still gives to the touch — about 10 minutes. It should not have browned at all, and the butter sitting in the cray will *not* be sizzling; if you get to the roasted, browned stage, with the butter sizzling, the flesh will be dry and tough.

6 Remove from the oven making a lot of noise, and a lot of fuss as you do it. Pour the melted butter and herbs from the carapace into a jug, and remove the flesh from the shell. It won't hurt if you use an oven glove.

7 Present with the legs, for all to grab, with the butter poured over the flesh. Keep the shell for a soup, later in the week. Sprinkle the flesh with extra lime juice and black pepper, and serve with chunky, crusty bread.

Note: If you are more disciplined and less of a show-off, you will keep the legs for tomorrow's soup.

WINE ✤ *What do you serve? Champagne of course! If you can afford French champagne, go for it. Some Australian makers are nipping at their heels. I like Croser, Yellowglen Cuvée Victoria, Domain Chandon and Seppelt Vintage Brut.*

♥

## A THAI-INFLUENCED CRAYFISH SOUP

There is nothing so rich in flavour as the stock made from a late and lamented crab or crayfish. It is so powerful it is not recommended for households that contain pregnant ladies. My wife, when heavy with child, once threatened to pour the boiling stock over my head. I'm still not sure whether it was the changes in physiology etc., that caused such an excess of behaviour, or the fact that she was kept from strong drink for nigh on forty weeks.

But if you are going to take a financial plunge and buy a crab or cray, then you *must* make the soup; and not just because it fits into the 'more meals per dollar' category of sensible home economics, but because the essential flavour of the cray, certainly, is best discovered from slow cooking in a pot of wine and water and aromatic vegetables.

It happened that the appearance of the cray corresponded with: (i) an improvement in my understanding of the mixing and matching of the flavours that are so integral to Thai cooking; (ii) a craving to try that old-fashioned French soup which goes under the rather flash handle of 'velouté'. Velouté translates literally as 'like velvet', so if you make this soup and the resulting liquid has the consistency of sand, then you sure as hell ain't made velouté.

The list of ingredients is long, but don't be put off. The method is easy.

♥   ♥   ♥   ♥   ♥

**1 kg ripe tomatoes, skinned, chopped roughly (for the final soup)**
*You can use tinned tomatoes if you wish.*

**salt**

**2 leeks, chopped roughly**

**50 g butter**

**¹/₂ bottle white wine**
*If you can't afford it, water will do.*

**the rest of the bottle of water**

**¹/₂ dozen black peppercorns, crushed**

**2 chillies, sliced finely**

**1 walnut-sized piece of ginger, or galangal if you can get it**
*Galangal is the authentic Thai ingredient — it has the look of ginger and an aroma reminiscent of bubble gum.*

**2 cloves garlic, sliced finely**

**¹/₂ kg ripe tomatoes, skinned,**

chopped (for the stock)

**2 carrots, chopped roughly**

**2 parsnips, chopped roughly**

**the shells and excess flesh of as many crayfish as you have cooked**
*If you know you are to make a soup, then reserve the legs when you cook the cray. Clean, then crush the shells into reasonably small pieces, like the pieces left after you drop (tragically) an Easter egg.*

**35 g plain flour**

**250 ml tin of coconut cream**

**3 stems of lemon grass**
*Remove the green tops and the tough outer sections.*

**the mustard from the cray's tummy**

**bunch of coriander**

**plenty of fresh herbs**

1 Cook the kilo of tomatoes in the microwave with a little salt, uncovered, for 25–30 minutes, until most of the moisture is gone and the kitchen is filled with the rich, essential aroma of tomatoes. Check the cooking occasionally, as there can be burn spots in the microwave. If you don't have a microwave, do it slowly and carefully in a heavy pot on a low heat.

2 Soften the leeks in half the butter, add the white wine, and cook for about 5 minutes until the leeks soften. Then add the water, black peppercorns, chillies, ginger (galangal), garlic, the half kilo of tomatoes, carrots, parsnips and the cray shells, and allow the lot to bubble away, at a simmer, for about an hour. Keep watching, stirring occasionally, removing any impurities which rise to the surface. Beware pregnant ladies.

3 After an hour or so, check the flavour. The aroma should tell you there is a cray about. If the essence has come through, put the lot through a sieve, forcing out every last ounce of flavour. Sieve again through muslin or kitchen cloth to remove any odds and ends that may still be around.

4 In a separate, heavy-bottomed pan, melt the other half of the butter gently over a low heat and add the flour gradually. Mix together with a wooden spoon and keep stirring for at least 10 minutes, until the flour is cooked. The flour must not be allowed to brown. It should be golden and not crumby.

5 Add the crayfish stock gradually, working it into the flour with the spoon. Off the heat, add the coconut cream, the lemon grass and the earlier-cooked tomato purée (and more chilli if you wish, or, if you are a desperate heat and Thai fan, some red curry paste). Cook gently for about 20 minutes. Towards the end of cooking, whisk in the reserved crayfish 'mustard' and add the coriander, tied with a string so it can be removed easily.

6 Taste for seasoning. If you're happy with the flavour, remove the coriander and strain the rest.

7 Warm the leg meat gently in a little melted butter — warm it, don't cook it! — and place the crayfish at the bottom of some soup bowls. Pour the soup over the top, sprinkle with the herbs, and serve with buttered toast.

♥
## YABBIES WITH A TOUCH OF COCONUT

Y abbies are about the only swimmer I have any luck with on a consistent basis. Get some smelly meat, tie it to a piece of string, toss it in the water, tie the string to your big toe, relax into one of those chairs with no legs and a solid back, and you're in heaven. If you fall asleep, there's a good chance the biggest yabby will knock off the meat, crawl up the string, and have a go at your big toe.

Once you stop screaming, you'll realise that yabbies are pretty handsome, too, if you're keen on that sort of thing. Brilliant of colour, huge of nipper, rather dominating when you put them gently on your best crockery. But that's about all there is. On a size-to-meat value, and get-up-and-go flavour, there's not much to write home about.

The best thing to do with them is to use their texture and romance, and mix these never to be underrated ingredients with some subtle but catalytic spice; something from Thailand.

We Aussies have fallen in love with the taste of the Thais. It seems to me this has much to do with the 'almost' western taste of much of the cooking of Thailand. Sure, it can be hot, as in given a big hit of chilli, but in the best of Thai cuisine, the chillies are there to enhance, not to dominate. That, as a matter of fact, applies to any cuisine which uses chillies — enhance, not dominate. Don't be intimidated by chillies. Plant them and grow them, pick them, chop them and dry them, and you'll gain a new respect for them, a new understanding — and these red and green friends will become as indispensable to you as they are to me.

Mix chilli with coconut cream and coriander, throw in some lemon grass, and you're well on the way to Thailand; as simple as that. Even if you don't make it there, on the trip you'll find something in yabbies you didn't know was there.

There is really nothing to cooking the yabbies (ho, hum, same old story). A pot of boiling water; 5 minutes for the large ones (tipping the scales at about 100 g), and a couple of minutes for the smaller. Straight from the water to a hot pan, and spruce them up with a few drops of chilli oil. Serve them as they are, with a nutcracker for the claws and the sauce on the side.

❤   ❤   ❤   ❤   ❤

**live yabbies, as many as you like, or are lucky enough to catch**
*Beware of yabbies which have passed on. They deteriorate rather rapidly. I wouldn't touch them unless they were alive and pinching. If you're buying, pick those of a similar size.*

**1 stalk of lemon grass, as fresh as you can find it, sliced finely**
*Discard the green tips and use only the thick core. Lemon grass (the Thais call it takhrai; its botanical name is cymbopgon citratus) would not have been available in Australia not so long back, but it's readily for sale these days. It provides a wonderfully subtle flavour of lemon, without the acid. It should be firm and green to the tips, with not a trace of brown anywhere. The difference in flavour between the very fresh and the little tired, is marked. If you can pinch a few rooted stems from a friend, do so, and grow it. With love, it is happy in most environments, although the more humid, the better.*

**1 chilli, chopped finely**

**1 clove garlic, chopped finely**

**6 caps (about a dessertspoon in each) of Thai fish sauce, Nam Pla**
*This is one of the numerous fish sauces found in many cultures — even the Romans had a condiment made from fish fermented with salt. It's a little on the nose, but judiciously used with odds and sods, it provides for a delicious underflavour. Thai cookbooks suggest using it on its own as a table condiment. I think you would need to get used to that idea.*

**200 ml coconut cream**
*You can make your own if you like, but it's hardly worth it. Note that it's not the so-called milk which comes when you crack a nut. It's the flesh — grated, boiled with water, and then squeezed — which does the job. The tinned product is fine for making sauces and curries. By the way, if you have a cholesterol problem, coconut milk is high on the list of out-and-out taboos. Coconut oil is very high in saturated fats. Sigh.*

**small bunch of coriander, chopped roughly**

**juice of 1 lime or lemon**

**2 teaspoons chilli oil**
*Beware: this is red hot! and optional.*

1 Bring a pot of water to the boil. Throw in the large yabbies first, taking care to avoid the nippers, and gradually the smaller, down the scale. Total cooking time for the fearsome 100 g yabbies is about 5 minutes.

2 While the yabbies are doing their darnedest, start on the sauce, which will only take a few minutes. Mix the lemon grass, chopped chilli, garlic and fish sauce into the coconut milk, and bring to the boil, slowly, preferably in a wide saucepan. When it has boiled, reduce to a simmer and cook gently

for about 5 minutes, reducing, reducing. Remove from heat and add coriander and lime juice; mix with a wooden spoon and set aside. Leave for a few minutes and taste for seasoning. If it is lacking, add a couple more caps of fish sauce, stirring through. Return to the heat and bring to a simmer again, cooking for another 5 minutes, then set aside in a warm bowl.

3 When the yabbies are cooked, drain them and toss them into the still hot pan in which you made the coconut sauce. Sprinkle the lot with a teaspoon or two of chilli oil, and toss on medium heat for half a minute. Put the yabbies in a large bowl and heat through the coconut sauce if necessary.

4 Serve the bowl at the table, with the sauce at the side for dipping the flesh in. Or, for a more substantial meal, steam some rice, work the sauce through the rice, and serve with the yabbies on top.

WINE ❖ *Forget the wine — go for beer or Chinese tea. If beer, I like a Cascade or a Dutch or Danish style.*

♥

## STEAMED FISH WITH LOTS OF COLOUR

The best way to present fish is simply. Makes sense. Cook it simply, and serve it with something moist and colourful and delicious on its own — without intruding on the subtle flavour of the fish. This is the cooking of the restaurants of the eighties. Gentle flavours, served with colour, all put together simply.

Fish is a prime target for this sort of cooking. The freshest of fish, matched with the rich reds of tomatoes, bold greens of broad beans, against the pure white of steamed fish. Mixed with the best of oils and vinegars, you have total simplicity, and very healthy to boot.

♥   ♥   ♥   ♥   ♥

3 luscious, ripe, red tomatoes, skinned and chopped as roughly as you like

salt

60 ml best virgin olive oil

1 chilli, chopped finely

dozen broad beans, or peas, broccoli, spinach, sugar peas, asparagus

black pepper

some balsamic vinegar

the freshest fish in the market (preferably one with white fillets), skinned and boned by your fishmonger

*Orange roughy is delicious presented like this.*

1 Hours before you get to the cooking stage, even the night before, give the tomatoes a good dose of salt, cover them with the olive oil, and sprinkle the chilli about. Every now and then, toss them around with a wooden spoon, as indelicately as is reasonable.

2 Pod the broad beans, and cook them in their inner pods for about 2 minutes. Cool quickly under cold water and remove the delicious inner bean from the pod by squeezing between your fingers. Set aside to be re-heated.

3 When you're ready, and it's ready, force the tomato – olive oil

mix through a fine sieve and add the black pepper. You will be left with a very fluid, richly flavoured and coloured tomato purée. Taste, and add the balsamic vinegar drop by drop. If you haven't any balsamic vinegar don't despair. Any vinegar will do, but you should make an effort to get a reasonably cheap bottle of balsamic for the cupboard. It has a sweetness which you must taste. In this dish, the vinegar is to provide a middle flavour to the tomato–olive oil combination, without much addition of acid, already there through the tomatoes. What you are creating is the bottom of a salad bowl after a particularly delicious tomato salad. You know, the part you dredge with crusty bread when no one is looking.

4 Cook the fish any way you feel comfortable. You don't need a steamer to steam, although it does help. A tough plate sitting in a little boiling water, the fish covered with wrap will do a similar job. If you do have a steamer, sit the fish on a full head of steam, cover and cook for a couple of minutes, depending on the thickness of the fish. Test (carefully) with your forefinger. The fish should be firm, but still give to the push.

5 Re-heat the vegetables, warm through the sauce, whisking as you do, and spread it thinly on the plate. Place the fish in the middle and spread the pretty green vegetables all about.

WINE ♣ *There are a lot of white wine styles that would work here. In Australia, you generally pay for what you get. If it's a special night, splurge and get an appropriately priced bottle — if not,* *lower your sights. A winemaker friend and I had a great bit of orange roughy and a Rhine riesling from Delatite not long ago.*

♥

## SELF-SAUCING FISH

Y ou can get a similar result all in one go by cooking the fish on top of a mix of aromatic vegetables and olive oil, and covering the lot with foil. The fish cooks in the steam coming from the vegetables. At the end of it, you are left with a moist fish and a richly flavoured sauce from the renderings of the vegetables. It may well be the fish version of a self-saucing pudding.

♥   ♥   ♥   ♥   ♥

4 waxy potatoes, peeled and chopped into quarters

2 carrots, chopped roughly

2 parsnips, chopped roughly

1–2 leeks, depending on their size, chopped crossways

8 tomatoes, peeled

2 chillies, chopped finely

2 cloves garlic, chopped finely

salt

1 ½ cups good quality virgin olive oil

2 sprigs of rosemary

a little soy sauce

black pepper

2 teaspoons full-flavoured vinegar, preferably balsamic vinegar or sherry vinegar

fillet of fish per person

This method works best with thinnish, firm fillets — perhaps bream, whiting, snapper, the Dory family, red mullet, gurnard or the like. Ask your fishmonger to remove the fillets, giving you any bones left over. Remove any tiny bones with your eye-brow plucker. Please don't use the one at the back of the bathroom cupboard.

**juice of 1 lemon**

**bunch of chives, chopped finely**

**a little parsley, chopped roughly**

**1** Partly cook the potatoes, carrots and parsnips in a pot of boiling water for about 15 minutes. Drain and place them into a wide, heavy-bottomed pan; add the leeks, tomatoes, chillies, garlic, fish bones, salt and olive oil. Keep aside the rosemary until the end of the cooking.

**2** Cook slowly on a low heat until the tomatoes have become pulp and rendered all their juice. The root vegetables and potatoes should have cooked through. Add the rosemary and soy sauce. Remove the bones and rosemary from the pan and test the sauce–vegetables for seasoning. Adjust as necessary. Mix the vinegar through.

**3** You are now ready for the fish. Place the fish on top of vegetables and cover pan with foil. Cook on high heat until fish has changed its colour. It should be moist and firm, yet give to the touch.

**4** Put the fish in a deep bowl, giving it a squeeze of lemon juice. Spoon the juice from the pan first, and then some of the vegetables. The dish should look attractive and not be a sloppy soup. Sprinkle with chives and parsley. Serve with a spoon and fork.

WINE ✤ *The Henschke vineyard in the Barossa has earned a marvellous reputation for producing great reds — big, rich and spicy. They also make lovely whites. My favourite wine would go well here — the semillon: big, aromatic and honey-like.*

♥

## SKATE, JUST FOR THE HELL OF IT

Skate are gentle fish, put on earth to scare the daylights out of scuba divers. They are almost all wing and seem to fly through the water, casting dark shadows on all beneath them. Imagine you are drifting serenely a few metres beneath the surface and suddenly all goes black. You would have to think the party was over, lost at sea. But fortunately, skate are not interested in humans. They are, it is said, sensitive to music. I remain unsure whether that's music as in Mozart or INXS.

Forget their looks and size, and worry about their taste and wonderful flavour. These are fish you can really bite into — they have a dense flesh, without being tough, and a real personality. When you eat these fish, you know what you are eating. And their bones are filled with gelatine, making them a must for thick, jellied stocks. There's nothing to cooking them, although the density of the flesh — like that of flake and salmon and monkfish and flathead — makes skate a moral for pan-frying.

Skate are sold in fillets, often skinned, but rarely removed from bones or cartilage. The skin is as rough as the roughest five o'clock shadow, but it comes away easily with a sharp knife. The flesh is attached to flat cartilage, and you will

notice it looks like a row of cylin-
drical bones, like large spaghetti.
Again, the flesh is easily removed,
simply by sliding a sharp knife along
the cartilage.

There are many ways to cook
them — grilled, poached, pan-fried,
or fried in batter. I tried one once at
Le Cirque, a brilliant New York
restaurant, where the chef served it
as part of a warm salad. The fish
was tossed in a little flour and hit in
a hot pan until the flour crisped and
browned. It was then sprinkled with
lemon juice and placed securely atop
a pile of tiny greens, all tossed in the
most wonderful, sensual olive oil. If
the fish is not a huge one, and therefore not too muscled, the spaghetti-
like flesh actually flakes apart and
looks a little like chips tossed
through the salad.

Skate is delicious simply grilled
and covered with a little lemon juice,
salt, and melted butter. The poms go
gaga over skate in black butter,
which is really brown. The butter is
allowed to sizzle in the pan until it
browns, and then the fish is cooked
in the butter.

Believe it or not, skate makes for
a beautiful filling for a sandwich.
Try it not cold, not hot, in chunky,
crusty bread, sprinkled with a little
black pepper, a touch of chilli and
chives and a little lemon juice.

WINE ✤ *Some of the more 'chablis-*
*like' or austere chardonnays are the go*
*here. Try the Heggie's from the Eden*
*Valley or Domain Leasingham from*
*Clare.*

♥
## FLAT OUT FOR FLAVOUR: OR SOLE MAN, SOLE

D on't be discouraged if you
don't have enough pans
for a sole party, man. Fil-
lets of flat fish like sole, or dory, or
flounder stand up beautifully to most
forms of cooking: frying, steaming,
poaching. Just keep a good eye on
the show. Remember, it's unusual to
find a fat, flat fish. They will cook
very quickly if they are filleted.

1 You can ask your fishmonger to
fillet the fish, but try it yourself
first, then you can tell him/her what
to do next time. Start with a very
sharp knife — that should go without saying when it comes to fish of
any sort. It doesn't have to be a boning knife, but a flexible knife of that
style will certainly help. Make an in-
cision near the tail, ease a little skin
away from the flesh, and then rip
the rest away. Sounds tough, is easy,
if the fish is very fresh; if it's not you
shouldn't have bought it. Now, run
your knife down the backbone until
it touches the chest bones. Run the
blade between the flesh and the large
skeletal bones, and draw the flesh
away gently. Soon as you know it,
you'll have four fillets and a skeleton
that looks like it came out of a Tom
and Jerry cartoon. Don't throw the
bones away. You can see at a glance
at the carcass that this is one fish full
of gelatine, just the thing for a stock.

Do something grand with the
bones.

2 If you make a stock, do it with
all sorts of aromatics — leeks,
carrots, parsnips, fennel, bay leaf,
black pepper, a couple of chillies,
ginger, some white wine and water,

and finish off with a few skinned tomatoes, some chopped lemon grass and half a bunch of coriander.

3 The fillets will cook quickly, by any of the methods already mentioned. They are wonderful steamed over the bubbling stock and then added, very late, to the stock itself, reduced to a simmer.

4 Serve at the bottom of a deep soup bowl, with the stock, vegetables all about, just covering the lot. Toss in some chopped coriander.

5 If you have a large pan, flour one side of the fish lightly, and fry, floured side down, in a very hot pan for a couple of minutes, until the fish is sizzling and the flour is well browned. Put pan and all into a hot oven and cook until the fish just gives to the touch, 5–7 minutes. Serve with salt, black pepper and a fresh, sliced lemon.

WINE ❖ *Have a search around for a gewurztraminer from Alsace. (Hugel is the most widely available.) Serve it cold — delicious.*

♥
## ESCOLAR. NEVER HEARD OF IT?

I bet you have never heard of escolar, or, by its more common name, butter fish, or, by its less common name, oilfish. You're in good company. Ask fishmongers, fishermen, fishing experts: escolar? Never heard of it.

Escolar etc. is one of the greatest gifts given to the palate by the sea. It is firm and deliciously, yet subtly, flavoured; it melts in the mouth (thus, I guess, the reason for one of its monikers); and it has no bones. My younger daughter, who is something of a trawler for food in our house, took to it like a soprano to 'Oh Come All Ye Faithful'.

These fish, according to the CSIRO, grow a bit like a decent soprano — to 300 centimetres — and that's a pretty big fish. They are always displayed as fillets, but sometimes a designer fish shop will stick the whole fish in all its glory in the shop front, to make you goo and gaa and then slip inside to shop around. You'd get a bit of a fright if you saw escolar in their natural habitat. They drift around the continental shelf from New South Wales through to Western Australia, at depths between 100 metres and 800 metres. No wonder their eyes are said to be 'phosphorescent'.

The CSIRO says there have been '2 or 3 samples caught off Portland', and regularly has reports of them being landed off the east coast. And here's the rub: 'They are never caught in large quantities.'

Which is why most of us have never heard of them. They come as a by-product of gemfish fishing, but there is more bad news here. Limits are being placed on the gemfish catch, so there could be even fewer escolar around town. You can only hope, I suppose.

But whenever they are around, grab them.

There's one bright side. For some reason or other, escolar is never expensive, although according to its Latin name, *ruvettus pretiosus*, that may not always have been so. The Latin word *pretiosus* means costly, precious, of great value. I suppose escolar's relative cheapness these days has something to do with its size — at the wholesale end — and the fact that so few of us have heard of the fish, much less tasted it, so there is hardly likely to be a rush for it. But now you know, please don't let escolar pass you by. Sea perch used to be like that, before it became orange roughy.

♥  ♥  ♥  ♥  ♥

**2 onions, sliced in rings**

**1 clove garlic, sliced finely**

**2 stalks of lemon grass, chopped**
*If you can't get it fresh, you are almost certain to get it frozen in an Asian supermarket. Don't bother with the dried variety. You can make this dish without lemon grass, but the difference is quite remarkable.*

**1 knob of ginger, sliced finely**

**200 ml tin of coconut cream**

**2–3 hot chillies, depending on your chilli rating**

**1 cup fish stock if you have it, if not, ½ cup water**

**handful of coriander**

**escolar, or any other firm-fleshed fish that has fillets which hold together and are on the thickish side — about 4 cm — such as flake, salmon, snapper**
*Half a kilo of escolar fillets will easily serve five people.*

**a little flour**

**salt**

**black pepper**

**juice of ½ lemon per person**

**a little butter**

**1** Toss the onions and a little oil into a pan, cook very slowly for 20–25 minutes, until they brown and taste sweet. Add the garlic, lemon grass and ginger after about 10 minutes, then the coconut cream and chillies when the onions are done. If you have some fish stock it is a wonderful bonus. Add the stock, or water, and coriander and allow to cook gently for another 5–10 minutes, until the sauce thickens. You must be careful not to leave it too long. It must be of a thick, but pourable consistency, not sticky. Set aside.

**2** Heat your oven to flat out. Prepare the fish. You need to dust the fillets in flour on one side only. I am forever annoyed, in inferior restaurants, at eating fish which have been floured on both sides and put in pans with several other fillets. The result? The flour steams in a pan which is overcrowded, and thus not hot enough, and is never cooked. I'm sure you have done it yourself.

**3** So, heat a little oil in a large pan (one which can go in the oven) and put in the fillets, one at a time. Make sure the pan sizzles when you put in the fish, and then move each fillet about a bit so that it does not stick. You might need to add a little extra oil as you go. When you have all the fish in place and sizzling away, put the pan into the oven. It will take about 10–15 minutes to cook, depending on the size of the fillets. You can test to see if the fish is done by pressing it with your finger. When it's ready, it doesn't fight back. You can also, like a cake, test with a knife. Why not?

**4** Set the fish aside in a warm spot while you re-heat the sauce.

5 You can serve the fish white side up, or crisp, whichever you like. I like it both ways. Sprinkle the fish with a little salt, black pepper and lemon juice, and rub some butter over the top. Serve the sauce separately, or with a little rice, or couscous. If you can't be bothered making the sauce, sprinkle some fresh herbs — tarragon, chives, or parsley are perfect — over the fish and moisten with a little butter, or virgin olive oil, or a mild vinaigrette.

WINE ✤ *The people of Cowra must be happy that it's producing some lovely chardonnays — something to remember it by other than a prison. The Rothbury Estate's Cowra Chardonnay is worth a look — it's rich but has good complexity and depth of flavour.*

♥

## FLAKE, FOR THE MEMORIES

R emember the 'good old days'. Remember when Gough Whitlam was the leader of the Opposition, Bob Hawke had black hair and silly glasses, you still had Sunday roasts, and fish shops — the first of the fast food outlets — did a roaring trade on Fridays?

Remember? Remember those shops which had piles of already-fried fish in thick batter sitting before your eyes, and at your order he (always he) would toss one into the foaming oil? Re-cooked fish! how did we put up with it? And fish wrapped in paper? Didn't we realise that on top of the double cooking, the fish would keep cooking in the insulated bag?

We were so dull then, so locked in our set ways, and the way we ate fish was as good an indication of our life as anything. We always had flake, for three reasons: it was uncomplicated — it didn't have bones; it was very cheap; and we were all so unsophisticated that we didn't understand what all these other fish were anyway. It was only much, much later that I knew that flake was in fact shark, and usually the less than fearless gummy shark.

For some strange reason, one of the strongest memories I have of that period of eating was the great 'mercury in the flake' scare. Our favourite fish, as identifiable with Melbourne as guacamole is with Mexico, or sushi with Japan, was under siege by some crazy metal which we knew only as something to do with thermometers. But the remarkable thing was that nobody seemed to care. Here was our life-blood being threatened by a poisonous metal, and nobody gave a hoot. What was no more than a ripple on the waters of the bay in those so-called halcyon days, would be a national scandal today, enough to bring down the government.

Mercury in the flake! Green or not, you would have to scream blue murder. Well, flake is back. Still without any bones, not cheap any more, generally imported from New Zealand, still tasting very fishy, and worth trying again.

♥ ♥ ♥ ♥ ♥

### (I) STEAMED/BAKED

**1 thick, steak-like fillet of flake per person**

**salt**

**a little lemon juice**

a little butter

herbs

black pepper

1 If you are cooking for several, it is best to 'steam' the fillets in their own juices. Heat a little oil in a pan which can go to the oven. Gently place in the flake pieces one after the other, pushing them about the pan so they don't stick. Place them close together, and put the lot into a hot, flat-out oven. Bake for about 10–15 minutes, checking after about 8 minutes. You will feel the fish is tender to the touch, not fighting back.

2 Sprinkle some salt over the fish, and drizzle some lemon juice all about.

3 Serve as is, with no more accompaniments than a little melted butter, some chopped herbs, black pepper, some green vegetables and a little salad. Flake has such a distinctive flavour and lovely texture, it doesn't need any intrusions when cooked like this. Whatever you do, don't douse it with the same cheap vinegar we used to ask for all those years ago. Potato cakes? That's a different matter.

### (II) FRIED IN THE PAN

a little flour

1 thick, steak-like fillet of flake per person

½ cup white wine

juice of 1 lemon

50 g butter

salt

black pepper

1 This is best for two, so that you can be sure the pan is not going to be cluttered. Flour one side of the fillets and oil the bottom of a pan that can go into the oven.

2 When the oil is very hot, place the fillets in the pan, flour side down, one after the other, pushing them about the pan so they don't stick. There must be plenty of room between each fillet. Keep cooking on a high heat for about 90 seconds, until the oil and flour and fish start to sizzle, and then put the lot in a flat-out oven. Cook for about 8 minutes, maybe more, maybe less, until just done.

3 Remove from oven, put the fish on a warm plate, and add the white wine and the lemon juice to the pan. When the wine has just about reduced, remove from heat, and swirl the butter, salt and pepper into the pan, until the butter just melts. Pour the sauce over the fish and serve with two shillings worth of chips, two potato cakes and a pickled onion.

WINE ✤ *You need a white wine with guts. Generally, whites that have been matured in oak casks are full flavoured — they have to be to stand up to the oak. Try a good big chardonnay or semillon, preferably with at least three years bottle age.*

♥

## FISH OF THE DAY WITH ROSEMARY

Every garden should have a bustling rosemary bush. There are few other flavourings which are always available at your back door and add so much life to so many dishes. Toss rosemary with tomatoes, soy and chilli and you've got hold of a true winner; cook down some cream and rosemary and you've got one of the simplest of simple sauces, perfect with any fish. Swap the cream for the coconut cream, and you're in the tropics.

♥　♥　♥　♥　♥

2 onions, chopped

1 clove garlic, sliced finely

1 walnut-sized piece of ginger, sliced finely

3 tomatoes, skinned and chopped roughly

some fish bones — snapper or John Dory if possible

2 cups water

2 cups sweet white wine

*The better the wine, the better the sauce. If you haven't sweet wine, use dry.*

1/2 dozen sprigs of rosemary

the freshest fish in the shop, at the best price

100 ml cream

salt

50 g butter

black pepper

1 The base of the sauce can be made well ahead, but equally, it can be made on the job if you are as ill-prepared as I usually am. Soften the onion, garlic and ginger in a little olive oil over a gentle heat — about 10 minutes. You might have to add a little water here and there.

2 Add the tomatoes, fish bones, water and wine, and cook gently for about half an hour, checking regularly to make sure the liquid doesn't disappear. Add most of the rosemary and set aside to cool. The lovely oils and flavourings will give to the stock as it cools.

3 After an hour, strain the stock, toss in the rest of the rosemary — bar one sprig — and set aside.

4 Cook the fish any way you like. Steam it, fry it, bake it.

5 While the fish is cooking, make the sauce. Strain the stack, remove the rosemary, and add a fresh sprig. Heat a cup of the stock and whisk in the cream. Allow the mix to bubble away gently for about 5 minutes on a low heat, stirring all the while. The mixture should reduce heavily, and all the cream flavour will disappear. The sauce should reek of rosemary. Season with a little salt.

6 Take off the heat and whisk in the butter, taste, and adjust the seasoning.

7 Put the fish on a plate and pour a little sauce over the top and down the sides. Don't drown it, just give it a little, to draw out its flavour. Turn the pepper mill over the top and give it a squeeze of lemon juice. If you have some fresh thin noodles, toss them through the sauce and serve next to the fish.

WINE ✦ *Red wine with fish — you've got to be joking! Try it just once. Geoff Merrill makes zingy reds with great finesse. He makes a lovely rosé style, released under his Mt Hurtle label.*

♥
## FLASH FISH, SIMPLE SAUCE: KING GEORGE WHITING

King George Whiting is always expensive, always delicate in flavour, and should always be cooked gently and watchfully. It has a delicious texture and a lovely flavour. It can be cooked any way really — it is great in batter and deep-fried, as many expensive restaurants have discovered; wonderful with its skin left on and steamed; perfect baked; marvellous wrapped in foil and cooked, with tarragon, on a grill or in the oven. For all that, this is really a recipe for its partner, that under-rated vegetable, spinach.

♥   ♥   ♥   ♥   ♥

1 bunch of spinach, cleaned of any dirt or sand

1 cup pine nuts

1 onion, chopped finely

1 clove garlic, sliced finely

a little ginger, chopped finely

2 chillies

1 cup whipping cream

black pepper

salt

nutmeg

1 fillet King George Whiting per person

*Ask your fishmonger to bone it and skin it. It's not hard to do yourself, but King George Whiting is rather too expensive to risk leaving delicious flesh hanging on the bones.*

80 g butter

1 lemon, sliced finely

bunch of tarragon, leaves chopped

1 Steam the spinach until it has lost its stiffness and become really green. Wring it out like a washer until it is as dry as you can get it.

2 In a dry pan over moderate heat, toss the pine nuts until they brown. Don't let them burn.

3 Gently cook the onion, garlic and ginger in a little olive oil until they soften and become translucent. Add the chillies, spinach and pine nuts, working them about the pan until well mixed.

4 Remove from the heat, and purée in a whizzer, slowly adding the cream through the spout. Taste, season as required with the pepper, salt and nutmeg. Set aside while you cook the whiting.

5 Cover the fillets with the butter (about 20 g per portion), lemon slices, black pepper, salt and plenty of tarragon, wrap in foil, and cook in a 220°C oven for about 10 – 15 minutes depending on their thickness.

6 Gently re-heat the spinach mix and spoon onto a plate. Pour the sauce from the foil on top of the spinach and place the fillets gently on the side.

WINE ✤ *From parts of the McLaren Vale you can look out on the sea to where the whiting live. Wouldn't it be nice if you could coax them in with a chilled bottle of white! The Wirra Wirra winery in the Vale makes lovely whites, as does Scott Collett at Woodstock. Try their chardonnays and semillon/sauvignon blanc blends.*

♥
## OCEAN TROUT IN A FROTH

Not so long ago, the only place you could get hold of salmon was from the freezers of the big department stores — and it would have arrived there via long and expensive trips from Scandinavia, Canada, and occasionally Scotland. No more. A superbly efficient salmon and ocean-run trout farming industry is flourishing in Tasmania — flourishing in terms of product and availability, still to find its feet financially — and the benefits belong entirely to the consumers.

Tasmania produces two products, North Atlantic salmon and ocean trout, which may differ marginally as far as family lines are concerned, but taste so similar even experts have trouble picking them apart. Then there are the old reliable inland cousins, rainbow trout, heavily farmed, and never ultimately satisfying to my palate, and a new chum, from New South Wales, called brook trout. Rainbow trout is pale and reliable, but never stunning; brook trout is of a fiery colour and slightly finer flake than salmon or ocean trout; Atlantic salmon is usually a rich deep orange in colour and ocean trout is fading towards pink. They are all expensive.

But what the hell. Salmon is the sort of fish you must taste at least once in your life, to know how good it is. I first tasted brilliant wild Scottish salmon in a wonderful, now defunct restaurant in Albertville in the French alps; a decent chunk of the fish was cooked rare, and doused with the most wonderfully balanced of vinaigrettes and delightful fresh herbs. The dish needed nothing more. The fish spoke for itself.

And so it is with these Tassie darlings. Whatever you do with them, keep it simple, and let the fish do the talking. Perhaps the best way to cook them at home is in a very hot pan, lightly oiled. Dip one side of a thick fillet in a little flour, shake away any excess, and then drop the fish, flour side down, into the oil, moving it about so it does not stick. When it is really sizzling, put the pan into a 220°C oven and bake for about 5 minutes, depending on how thick the fish is. Serve with a little salt, some black pepper and a good dredge of lime or lemon juice. If you've got some lovely fresh vegetables, tossed in a vinaigrette on side, and some delicious mashed potatoes, you have a perfect dish. But …

… sometimes you want to be really flash and show everyone how smart you are. Try this. It's something between a sauce and a soup. It is times like these when the English language is inadequate. We have all sorts of words to describe the wind — from a flighty zephyr to a fearsome hurricane — but a soup is a soup until it becomes a stew. This is a mix of stock, an egg yolk to provide air and frothiness, a little cream, some vegetables for crunch and some mussels. You can't have a fishy soup — whether a zephyr soup or the hurricane version — without mussels.

♥　♥　♥　♥　♥

### THE MUSSELS
4–5 mussels per portion

a little white wine, if you have some open; water if you don't

½ lemon, sliced

### THE FISH

**100 g ocean trout per person**

*If you can't afford ocean trout, go for a small tuna, or yellowtail, or mackerel. All of these fish have a flesh that requires little cooking. In the case of the tuna, I usually prefer it raw, but for this dish it can be seared on each side. Funnily enough, neither ocean trout nor Atlantic salmon taste remarkable in their raw state. They need that searing process to bring them to their best.*

### THE SAUCE

**2 egg yolks**

**1 cup fish stock**

*If you have none, use the reserved stock from the mussels, straining again to remove any loose sand.*

**zest of 2 lemons, chopped finely**

**1 chilli, chopped finely**

**salt**

**black pepper**

**a little cream**

### THE VEGETABLES, CUT INTO JULIENNE

*Whatever is available is fine. The vegetables are for texture, as well as flavour. Try these:*

**4 spears of asparagus per portion**

**1 small leek, sliced along its length, each piece about 10 cm long**

**some snow peas, sliced along their length**

**1–2 baby carrots, sliced similarly**

**1 zucchini, sliced in lengths, thinly**

**tarragon, chopped**

1 Put the mussels in a pot with the wine and lemon slices and cook, covered, just for a few minutes until the mussels have opened. Set aside to cool. Remove the mussels from their shells, discarding any which refuse to open, strain, and retain the mussel stock. Set the mussels aside.

2 Ask your supplier to bone the fish. If you do it yourself, the way to do it is with a very sharp knife worked closely along the backbone. The trout has tiny bones which then have to be removed carefully by hand. Use eye-brow tweezers.

3 Slice the fish into pieces about 5 cm wide. You will have fish slices not unlike fish fingers (God forbid the comparison!).

4 Whisk the egg yolks in a stainless steel bowl over a low heat. (You can do this over a saucepan of boiling water if you wish.)

5 As the yolks thicken, add a little stock, the lemon zest, the chilli, salt, black pepper and some cream. As the yolks get warmer and you are whisking vigorously, the mix will lighten, becoming frothy and pale. Keep tasting and adding as much stock as you think it needs to reach the right fish/lemon/vegetable flavour. When the flavour is right, set aside in a warm spot. (If you are cooking over boiling water, you could take the saucepan from the heat, allow any accumulated steam to escape, and leave your sauce there. The sauce should never be much above warm, as, if it gets any hotter, the yolks will curdle.)

6 Pre-heat your oven to its maximum. Warm any stock you have left. If it has all been used for the sauce, slice a lemon into a half litre of water and bring it to the boil. The mussels will be re-heated in this lemon stock.

7 Cook the asparagus in boiling salted water. They will need only a few minutes, depending on their thickness. Make sure they are cooked more than *al dente*.

8 Cook the vegetable julienne in the same water as the mussels. The vegetables will need about 45 seconds.

9 Heat a little oil in a saucepan which can go into the oven. When the pan is very hot, slide in the salmon (or tuna or yellowtail). After 30 seconds turn the fish over. If the fish is thin, that may be all the cooking that is required. Just leave it in the hot pan, away from the heat, while you prepare your bowls. If the fish is thicker, it will probably need about a minute in the oven. Remember, the retained heat from the cooking process will continue cooking the fish after it has been removed from the heat source. The fish should be served rare to medium, like a fillet steak.

10 Check the temperature of your sauce as the fish is 'resting'. If the sauce has cooled too much, whisk it again over the boiling water or the gentle heat, until well warmed through, without being hot.

11 Arrange the vegetables in a mound in the centre of your bowl. (The fish will sit on top of the mound and should be free of the frothy sauce.) Pour the sauce about the vegetables, place the mussels symmetrically about the mound and put the fish on top, sprinkled with chopped tarragon. If you wish to be really flash, finish the presentation with the asparagus spears crossed on top of the fish.

12 Remember, you can also serve the fish and the sauce alone, using the same methods. What you have above is rather a special restaurant-style dish. But it tastes just the same without the add-ons.

WINE ✤ *You will need a chardonnay with some zip. A lot of Aussie chardonnays tend to get a bit broad, lacking the 'backbone' needed to hold this dish. Have a search for the Pierro Chardonnay from the West or the Prelude from Leeuwin Estate. De Bortoli's from the Yarra Valley or Tim Knappstein's are other options.*

♥

## MUSSELS IN PUFF PASTRY

This dish and the next were consistent winners during my restaurant days. We served one or the other or variations day and night, week in week out, and never once thought of how much butter was in them. I offer them to you now, to allow you to note how times change and how we must learn and change with them; but only after we have thought about the hows and whys, and decided positively that yes, this is the way to go. And then, and this is where I fall down oh so often, the discipline to hold the line, hold the line.

I guess all recipes evolve, either from your own work, or from another's base, or from a combination of both. This mussel and asparagus tart started simply as a piece of warm bread, some butter, some mussels and some vegetables, all snatched together as a quick, late lunch after service. It became complex, not in its presentation, but in its preparation. The labour of preparation is worth it, for the ease of service. Dishes like this are marvellous for a very special list of dinner guests. If they are not worried about butter.

And don't be concerned about the number of steps. Most of them are independent of the others, and can be done separately and simply. You don't need to be an octopus to succeed here. Just committed.

♥    ♥    ♥    ♥    ♥

**2 mussels per portion and another half a dozen mussels for a mussel 'mix'**

**¹/₂ onion, chopped roughly**

**1 stick of celery, chopped roughly**

**a few rashers bacon**

**2 hot chillies**

**150g butter for the inside of the tarts**

**bunch of basil**
*Basil is now available all year round, praise the Lord.*

**500g puff pastry**
*You must make your own for dishes like this (see page 240). It is so much better, the commercial, frozen alternatives are not even worth considering. If you haven't the time to make it, buy it from a favourite pastry shop.*

**a template in the shape of a diamond**
*It should be about 15cm long and about 10cm wide. From this you can shape your pastry.*

**1–2 cobs of corn, depending on the size**
*Slice the corn from the cob using a very sharp knife.*

**6 spears of asparagus per portion**
*Break away the woody bottom and discard. Retain the best end (about 10cm is plenty) and slice the remaining section very finely across its width.*

**1kg peas**
*Only use peas if you believe them to be at their best. There is nothing better than the best peas, nothing worse than the worst. If not peas, new broad beans.*

**egg yolk and milk for an egg wash**

**50g butter for the sauce**

**juice of 2 lemons**

**a little good-quality white wine, if you have some open; if not, use some water**

**salt**

**pepper**

1 Steam the mussels in a little bit of water with the onions and celery in a closed pot. When the mussels open, take them from the heat. Retain the mussel juice from the cooking process.

2 For the mussel paste: Cook the bacon quickly in a hot pan, or in the microwave, and allow to cool. Drain off any excess fat. Chop the bacon, the chillies and the half dozen mussels very finely. With your hands, work the 150g butter until it is very soft. In a bowl, mix the chopped ingredients with the butter, a little mussel juice and about 25 basil leaves, snipped roughly. Refrigerate until the mix is firm.

3 Cut the pastry into two and roll out each half as thinly as you can, making sure no butter exudes from the dough. Place in the refrigerator until quite cold. You will need tops and bottoms for each portion. Cut the pastry into diamond shapes,

using the cardboard template. The top needs to be slightly thinner and cover more area than the base, so you will have to re-roll the top gently to make it larger. Prepare the top by folding the short corners gently together, and cut slats in the pastry from one narrow end through the middle to the other narrow end. Flatten the pastry once more. You will now have a 'windowed' top.

4 Now to stew the vegetables for the tart. Take half the mussel and butter paste. Set your oven to 180°C. Spread the corn, chopped asparagus ends and peas on a tray to go in the oven. Dot the mixture with the mussel paste and allow to cook slowly in the oven, until the paste has melted and the asparagus bits have softened. You may need to take the tray from the oven once or twice to work the vegetables about a little. Make sure the paste really does get into the vegetables. When the vegetables are done — about 12–15 minutes — take them from the tray, and allow to cool in a bowl.

5 Place the puff pastry bases on a cold baking tray. Take the other half of the mussel paste and rub a little on each bottom. To a dessertspoon of the prepared stewed vegetables, add two mussels per portion. Work the mix into a little mound and place each mound on the pastry bases. You might need more or fewer vegetables.

Moisten the edges of the pastries and join top and bottom together carefully, slicing away any untidy edges. With the back of a fork secure the joins. Refrigerate.

6 Pre-heat the oven to 200°C. Whisk the egg yolk with a little milk and paint the top of the pastry with a brush. If you don't have a brush, use your fingers or a paper towel. The egg–milk mix will ensure the pastries are a gorgeous golden brown colour when cooked. They will take at least 30 minutes to cook. When properly cooked the pastry flakes away like segments of old tiles. Don't undercook the pastry. It should look as though it is only seconds away from being burnt.

7 The sauce: The sauce is nothing flash. Chop the butter into cubes. Bring the lemon juice to the boil. Add the wine/water (and some chopped leeks if you like). When the mix has boiled, remove from the heat and whisk in the butter. Take it easy, and it will emulsify quickly and easily. Taste for seasoning — it will certainly need salt, definitely pepper. Leave the saucepan at the side of the stove in a warm place. Taste for temperature just before serving. If it has cooled too much, just add a little more water and, holding the pan a few centimetres above the heat, just whisk it a little more.

8 The vegetables for the plate: When the tarts are cooked, set them aside while the asparagus tips cook in boiling salted water. The tarts will be very hot when they come from the oven. If they are left aside for a minute or two, the top layer of somebody's mouth will probably be saved from burning! The asparagus tips will take only a few minutes, depending on their thickness. They are done when a knife cuts through them easily, but with resistance.

9 Pour a little sauce onto the plate. Arrange the tarts in the middle

and criss-cross the asparagus spears on either side.

There is no doubt this is a brilliantly flavoured, superb dish, despite the apparent complexity of its making, or more likely its description, and it should not be removed from your diet forever just because of the butter. I would say try it once a year and love it, and look forward to it again the year after. And don't serve it with a rich main course, or a rich dessert: they might have to carry you from the table.

There are all sorts of variations to this basic dish. Without the mussels, it makes for a perfect vegetarian number. You can replace the butter inside the tart with a low-fat cheese like ricotta, and the mussels with spinach, and drizzle the tart with a richly flavoured virgin olive oil.

Oh, an afterthought: if all that means not much at all, and you want to be mischievous, melt a little butter on the top of the tarts when they come from the oven!

WINE ♣ *You need a counter-puncher here — something to cut through the butter. Try a good bubbly. If French, Louis Roederer N.V. or Bollinger. If vintage, try one from a well-known house.*

Now, read on ...

♥

## A PARCEL OF MUSSELS

There's another, even more impressive-looking version of the previous dish, which is easier to prepare — crêpes instead of puff pastry — and can be made well in advance. In the end, it looks like a purse. Flavour and wit together. It was one of the most consistent dishes on the old restaurant menu, and one of the most consistently applauded. It does take a little effort and skill, but it is still worth it. The applause will be deafening.

♥  ♥  ♥  ♥  ♥

### THE CREPES

100g flour

1 teaspoon sugar

pinch of salt

250ml milk

2 eggs

1 dessertspoon oil

### THE MUSSELS

60 mussels

1 lemon, sliced

150g butter, softened

200g almonds, chopped finely

1 clove garlic, chopped finely

bunch of basil, leaves removed from the stems

2 chillies

1/2 cup cream

12 cherry tomatoes

150g sugar peas

1 leek

1 I've had my highs and lows with crêpes. Often they have stuck to the pan, or been too thick, or burnt. But if you get organised, and do it with coolness and care, nothing can go wrong. If you have a seasoned crêpe pan, then good luck to you. If not, just clean assiduously a heavy-bottomed pan and wipe it thinly with oil.

2 Mix all the crêpe ingredients together, whisking lightly so as to

dissolve the sugar and salt. Set aside in the fridge for a few hours.

3 When you are set to go, heat the pan until it is too hot to touch. The best way to make sure the crêpes are thin is to pour on some batter, then pour it off straight away. Let the crêpe cook until the top bubbles a little. Lift the side to check. Flip with an egg slide or spatula. Feed the first one to the dog. It always disappoints. Keep making until you run out of batter.

4 Steam the mussels in a little water and lemon slices until they open, discarding any which do not open. Remove the beards as you pull the mussels free. Retain some of the mussel 'milk', straining to remove any sand.

5 Knead together the butter, almonds, garlic and basil.

6 Whizz together 20 of the mussels, one chilli and the cream until it comes together, just holding its own. It will be neither runny nor thick.

7 Chop the cherry tomatoes and the sugar peas and mix with the rest of the mussels in a bowl. Add the mussel cream to coat the lot, mixing through with a wooden spoon. Now to bring it all together. Blanch the green top of the leek in boiling water and slice into 'strings'.

8 In the middle of a crêpe, put a decent nob of the almond–basil butter and a handful of the mussel vegetable mix on top, allowing 5 mussels per person. Gather the edges of the crêpe together, enveloping the mussels and the mix, and tie securely with the leek 'string'.

9 Bake in a 200°C oven for 15–20 minutes. The job is to get the contents heated through, not to provide any more cooking. You may have to cover the top with foil to stop it from burning. Serve with a little melted butter and lemon sauce, as before.

10 If you can't be bothered making crêpes, you can get a similar result, with less work, using filo pastry. Just follow the filo instructions on the packet and start from step 4.

WINE ✤ *Rhine riesling from the cooler areas — Eden Valley, Clare, Coonawarra or central Victorian Highlands. You are looking for the lime/lemon floral character these wines display when young.*

We're still on a butter kick, now read on …

♥

## PRAWNS IN A BUTTER AND BLACK PEPPER SAUCE

I have flirted and failed with diets for so long I cannot look at the word these days without being riddled with guilt and self-doubt. I know all the reasons why a sensible diet should be part of my life. I eat too much, liking food for its delicious flavours and tastes, that I just can't ignore the things I have loved all my life. That makes me a failure too, not being able to provide a regular sort of cooking which is not only healthy but leaves you feeling good, then, during the night and the next morning. I try it on for a while, then fall to temptation.

I have seen people who have succeeded. During the restaurant days, one of my favourite customers was a devotee of the Pritikin diet, a man who was absolutely content to live without butter, cream, eggs, sugar, salt and grog. I looked at him and saw a man with sparkling eyes, of clean skin, a man oozing satisfaction with his life, his lifestyle and his diet.

I was so drawn by his appearance, I went for it with a gusto: on the first day, fruit for breakfast, fruit for lunch, then a big dinner of steamed potatoes puréed with poached onions, chillies and garlic; more steamed vegetables with mint; bowls of mangoes and raspberries; the weakest tea; and no grog. It worked — I felt great, didn't fall asleep in the after-dinner chair, and bored the pants off everyone else in the house.

I tried it the next day. Fruit, fruit and more fruit during the day, then at dinner: eggless pasta with tomato sauce and snow peas; steamed fish on a purée of spinach, lots of lemon juice and black pepper; apricots, lightly stewed in lemon juice; more *intense* conversation about the pros and cons of eating to live. Now my wife had fallen asleep in the chair.

The diet failed because: (i) I became a bore, a sort of live-in Billy Graham; (ii) I needed a drink; and (iii) I wanted to celebrate a special occasion and didn't fancy doing it with mango, mineral water and mumbo-jumbo. Could you? I went back to my worst ways. Absolute worst. Read on and you will understand what I mean.

Buy your prawns from your favourite and trusted fishmonger. Fresh is best, of course, but they are not always available at retail outlets. If not, don't buy soaked green prawns, buy them frozen and defrost them yourself. There is an argument that frozen prawns can be better than fresh, unless you can get them while they are still kicking. The crux of the argument is this: if they are frozen quickly, preferably straight out of the water, and maintained at the correct minus temperature, then there is no chance of any deterioration. There's plenty to that argument — as long as you know your supplier.

♥    ♥    ♥    ♥    ♥

**bunch of basil (or chives if you can't get basil), leaves removed from the stem, snipped in half**

**100g butter, chopped into blocks, softened**

**200g bacon, cut into strips, fat removed**

**2 cobs seasonal corn, corn sliced from the cob**

**4 prawns per person, shelled and de-veined**

*Keep the shells for a prawn stock. You can freeze the shells if they are fresh.*

**1 dessertspoon black peppercorns, crushed under the back of a knife**

**1 clove garlic, chopped finely**

**juice of 1 lemon**

1 Rub the basil into the softened butter and refrigerate until firm. This, and no more, makes for a terrific sauce on its own. Somehow or other, melted basil butter imparts a brilliant flavour of basil. Try it and see.

2 Heat the oven to 220°C.

3 This dish takes no more than a few minutes, but it all happens

together. The sauce is made just as the prawns are cooked, the toast is toasting, the corn is cooking, and the bacon is frying. It sounds tough, but any octopus can do it.

4 Cook bacon first, simply, in the microwave on some absorbent paper. It takes but a minute. Drain any excess fat and keep warm.

5 Steam the corn kernels in a colander over boiling water. This will take a few minutes. Taste and check, and set aside to be re-heated.

6 Prawns are the easiest fish in the world to cook, once cleaned of shell and co. Heat some oil in a heavy pan which can go into the oven, and toss the prawns in the hot oil, making sure each has plenty of room to sizzle. After 30 seconds of sizzling on one side, turn for 30 seconds on the other. Remove pan from the heat and cover the prawns in the basil butter, black peppercorns, garlic and lemon juice. Put them in the oven for a couple of minutes, until the basil butter has started to melt. It must not get to the sizzle stage. Remove from the oven and swirl the prawns and butter about, allowing the heat of the pan to melt the butter. It must not become oily.

7 Serve the prawns and pour the sauce, bacon and corn about. This is wonderful if served over a waffle, or crumpet, or very good toast.

WINE ✤ *There was a time when Rhine riesling was the ant's pants — the flavour of the month, or year. But that's going back to the late seventies. It's not now and that means you can buy oceans of good Rhine riesling for under $10 — a lucky country!*

And now, for the last butter indulgence ...

♥
## BUGS OR SCALLOPS IN A TARRAGON BUTTER

You must learn from your mistakes. It was during one special dinner that a disastrous series of events, interspersed by one or two *sacre bleus*, led me to one of the most delectable treats I have tasted. Certainly the meal was the best part of an hour behind schedule, but the result was remarkable.

By great good fortune, I had came across a windfall of Moreton Bay bugs just before the big day. The bugs — often called the bull-dozers of the deep so exquisitely designed are they — were delectably fresh, not alive, unfortunately, but next best. Bugs have a durability beyond most creatures of the deep. They last much longer than most crustaceans and so are an ideal Friday purchase for use on any day of the weekend. Even Monday. Don't try the same with prawns. Buy prawns and eat them quickly.

My idea with the bugs was simple. Hit them hard in the pan, toss them into a red-hot oven, cover them with butter mixed with tarragon, and roast them very, very quickly. It didn't quite turn out that way.

The oven went off without anybody knowing it, and when the time of service was expected, the bugs were sitting cold and wan all over the bottom of the oven.

I turned on the oven flat to the boards, and waited and hoped. This was not one of those modern numbers which goes from zero to red-hot in a flash. This was marginally ahead of a wood-burner, marginally. After several inspections, I noted something quite extraordinary. As the oven slowly warmed up, the butter melted gently and the bugs seemed to cook lazily, blending into the butter.

It was too puzzling for me. I took one of the bugs from the dish, and was knocked over by the (i) buttery texture of the seafood; (ii) superb blend of flavour of the tarragon and the bugs; and (iii) the ripping, pungent flavour of the sauce which had not, surprise, surprise, separated into ghastly oil, flecked with powdery particles of 'milk'.

Quite simply, these were the best flavoured Moreton Bay bugs I have ever tasted. And the dish can be reproduced without the tension, by starting with a low oven and cooking the bugs very slowly.

❤   ❤   ❤   ❤   ❤

**about 3 medium bugs per person**

*Bugs vary in size so much. You can use prawns, yabbies, scallops or even mussels for this dish; just give them less time in the oven. Prawns are less dense than bugs and take less time to cook, whether in this way or on top of the stove. If you use scallops, switch herbs to chives; for mussels, use basil.*

**at least a bunch of tarragon, the leaves plucked from the stalk**

*Tarragon is a summer herb, but it is still readily available in winter these days. There are smart herb growers in the Northern Territory and Queensland. Tarragon is unquestionably the best match for this dish. You should grow some. It is easy to grow, and sprouts every year. Make sure you buy French tarragon, never Russian.*

**2 heads broccoli, each stem cut from the main stalk**

**150 g butter at room temperature**

**handful of beans per person**

**handful of sugar peas per person**

1 The bugs are very difficult to remove from their shells. Their armour and sharp-edged defence system has been around for zillions of years. Grin and bear the cuts as you slit with a knife down the guts and rip the armour away, leaving the translucent flesh. Eliminate the waste system.

2 Prepare the tarragon. Be patient. It takes time to tear the stems away from the main stalk. When this monster has been done, chop the leaves roughly.

3 Work the butter in your hands in a bowl, until the butter softens. Its ideal texture should be like face cream. Once there, work in the tarragon. Return to the fridge until firm.

4 Heat the oven to 180°C. Put the bugs on a baking tray and cover with about three-quarters of the butter, separated into nuts. Set aside.

5 Ditto the broccoli, with the other quarter of butter, in a separate baking tray.

6 Boil some salted water and quickly cook the beans and the sugar peas. Once cooked, refresh them under cold water and set them aside for re-heating. Keep some salted water boiling on the stove.

7 Put the bugs in the oven on the top shelf, and place the broccoli

underneath. Cook both for about 20 minutes. The bugs will be pure-white and swimming in tarragon butter; the broccoli, also swimming freely, should just give to the knife. Taste each to be sure. In fact, taste on the way through. Your oven tempera-ture might be lying. Twenty minutes could be 15 or 30. By the way, this is a wonderful way to cook broccoli for any sort of accompaniment.

8 Moments before the bugs are ready, re-heat the peas/beans, toss them into a bowl, and cover them with the broccoli and butter sauce.

9 Serve the peas/beans/broccoli in your best bowl in the middle of the table.

10 Serve the bugs as they are, or over freshly made pasta, or with steamed rice, or, for a taste of heaven, on crunchy toast.

WINE ♣ *Bugs and good chardonnay. If possible, look for something with some age on it. A Tyrell's Vat 47, 1984 would be stunning here.*

That's it, no more butter ... read on for the denouement.

♥

## COMMON SENSE AT LAST: POACHING ORANGE ROUGHY

The previous butter-soaked fish dishes came from my restaurant days, some-where between 1983 and 1988. The following was written in May, 1990, when the penny was starting to drop.

I think I must be falling for this health propaganda in some sort of subconscious way. Not so long ago, if you gave me a fish to cook, I'd pull out the butter, split a lemon, and go for broke with a simple sauce of plenty of butter, a little lemon, a touch of salt, a few herbs and several twists of the pepper mill.

Suddenly I've turned. Here we were, a gorgeous slab of orange roughy before us, and me pro-nouncing that we were going to have a meal without any naughties. No butter, no salt, no grog. She sneered and mumbled something which sounded like: 'Here we go again, another hare-brained scheme.'

I looked up and said: 'What did you say, pet?'

She gazed into my eyes and said: 'I said "that sounds like a pretty fair scheme."'

I had turned to health after a meal out the night before when a perfectly respectable piece of orange roughy was slaughtered by an ap-palling chef. The menu read some-thing like: 'Fish of the day (orange roughy) with bearnaise sauce.' We were eating in what purported to be a restaurant in the French bistro style, and I had my mind on a gen-tly fried fillet, attended by a neat spoonful of bearnaise, tarragon pop-ping out left and right. Maybe a sim-ple salad on the side and perhaps a potato or two.

What did I get? A fish that had hit a pan so hot its edges had curled, and the poor dear was still swim-ming, this time in the most revolting reservoir of split butter. Even after I had wiped most of it away, there was still a litre or two hanging about.

It showed a total disregard for the customer, surely, but what about the poor fish? In spite of the hype surrounding orange roughy it really is a lovely fish, gentle in flavour, just tough enough in its personal infrastructure to hold together when cooked, but gentle enough to be so, so tender to the bite. It's got plenty going for it. In the pan that is. Reserves of orange roughy, or sea perch (centurians when they reach the pan) are not only dwindling, but are in danger of fading away through overfishing. Remember, your children might like to try this fish before it disappears.

I offer this recipe as a way to use orange roughy if you must, but take it as appropriate for any fish, particularly those with a finely flavoured, slightly soft flesh.

♥　♥　♥　♥　♥

**orange roughy fillets — about 200g per person**

**½ lemon, sliced**

**some herbs — tarragon is great, or parsley, or chives**

**1** In a pan, big enough to hold at least two fillets about 5 cm apart, pour water to the level of about one centimetre. Toss in a few slices of lemon.

**2** Heat the oven to flat out. Bring the water to the boil on top of the stove, and gently glide the fish fillets in. Allow the water to come to the boil again and move the fillets about a bit with a slide, to ensure there is no danger of them sticking to the bottom.

**3** Put the fish, pan, water and all into the flat-out oven, and leave them for about 8 minutes, depending on the thickness of the fish and the heat of your oven. Test regularly.

**4** Remove, allow the fish to drain, and serve the fish in all its glory, sprinkled with chopped herbs.

**5** Any of the following makes a good accompaniment: mashed potatoes; mushrooms 'baked' in a microwave or slow oven until their moisture is eliminated, then tossed with a little beef stock, or madeira; a salad of spicy cress, tossed with a little Ricotta, olives and roasted red pepper strips; or, if you can't go cold turkey, a speck of butter, melted in a little of the water in which the fish was cooked; and, of course, lemon juice and black pepper.

WINE ✤ *The first white wine that changed my life was a Brown Brothers Rhine riesling — it was under the old, white Milawa label and I was under-age. I decided I had to be a winemaker. I still like Brown's Rhines, especially the King Valley range.*

♥

## SNAPPER IN A TOMATO SAUCE

My past has come back to haunt me. As I read my cholesterol level on the lab sheet at 20 per cent higher than the optimum, my mind raced back through all those throwaway lines from food columns of the past: 'drown the lot in butter'; 'serve with cream or ice cream, or better both'; 'cholesterol scholesterol'; and worse.

Now I have to decide (again) whether to join the rest of the world and become an obsessive bore about health and fat levels in the blood, and find out what 'lipid' really means; and whether polyunsaturated is a dry parrot, or is to become an important part of my vocabulary; and whether there is a decent full-flavoured margarine anywhere to be found; and how to make a soufflé without egg yolks. I have to think of life after apple pie and ice cream, and say farewell to chocolate mousse and Lord knows what else.

My first response was to adopt a facade of being reformed while sneaking into the cupboard when nobody was looking, but then I rang Wendy Morgan, a food and nutrition consultant with the National Heart Foundation. We were talking about not much at all, when I thought I'd mention my cholesterol level.

'6.6,' I said, expecting her to say something like: 'Aaah, that's not too bad. I've heard of much worse.'

She didn't.

'That's too high,' she said, and I went white. She went on to tell me I must make changes in my diet. And I found myself nodding, looking on the one hand at my note-pad, and on the other at my Maker.

'Look at what you eat,' she was saying, 'from the very beginning of the day and work through all the things you like. Especially note all the hidden sources, like biscuits and pastries, and sausage rolls.'

On and on she went, listing with unerring accuracy all those things I love.

'Give me a break,' I said. 'Isn't there anything I like, that I'm allowed to like?'

'That's better,' she said. 'I'd much prefer to talk about the positive things.' She wasn't talking long.

'All fruit and vegetables,' she said, which would put you into the Robinson Crusoe class. 'Bread is an excellent food, and polyunsaturated margarine is okay. Definitely not coconut oil, or coconut milk.'

'Coconut milk,' I said. 'What about all those Thai dishes?'

Then the pressure started to ease. The Thais, said Ms Morgan, obviously have a well-balanced diet, which allows them to hop into such things occasionally. Suddenly there was light at the end of the tunnel. The message was one of common sense and balance. If you have loads of butter for breakfast, lunch and dinner, and wash it down with cream at the end of the night, then you are crazy. Use your scone and go for balance, and, to make it interesting, look at twists to the old ways. You won't miss it, I consoled myself, just like you never missed sugar in your coffee. The upside is worth it. The old cholesterol counter will stop ticking, and the heart will beat regularly again.

I went straight into attack.

♥ ♥ ♥ ♥ ♥

**1 medium snapper or similar fish of about 2 kg**

**1 onion, sliced**

**1 clove garlic, sliced finely**

**4–5 tomatoes, skinned and cored, or a small tin of tomatoes with no added sugar or salt**

**1 chilli, chopped roughly**

**salt**

**rosemary**

**black pepper**

**the best virgin olive oil (gets the thumbs up from nutritionists)**

**a stack of broad beans, removed from outer and inner pods**

We had been to the market, and spied some fantastic snapper at a fantastic price. Only one problem. They were two kilos each. I couldn't resist the wonderful shining eye of the fish. It had come straight out of the water. But none of our pans were big enough, and I didn't want to fillet it. What to do?

1 Scale and clean the fish in the back yard. One of the hazards of buying late at a busy market is they won't do any extra business for you. With fish, I'm not sure the savings you make are worth the trouble at the other end. One thing is for certain. Don't attempt to scale fish indoors. Until next Christmas twelve months, you'll be finding scales in places you didn't even know there were places. Do it outside under a running tap.

2 Back indoors. Cook the onions and garlic gently in a high-sided pot which can go to the oven. A heavy-bottomed stew pot is best. The onion slices need to be cooked slowly for about 10 minutes, until they have softened and changed colour and texture. Add the tomatoes, chilli, salt and rosemary, and keep cooking on a low flame for another 10 minutes. Season with black pepper. Set aside.

3 Now for the fish. Splay the underside of the fish, so the chest cavity is wide open, and sit it on top of a pile of onions and tomatoes. You might have to twist it about so it follows the turn of the pot. Rub some of the oil on the fish, put the lot into a 230°C oven, and cook for 30 minutes. You should baste the fish with some of the sauce and a little oil every now and then. With a few minutes to go, cook the broad beans in boiling salted water. They need only a minute.

4 Serve on a platter in the centre of the table, with the sauce on the side. Allow each and every diner to ease his/her required amount of fish from the bone and pour some of the sauce around. Make sure there are plenty of broad beans and piles of other appropriate vegetables about: Brussels sprouts, broccoli, cauliflower and pumpkin.

Where to now? The truth is I flit between the one and the other. When I'm busy and tired I go back to the old ways, to familiar ground I guess. It's the food version of returning to the womb. But despite that I am getting more sensible, understanding my body and its needs. Don't become an evangelist and bore the pants of yourself and your friends and colleagues. Take it easily and slowly, but make sure you are aware of sensible diet when you are feeding the kids. Their future is in your hands.

WINE ❖ *Marsanne is one of those white wines that no one seems to drink when it's ready. I remember savouring a '53 Tahbilk Marsanne as a Roseworthy student with Mr Eric Purbrick. It was beyond my limited abilities to describe. I had half a glass left and was making little groaning noises when Mr P. topped me up ... with a '63 cabernet! 'Rosé, boy,' he said, quick as a flash.*

*Try a Tahbilk or Mitchelton marsanne, 5–6 years old.*

## ♥
## A PRAWN SALAD WITH GNOCCHI

There are some old delicacies that just wouldn't be the same without cream. Gnocchi is one of them. And the sauce that comes from belting down prawn stock with cream is just one of the most intense flavours of cooking. That's the simple way, one-directional cooking, and by and large it's fine. But now and then there's a chance to work at the edges and lift a one-directional dish into something really special, startling even, while never getting complicated.

This recipe is for one of those times. The addition of a sharply flavoured dressing, some crunchy vegetables, a surprising colour, and some nutty crunch, will lift the simple into the superb.

♥    ♥    ♥    ♥    ♥

### THE CREAM SAUCE

**the heads and tails from the prawns**
*When you clean the prawns, remove the 'vein' running through the back of the prawn. It won't kill you if you miss a bit, but it's best to get rid of as much as you can! Retain the shells.*

**a little white wine (forget it if you haven't any handy)**

**all the aromatic vegetables you have around: carrots, celery, leeks, onions, garlic, ginger, herbs from the garden**

**1 l water**

**fish bones from a flat fish like John Dory or sole or the like**

**½ cup of cream**

### THE DRESSING

**walnut oil, of the highest quality**

**a little mild vinegar, mixed with lemon juice**

**salt**

**black pepper, freshly ground**

**3 prawns per person, shelled and cleaned**
*Retain the shells for a stock. Try to get fresh (green) prawns. If you must use frozen prawns, the frozen variety from South Australia is excellent.*

**pumpkin gnocchi (see page 34)**

**cashews for texture, and a lovely flavour combination with the 'nutty' cream**

**carrots, sliced into 'matchsticks'**

**hijiki — dried seaweed strands**
*Marinate it in stock or water for a few hours. It provides a lovely black colour and a real taste of the sea.*

**as many asparagus spears as you think reasonable**
*If you can't get asparagus, you can make a version of the dish using excellent beans or sugar peas.*

1 Cook the shells of the prawns with the white wine, the aromatics, water and fish bones, and reduce slowly but heavily. It will take about an hour. Strain. There should be no more than half a litre of stock. Reduce by half and set aside to cool. Remove any scum which may rise to the surface. The colour of the final stock depends on the type of prawns.

2 Add the cream to a cup of stock and cook down until the cream has thickened and the flavour is just right. There should be no flavour of cream, but plenty of the prawn shells. Add salt and pepper.

3 Make the walnut dressing by whisking the walnut oil into the mix of vinegar and lemon juice. Add salt and black pepper to taste. As with any sauce, you must taste. You cook for your palate! It doesn't matter if the dressing doesn't emulsify. Just whisk it together before you assemble your salad.

4 Toss the prawns quickly in a hot pan, just to seal, then finish in a hot oven until just done (warm in the middle), no more than 2 minutes.

5 Cook the gnocchi in boiling water and toss with the cashews in the hot cream sauce. Use a slotted spoon to take the gnocchi etc., from the sauce. There should no more than a tiny pool of cream sauce on the plate; the idea is for the gnocchi to 'take in' the cream, and there is no need for more sauce around the gnocchi.

6 Cook the carrots and the hijiki quickly in boiling water. Cook the asparagus for several minutes until tender, but still giving firmly to the touch.

7 Arrange the gnocchi in the centre of the plate, with a few cashews. Put the prawns on top — if they are large, it might be a good idea to slice them in half. Toss the carrot and hijiki and asparagus with the walnut dressing and put on top of the prawns.

WINE ♣ *I'm not the greatest fan in the world of sauvignon blanc, but it's just right here. Cloudy Bay and Moreton Estate from New Zealand, or Yarra Ridge and Katnook from Australia would go very well.*

♥
## SCALLOPS ON THE HALF SHELL WITH A LITTLE SOY

For years we suffered the flavour loss which comes from that shonky fishmongers' method of profiting by soaking scallops, purportedly to clean them of any muck from the sea. All they did was rinse them of their best, most subtle flavours, and add large volumes of water, water we paid for on the scales.

Then one or two fishmongers realised that flavour was more important than inflated profits, and decided to serve them 'dry' — an ironic title if ever there was one. 'Dry' scallops are really scallops soaking in themselves, and are brilliantly flavoured of themselves and the sea. And finally, intrepid divers in the beautiful waters off Port Lincoln in South Australia were able to bring us scallops not only 'dry', but still alive, still sitting on their shells.

This is truly glorious eating, and the most simple perfection you can imagine. They are not cheap, never will be, but that comes from limits to the catch, and the fact they all come from individual labour. Worse, they are not readily available from regular fish shops about town, but special fishmongers should be able to get them if they are prepared to make the effort. And when you see the bill, just close your eyes and think of them as a true treat.

♥   ♥   ♥   ♥   ♥

4 dessertspoons soy sauce

$\frac{1}{2}$ hot chilli, chopped finely

$\frac{1}{2}$ clove garlic, chopped very finely

juice of ¹/₂ lemon

1 shallot, chopped finely, or a small onion

dozen chives, chopped finely

black pepper

2 tomatoes, skinned, seeded, and chopped into tiny cubes

¹/₈ teaspoon sugar

at least 6 scallops per portion, cleaned gently to remove any waste material or grit

1 Mix all the above together (except for the scallops), gently but firmly, so that whatever has to dissolve, dissolves, and whatever has to cling, clings. Set aside for about 10 minutes.

2 Spoon the mixture about the outside of the scallops reposing in the shell.

3 Heat the oven to 250°C and put the scallops on a tray, taking care not to lose any of their juices. An excellent method is to use a muffin baking tray and place each scallop into the muffin slots with a little water underneath. Bake for 6–8 minutes, until the scallops are just done. That may seem a long time, but scallops seem to take quite a time to get to like the heat in the oven. Whatever you do don't overcook them. They should be just, and I mean *just*, done, giving to the touch, but far, far from tough. The best thing to do is to check after about 5 minutes. Don't waste this taste of luxury.

4 Serve straight from the oven, with stacks of crusty bread to wipe up the magnificent lightly crunchy sauce, which now includes some of the juice of the scallops. Add a touch of black pepper to each.

5 This recipe is just as appropriate if you can't get scallops on the shell. It is just as tasty with shelled scallops, and magnificent with squid. Just heat the sauce through gently, letting it get to the boil, and no more, and set aside. Pan-fry the scallops or squid, and when they are cooked, toss the sauce through them.

WINE ❖ *Scallops are rich little fellows. You need a wine that's light, crisp and dry. Try a bottle of French Sancerre or Pouilly Fumé. Compare the style to the dry Australian and New Zealand sauvignon blancs which are made from the same grape variety.*

♥

## A TOUCH OF INDIA, AND SCALLOPS

S callops don't need much assistance really. If you're adding extras, make sure they are not of the sort which overwhelms. Allow the scallops to speak for themselves, and go for them as a light main course, perhaps preceding your best plate of cheese.

Onions, cooked slowly in the pan are a perfect accompaniment for just about everything.

♥    ♥    ♥    ♥    ♥

### THE ONIONS

4 onions, sliced into rings

### THE SAUCE

(from an idea from Julie Sahni's terrific book, *Classic Indian Cooking*)

1 dessertspoon coriander seed

6 star anise

1 dessertspoon cumin seeds

2 onions, chopped finely

1 clove garlic, chopped roughly

1 walnut-sized piece of ginger,
sliced roughly

2 chillies, chopped finely

3 dessertspoons turmeric powder

2 dessertspoons tomato paste

2 cups fish stock, if you have it;
water if you don't

250 ml whipping cream

salt

black pepper

lemon juice

½ dozen scallops each

chives

**1** The onions. Heat a little oil in a pan and add the onion rings. Cook slowly until they turn brown, stirring constantly so they don't stick to the bottom of the pan. This is a slow, tedious process, as the onions gradually go through several colour changes and changes in consistency. As they give off their moisture, you might need to add a little water here and there. The onions are ready when quite brown, and have lost much of their bulk. Set aside for re-heating later.

**2** Now for the sauce. Dry roast the coriander, star anise and cumin in a hot pan, working the spices about the pan with a wooden spoon. The aroma is incredible. When they have roasted sufficiently, a few minutes, and your nose is tingling, re-move from the heat and grind, stamp upon, or whizz up the spices. Your 'second' coffee grinder is best for do-ing this.

**3** Add some oil to the spice pan and gently fry the onions, garlic, ginger and chillies until the onions change colour and soften — about 5 minutes. Add the turmeric, mixing it through thoroughly, the roasted spices, tomato paste and the stock/water. Reduce gently until the mixture thickens, and then purée. It should be quite thick — there will be enough to form a base for several meals.

**4** To 2 large tablespoons of the sauce base, add the cream and cook gently, stirring constantly. Cook until the cream has reduced and cooked through. Strain through a fine sieve. The sauce should have a rich orange-yellow colour. Test for seasoning and add lemon juice to taste. Keep warm. Heat the oven to 220°C. (You can approximate this sauce by cooking some onions with garlic, ginger and curry powder, and then working cream through.)

**5** Cook the scallops in a hot pan in a little oil, giving them each plen-ty of space. Toss them about until they are all sizzling, and then place in the oven for 3–5 minutes, until firm and just done.

**6** While the scallops are cooking, re-heat the onions and toss the chives through. Add a little sauce to the scallops and serve with the sauce clinging to the scallops and a spoon-ful of the caramelised onions on the side.

WINE ❖ *Traminer and I have a love–hate relationship. Too many Australian wines from this grape have an oiliness I don't like — but the best ones are good. Try Orlando Flaxmans or some blended with Rhine riesling like Krondorf.*

♥
## FISH FOR THE KIDS

There are no rules for cooking for children. It's as much a case of pulling out whatever they liked yesterday, adding two tablespoons of hope, a couple of wild jokes, and mixing it all together gently with patience; when they won't take that, give them what they wanted in the first place.

Just persevere. Every now and again, you will find they'll take what they are given and enjoy it; before you know it, they'll be eating what you're eating, liking what you like, asking for favourites, your favourites. Even then don't expect them all to be the same, despite the same family structure, routines, emphases. They'll be chalk and cheese. One might eat anything and plenty of it, from birth; the other will take favourites and little of them, from first taste, and nothing else; and the third will be a bit of this and a bit of that.

I learnt these things very early. Number one daughter loves Weet-Bix; she adores strawberries. So why not the two together, as a treat? Wrong. She threw the lot across the table, and screamed for 20 minutes.

They all love muesli bars. So let's make our own. Wrong again. They look the same as the commercial, they taste pretty much the same, but they don't come in wrappers. Not interested.

Then there was fish. For weeks I tried my son with fish. No way. Then by a miracle, he happened by when I was trying a batch of finger-sized mackerel in the deep frier. This is a richly flavoured, rather oily fish, as often as not eaten raw, smoked or pickled, rather than cooked. However, given a light batter and cooked very quickly in small pieces, it became something of joy. And he loved it. Now he eats fish of all shapes, sizes, flavours.

♥　♥　♥　♥　♥

**1 medium-sized mackerel, boned and skinned by your fishmonger**
*Remove any extra bones carefully. There is nothing worse than biting into fish in batter and discovering a surprise. This is doubly true when feeding children. Any firm, well-muscled, well-flavoured fish will be fine.*

**a little flour to coat the fish**

**salt**

**black pepper**

**1 egg yolk**

**1 cup iced water**

**1 cup sifted flour for the batter**

**oil for deep frying**

1 Slice the fish into bite-size pieces and rub them through a little flour. Sprinkle a little salt and pepper over the fish.

2 Lightly whisk the yolk and add the water, beating lightly together. Add the cup of flour all at once and mix gently with a fork, until it is just together. Don't worry if it is lumpy.

3 Heat the oil to 170°C. Test with a little batter. It should sizzle and cook instantly.

4 Dip the floured fish into the batter, drop into the oil gently, and cook until the batter is golden — no more than 45 seconds. Drain on absorbent paper and serve simply with wedges of lemon, or mayonnaise, or tartare sauce …

# VEGETABLES FOR ALL TASTES

Y ou don't have to be a vegetarian to love vegetables. All you have to do is to love essential, splendid flavours, enjoy flamboyant shapes and colours, and look on vegetable cooking as one component of the kitchen craft which is forever changing and surprising.

Vegetables are remarkable for their ability to provide so many different textures, for so many different roles, at such affordable prices. The humble potato will support a book, so numerous are the opportunities to cook with it. Broccoli is wonderful straight from the garden, delicious blanched to pick up a fruity, full-bodied dip, doubtless based on some vegetable; gorgeous when cooked until just tender, then covered with a cheese sauce; and super duper whizzed with chicken stock, spices and herbs to make for a bright and beautiful soup.

Spinach can act as a salad, a soup, a sauce, an accompaniment; or it can paint pasta. Zucchini provides colour, texture and flavour to a vegetable stew like ratatouille, pizzazz to pasta when grated like spaghetti; and the flowers are the most delicious containers for all sorts of stuffings.

Vegetables can be taken raw, or baked, steamed, fried, or boiled; they are happy as bridesmaids to meat and fish, chicken and pork, and happier still as the bride and groom; some of them even make for splendid desserts.

The only thing wrong with vegetables is vegetarianism; vegetarians would often have you believe that they are more wholesome than meat eaters, better people because they are making a sacrifice by eschewing meat. Don't believe them. Vegetarians have the best of all worlds, with access to vats of colour and crunch and limitless flavour variations.

The latest data on eating suggests the best diet is a pyramid, with bread, grains and legumes the foundation, vegetables and fruit next. As the pyramid gets tighter and tighter we run into chicken and meat and fish. And scorned, at the top of the pile, are nasties like fats and oils.

I keep on reading such things and making resolutions, and then breaking them. But perhaps subconsciously, I have already enveloped vegetables as my flavour base. Thus the long list of pasta and rice dishes up front, and now some down-to-earth, basic, yet enthusiastic flavours.

You know something: the more I think of it, the more attractive vegetarianism is — if it wasn't such a social nightmare.

## What You'll Need

1 **The personality to take hold of vegetables with an enthusiasm the crop has not seen before.** Don't look at vegetables as accompaniments. Make it your life's aim to make at least one more meal a week based on vegetables.

2 **As ever, you need an excellent rapport with your fruiterer.** Excellent relationships take on a new twist at the fruit shop. My favourite fruiterer is one who won't faint when I pick up a pea from the pile, pod it, and toss the little green orbs down the hatch. There are so many times in the year when produce is less than perfect; and other times when it's perfect when you believed it couldn't be. And the infuriating thing is, you can't tell a perfect pea from its pod. The only way to know is to try and see. I'm not suggesting you should munch an apple and put it back, or poke an avocado, or crunch the celery, or snap the asparagus. But you should believe that if a test is necessary, then you're in the right shop to do it.

3 **The curiosity to try something different with an old favourite.** This is the essence of all cooking, but it is particularly appropriate with vegies. So, just because cauliflower is great with white sauce, why not try it baked with onions and garlic, or tossed in a wok with soy and chilli,

or steamed and sprinkled with garam masala, or whatever you think of next?

4 **And definitely a microwave.** You haven't tasted a pumpkin until you've cooked it in the microwave; how else would you 'roast' garlic cloves in under a minute? Is there any other way to cook eggplant? And tomatoes, and chutneys and sauces. The microwave is the key to vegetable-cooking stardom.

# THE RECIPES

♥
## MASHED SPUDS, THE WORLD'S GREATEST DISH

My favourite dish as a child was mashed potatoes on thickly buttered white bread. Later (not so long ago) I added fresh herbs and cut down on the butter on the bread, but not in the potatoes. It is still my favourite.

I can't think of anything more acceptable to eat at any time, at any place. No matter how far up the market you go, you'll find potatoes, and classy chefs working their whisks off to do something just a little different, just a little better than the joint down the road.

At Restaurant Guy Savoy in Paris, I remember the combination of finely sliced potatoes and truffles as a true classic. Finely sliced potatoes with a touch of mash to hold them together and shaves of fresh, very expensive truffle in between.

Flash restaurants do flash things with mashed potatoes too. Restaurant Robuchon in Paris is rated one of the best in the world; I haven't been there, after being turned away at the front door one forlorn day, but those who have don't talk about the crayfish, or truffles, or lamb, or pheasant — they hold forth about the mashed potatoes.

Greg Brown at Melbourne's Browns restaurant helped me out with his recipe for something similar. It's hardly the simple mash of my mum: it's made up of one-third mashed potatoes, one-third cream, and one-third butter, and seasoning. Yikes! There's more. You add the cream to the mashed potatoes in a pan, then finish the dish with the butter. And then you pass the whole lot through the finest of sieves

*four* times before serving. Yabba dabba doo!

That sort of labour is one of the reasons you pay big money to eat at flash restaurants. Mashed potatoes at home are not like that, but they must be more than just well-cooked potatoes, given a bit of life with butter and squashed. They should be filled with all sorts of surprise flavours. They don't have be whizzed to a purée, but are lovely with a little chunkiness, letting you know there's still a little bit of the rustic in our lives.

♥   ♥   ♥   ♥   ♥

6 large floury potatoes, in their skins

1/2 l milk

50 g butter

1/2 bunch of parsley, chopped roughly

small bunch of tarragon leaves removed from the stem, or chives, chopped roughly

black pepper

salt

1 Boil or steam the potatoes until they take easily to the knife. You might think you have too much. You can never have too much mashed potato.

2 Allow them to cool a little, peel them, and mash roughly with a masher or the back of a strong fork.

3 Bring the milk to the boil and add it to the potatoes on a gentle heat, stirring it through as you go. It is better if there is little re-heating to be done, but the difference in flavour, given all the things that can

happen at home, is so minute it won't be noticed.

4 When the potatoes are well warmed through, fold in the butter and add the herbs, black pepper and salt. The herbs should be rather chunky as well. Mash again, as before, making sure the milk is well incorporated. This dish should feel rustic, right to the end.

♥

## IRISH POTATOES

This all started with several slugs of Irish Whiskey. I had always believed that Irish was just another version of Scotch, and Scotch was the one and only whisky. It just goes to show how wrong you can be, and how there's something new to learn in this business every breathing moment. The truth is the Irish were making whiskey (note the 'e') 700 years before the Scots started making whisky.

Irish has a cleaner, less harsh flavour than Scotch and it leaves the bubble-gum perfumery of bourbon for dead.

And then I started thinking of potatoes; not because of the generations of Irish in my blood, or the Irish in my blood from the drinking session, but because there's a taste there that seems made for potatoes. It sounds crazy, the product of a lush. It isn't.

♥   ♥   ♥   ♥   ♥

500 g floury potatoes suitable for mashing

bunch of tarragon

a little cream

a good pour of best olive oil

30 g unsalted butter

salt

black pepper

a few teaspoons of Irish whiskey
*Any of the five brands which make it here is fine.*

80 g of your favourite melting cheese, grated

1 Cook the potatoes in plenty of salted water until they give like butter to the knife. Heat the oven to flat out.

2 Peel the potatoes and mash with a masher or fork, depending on how you prefer your mash.

3 Add the chopped tarragon, cream, olive oil, butter, salt and several turns of the pepper grinder. Mix the lot together powerfully.

4 On a flat-out flame, heat a little olive oil in a heavy pan which can go to the oven. When the oil is hot, toss in the mash and flatten the mix so that it touches the edges. Cook for a minute or so on high, and then put the pan in the oven.

5 Heat through for about 10 minutes, remove and mix the grated cheese through.

6 Spoon the potatoes on the plate, make a little well in the pile, and mix the whiskey through them. Have a sauce boat of whiskey handy for top-ups.

7 You can do the same with baked potatoes. When they are done, slice the tops, fluff up the potatoes, and add a few drops of the whiskey. Finish with butter or olive oil, and salt and pepper.

WINE ✤ *One day, get two good tasting glasses and compare a nice Irish whiskey with a good Scottish malt. I believe the overall difference is that the Irish has a herb/spice aroma whereas Scotch is more peaty, smoky and oak-influenced. Maybe the herb-like character is why the Irish is so good with mashed potatoes.*

♥

## A CURRY OF NEW POTATOES WITH TOMATOES

T his has nothing to do with mash, or truffles, or whiskey, but more to do with some fiddling I've been doing with potatoes since several happy visits to very good Indian eating houses. It is best made the day before you want it.

♥　♥　♥　♥　♥

### 3 onions, sliced

### 1 clove garlic, sliced finely

### 2 solid dessertspoons of garam masala (a hip Indian term for a spice mix)

*Make your own mix. A suggested version is: 2 tablespoons coriander, 2 tablespoons whole black peppercorns, 3 hot dried chillies, 1 tablespoon fennel seeds, 1 tablespoon caraway seeds, a few dried curry leaves, 2 tablespoons cumin seeds, 2 tablespoons mustard seeds, 1 tablespoon of fenugreek seeds, all whizzed up in a coffee grinder. Add a tablespoon of ground turmeric for colour. But really it's what you have in the cupboard: a mix of heat, sweetness and subtlety.*

### a little water

### 6–8 firm waxy potatoes, peeled and cut into medium-sized pieces

*They must hold their own when cooked. Pontiacs (the pink skinned variety) are the type most likely to be available at your fruiterer. Patrone, a newish yellow variety, is ideal.*

### 8 skinned cooking tomatoes, in season (or a small tin of tomatoes, with juice), mashed

### 1–3 chillies, depending on how hot you like it

1 Put the onions, garlic, garam masala and a little olive oil in a large pan. Cook very slowly on a low heat until the onions caramelise and become very tender. This will take at least 20 minutes, and you might need to add a little water here and there. There are no short cuts — just dream of nice things as you watch and stir. The aroma makes it worthwhile anyway.

2 Transfer to a saucepan and add the potatoes and the tomatoes (and chillies if you wish). Cook slowly on a low heat until the potatoes are done and the sauce has thickened. The idea is for the tomatoes to cook into a thick spicy sauce, hugging the potatoes. It will take about a half an hour, and again it needs a deal of watching and stirring gently. It needs a little touch to know whether to add a little water here and there to prevent sticking, or just to stir a little harder.

3 Leave overnight to allow the flavours to mingle, and then reheat gently.

WINE ✤ *Drink beer.*

♥
## RACLETTE, THE CHEESE

Discovering Raclette (i): We had just settled into the plush seats at Two Faces at Delgany, that brilliantly restored castle/hotel at Portsea, Melbourne's Riviera. Unused as we are to such style and service, we were still holding on to that moment of self-consciousness as the waiters scurry about and smile glowingly, and you ask about the wine list etc., and there is small talk all about, and you wonder when they will disappear so you can exchange that opening titbit of gossip etc. Suddenly I looked at the missus, glowing across the table, and said, quite loudly in retrospect: 'This place smells like a cowshed.' If looks could kill, I would have been stone dead.

'It's the cheese, you idiot,' she hissed. I looked around, and there, at the table behind, was a couple hoeing into a dish of asparagus, over-baked with Raclette.

Discovering Raclette (ii): We had been here and there, and decided to call into a favourite cheese shop where we stocked up with all sorts, including a decent slab of Raclette, sliced very finely. I tossed the lot into the car, and we drove home, humming and whistling. We unloaded the kids and, when it was all over, their mother returned to the car, rummaging about in the mess in the back.

'What on earth are you doing' I asked.

'I think one of our darlings has left something behind. The car stinks.'

'It's the cheese, you idiot,' I hissed.

15–15.

It's extraordinary when you think about it. So much of the cheese we eat and love smells like all those things on earth we prefer to leave to others: the inside of a horsebox; a pair of well-worn socks; a kid's lunch-box after a week's holiday; bathers in the boot; nappies in the night. Put all the above together and you've got Raclette.

Raclette has been made for centuries in Switzerland, but it is only since 1988 that Australian-made has been readily available, thanks to a joint venture between a Swiss company and Haberfields, a long-time milk supplier at Wodonga on the Victorian – NSW border.

The cheese itself has given its name to a famous mountain dish. The hardy Swiss mountain folk would stick a great chunk of Raclette on the end of a knife and poke it in the fire. As soon as it started to melt, they would remove it and scrape it over oven-baked potatoes. The French 'to scrape' is *racler*.

Raclette is the most perfect of melting cheese, and although its joy in a fresh bread sandwich should not be underestimated, I would not put one in your child's lunch-box. It could cause some embarrassment.

♥  ♥  ♥  ♥  ♥

¹/₂ dozen potatoes for mashing

¹/₂ cup milk

100g butter

bunch of tarragon, leaves pulled
from the stem

salt

black pepper

dozen slices Raclette (about 150g)

*When buying this cheese, ask your supplier to slice it for you.*

**1** Cook the potatoes until just done. When they are just about cooked, bring the milk to the boil. Mash the potatoes roughly with a fork and add the milk, butter, tarragon, salt and pepper. Set aside to cool in an oven-proof dish. This can be done well in advance.

**2** Heat the oven to 200°C. Spread the cheese over the potatoes and heat through in the oven. It should take about 15 minutes. Season with black pepper and serve.

WINE ✛ *Wine is not scared of Raclette! With these spuds the Swiss would probably serve a crisp, dry white made from the chasselas grape, or a light-bodied pinot noir. Chasselas and I have never been able to dance together, so I'd go for a pinot.*

♥

## BABA GHANOUSH, VIA THE MICROWAVE

Eggplant and the microwave are as happy as peaches and cream. Big, bold, shiny, hard to cook by conventional methods, and full of water: eggplant is just the combination this space-age machine delights in. Just prick the vegetable a few times with a fork, shove it through the door, and what do you have? Absolutely perfect eggplant, firm yet soft, cooked through yet holding its own, ideal in colour, texture and flavour.

And remarkably, it has no need of the salt dredgings which come with usual cooking processes. Don't ask me why.

Cooking eggplant like this means you can have that delicious Middle Eastern dip, baba ghanoush, as quick as a flash.

♥   ♥   ♥   ♥   ♥

**2 eggplants, about 350g each, stem attached**
*Eggplants should be firm and glossy.*

**1–2 cloves garlic, unpeeled**

**2 soup spoons tahini, the paste made from sesame seeds**

**juice of 1 lemon**

**1 teaspoon salt**

**1/2–1 chilli, chopped finely**

**1 teaspoon ground cumin**

**1/2 cup first quality virgin olive oil**

**handful of parsley, stems removed**

**black pepper**

**1** Prick the eggplants all over with a fork, put on a plate, and cook in the microwave on high for 6–10 minutes, depending on the power of the machine. You will know when the vegetables are done when they are tender to the touch and the skin has changed colour from deep purple-black to purple-green-brown.

**2** Allow the eggplants to cool, then peel while you cook the garlic. The eggplant skin will come away easily, like an orange peel. Put the garlic on a plate and cook in the microwave very quickly, about 1 minute. You will know when it's done when the kitchen is filled with the sweet aroma of garlic. Don't let it overcook, or it will shrivel into nothing.

**3** Allow the garlic to cool and then squeeze the bulb from the skin.

**4** Mash the eggplant and garlic together, then whizz with the tahini, lemon juice, salt, chilli, cumin and finally the olive oil. Whizz until it has become a thick purée/dip.

5 Chop the parsley quite roughly and work it through the dip. Serve with Middle Eastern bread. Goes well with steak, veal, chicken, and is a hoot with fried sardines.

♥

## RATATOUILLE

There are none so blind as those who will not see. For some time I had wondered about the origins of ratatouille, and then I looked at the flourishing vegetable garden and saw tomatoes blooming, and chillies and peppers blushing, and garlic popping from the ground, and zucchini taking over, and finally, surveying it all rather imperiously, the purple flowers and luscious purple fruit of the eggplant. Throw them all together with a little onion and you have ratatouille.

It is a dish which eased its way onto the menus of classy restaurants a few years back, as the chorus to a less than substantial main course. The clever thinking being that if the main event is a little dodgy you can win them with a reasonably cheap, easy to make, easy to serve vegetable stew with an exotic name.

Good thinking it was, too. Ratatouille has that fine ability to mix and match with just about anything, yet the dish still stands firm on its own. There are no prima donnas in well-made ratatouille. Nothing stands out; all stand equal, but apart. But first among equals, the prime minister of the party, must be the eggplant. If Gough Whitlam had been a vegetable, I am sure he would have been an eggplant, although of course he would have taken the French name and been known as an aubergine.

The eggplant is one of those vegetables that grandmothers, and less-than-modern mothers know little about, even though it has been around since Adam was in short pants. It is probably not greatly favoured because it has never been really cheap, and is never that easy to prepare — in the sense that beans and peas and cauliflower and potatoes are. There's this salting business, and the skin, and the old bogey of the cauli you know is better than the eggplant you don't.

You usually have to salt eggplants to draw some of the excess liquid and bitterness out. Eggplants also sop up oil from any part of the pan.

None of this is a worry with ratatouille. The more the eggplant soaks up the better, which is why the stew, like all stews I guess, is better the day after it has been cooked. Give the boys and girls time to get to know each other. Then you can be sure you are voting for a winner.

The traditionalists prefer to cook each of the ingredients in separate pans, so that each is cooked just the right amount. I can't see the need for that. A little care, and a lot of observation, and you achieve the same result. Any minor imperfection is worth not cleaning four extra pans.

WINE ❖ *Good French chablis has a knack of cutting through the oil that eggplant tends to soak up. French chablis is not everyone's cup ot tea — in taste or pocket — but it's worth a treat.*

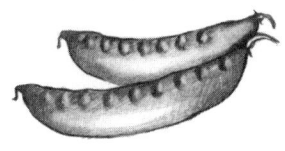

♥  ♥  ♥  ♥  ♥

2–3 middle-sized onions, sliced

6 Roma tomatoes, peeled and
chopped roughly

equal volumes of red peppers,
eggplant and zucchini, all chopped
into walnut-sized pieces, skin on

2 cloves garlic, sliced finely

2 hot chillies, chopped finely

bunch of basil

handful of olives, pips removed
(optional)

2 teaspoons salt

plenty of black pepper

best olive oil for the plate

**1** Cook the onions slowly in a little olive oil, stirring so they stew
and soften, rather than fry. You
might need to add water if they get
a little cantankerous in the pan. Let
them stew away for about 15 minutes before you add the tomatoes
and peppers.

**2** Cook slowly, adding the garlic
and chillies, until the tomatoes
are quite soft and the peppers are
soft, but still holding their shape.
Add the eggplant and salt heavily.

**3** Allow mixture to stew away for
a few minutes on a low heat,
then cover and cook on a low heat
for another 15 minutes, checking to
make sure there is no burning. When
all the vegetables have softened, but
the pepper and eggplants retain their
shape, add the zucchini.

**4** Stir about and then cook, covered, for another 10 minutes,
until the zucchini is soft to the knife.
Add the basil and the olives, and

mix through gently. Adjust for seasoning (salt). Twist the pepper mill
around and around, and leave, covered, off the heat until it cools.

**5** Re-heat gently to serve, swirling
some olive oil about as it goes to
the plate. You can serve the ratatouille in a variety of ways: cold, in
a sandwich, warm as a vegetable, or
hot with pasta. Serve it hot, pep-
pered anew, and covered with large
slivers of Parmesan.

**6** Once you've done it on the
stove, do it in the microwave; the
same rules apply, but it doesn't
make too much difference, either in
flavour or in time.

♥

## EGGPLANT AND CHEESE SOUFFLE

**R**estaurants rarely treat eggplant as much more than
an occasional accompany-
ing vegetable. The only place I have
seen eggplant treated as a star is at
Browns, the flashy Melbourne restaurant, where Greg Brown shows
just how lovely eggplants can be.

His version is as simple as simple.
Just cut the eggplant in half — either
way — score it, salt it lightly, rinse
to remove the salt, bake in a 200°C
oven for about 15 minutes (for a
medium-sized vegetable), remove,
and cover with your version of pesto
containing more than the usual
amount of Parmesan. Then, just put
it under the grill for about 3 minutes
(that's a restaurant grill — the home
version might take longer, and is
best completed in the oven), and
that's it.

It gets such a thick, rich flavour,

you are sure as sure you are eating mushrooms.

This is very much an attribute of the eggplant. If you cook eggplant slowly, it takes on very much the flavour of the mushroom.

It's a good idea to mix it with basil and cheese, whizz it until strong, add some vegetables, fold in some whipped egg whites, and make a soufflé/pudding.

♥ ♥ ♥ ♥ ♥

4 medium eggplants

a little lemon zest

100g cheddar cheese, cubed

20 basil leaves

1 egg yolk

1 chilli, chopped finely

black pepper

5 egg whites

*This number will give you a medium light soufflé/pudding. If you add a few more, the end result will be much lighter, much fluffier.*

2 teaspoons sugar

1 zucchini, sliced, and briefly cooked in a little olive oil until softened

1 red pepper, skinned and sliced in strips

Parmesan or cheddar for grating

tomatoes for sauce

*Just cook down the tomatoes with a little chilli, herbs and salt until very soft. Whizz with a little first-grade olive oil.*

1 Toss the eggplant into the microwave and cook on high for about 10 minutes, or until they take a knife like butter. Peel and toss the flesh and lemon zest into the whizzer.

2 Add the cheese, basil, egg yolk, chilli and black pepper, and whizz to a purée. It takes on a greenish hue, but never fear. That's another sidelight to eggplant, especially with the added basil.

3 Whip the egg whites in a perfectly clean bowl, adding the sugar gradually, until light and fluffy and holding soft peaks.

4 Flop a quarter of the whites into the purée and fold through. Then add the rest, quarter by quarter, folding and maintaining a lightness.

5 Butter a baking dish. Lay half the mix along the bottom. Lay the zucchini and red pepper on top of the base, then put the rest on top.

6 Bake in a 200°C oven for 20 minutes and then remove. Grate some Parmesan or cheddar on top and return to the oven for a few minutes.

7 Serve from the dish, with a warm tomato sauce about the edges.

WINE ✤ *A very good fino sherry — Spanish or Australian.*

♥

## HUMMUS, THE HIP DIP

H ummus was a hip dip in the days when we were all growing up and learning there was more to eating than roast lamb, carrots and tomatoes; and more to the Middle East and North Africa than the Pyramids and Casablanca.

Hummus is the happy marriage of dried chick peas and tahini, the paste made from zillions of sesame seeds. It might surprise you to know that chick peas start their lives as delicious green delicacies, but I have never seen them in this state, and I doubt many of us have. The fact they make the dried state suggests they must be pretty good fresh — otherwise why dry them for keeping? You certainly wouldn't touch them in their dried state, unless you were a horse. Farmers in the Mediterranean have been using dried chick peas for horse feed for generations, but fortunately they have also crunched them up and mixed them with tahini and oil and some spices, and given us hummus. Bless them.

♥    ♥    ♥    ♥    ♥

**450g  chick peas, soaked in water**
*You can buy them in tins, pre-soaked, and, as they are to be pulverised in the whizzer, it seems a pretty good idea to have a tin or two on hand for the start of an instant hummus.*

**2 cloves garlic, peeled**

**2 chillies**

**2 teaspoons salt**

**2 teaspoons cumin, ground yourself**

**juice of 2 lemons**

**2 soup spoons tahini (about 20g)**

**1 cup virgin olive oil**

1 Once the chickpeas have soaked, skim away any foam which comes to the surface, and cook gently in new water for 1–2 hours, until they have softened. Don't let them disintegrate — they should get just to the stage of tenderness. Once cooked, remove the skins and taste.

You'll understand why farmers feed them to horses.

2 Taste the tahini: it has a nutty, very attractive, but dominating flavour. That's why you don't need much of it.

3 Now put all the ingredients in the whizzer, and go for it. It will take not much time at all. While you are doing this, spare a thought for the thousands of years of hummus makers who sat and ground sesame seeds and ground chickpeas and then ground them together; and then ate the result and did it again. Test the flavour, by rolling it around on your tongue, until you feel the lemon juice, the garlic, the chilli, the cumin, the tahini, the olive oil and the chickpeas coming through.

4 Cover with a little more olive oil. It keeps for ages. Serve with chopped parsley.

WINE ❖ *I have a mate who's always late for dinner. Over the years, after much scientific research, I found that the only way of making her arrive anywhere near the rest of the crowd was to open a bottle of French Champagne. N.V. French fizz and hummus is a good blend — non-vintage because I can't afford vintage any more. My favourites have always been Louis Roederer, Bollinger and Tattinger.*

♥

## STUFFING ZUCCHINI FLOWERS

Zucchinis are wonders for the hack gardener. You plant them, leave them to the ladybirds, and keep picking from their foliage for months on end. You can eat them raw, grate them on salads, bake them, toss them into stews, and their beautiful flowers make for wonderful containers for all sorts of ripping flavours.

Stuffed zucchini flowers make even the most mundane plate look magnificent. The gorgeous green and white of the finely sliced vegetable, given that extra edge of style by the brilliant yellow of the flower. You can put anything inside — anything, that is, which requires gentle re-heating rather than cooking. One of my favourite mixtures is a combination of finely chopped and gently cooked onions and garlic, a mussel or two chopped very finely, and the lot held together by a mix of butter and basil. The butter melts and the flower loses its shape, but you just can't beat it for flavour.

A version of this dish which holds its own is one in which you replace the butter and basil with pesto. You can also dip the stuffed flowers in batter and deep-fry them, but I have never seen the sense in this. Apply common sense and let simple flavours do their best.

The secret to stuffing something so delicate as these zucchini flowers is to provide the same ground rules you would apply to stuffing pasta and calling it ravioli or tortellini: the filling should have a robust flavour, well and truly able to hold its own, but when encased, it should not overwhelm its host.

♥   ♥   ♥   ♥   ♥

**1 zucchini per person, complete with flower**
*These are available at smart fruit shops across town, but of course they are much better if picked direct from your garden. They should be picked when closed, either at the end of the day or first thing in the morning, and then treated gently. They are best if not washed, which is another reason for not spraying the vegetable garden.*

**1 other young zucchini, sliced very finely**

**1 carrot, grated**

**1 clove garlic, chopped very finely**

**3 small shallots, or 1 onion**

**1 tomato, peeled and chopped finely**
*Romas are best because of their dense flesh.*

**handful of chives, chopped finely**

**a few leaves of basil, snipped**

**a few nuts, chopped roughly**
*Use hazelnuts, unsalted walnuts or cashews.*

**¹/₂ stem of lemon grass, chopped finely**
*The zest of ¹/₂ lemon, chopped finely, is a good substitute in this case.*

**1 dessertspoon good olive oil**

**1 dessertspoon soy sauce**

**black pepper**

1 Mix all the ingredients, except for the zucchinis with the flowers, in a bowl and steam, covered, in the microwave on high for about 5 minutes. The filling is done when the carrots, zucchini and shallots have softened. The filling cannot be undercooked — the ingredients are young enough to eat raw anyway — but if you cook it too long it can dry

out. Remember, it is also going to be heated through again. Allow the mix to cool before filling the flowers.

2 Treat the zucchini and flowers very gently. Slice the zucchini along its length from the bottom almost to the flower, so it can be fanned. Taking care not to rip the flower, slice out the calyx (the zucchini's tonsils, I guess).

3 Gently fill the flowers with the mixture, and fold them shut. Steam for 8–10 minutes, until the zucchini is tender. The flower should still be firm and yellow.

4 Serve with a simple dressing made of the best virgin olive oil, a little lemon juice or balsamic vinegar, black pepper, salt and some chopped nuts. Use the same nuts you used in the stuffing.

♥

## ZUCCHINI OMELETTE

E ggs are hardly the food of the nineties, these days of healthy eating, but what the hell. I'm as aware as the next person that sensible eating makes for a good night's sleep and a productive, contented life, but that doesn't mean you dive daily into a pool of virgin olive oil, coming up only occasionally for a stick of celery and a raw carrot, with a rare treat of poached pears and yoghurt.

Don't think I'm scornful of the new order. I would reckon these days I'd take a meal of eggs about once a season, whereas it used to be more than once a week. We usually get stuck into eggs after getting our annual carton from a farmer mate who has chickens pecking the dirt

and eating delicious leftovers from the kitchen. The eggs feel great, have really yellow and rich yolks, and when broken fall exactly into their expected parts of whites and yolk. Poached, they hold together wonderfully, making every cook a genius. They have a flavour all their own. You have to eat them.

♥ ♥ ♥ ♥ ♥

**1 zucchini, grated**
*You could use carrot, corn, roasted capsicum, eggplant etc.*

**4 eggs**

**nutmeg, grated freshly**

**a little chilli, chopped finely**

**1 clove garlic, chopped finely**

**a little fresh horseradish, grated**
*Horseradish is one of those flavourings of which a little goes a long way. It's never really been a favourite because it has such a dominating, pungent flavour, but I guess much of that distrust has been because so little of it is available fresh. If you see it, try it. If you like it, plant it. It will grow and grow and grow.*

**salt**

**any fresh herbs, chopped roughly**
*If I could ask for one, it would be tarragon.*

**1/2 cup cream**

**1 dessertspoon full-flavoured virgin olive oil**

**Raclette or Parmesan cheese, or any flavoursome cheese, to be melted or grated at the end**

**black pepper**

1 After grating the zucchini, squeeze it gently in your hands to remove any excess moisture. Add the eggs, nutmeg, chilli, garlic, horseradish, salt and herbs (keep some

aside for garnish and seasonings), and beat the lot together with a fork until the yolks and whites are as one. Pour in the cream, and beat gently. Heat the oven to 190°C.

2 In a heavy-bottomed pan (a Le Creuset 20 cm pan is perfect), heat the oil on high until it sizzles. Remove from heat and run the oil all about the pan. Pour off any excess.

3 Return pan to the heat for a few seconds and add the egg mix. Leave on the heat for about 30 seconds and then turn off the heat.

4 Put the lot in the bottom of the oven and leave for about 20 minutes. Test after about 15 minutes. You will notice that the edges are firming up and the centre is undercooked. The dish is done when the centre, while underdone, is firm enough to hold its own.

5 Remove and leave in the pan on top of the stove for a minute or so. Grate some Parmesan over the top. Turn on the grill to high and slide the pan under the grill. Leave for a minute or so, until the cheese just melts. Remove and set aside for 30 seconds.

6 Run about the edges with a flexible knife to ensure they have not stuck. They should not have — the oil and the fast early cooking should have ensured that. Fit a plate onto the top of the pan and unmould. (If it doesn't unmould, don't despair, just take it straight from the pan.)

7 Sprinkle the new top with cheese and black pepper from the pepper mill, and put under the grill for 30 seconds.

8 Sprinkle with some herbs and serve. It's best taken in slices. Delicious, hot, warm or cold. And especially delicious on toast.

WINE ❖ *Have a bottle of chilled Rhine riesling taken straight from the fridge. We tend to try our rieslings too early in Australia — the best ones need three to five years bottle age before they flower.*

♥

## A SHARP TOMATO SOUP

Whenever you see Roma tomatoes in the market you know it is deep summer. These are the luscious variety used for thousands of years by Italians for pasta sauces. They are much denser in the flesh and seem to have less water content, and so more flavour, than the usual table tomatoes. They also ripen later, so, I guess, take in more of the sun. They usually arrive and depart from market in those old wooden fruit boxes which we used to turn into billy carts. They grow low to the deck and are usually dusty and even muddy. They are just about always left to ripen on the bush, as they have rather solid, protective skins. All this gives them a certain rustic authenticity. They are also usually very cheap.

I love them, any of a million ways, but especially as a rich, acidic tomato soup. I once gave this recipe to a friend who took it to Italy. The Italians loved it too.

♥   ♥   ♥   ♥   ♥

**8 Roma tomatoes, skinned**

*Just cut an X in the end opposite the stem and toss into boiling water for about 20 seconds. Remove, plunge in cold water, and the skin will come away easily.*

**2 teaspoons salt**

**²/₃ cup virgin olive oil**

**2 onions**

**2 chillies, sliced finely**

**2 cloves garlic, peeled**

**20 basil leaves**

1 Chop the tomatoes in half, sprinkle with salt, and cover with the oil. Mix them together with your fingers.

2 Cook the onions, chillies and garlic gently in a little oil until the onions soften, then add the tomato and oil mix, and slowly bring the lot to the boil.

3 Simmer for about 15 minutes, until the tomatoes have all but given up the ghost, then add the basil leaves. Cook for another few minutes, mixing through the basil.

4 Remove from the heat and put the mix through a mouli or a whizzer. Test the seasoning. You are likely to need more salt.

5 When you are ready to serve, bring the soup to the boil, whisking boldly. This soup does not keep all that well, but then I have never really needed to bother too much about that.

6 Serve with toast, smeared with butter mixed with chopped basil leaves.

**WINE ♣** *This is a wine killer of a dish. If in doubt, serve full-bodied sherry. Amontillado or oloroso. The Aussie sherry makers of note are Seppelt, McWilliam's and Mildara. Go for the top shelf — they are still ridiculously cheap.*

♥
## PUMPKIN, QUICKLY

I have always loved pumpkin, but that rough and tough and mottled skin was too much for anybody less muscled than Rocky I, II, or III, before he started to get weather-beaten and beaten. Butternuts were easier, but then I could never get them to taste the way mum's used to in the days when little old ladies roasted the pants off everything.

Then, in a fit of madness, I tossed a whole butternut pumpkin into the microwave, went and took a sherry, and waited for the bell. Wow! What a result!

This was old-time pumpkin, back on the top shelf. Full of sweetness, juicy, delicious.

1 Put a whole butternut pumpkin on a plate which can handle the microwave and bake on high for 25–35 minutes, until the skin has changed from lovely orange to tacky brown. A knife should pierce it like butter.

2 Serve sliced, peeled (the skin comes away easily), or scooped. Serve hot, warm, cold, or re-heated; as an extra, on its own, or on a slice of bread. Or whizz it up with a little chicken stock, some cream, caraway seeds and chives, and you've got a thick pumpkin soup.

♥
## PEA SHOOT SALAD WITH LIGURIAN OLIVES AND GOAT'S CHEESE

My beloved despairs of my habit of putting all her best efforts on buttered bread, turning anything from crayfish to roast lamb into nothing more than a sandwich.

It's something I will never grow out of, although I have thus far avoided reverting to type when in company.

At home there is nothing I will not put on bread: fish, veal, lamb, definitely poultry, chips and, above all, hot peas. During my restaurant days, I used to live on pea sandwiches followed by ice cream. The bread was always delicious, the peas plentiful and podded, and there was always a pot of boiling water on hand for a quick dip. This was more often than not lunch. Dinner, late, when desserts were going out, was likely to be leftover mashed potatoes ... on bread, of course. Followed by ice cream. So there you are, behind all the glamour of the flash restaurant, a pea sandwich, and ice cream.

This unfortunate joy of mine drives her to distraction, but I'm afraid she is taking it the wrong way. It is not discrediting her cooking — quite the reverse. This is my method of saying wow: you have retained the flavour, the essence of the food; let me present it to you with my kindest regards. A sandwich is the highest level of food. Nothing confuses.

I refer you to this rather quaint habit because it became my tasting medium when I ran into pea shoots at the local fruiterer. At first glance this was another of those strange vegetables popping up in flat polystyrene packages covered in plastic wrap.

They are usually labelled like wine — front and back labels explaining what the hell they are. This was no different.

'Pea shoots, as the name suggests, is the top of the pea plant.' (I dashed out the back to check our rather young pea plants. They looked just the same, although our shoots were bigger. I wasn't game to pick off any. They were too young, and it might have given the dog the wrong idea.)

'It has been a popular vegetable eaten by the Chinese for a long time. (I am amazed I have never heard of it before.) Now freshly grown in Australia (in Kilsyth). Use in sandwich, salad, soup, or any other way as your normal vegetables. Pea shoots are an excellent source of vitamins and minerals.'

On the back of the pack were the recipes. Garden salad: Mix pea shoots with cucumber etc. I flicked that. Cucumber is one of the few things I can't eat, and anyway, any salad with cucumber becomes a cucumber salad.

Egg and pea shoot soup: No. As above, just change cucumber for egg.

Fried: In 50–100 ml cooking oil. Doubtful. Too much oil.

I was thinking of something more simple. Pea shoots on bread and butter. I had some crusty white bread (white so as not to intrude on the flavour), some delicious butter and a full pepper grinder.

I warmed the pea shoots by dipping them briefly in boiling water, and planted a good handful on the bread. (They were warmed so as to just melt the butter.)

Aaaah. My youth came flooding back. Pea sandwich, without the bother of the peas falling off your bread, dripping down your neck, running across the table. Isn't it lovely that you can do these things without your mother scolding you? The wife ... that's another matter.

Whatever, these pea shoots are a great success. They taste just like peas, are deliciously fresh, hold olive oil and butter beautifully, and they're great on their own to chew. They make a wonderful salad base, in the same style as watercress.

♥   ♥   ♥   ♥   ♥

**handful of pea shoots**
*This method applies equally to any green which has a solid flavour of its own: thus watercress, mustard cress, spinach, whitlof, silver beet.*

**a few cubes of hard goat's cheese**
*Or cheddar will do as long as it's not too 'bitey'.*

**dozen olives**
*If you can get hold of those lovely, tiny, Ligurian olives, do.*

**a little lemon juice**

**a lot more of your best olive oil**

**black pepper**

**a little salt**

1 Mix the lot together in a bowl with your fingers.

2 Heat a heavy-based pan until it is very hot.

3 Add the mix, turn off the heat, and toss around until it is just warmed through. The leaves will be glistening with the oil.

4 Serve in the middle of lovely white plates.

♥
## RADICCHIO BRAISED WITH BLUE CHEESE, COMPLIMENTS OF STEPHANIE'S

When it comes to the re-awareness, or re-interpretation of dishes, or discovery of ingredients, then nobody works harder or does it better than Stephanie Alexander, the well-known restaurateur and brilliant writer on food and food matters.

I think if I could wish for anybody in the business to cook for me at home, it would be Stephanie. Her cooking and writing upholds all the values of home and community and the culture of Australia. There are no free swings with Stephanie. Just an examination of her life and her experiences, as put together on the plate. First it was lamb shanks on a flash menu, then it was scallops from Coffin bay, a pheasant like none other, a raspberry crumble as tactile today as it was when I first tasted it, and now, believe it or not, braised radicchio.

Before Stephanie's, radicchio was a pretty colour with a bitter flavour. Not now. Once I had tasted it braised, given an added flavour with blue cheese, I had to have the recipe.

♥   ♥   ♥   ♥   ♥

**1 round, firm radicchio, cut into quarters, then in halves again, maintaining the core**

**60 g butter ('a lump of butter!')**

**black pepper**

**2 teaspoons balsamic vinegar**

**100 g creamy blue cheese**
*Stephanie uses Gippsland Blue.*

1 Wash the lettuce to remove any grit, then drain well.

2 Melt the butter in a heavy pan. Add radicchio, grind pepper over each piece, and cook gently for about 5 minutes, turning pieces at least once. It should wilt, and take on a slightly forlorn look, without losing its shape.

3 Add the balsamic vinegar, turn up the heat to high, and cook for a minute, turning the radicchio in the syrupy juices. Remove from heat and set aside on a tray, tipping over any juices left in the pan. You can leave it now until you need to finish it.

4 Cover the radicchio with slim slices of cheese and cook under a hot griller (if proceeding directly and the radicchio is still hot) for a couple of minutes, or in a 220°C oven for about 5–10 minutes (if the radicchio is cold to start with) until the cheese has melted, and melded with the radicchio. Watch it. The cheese can burn if it gets too close to the grill, or too hot.

5 Serve with anything you like. It works brilliantly with veal, just as well with chicken, and it's not bad at all on its own. Stephanie tells me that many people at the restaurant push the radicchio aside and leave it for the cat. Oh well.

WINE ❖ *As an aside, there is always a debate among winemakers over what to serve with blue cheese. Frankly, red wine doesn't work. Try a port, vintage or tawny, or a botrytis white wine.*

♥
## SORREL SOUP

When my precious took the first slurp of my sorrel soup, I thought a horse must have tip-toed into the room and left a message on the easy chair at my back. Her eyes widened and took on a slightly acidic sheen, her nose shot up, and her lips curled the curl of utter contempt.

I knew exactly what had happened. Her lip is like a canary in a coal-mine. If it drops, something's up.

'Too much sorrel in the soup?' I ventured in my best mannered voice.

'Cor,' she shrieked, 'didn't ya taste it?'

'Well, as a matter of fact, I quite liked it,' I lied, and took to it with a gusto, just to, as they say at the footy, stick it up 'er.

She was right, of course. It was too tart, by half. I had forgotten to taste the main event. No matter how familiar you think you are with a flavour, taste it again. Do it with quinces, with cumquats, and especially with sorrel.

They are all extremely tart, with a surprising undertaste, but you've got to taste a little first, before committing the bunch to the pot —or risk the curled lip.

Sorrel is a marvellous weed which seems to take a while to consolidate, then keeps multiplying like mosquitos in spring. It *is* extremely tart, certainly the tartest leaf in the garden, and unlike rhubarb, it is served at that part of the menu which doesn't appreciate sugar assists.

There are dozens of recipes for sorrel soup in French recipe books.

Sorrell is also greatly recommended with omelettes. The Troisgros brothers have a signature recipe at their famous restaurant at Roanne, not far from Lyon: escalopes of salmon with a sorrel cream sauce. It is not much more than a heavily reduced fish stock, a little cream and a quick warm through of some torn sorrel. Why not try your own version?

♥   ♥   ♥   ♥   ♥

## STOCK

**You can avoid this part of the recipe if you wish, but it is at your peril**

*Those who will are those who enjoy raw lemons. The best stock is one heavily flavoured with lamb bones; a close second, that from a ham hock; third, a strong vegetable stock. Whichever you make, ensure there are a couple of parsnips, a couple of carrots, some celery, a few chopped onions, some fennel, garlic and a little ginger.*

**1 teaspoon curry powder, preferably your own**

**handful of sorrel**

*Tear off the thick stems and taste a little of a leaf. Tart, hey?*

**salt**

**black pepper**

**a little cream or butter (optional)**

1 Make the stock, ensuring there is plenty of liquid. Strain, and remove the vegetables. Pour the liquid into a whizzer along with the cooked onions, fennel, garlic and a little of the carrot and parsnip. You don't want much of the root vegetables. The soup should not be thick. Add the curry powder and whizz quickly.

2 Return to the heat, bring to the boil, and throw in the sorrel for about 30 seconds. Check the seasoning. It could need a deal of salt

and black pepper. Separately (in a microwave) re-heat the parsnip and carrot you set aside.

3 Whizz briefly the stock and sorrel mixture. Toss back in the rest of the slow-cooked carrots and parsnips for some chunkiness, and serve with some crusty bread. You can enrich the soup with some cream, or butter, or even an egg, if you wish.

WINE ❖ *I was once at a luncheon with an august group of wine people who were saying nice things about a 'masked' sherry. When unmasked, it turned out to be one I had blended. I was feeling rather chuffed, but soon horrified when, to a man, they popped the sherry into the soup and were racing. When in Rome … I tried it — it worked and I've done it ever since.*

♥

## AAAH, ASPARAGUS

I haven't always enjoyed asparagus. Again it comes down to the influences of youth. I seem to recall trying asparagus at a pub counter lunch years ago. It was mushy, yellowing at the tip and tasted aggressive. But not as aggressive as it smelt, afterwards, you know, afterwards. It was an altogether unpleasant experience, and not assisted by the fact that every time I saw asparagus in the shops it was at a top-shelf price. I decided to give it a miss until a few years ago when it was served perfectly cooked at a dinner party. You have to eat whatever is put before you at such shows, don't you? I ate, enjoyed, commented, and took to the little darlings with a vigour.

That afterwards effect has not changed, but now, thanks to the brilliant book, *On Food and Cooking*, by Harold McGee, I know the reason why. According to McGee, they have been worrying about it since before Australia was a light in Arthur Phillip's eye. In 1702 a Frenchman, Dr Louis Lemery, had some things to say about the vegetables in his Treatise on all sorts of foods. Wrote the doc: 'Sparagrass eaten to excess sharpen the humours and heat a little; and therefore persons of a bilious constitution ought to use them moderately: They cause a filthy and disagreeable smell in the urine as everybody knows.'

Thanks, doc. The culprit, according to McGee, is methyl mercaptan.

So the next time the subject comes up at a toffy dinner party, you can curl your upper lip, as Biggles used to do, and answer loftily: 'Oh really, old thing, don't you know methyl mercaptan when you smell it?'

Whoever invented asparagus cookers was a profiteer and, I suppose, a successful one, judging by the fact that they still are produced and they still sell. Who needs one? Forget all thoughts of cookers. All you need is a little salt, a little water and a pot.

♥　♥　♥　♥　♥

THE SAUCE

juice of 1 lemon

150g butter, cut roughly into cubes

salt

Parmesan, for grating, or your favourite grating cheese

500g asparagus

1 corn cob, the kernels cut from the husk

bunch of tarragon

handful of almonds, broken

black pepper

1 It all happens so quickly. One minute you are thinking what the hell can I cook, the next you are sitting down to the most perfect meal. Make the sauce first. This is probably my favourite sauce because:
(i) it works;
(ii) it is the simplest of simple;
(iii) it is suitable for anything from asparagus to sweet corn to John Dory.

All you have to do is heat the lemon juice, toss in the butter, cut roughly into cubes, whisk, add a little salt, and taste. And there you have it. The lemon juice should just come through. You don't want a pure lemon sauce, and you don't want a heavy butter sauce. The beauty of all this is you can add or subtract until the sauce is just right. There is only one thing that can go wrong — the juice could be too hot and the butter too soft. If that combination occurs you are almost certain to finish up with pure oil and water. If that happens, you just have to start again. Don't throw out the failed sauce. Let it settle, and you will have clarified butter to cook with.

2 Set the butter sauce aside in a warm place.

3 Bring some salted water to the boil. Toss in the asparagus and the corn, and cook for 5–6 minutes.

4 When the asparagus and the corn are cooked — the asparagus should take a knife easily — drain, and place the asparagus in a criss-cross pattern on a plate, with

the corn dribbled about. Pour the sauce over the top, and sprinkle with the cheese, tarragon, almonds and black pepper. Asparagus like this is terrific with risotto; great with pasta, with more butter in the sauce; and an absolute star with your own freshly baked puff pastry.

If you've seen a very pale version of asparagus in a few shops about town, don't turn white with horror. This is one of those delicacies which Europeans have grown to love and expect with the seasons, and now it's available in Australia. A few growers are devoting time and energy to growing the white version.

There is, I should point out, nothing different about the species. It is just that the asparagus is not allowed to see the sun. As the spear grows, it is mounded with earth, and thus it misses out on the green-ness that comes from exposure to the sun. The flavour that develops in the spears is more intense, more of the real asparagus flavour. Even then, it is rather subtle, and inclined a little to the walnut. I found a batch very juicy, very tender, and served it simply in some melted butter, a handful of torn basil leaves, some lemon juice and plenty of black pepper.

There is one very happy consequence of the white asparagus. It does not leave a signature tune in your urine. The unhappy side is the price. Because of labour it works out at rather more than $20 a kilo, even in season.

WINE ✤ *Sauvignon blanc with all its 'cut grass' character is a good foil for asparagus. Try a Sancerre or a Pouilly Fumé or a New Zealander.*

♥

## A COLOURFUL PASTRY: A FRENCH ROUTINE WITH GREEK FLAVOURS

I made this up on the telephone. An old friend had organised a picture shoot of his home for *Belle* magazine. The shoot was to include a few restaurateurs and me, and our food. My job was to provide the entrée. I wanted something which would work in pictures, as well as flavour. I was thinking Greek, and I was thinking French, and this tart — derived from the classic French jam tart, but using predominantly Greek flavours — tumbled out. It is marvellous.

♥   ♥   ♥   ♥   ♥

**2 (400 g) tins of tomatoes, the tomatoes chopped roughly**
*Obviously, use fresh in season.*

**1 clove garlic, chopped finely**

**2 chillies, finely chopped**

**bunch of fresh English spinach**

**250 g goat's cheese**

**50 g pine nuts, or more to taste**

**salt**

**black pepper**

**1 kg puff pastry**

**2 tablespoons chopped chives**

**egg wash (1 egg yolk whisked with 1 tablespoon water)**

1 Place the tomatoes, garlic and chillies in the microwave and cook down until the mixture has reached the consistency of a thick sauce. Remove, purée and allow to

cool. The mixture should be thick enough to be spreadable but without extra moisture seeping through.

2 Steam the spinach until cooked, either in a steamer or in the microwave. Allow to cool and squeeze out any excess water.

3 Put the spinach in a whizzer with the goat's cheese, half the pine nuts, and salt and black pepper to taste. Purée, then set aside.

4 Roll out the puff pastry to make a long rectangle about 30 cm x 40 cm. With a very sharp knife cut four sheets 30 cm x 10 cm (two for bases, two for tops). Put the bases onto the baking tray. Divide the tomato purée over each base until it is about 2 cm from each edge, then spoon the cheese and spinach purée down the middle of each. Sprinkle with pine nuts and plenty of chives and black pepper.

5 For the tops, fold the pastry in half along its length and make cuts along the length, about a centimetre apart, creating a lattice effect. Brush the edges of the pastry base with a little water and place the tops on gently, making sure they cover the mixture and sit neatly on the bases. Crimp the edges with the back of a fork and brush the tops and sides with egg wash.

6 Bake for 30-35 minutes at 195°C. Let cool slightly before serving. Serve in 5 cm thick slices, on a little tomato purée.

WINE ✤ *A good New Zealand sauvignon blanc would be nice.*

♥
## CAULIFLOWER WITH ONIONS AND GARLIC

C auliflower happens to be a wildly under-rated vegetable, and it's served poorly, more often than not. A cauliflower, picked at its peak in the middle of winter, has a feel and flavour like few other vegetables. Cauli should be cooked longer than is conventionally believed. I like to cook it until it takes a knife easily, without getting near to being soft.

♥  ♥  ♥  ♥  ♥

1 onion, chopped finely

1 clove garlic, chopped roughly

1/2 cup virgin olive oil

1 head of cauliflower, fresh, pure-white and firm

*Cut the cauliflower away from its 'struts' and cook only the small, individual flower heads.*

100 g best beans, cut in half

salt

black pepper

1/2 bunch of chives, chopped

1 Heat the oven to 200°C.

2 Cook the onion and garlic in a little of the olive oil, until the onion softens — about 5 minutes on a gentle heat. Add the cauliflower pieces and the rest of the olive oil, just warming the oil through on top of the stove and making sure the onions and garlic mix well with the cauliflower.

3 Put the whole lot into the oven, and allow to cook gently, turn-

ing the cauliflower occasionally. It should take about 20 minutes. This can be done in the microwave, but then you'll miss the gentle browning which comes from the oven. It still tastes great.

4 While the cauliflower is cooking, toss the beans into boiling water until cooked.

5 Toss the beans through the cauliflower mix, sprinkle with salt, black pepper and chives, and serve as an accompaniment to your best roast, or tossed through pasta.

♥
## PINE MUSHROOMS, COLOURFUL PALS

There's an old rule which pops up whenever mushrooms pop up in the fields and paddocks and forests. Don't eat any which display blazing colours. But, like all rules, there is a wild exception. Pine mushrooms are bright orange, and their gills turn green when you rub them. If ever nature was trying to warn you off, it could not choose better colours. Anybody who suffers mushroom poisoning is more likely than not to turn orange then green.

Don't be put off by the colours. Pine mushrooms cop their name because of their affinity with pine trees, but searchers have given them another descriptive title. They've also been called saffron milkcap. The saffron is self-evident. The milkcap is a neat touch. Pine mushrooms are most positively identified by their dimples, usually half filled with moisture. So when in doubt, look for the dimple in the middle.

There is really no big deal about cooking them. Rub away any dirt or pine needles. Chop them as roughly as you like, throw them into a pan with as little or as much garlic as you can cope with. Sprinkle with a little of the best olive oil you have, as much butter as your heart will take, salt, freshly ground black pepper and plenty of thyme from the garden. Work the lot around the pan over a low heat. The mushrooms will give their moisture to the pan and mix deliciously with the butter. When the fungi have just softened they are ready to go. The butter will be a gorgeous yellow colour. Throw in a hat full of chopped parsley. To give the dish a little crunch, mix in some just-cooked beans and throw the lot through some freshly made pasta. In fact you can cook any mushrooms like that — just make sure you don't lose sight of the main event.

WINE ❖ *A hearty red. Try a shiraz from Clare or the Barossa — Birks, St Hallets or Rockford come to mind.*

♥
## ANTIPASTO

I was getting a little tired of all the salt-laden antipasto around town: all sorts of olives, prosciutto, pickled vegetables, the ubiquitous bottled artichokes, sun-dried tomatoes, sardines and such. Too much salt; too much deadening of the palate, but worse, not enough hard work from the kitchen. Then I went to Sydney and tried the antipasto at Taylor's.

This is the way antipasto should be. Something rather special, a palate tickler before the main event, not just a trendy name for cold meat and salad. Forget that. Antipasto might be an easy number at home, but when you're in a restaurant, it sure as hell should not be easy. I have an old and trusted routine in restaurants: never order a paté or terrine, because all the work is done earlier in the day, or often the day before. A great restaurant is one which responds to the pressure of the moment.

Taylor's is a restaurant pretty much on its own in this country. A pair of dinky-di Australians, Ann Taylor and Ian McCulloch, each untrained in the ways of a professional kitchen, but with a love of food, travelled to Europe, fell in love with the food of Italy, tasting dishes they had never seen in this country. Plenty of us have done that. The secret is to turn it into something more than fancy home cooking.

The pair recognised there was a gaping hole in the market back home, and went for it. Fortunately they had the nous to turn a vision into a classy restaurant. And Taylor's is on the eve of its tenth anniversary, with Taylor and McCulloch still calling the shots. And something else hasn't changed.

The restaurant is an expensive renovation of a gorgeous early Australian sandstone building (1840s) in a bits-and-pieces part of Sydney's Surry Hills. Out back is a cracker-jack extension: outdoors they call it, but it's actually a glass house, allowing visual access to the garden and the handmade bricks of the out-house, without the wind and rain and desperate heat and cold. There are heaters for the winter, and, please allow me to stray from the immediate point, the antipasto

comes from the kitchen, and it's as good as you can get.

Consider some of what is offered — all at room temperature, note:

♥ Salad of baked butternut pumpkin with avocado, a few drops of olive oil hanging about; brilliant.

♥ Field mushrooms sauteed with lemon and mint, with a rich thick tomato sauce just holding the mushies; a ripper.

♥ Steamed asparagus with tomato vinaigrette — as called, with the tomato chopped finely, mixed with the finest of chopped onions; a bottler.

♥ *Involtine di melanzane*, which translates to grilled eggplant and Ricotta roll — a fine slice of eggplant wrapped around Ricotta; a bewdy.

♥ Baked spinach and rice frittata — a slice of a large quiche-like pie.

The display was just lovely, and the mix of flavours and portions superb. There was air on the plate, and there was a need for more when it was over. This was true antipasto.

This is not, you must realise, a review of a restaurant. It's an indication of the style all restaurants should look to: simple food, given a touch of class in the hands of a pro. So what's it doing in a cook book? Simply this. Read again the list of items in the antipasto above. Is there any one of them that you could not do? Is there any one of them about which you would not say: 'Gee that sounds easy.' Get the drift? Take this as your dictum: for each dish, seek only the freshest ingredients, put some thought into its best face, and put it to plate with care, flair, and attention to detail. Love, I suppose. That's the best food, at home, or in a restaurant.

Ann Taylor was a bit taken

aback with the praise I was offering for such a simple display. But I think deep down she understood what I was on about. Her restaurant is all about careful planning and thinking and caring: 'We do plan things quite carefully,' she said. 'When we are deciding on antipasto, we do think about the shape, the keeping quality, the combination of food and the colour. Some of the dishes we think would be terrific just don't look too good on the plate.'

I didn't ask her for any recipes. As I said: anybody can make up the list above. Just do it carefully. Here's a few more to try, any way you like:

♥ Broad beans, braised, in their skins, in chicken stock with cabbage.
♥ Goat's cheese, and roasted peeled garlic roughly mixed together with some virgin olive oil and wiped on crusty bread.
♥ Warm broccoli, just on the edge of soft, with virgin olive oil, steamed spinach and Parmesan.
♥ Warm mussels with finely chopped olives and herbs in a vinaigrette flavoured with lime juice.
♥ Just-boiled eggs with onions slow-cooked in a little curry powder.
♥ And if you don't want to be flash, a pot filled with mussels and clams, and served with a large white napkin for the neck, just as the sun sets.
♥ And for those of you who really can't be bothered, hot sugar peas, straight from the boiling water, on thickly buttered bread, eaten in a hot bath.

WINE ♣ *'Not sherry again,' I hear you cry. The fact is, it is the perfect apéritif. Good, complex fino sherry is one of God's gifts, and in this country is so cheap. Try Seppelt D.P. 117 for a treat or Mildara George for everyday drinking. Okay,* méthode champenoise *is another go.*

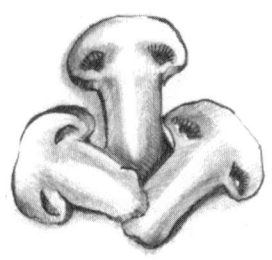

# LAMB AND BEEF, PORK AND VEAL

The best way to cook meats well at home is to cultivate a good butcher. And the best way to cultivate a good butcher is to open an account.

Accounts are strange social instruments. They guarantee a happy repartee until one party lets down the other. So, you will get to know your butcher, and he will get to know you — probably too well. But that risk is worth taking if you are sure to get the quality, the cuts and the special favours that good butchers are able to provide.

I used to treat butchers like barbers and taxi drivers until I had a desperate need to start an account — the desperate need being that there was no ready money to handle the bill on a daily basis. Opening an account meant a lot of smiles, a good banter, urgent phone calls, deliveries and a dirty, crumbled cheque at the end of the week — and everybody was happy.

If your butcher refuses the idea of an account, don't take it to heart, just take your business elsewhere. The truth is, any butcher who is worth his saltpetre will welcome a customer asking strange questions. Butchers really do get bored with whizzing saws and pulsating mincers and barbecue chops and scoops of nondescript mince; they yearn to be recognised as creative giants, to treat piggies' ears in the style of Vincent Van Gogh.

If it all works out, you will come away with a few good jokes a week, a little in-house gossip, and most of your preparation will have been done before you get home. Good cooking depends on quality preparation. And with meat, and fish of course, the butcher can fillet and tie and slice and fiddle in his sleep. Put him to the task.

## WHAT YOU'LL NEED

1 A heavy-based metal pan which can go into the oven. Most meats are best started on top of the stove, and finished in the oven. This browning process was once considered necessary to 'seal' the meat, but research has shown that to be so much bosh. You try it and see. Brown a piece of meat all over, then leave it on a plain white plate. Check after half an hour. Look at all the juice sitting in the plate.

The advantages of browning in the pan are two-fold:

(i) The browned crust has a flavour all its own. Remember the well-cooked lamb of the old days?

Remember how dry the middle was? But, remember how delicious the almost burnt crust was?

(ii) If you get the pan hot, and the meat hot, it takes much less time to cook in the oven.

**2** **A large stock pot, with a heavy base, sitting on a large, dedicated, flat-topped cooking range.** Aaah, I'm dreaming. A large pot, a very expensive flat-top cooker, and a stock bubbling away day and night. Imagine the aromas, imagine the soups and sauces at call. I'm still dreaming. One day I'll have this; one day.

**3** **Sharp knives are always important in the kitchen, but less so for preparation when you're dealing with meat.** Remember, the butcher does all that. You will need a sharp knife for carving.

**4** **A crackerjack pepper mill.** This is more fundamental to my eating than just about anything, except perhaps flash olive oil and Parmigiano Reggiano. You must have freshly ground pepper, or no pepper at all, and there is nothing more frustrating than a poorly made mill. Invest heavily in one which works all the time.

**5** **A good friend from the Orient, and another from the sub-continent.** Meats and spices and long, slow-cooked dishes are enough reason to take a sabbatical in Bangkok, or Bombay, or Singapore. To succeed in this form of cooking, you need a good look at a good cook at work. You need to see and hear, feel, taste and smell the spices sizzling, the stock bubbling, the meat falling from itself and sliding about your tongue before its last hurrah.

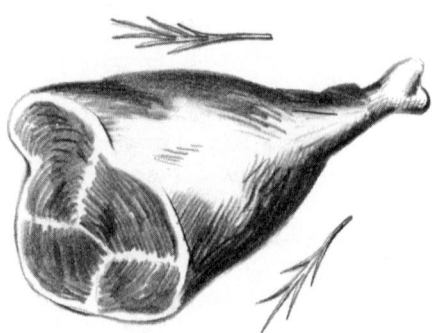

## THE RECIPES

♥
## RACK OF BEEF, ROASTED

If you have sought and found the butcher of your dreams, you will never be concerned about tough steaks again. The best butchers choose the best cuts from the best cattle; but that's not the end of it. You can be sure they love their meat and treat it tenderly, with the utmost respect.

You'll never buy pale fillet from a fair dinkum butcher, never worry about chewy porterhouse, never pay for the fat left on poorly trimmed meat. You will know he is a star when you see lamb and beef looking a little crusty from time exposed to the crisp air of the cool-room. Beef and lamb, and hare as well, if you're into it, are all greatly enhanced by time on the hook. The flavour develops, especially in the game, and a subtle undercover operation by enzymes in the meat tenderises it remarkably. Beef cuts like porterhouse or rump will need at least ten days — better three weeks — before getting it all together. Lamb needs a week. There is an old tale about hanging hare: when the string breaks, the hare is ready!

I can't imagine a better dinner party, or Sunday lunch, than the rack of beef, cooked on the bone and sliced at the table. Plead with your butcher.

♥   ♥   ♥   ♥   ♥

**a 2 kg side of beef, including the heavy bones, is plenty for 4 people**

**salt**

**black pepper**

**12 baby carrots**

1 Heat the oven to flat out. Lightly oil a pan which can go to the oven, and, on top of the stove, brown the beef top and bottom. This is to encourage the delicious flavours which come from the browning of the meat. There's little better than the brilliant flavour of crisp beef, especially when it surrounds a tender, rare middle.

2 Once you have heated the pan and the meat, sprinkle the lot with salt and grind and grind and grind the black pepper all over the meat. Put the lot in the oven and cook for at least 30 minutes.

3 While the beef is cooking, cook the carrots until tender (a few minutes in the microwave). When tender, toss the carrots about the beef and put the lot back in the oven.

4 After 30 minutes, remove the pan and check the beef. It should be well browned, but when pressed it will give easily to the touch. If you wish, slice through to see how it is travelling. It should be still quite rare, but the heat should be making progress. If you think it's right, leave out of the oven, covered, in the hot pan. Leave for about 20 minutes, while you get the rest of the show organised.

5 Serve very rare, with each person getting a good portion of the browned outside. Serve with the carrots, now impregnated with much beef juice.

6 De-glaze the pan with a little red wine, the juices which have

flowed from the waiting beef, season, and pour over.

WINE ❖ *Claret and roast beef — pillars of the British Empire. Claret was the generic term used to describe the red wines from Bordeaux. In Australia we pinched it to describe any full-bodied, dry-finish red. Bordeaux wines are generally made from a blend of the grape varieties cabernet sauvignon, merlot and cabernet franc. Historically, Australian winemakers blended the shiraz grape with the cabernet sauvignon to make the 'claret' style.*

♥

## THE PERFECT STEAK, VERY RARE; A PARABLE FOR MEAT LOVERS

It took me a long time to decide how best to serve a steak. The 'How rare is rare?' syndrome. But it all came together one dreary winter's night when the front door of the restaurant was swept open and into our presence came a gentleman who was wearing the clothes he had received at Christmas, 1957.

'A table for one,' he announced and promptly sat at the table closest to the exit.

I shrugged my shoulders and handed him the menu, certain that the $20 minimum price would see him out the door as quickly as he had arrived.

'Hmmm,' he said. 'I will have a steak — very rare.'

What could I do? I rushed it into his presence. He cleaned the plate and called for a coffee. He sat on the coffee for at least an hour, his eyes darting around the restaurant. Finally he waved his hand.

'The bill, my good man,' he said.

No sooner said than done. He gave me $25 and offered me the change. I thanked him profusely and

led him to the door. He grabbed me by the arm, and took me aside, confidentiality all over his person.

'You didn't think I'd pay, did you?' he whispered.

I was about to act shocked, when he said, slightly more loudly, 'I shouldn't tell you this, but I have access to more money than anyone you are ever likely to meet.'

I stuttered a few words, and he took me closer.

'I,' he said, 'am Jesus Christ.'

With that, he was gone.

Learn from the parable, as we did. From that day forward we served our beef rare, very rare.

The best form of very rare beef is steak, fair dinkum steak with a thick, flavoursome crust surrounding tender, rich, bloody, red beef. Too often the beef is overcooked and there is little crust to speak about. There are a few rules you must follow to get it right.

(i) Make sure the meat is quite thick: 3 cm thick is ideal, 5 cm is getting a bit thick.

(ii) Use a minimum of oil, or else the meat will stew and remain soft and flabby.

(iii) Use a heavy-bottomed pan, something which holds heat evenly.

(iv) Be patient; don't sit over the meat with tongs turning and turning and turning. A thick, brown crust is possible on one side only.

♥   ♥   ♥   ♥   ♥

## THE MEAT
### The cut of your choice
*Fillet is sure to be tender, but you need to be sure your butcher is supplying you with fillet with plenty of age on it — and not just age in the cool-room, but age on the hoof as well. Rump and porterhouse have all the flavour, but from most*

butchers they will be tough and chewy. If you are buying these cuts, make sure they have been well hung, so all the chemical things that need to be done, naturally, will have been done, and the meat will be tender.

## A SIMPLE SAUCE

½ cup water

3 teaspoons soy sauce

2 tomatoes, skinned and chopped roughly

1 hot chilli, chopped finely

1 walnut-sized piece of ginger, sliced finely

1 branch of rosemary

1 clove garlic, sliced finely

salt

small bunch of chives, chopped finely

1 About 10 minutes before 'go', heat the oven to 200°C. Put in some plates to warm.

2 Make sure your pan is perfectly clean. Brush the pan with a little oil, and heat the pan until it is very hot. Place the steak into the pan. It should sizzle immediately. Move it about the pan gently, so that it gets a good coating of oil, starts to get a crust and is not about to stick.

3 Be patient. All you have to do now is wait and make sure the meat does not stick to the bottom of the pan.

4 Just keep watching. The meat should be sizzling and a greyness will be creeping up the sides. The first and only turn will come after about 2 minutes. The meat should

then have a rich, brown crust.

5 After turning the steak, move it about again and leave it on the heat for about 30 seconds (for a steak of 3 cm — twice as long for a 4 cm steak). Put the pan in the oven for a minute. The meat will be very rare. If you must have it cooked more, then leave it for as long as you like.

6 Remove steak from the pan, lightly salt, and leave on a warm plate. Turn off the oven, but leave the steak in it.

7 The pan should be very hot. Add the water and work it around the pan with a wooden spoon to pick up any meat left on the bottom of the pan. Allow to bubble, add the soy sauce, and leave it to reduce.

8 Turn down the heat. Add the tomatoes, chilli, ginger, rosemary, garlic and a little salt. Stir and allow to bubble away until the tomatoes soften. Remove the rosemary. Take the steak from the oven, and pour any exuded juices from the plate into the tomato sauce. Turn up the heat, and cook for 30 seconds on high.

9 Spoon some sauce and sprinkle the chives over the steak, and serve with a simple accompaniment.

WINE ❖ *Shiraz, when it's good and young, can have a lovely 'black pepper' aroma. I am hopeless at putting down wines — for someone who has spent nearly fifteen years in the wine industry, my cellar is miniscule. But I like young shiraz — central Victoria, Barossa or Coonawarra. Try a Rhone hermitage for a change.*

♥
## BEEF WELLINGTON FOR REFORMED ROMANTICS

The first time I cooked for show I went for broke: Beef Wellington with all the trimmings. The occasion provides vivid memories. I had just moved into an unfamiliar house, I had no idea how the oven worked, and would not have picked the difference between a beef fillet and a shoulder of lamb.

Such a bull-at-a-gate mentality has been my life's burden. I thought it would be a good idea to build the dog a kennel. Much sawing and nailing later, I had concocted a shell. Problem (i) the dog didn't like it; problem (ii) when we shifted house, the kennel fell apart. I don't always maintain my enthusiasm. I set up a dark-room in the bathroom — once. I planted herbs in rows expecting an instant olde worlde herb garden. The dog dug them up and I gave up.

I am glad to know there are others like me, but generally the madness only grabs them when it comes to cooking. The vision of guests arriving for lunch or dinner seems to provoke some instinct in us to attempt the damned near impossible, and hope for the best. It is a rare dinner date when the host has not attempted a completely new recipe, one followed slavishly from a new cook book.

On this occasion I used the Beef Wellington from Simone Beck, Louisette Bertholle and Julia Child's *Mastering the Art of French Cooking* I. It went for page after page, and suggested combinations of dux-elles, which I had never heard of, and duck livers, which the butcher did not have, and muslin cloth to wrap the beef, which was impossible to obtain. Was I KO'd? Of course not. I bought the pastry, dirtied more pots than you could imagine, and blustered on, praying all would be well.

By some miracle (or, more likely the genius of the cook book, as relevant today as it was when unveiled in 1961), it was. Or my guests were too darned polite to say it wasn't. Of course we are all delighted when a host makes an obvious attempt to please, but I have learned since that you can please even more if you keep it simple, do plenty of pre-cooking, knock out hunger by trays of easy nibblies, and go for roasts or other old favourites which keep the host in the dining room and out of the kitchen.

What follows remains true to traditional Beef Wellington in flavour alone. It will take one tenth the effort, and one twentieth of the cooking talent.

♥   ♥   ♥   ♥   ♥

### THE PASTRY

**500g puff pastry**

*If you haven't your own handy, or haven't the inclination to make it, go to the best pastry shop in your region and convince the proprietor to sell you some. They will do it if you ask.*

**an egg yolk, lightly beaten with a little milk, and a pastry brush**

**200g fresh duck livers**

**250g bacon, fat removed**

**2 onions, chopped finely**

**200g mushrooms, chopped finely**

bunch of chives, chopped finely

the centre piece of a beef fillet, about 150g per person

salt

pepper

1 Heat the oven to 200°C. Roll out the pastry until quite thin, about the thickness of two twenty-cent pieces. Cut out diamonds, squares, circles, whatever takes your fancy, to about the area of the palm of your hand. Allow to rest in the fridge for 15 minutes, or in the freezer, briefly.

2 Remove the pastry from the fridge and paint the top with the yolk–milk mix. Grease a baking tray and bake the pastries for about 25 minutes, until the tops are a golden brown, the bases are firm and the layering has reached its peak. The beef will be cooked separately and slices will be placed into split pastry shapes (see step 6). Set aside the pastries to cool. Ideally this will be done just before the meal, but it can be done in advance — preferably within 3 hours.

3 In a hot pan, fry the livers until they just firm up. They should be still pink in the middle, but not rare. Set aside to cool. Heat the oven to flat out.

4 Fry the bacon until just cooked, then the onions in a little oil and butter until they soften. Add the mushrooms and cook slowly until they are quite soft. Remove from the heat, add the cooked livers, and chop the mix very finely. Stir the chives through. Set aside.

5 In a baking tray, roast the beef until it is done to your liking. I suggest it should be served very rare, cooked just enough for it to be warm to the touch in the middle. For the middle portion of a large fillet, that would be somewhere around 15 minutes in a hot oven. Just keep looking. When you reckon the beef is just short of cooked to your liking, remove from the heat and leave, covered, in a warm place.

6 Turn down the oven to 200°C and warm through the puff pastry diamonds etc. Cut through each one to provide a hat and a base. Rub some melted or softened butter over the lid to make it glisten.

7 Gently warm the mushrooms-liver–bacon–onions mix. Wipe some on the bottom of the pastry.

8 Slice the beef quite finely, season with salt and pepper, and lay the slices on top of the mushroom mix. Place the pastry lid on top. Best served with a simple beef stock sauce, or a wine sauce retrieved from the cooking pan.

WINE ✤ *This calls for one to crawl underneath the house about a day before the beef is to be served. Grab a bottle of old red and stand it up on the sideboard. Just before the guests arrive, decant it — into a special decanter if you have one, or just transfer the wine carefully into another clean, empty bottle. You are ridding the wine of some sediment that might be in the bottom of the bottle.*

♥
## CHONG'S BEEF RENDANG

I've always believed you have to have been born in the Orient to be a dab hand at making curry, or slow-cooked meats, or spicy sauces. How else can you get close to understanding the flavours that come from a teaspoon of this, a cup of that, an infusion of something else? These are the smells and flavours that become second nature to those lucky enough to be born in a house of spice.

We're not just talking of one lifetime here. We're talking of generations on generations. And we're talking about a way of life.

Cook books, guide books, travel essays, tourism, and back home, multi-culturalism, all help a little bit, but in the end nothing teaches like experience — taking it all in from the experts. You need to see, and hear, and smell, and taste. You need to be with the dish from the beginning to understand how it comes together. You need to smell the difference a soupçon of fenugreek, or fennel seeds, or cardamom pods will make on the way through, and to the final result. You need to ask why some spices need to be roasted, why some don't, and why some are happy each way. You need to be told why chilli, and why not; why tamarind water and why not; the difference between galangal and ginger, lemon grass and lemon zest, fresh and dried. You need to see the way a dish bubbles: fast, medium, slow, slower; and when done is done.

Simple if you happen to come from Bangkok, or Kuala Lumpur, or Delhi, or Jakarta, or Phnom Penh, or Hanoi. Not quite the same if you come from Bondi or Burwood or back of Bourke.

Whenever you come across a dish you enjoy, ask about it; ask how it came together, ask for the recipe. You'll get it, and you'll know then exactly how it should look, feel and taste. That's how this dish came into my repertoire. I took lunch in an oriental garden in the inner suburbs of Melbourne. The host, Chong Weng-Ho, a proud son of Malaysia, put on a magnificent spread: the flavours were clean, the combinations flawless and the presentation simple, yet ultimately appealing; every dish was completely appetising, with not a touch of excess oil or fat.

The day's highlight was the Beef Rendang, so dry, yet so moist and tender at the same time.

'How is it so?' said I.

'Most people', he said, 'don't cook it long enough.'

♥  ♥  ♥  ♥  ♥

### 2 kg beef shanks

*Clean the meat as tightly as you can, eliminating any sheaths and sinews. From 2 kg you will end up with about 600 g of waste. Chop the beef into similar-size pieces.*

### 2 onions, quartered

### 4 cloves garlic

### 1 walnut-sized piece of ginger

### walnut-sized piece of galangal root

*Galangal root is from the same family as ginger and looks a little like its rougher brother/sister. Its aroma is more in tune with a sweet shop than a bar. Galangal can be found dried, sliced and powdered. The powdered form is known as Laos powder.*

4 chillies — more if you like them

1 teaspoon coriander seeds

1 teaspoon cumin seeds

1 teaspoon fennel seeds

enough coconut milk to cover the beef — about 2 tins

2 teaspoons salt, perhaps more

2 stalks of lemon grass, top green section and tough outer leaves removed, sliced finely

1 cup tamarind liquid: tamarind is a pulpy pod resembling a large pea pod, native to India, and is a terrific souring agent

*It is brownish-black and tastes like a sour prune. When fully mature, tamarind pods are peeled and pitted and the pulp is compressed into cakes. Only the pulp form is suitable for cooking, as the pure juice is too acidic. To make tamarind water from pulp, soak a piece of tamarind — the size of a blood plum — in boiling water, or put pulp and water into a microwave and heat until boiling. Squeeze as much juice as possible through a sieve. It is remarkable to note the difference in flavour that tamarind water gives to a slow-cooked dish. Even after several hours cooking, its subtle sourness still comes through.*

3 large, whole carrots, peeled only

2 teaspoons crushed black peppercorns

some parsley or coriander, chopped

1 Brown the beef in the same heavy-based pot you intend to use to cook the dish, cooking only two or three pieces at once. Be careful not to burn the pot or the beef.

2 Whizz the onions, garlic, ginger, galangal and chilli with a little water. Grind the coriander seeds, cumin and fennel in a grinder until they form a fine powder.

3 Toss the beef with the onion–garlic mixture, cover with the coconut milk, and mix through the ground spices and the salt.

4 Bring to the boil and reduce the heat to low, so the pot merely bubbles. Add the chopped lemon grass and the tamarind water. After about an hour, add the carrots. Carrots are not part of the original recipe, but I can't stand the thought of a slow-cooked dish without carrots. After another half an hour, add the peppercorns.

5 It should take about two and a half hours before it is close to done. The liquid will have just about evaporated, or been taken up by the beef. Check the seasoning. If the beef is cooked just right, and there is still too much liquid, remove the beef and reduce the liquid, stirring all the way. Add back the beef, stirring through again. At the end, the beef should be just touched by a thick, flavoursome gravy.

6 Sprinkle the parsley or coriander over the meat. It can be served hot, or warm, or at room temperature.

WINE ✤ *Pinot meunière is a variety used in the Champagne district of France to make bubbly (blended with chardonnay and pinot noir). We are using it in small quantities for Aussie sparklers now, but Bests at Great Western have made a dry red wine from the variety for years. When young, it's fresh and fruity, not unlike a pinot noir. The interesting thing is, it does age well. Serve it slightly chilled, young or aged. By the way, the sediment won't hurt you; it is just the tartrates that have fallen out of the wine during maturation.*

♥
# BEEF VINDALOO FROM CHISHTI'S

I fell in love with a tiny Indian restaurant in Melbourne's inner suburb of Fitzroy, and was particularly enchanted with the chef's version of beef vindaloo. I adhered to my principle of asking for special recipes. Harjinder Singh Bhogal, who was in the midst of writing his own cook book, was happy to oblige.

♥　♥　♥　♥　♥

### THE MARINADE
2 tablespoons vinegar

1 tablespoon mustard oil

pinch of salt

10 curry leaves

1 tablespoon cumin seeds

1 teaspoon ground coriander

1 teaspoon red chilli powder

$^1\!/_2$ teaspoon turmeric

2 cups plain yoghurt


500 g beef from the rump, chopped into walnut-sized chunks


2 tablespoons fresh ginger

2 cloves garlic

3 green chillies

2 tablespoons ghee or oil

2 onions

3 tomatoes

1 teaspoon cloves

pinch of turmeric

2 or 3 bay leaves

1 teaspoon mustard seeds

1 teaspoon garam masala

*Harjinder's spice mix comprises bay leaves, coriander seeds, black pepper, cloves, green cardamom pods, brown cardamom pods, cumin and cinnamon, whizzed to a chunky powder.*

1 teaspoon fresh coriander


1 Make a separate mixture of vinegar, mustard oil, salt, curry leaves, cumin seeds, ground coriander, red chilli powder, turmeric and yoghurt. Marinate the beef in the yoghurt-based mixture for at least 12 hours, turning it occasionally.

2 Grind a mixture of fresh ginger, garlic and green chillies.

3 Heat ghee or oil in a saucepan. (Many Indians prefer ghee, but oil is also excellent for curries.) Brown the onions. This will take about 20 minutes. Be watchful.

4 Add crushed and peeled tomatoes, ground ginger mixture, another pinch of turmeric, cloves, mustard seeds, bay leaves and garam masala. (Home-made garam masala makes a big difference to the taste; however, there are many commercial varieties available.)

5 Cook until mixture forms a rich sauce. Add marinated beef and cook on a medium heat for 45 minutes or until tender. Serve garnished with fresh coriander.


WINE ✤ *A beer with good hops character is my preference here. Try Hahn's from Sydney or Cascade from Tassie. Depending on your chilli fire-power, a big jug of iced water is the go.*

♥
# BEST BURGERS

A hamburger might very well be the most popular feed on the globe; at least the western part of it, anyway. Not surprising really. You get a filling feed, simply, quickly and cheaply, with a minimum of effort.

The irony is you can achieve a hugely superior product at home, simply, quickly, cheaply, with a minimum of effort. The trick with burgers is to follow a few simple rules:

(i) Don't buy mince from your butcher. This is usually the scraps from inferior cuts of meat. If you're observant when at the butcher's, you will notice a couple of receptacles for leftovers from the slicing, filleting and paring. The one is for the bin, the other, more than likely, is for the mince. So the mince could be a homogenous mix of ox, lamb, pork, chicken, or whatever. In the end, after a trip through the finest grade in the mincer, it tastes like not much at all.

(ii) You don't need prime, prime cuts, but those which combine prime tenderness with prime flavour. So, for an extra special beef burger, you should go for the best cut of fillet, but with lamb, the leg will do just nicely.

(iii) Make sure you have a pair of heavy, sharp knives, to reduce the meat to a burger consistency, without losing its essential flavour and identity. If you can't face such a prospect, get your butcher to do it.

♥ ♥ ♥ ♥ ♥

**1 kg of the meat of your choice**
*That's about half the leg of lamb, or a portion of a leg, or half a first-grade ox fillet. For the lamb, get your butcher to bone it, remove any sinews, then cut it into cubes, and mix it with a weight of pork fat equal to one-third the weight of the cleaned lamb.*

**2 eggs**

**250 g bacon, just cooked, chopped roughly**

**2 chillies, chopped finely**

**1 clove garlic, sliced finely**

**¼ cup soy sauce**

**1 bunch of strongly flavoured herb like dill or tarragon or parsley, chopped roughly**

**1 small piece of ginger, sliced finely**

**1 cup breadcrumbs**

**100 g chopped dried apricots**

**2 onions, chopped and sweated in a little oil until soft**

**2 cups melting cheese, grated**

**salt**

**black pepper**

**a little flour**

### THE 'TOPPING'

**1 dessertspoon mild mustard**

**50 g almonds, chopped**

**1 red pepper, skinned, seeded and chopped into tiny cubes**

**½ bunch of parsley, chopped roughly**

1 You are still at the butcher's. When the lamb (or beef) has been mixed with the fat, ask your friendly butcher to chop the mixture with a pair of heavy knives, one in each hand, until the lamb/beef pieces have been reduced to the size of peas. The fat will hold it all together.

**2** Back home. In a large bowl, break the eggs into the meat–fat mixture, and add the bacon, chillies, garlic, soy, herbs, ginger, breadcrumbs, dried apricots, chopped onions, half the cheese, salt and black pepper. Mix first with a wooden spoon, then with your hand, bringing it all together so that any part is the same as any other part.

**3** Form into hamburger shapes and sprinkle with flour. Set aside while heating the oven to flat out.

**4** Rub the mustard over the top of the burgers, and sprinkle the almonds, chopped peppers and parsley over the mustard.

**5** In a large pan which can go into the oven, heat a little oil until sizzling. Ease the burgers into the pan, one at a time, so that each sizzles. Keep them well spaced so they do not stew. As soon as the bases are firm and browned, put the tray into the oven.

**6** Cook for 8–10 minutes, sprinkling the rest of the cheese over after about 5 minutes. The burgers should not be well done. Remember you are using premium or semi-premium cuts. They should be cooked medium–rare, the topping should have heated through, and the cheese nicely melted. The burgers taste best with a good serve of moist tomato sauce/relish, or plum sauce, not in a bun, but as an open 'sandwich'.

WINE ✤ *What happens if I recommend someone's wine to go with hamburgers? What a backhander! But these are special hamburgers. Try a 3- to 4-year-old shiraz or hermitage (same thing) from the Hunter, central Victoria or the Barossa.*

♥
## LAMB STEAKS IN A SIMPLE SAUCE

**L**amb chops are so familiar to all of us that they are rarely considered first-rate cooking. Nothing, to my mind, could be further from the truth. The bones pared to the loin and the chops cooked on a barbecue or grill make for a classic dish, beautiful to look at, delicious to the taste. The confusion comes from the fact that few of us bother to clean the chops properly, removing — for another day — the fatty extras hanging around the bones.

Never forget, the chop bones are hanging on to the prime cut of the lamb, the loin. If you remove the bones and all attendant fat, what you will have left are tiny, but tender steaks, so simple to cook, and so satisfying.

♥　♥　♥　♥　♥

**16 lamb chops, taken from the mid-loin**
*Ask your butcher to select the thickest chops from several different loins, so you will have identically sized portions. Make sure the chops are cut at every second bone, forming double chops. Each person will have two of these double steaks.*

**6 tomatoes, skinned and chopped into quarters; or 250g tin of tomatoes, no added salt or sugar**

**1 cup red wine**

**1/2 cup good quality port**

**1/4 cup soy sauce**

**a little water**

**2 sprigs of rosemary**

**2 teaspoons brown sugar**

salt

**black pepper**

**1** You must bone the chops, re- moving all the meat. This is very simple. All you need is a sharp, flexible knife. Just run the knife as close to the bone as possible. Lamb chops have a great deal of tender meat hanging about the loin, en- cased in fat. This is the stuff you chew on at barbecues. While you are trimming, save this for a stir-fry or some burgers.

**2** Once the boning has been done, you should have four plump medallions, the scraps and plenty of lamb bones for a stock. Heat the oven to 250°C.

**3** Heat a little oil in the pan until it sizzles. Add some lamb fat and some of the trimmings, and then the bones, mixing them about the pan.

**4** Cook the bones etc. in the oven until the bones have browned — 15–20 minutes. You should stir them here and there.

**5** Remove from the oven, drain away the fat, retaining a little for later, and pour in the wine, port and tomatoes. Stir the bottom of the pan, bringing up any sediment.

**6** Cook on a high heat on top of the stove, reducing the mixture heavily. You will need to stir it about to make sure the tomatoes don't stick. Add the soy, rosemary and sugar. The tomatoes will soften and disintegrate after about 10 min- utes. You might need to add a little water on the way through.

**7** Remove the bones and reduce again. You should end up with about a cup of sauce. Pour into a smaller pan, and discard the rose- mary.

**8** In the pan in which you cooked the bones, cook the lamb steaks in a little of the reserved fat. Put them into the pan one at a time, moving them about gently so they do not stick. Cook on high heat for a couple of minutes, still moving them about. When they have a thick, brown crust, turn, again mov- ing them about to ensure they do not stick. Cook on the turned side for about 30 seconds, then put the lot into the still-hot oven.

**9** Cook for between 5–8 minutes, depending on the thickness of the lamb. Then set aside in a warm place for several minutes. The tim- ings will depend on the thickness of the cuts. The only constant is this: the lamb must be pink, pink, pink. Not rare, not well done. Season with salt and black pepper.

**10** Re-heat the sauce, adding any juices from the resting steaks and swirling a little through the lamb pan to pick up any extra sediment from the lamb cooking. Serve with mashed potatoes and green vegetables like broccoli, or beans, or peas. Serve the sauce on the side.

WINE ✣ *There's something about lamb and Coonawarra cabernet. Mil- dara's master wine maker, Jack Schultz, said to me once: 'You have to be a real dill to make bad Coonawarra cabernet.' He's right. The best years of the eighties are generally the even ones — '80, '82, '84, '86, '88 and '90.*

♥

## THE LOIN OF LAMB, TOUCHED WITH GARLIC, ROASTED, AND SERVED PINK IN A REDUCED PORT AND LAMB STOCK SAUCE

The title will tell you where this recipe came from. Notice the formality and the nonsense added to give it a style of its own. It's a menu item from the old restaurant, and menu writers, especially me in my heyday, do get carried away with detail. I sometimes think quality restaurants would be better off serving:

(i) what they liked on a particular day, and what was freshest and best; or

(ii) pork, lamb, chicken, beef, fish, game, or vegetarian. Full stop. No description. Just trust me and see.

Can you imagine a written menu at home? What's fresh, what's best, and what's available. That's the recipe for success. For me, when it comes to meat, that means lamb more often than not. This dish, I must say, was one of the proudest of our restaurant days. It looks beautiful, arranged in a circle about a pile of mashed potatoes, it tastes marvellous, and it is wonderfully easy to prepare and to cook. It works just as well at home.

♥  ♥  ♥  ♥  ♥

**A whole loin of lamb will provide three, maybe four portions**

*Ask your butcher to de-bone the lamb, making sure the fat (which will then resemble a flap) is left on. The idea is to roll the lamb in its own fat, encasing on the way slices of garlic and black pepper, tie it up and roast it. Your butcher will* do all this for you if you take the sliced garlic to him. Keep all the bones, if you wish to make a sauce. It is not really necessary. The lamb has enough flavour on its own and sauces take plenty of time. That's the job for the restaurant. (If you are buying whole loins, ask the butcher to keep the tiny lamb fillet attached at the loin. It's as tender as butter. Freeze it until you have enough for a meal. See page 137.)*

**2 cloves garlic per loin**

*Slice the garlic very finely. You can use as much as you like. The garlic is generally discarded at the end, unless, like me, you like chewing it just cooked.*

### A SIMPLE SAUCE

**1 onion, chopped roughly**

**1 clove garlic, chopped roughly**

**1 piece of ginger, similar in size to the garlic, chopped roughly**

**thyme, rosemary**

**1/2 cup port**

**1/2 cup red wine**

**a little water**

**20g brown sugar**

**salt**

**black pepper**

Preparing the meat: You really should do this yourself first, so you can instruct your butcher in the future. It's not too difficult to de-bone lamb. Just work a sharp knife along the bones, taking care not to slice through the fat. It's much easier the second and third times. Trim away all excess meat, the tough outer skin from the flap, and any of the tough and generally inedible sinews attached to the loin itself. Pound the flap until it is quite thin, taking care not to break through the surface. Season the lamb with freshly ground salt and pepper, and then layer it with very finely sliced slivers of garlic. Lamb and garlic are the very best of bedfellows. Do not be worried about an overpowering flavour of garlic. Its purpose is to bring out all the flavour of the lamb, a job it does admirably.

1 Roll the flap around the loin, enclosing all the meat (and garlic). Cut the loin into the portion sizes you require and tie each roll securely with string.

That's really all there is too it, other than a bit of cooking.

2 Heat the oven to its maximum.

3 Brown the loins in a hot pan and place in the oven in the same pan. This step is not necessary, but it gets the pan hot, and the lamb hot, thus speeding up the cooking process.

4 The lamb should be medium–rare (pink) when it's served. With the flap tied around it is difficult to test whether it is done if you employ the usual 'finger-pressing' method. In the hottest oven, using the hot-pan cooking method, it should take no more than 12 minutes to be cooked, but the time will obviously depend on the thickness of the loin. It is perfectly okay to cheat. Take the lamb from the oven and slice it halfway through to inspect. It is cooked when it feels just warm in the middle. If it's stone-cold put it back for a couple of minutes more. If warm, remove it, and leave it in a warm spot. The cooking process will continue through the retained heat in the outer section of the lamb.

All meat should be cooked like this. I'm sure the reason why our parents always cooked meat through to the bone is they didn't understand the fact the meat continued cooking *after* it was removed from the oven. A happy consequence of this long cooking time was the gloriously flavoured crust on the meat and the deliciously tender roasted pumpkin and potatoes. The only way to get these vegetables to taste the same these days is to replicate the old ways, and roast them in a little beef or lamb stock.

This dish is delicious with the simplest of accompaniments — mashed potato and peas, and the lamb will more than stand up on its own without a sauce. It is moist, tender and reeking with flavour. Just slice the string, unroll the flap and cut it away from the loin. Decide whether you wish to serve the garlic scattered about, or discarded. Serve the loin sliced like coins.

You can make a complicated lamb stock, with bones and port and wine, but I have never done it at home, and I'd be amazed if anybody these days has the time to make complex sauces while maintaining a happy household. But there is another way.

5 A simple sauce: This will make a couple of portions, so be frugal with the sauce. Make the sauce while the lamb is cooking. Brown the bones and any pieces of leftover lamb meat in a hot oven. Be careful not to burn the lot. Remove the bones, pour away any fat and cook the onion, garlic and ginger gently until they soften. Add the port, red wine, water, brown sugar and herbs.

Use a wooden spoon to work away the sediment left from the lamb and bones. Reduce heavily over high heat until jammy. Season. There will be only a couple of teaspoons of thickly flavoured sauce.

WINE ❖ *Coonawarra's a funny place. Flat as a billiard table — in winter the wind screeches across it — but it makes Australia's most consistent premium red wines. The south-east of South Australia, where Coonawarra is nestled, produces some of the country's best fat lambs. Maybe that's why I cannot go past a good Coonawarra red for this dish.*

♥
## LAMB FILLETS

You might see lamb fillets in the butcher's display tray. Be wary. These are more likely to come from mutton than lamb, and, although still tender, have a very gamey flavour, which may not appeal to too many modern palates. This is the flavour of big, fat sheep, coming from years of roaming wild pastures.

If you want fair dinkum lamb fillets, order them from your butcher. Ask him to pull away the fillets from a dozen lamb loins and save them for you. The lamb fillets need no expertise to cook: just hit them in a hot pan, making sure they do not stick. Turn them to brown on each side, and finish in the oven for a minute. Set aside for a few minutes, season with salt and black pepper, and serve, sliced, with mashed potatoes and the juices from the pan and the cutting board.

♥
## ROAST LAMB WITH GARLIC AND MASHED POTATOES

A large leg of lamb is, more often than not, too much: too big, too long to cook, too hard to get perfectly pink all the way through. But, if you get your butcher to cut a leg into its individual segments, running his knife along the inner tracts of muscle and sinew and fibre, you will get all the delicious flavour of the leg in a fraction of the time, with none of the effort, and it will be wall-to-wall quality.

A leg will give you several pieces of varying sizes, the average fitting neatly into the palm of your hand. Certainly you can do this all yourself in half a day, but your friendly butcher will be *happy* to do it for you in a few minutes.

The largest piece is perfect for four people; the smallest, not much bigger and similar in shape to a banana, is ideal for two. The hit-and-miss nature of cooking large roasts — with all their different muscles — is eliminated, and the meat is very easy to carve.

They are also easy to stuff, if that be your way, and lend themselves beautifully to flavouring with herbs and, my favourite partner with lamb, garlic.

There is only one set of accompaniments to serve with lamb prepared like this — three veg, just like mum used to make. One of them must be mashed potato.

♥ ♥ ♥ ♥ ♥

**2 nuts of lamb from the leg is more than enough for 4 people**

**black pepper**

several cloves of garlic, peeled and cut along their length as 'bullets'

salt

½ cup port or red wine

**1** Make deep slits into the lamb with a sharp knife, and rub some pepper into the slits. Insert a garlic 'bullet' into each slit. Rub with olive oil.

**2** Turn the oven to full bore. Heat a pan on top of the stove and sizzle the lamb in a little oil until it is brown all over. Salt lightly, and turn the pepper mill all over, not lightly. Place in the oven for about 15 minutes, depending on the thickness of the lamb. Keep checking, even if you have to slice through the lamb to see whether it has been done. It should be right when it gives to the touch, without being wobbly. It should be removed from the oven before it is completely cooked, as the cooking process continues outside the oven. When it is just about right — warmed right through to the heart — turn off the oven and sit the lamb on the oven door.

**3** Leave it to rest on a warmed plate for about 10 minutes, while you get the rest of the meal organised. Remember, the lamb must be served pink — don't listen to your grandmother.

**4** In the pan, splash in the port or wine, on a high heat, using a wooden spoon to remove any sediment left by the cooking of the lamb. Reduce heavily, adding salt and black pepper, and any juice which has run from the waiting lamb. Serve the sauce drizzled over the lamb slices.

WINE ✤ *Roast lamb and red are perfect partners. A couple of safe bets for this are Jamiesons Run from Coonawarra and Penfolds Bin 389.*

♥
## LAMB SHANKS

I started a career on ABC radio with a recipe for lamb shanks, and the place went wild. People were writing in from mansions and caravan parks for what is nothing at all really — just a simple mix of lamb shanks and water and vegetables, and patience.

It gave me great heart that some of the old cuts and old ways are still keenly considered, perhaps just needing a memory prod.

The beauty about cooking the gelatinous cuts of meat such as shanks of lamb or veal or beef is that one effort contributes to three or four meals, depending on your appetite. And even when the meat has disappeared you can often rely on a little stock to give a soup a boost. And every time I cook a dish like this I wonder why there is not a permanent place on the stove for a bubbling stock. Space I guess, or a lack of large, dedicated stock pots.

Lamb shanks really taste a lot better if cooked in a stock of their own, but I'm not about suggesting you make one especially for this dish. Perhaps you should if you want to impress guests; otherwise cook the shanks in water and let them provide their own stock.

If you have plenty of stock on hand, enough to cover the lamb, then it is best to cook the dish slowly in a covered pot; if you are cooking with water, cook them uncovered to intensify the flavours.

♥   ♥   ♥   ♥   ♥

**6 lamb shanks, sawn in half crossways by your butcher**

**2 cups red wine**

**2 cups port**

*The red wine and the port will not be necessary if you have a lamb stock.*

**4 carrots, sliced in wide pieces**

*You can use more or less, as you prefer.*

**2 leeks, sliced like the carrots**

**6 cloves garlic, peeled**

**2 chillies**

**lamb stock or water to cover**

*You can make a lamb stock by roasting some lamb bones and some veal shanks in the oven, draining the fat away, deglazing with some red wine, adding carrots, celery, leeks, and salt to taste, and covering the lot with water. Cook gently for a couple of hours. Drain, cool, and remove any fat which has come to the surface. Save the veal for a splendid meal, later in the week.*

**salt**

**black pepper**

**bunch of rosemary**

1 When you are ready to go with the shanks, brown them on top of the stove for a couple of minutes, then roast them in a hot oven for about 15 minutes until they are sizzling. They should have browned (not burned) pretty well all over. Remove and drain the pan of fat, and de-glaze with the red wine and port, cooking it hard to a fast boil for several minutes. Add the carrots, leeks, garlic, chillies, and shanks, cover with the stock/water, and add more salt than you might think — about 2 teaspoons. You must check the seasoning on the way through.

2 Bring to the boil and then reduce to a bare simmer. Cook until the shanks are tender and come away from the bone easily — 60–90 minutes. The carrots will be a good indicator of when the shanks are done. They will be tender and full of their own sweetness and the flavour of the lamb stock. The lamb must not be dry — you can overcook a stew — but pink to the bone. When the lamb is cooked, toss in the rosemary to infuse the sauce as the pot cools down. Allow to cool so that the fat will come to the surface.

3 Remove any fat, and the rosemary, and re-heat. Serve in large bowls, with a large bowl in the middle of the table for the scraped bones.

Note: Much the same method should be utilised with ox tail, cut into segments by your butcher. Perfectly cooked ox tail needs a rich red wine and beef stock in which to cook. If the ox tail starts in the stock, and there are many carrots and waxy potatoes drifting around, you can be certain of pure delight. Pure, pure delight. In each case — lamb shanks and ox tail — if the meat is removed from the bone, it makes for a superb pasta dish, far better and more satisfying than the usual bolognese sauce made with mince.

WINE ✤ *I guess that before wine became a natural part of Australian meals, a pot of tea would have been served with this dish. I have nothing against tea, but I'd prefer a hearty red. The Langhorne Creek district of South Australia makes perfect reds for this dish — Potts, Metala or Wolf Blass.*

♥
# JAMES MAVROS' LAMB'S NECK

Aaaah, a pleasant day in the country. Lunch was a leg of lamb, a lamb, I might add, which had been born, raised, and slaughtered not all that far from the table on which we ate. The post-lunch recovery was spent assisting (more accurately, watching, bemused) the round-up of a flock of ewes and lambs, chasing a burly fox across a paddock or two (fruitless) and wondering why we Westerners eat sheep but not foxes, beef cattle but not dogs, chickens but not cockatoos.

I often wonder who took the first bite of some of the delicacies that grace our tables. Who was game enough to toss down the first oyster? How many thousands of gourmands gave their life searching for the latest fungus sensation? And who decided that under that stinking, oily, filthy, matted mass of wool, all capped by the thickest head in the animal kingdom, lay the most delicious of meats?

At the base of that head lies the neck, a cut of the beast to which I had not really given much thought until I ran into it in a tiny restaurant which charged tiny prices for the quality of its cooking. It's as simple as any other slow-cooked item, with one proviso. The neck has a few tiny bones drifting about here and there, so beware.

♥　♥　♥　♥　♥

2 lambs' necks, split down their lengths by your butcher and cleaned of any excess fat

*Inside the vertebrae is the sheep's spinal cord. When you see how thin it is, you will understand why sheep are not usually Rhodes scholars.*

salt

black pepper

3 cups port

10 small onions or 5 large onions, sliced into rings

2 cloves garlic, peeled and sliced finely

4 carrots, chopped into bite-size pieces

6 waxy potatoes, peeled and chopped to the same size as the carrots

at least a litre of lamb stock to cook the neck, but if you don't have it, use water — and you'll end up with not only a lovely neck, but a lovely stock as well

1 Heat the oil in a heavy-bottomed saucepan or stock pot. Brown the necks all over, making sure they do not stick or burn. Remove, pat dry and season well with salt and black pepper.

2 In the same pan, scrape up any sediment with a wooden spoon and de-glaze with the port, cooking fast and furiously for several minutes.

3 Cook the onions and garlic gently over a low heat until they lose their colour. This step could take 10–15 minutes. Every now and then, when the onions appear to be drying out, add a splash of port. The onions will soften, brown, and take up the port.

4 Put the necks on top of the onions, meat side down, so that the meat does not dry out, and

spread around the carrots and potatoes. Cover with the water/lamb stock.

5 The necks must now simmer, uncovered, for 2–3 hours. If you have lamb stock, do not cook on top of the stove, but covered, in a 200°C oven for about the same time. Keep a good eye on the show, making sure the mix does not boil vigorously. The heat should just cause the surface to ripple. After about an hour, remove the potatoes and set them aside, covered with some stock from the pot.

6 You might need to add a little water through the cooking, but don't be too heavy-handed. The lamb is done when the meat comes away from the bone easily.

7 Leave it overnight, so that any fat given off will solidify and can be removed easily. Once you've removed the fat, toss the potatoes back in and re-heat, covered, in a low oven for about 20 minutes.

WINE ✚ *I remember having this dish as James cooked it. We had a bottle of French red burgundy with it. It was great. A small group of heroes is making better and better Australian pinot every year. I like Bannockburn, De Bortoli (Yarra Valley), Coldstream Hills, Scotchman's Hill and Balgownie's. Unfortunately they are all still young wines. It will be interesting to see what they look like as 10-year-olds.*

♥
## STUFFED PORK NECK, THE LAZY WAY

T he lovely thing about being keen on food and cooking is that there is no end to the things you can learn. Here I was, strolling down a suburban street, minding my own business, when I happened upon a butcher's shop. I stopped to ponder on what appeared to be just another display of meat, only to spy a bundle neatly labelled 'pork neck'.

I thought I'd try it, expecting it to be one of those long, slow cookers, so I nipped in. And lo and behold, I hear the butcher telling me, slowly and carefully, the several ways to cook this cut, none of which takes any time and effort.

'Roast it whole,' said Martin Schaad, the Swiss born and trained butcher. 'Or cut it into slices and cook it in the pan like schnitzel. It will be beautifully tender.'

He spoke with a real and rare authority. In the fridge before him were all sorts of sausages and cooked meats. I had thoughts of pork neck, stuffed, so to speak, but was feeling lazy and took the lazy stuffer's way out — a couple of knackwurst, the deliciously mild veal and pork sausage from Germany.

I took the casing from the knackwurst, rammed them into the pork neck, put the lot into the oven and let it bake furiously for about 40 minutes, until the pork was just done. One point to note about tender pigs. Make sure you're getting the females of the breed, and never, never, never the males.

'Only the females,' said the butcher.

'Why?' I asked.

'The females,' he said, 'never have that, that, I have to use the word, pissy smell when they're cooked. Only the males.'

♥   ♥   ♥   ♥   ♥

**1 pork neck, boned by your butcher: 1 kg will serve six**

*The neck roasts beautifully because it is not completely lean. There is fat through it. The leg is never as good, nor the loin. They become dry with cooking. Not the neck.*

**2 knackwurst, or equivalent cooked sausage, skinned**

**2 cups good quality port**

**salt**

**black pepper**

**1** With a steel, force an opening through the pork and stuff in the sausage, being as delicate as you can. Tie up the pork, tightly but gently.

**2** Put the oven on full blast. Brown the pork on top of the stove until the pan is sizzling. Pour in half the port and put the pork and all in the oven.

**3** It will take about 40 minutes. After 20 minutes, check to ensure the port has not evaporated and add the rest, pouring it over the top of the pork.

**4** Remove from oven and set aside in a warm place. There should be enough port left for a sauce. If not, add more and reduce vigorously, taking up any sediment left in the pan. If there is sauce remaining, remove any obvious fat from the pan and reduce the rest until it thickens a little. Season.

**5** Slice the pork and pour the sauce over the top. It also makes for a delicious sandwich, cold, for lunch the next day.

WINE ♣ *I quite like Rhine riesling with pork. I have the kind of insides that make whale noises after a good feed of pork — riesling is a foil for the pork's richness.*

♥

## PORK SPARE RIBS; GNAWING AT THE BONE

Y ou have to be something of an animal to enjoy pork spare ribs. Enjoyment is gnawing away at fat and bones, ripping away tender meat, while the soy and pork fat drips down your chin. And enjoyment is dependent on you getting the best quality ribs — plenty of meat, mixed with just the right amount of fat and, naturally, the ribs of the female of the species.

Check your ribs before you buy, and make sure you are getting meaty value for money. There's nothing worse than a rib with more fat than meat. And one more thing, before we get down to business. If you are frightened of fat, don't read on. You might have a heart attack.

♥   ♥   ♥   ♥   ♥

**dozen ribs, sliced no thicker than 2 cm**

**THE MARINADE**

**1 cup soy sauce**

**just under ½ cup honey**

**1 cup dry sherry**

*We used Mildara supreme dry, which seems just right for this, is the right price, and is just right for a chilled apéritif as well.*

**1–2 chillies**

**1 fresh bay leaf, split into pieces**

*We have a tree; if you don't, a dry bay leaf is okay, or some fresh sage.*

**1 sprig of rosemary**

**a few sprigs of lemon thyme**

*If you haven't any, use parsley, or co-riander, or whatever fresh, flavoursome herb you can find.*

**1 walnut-sized piece of ginger, sliced finely**

**1/4 stick of cinnamon, rubbed between your fingers**

*Cinnamon might seem a little unusual, but it works wonderfully here. When you are getting into the fourth rib, you suddenly come across this flavour, and mentally say to yourself: 'Yikes, what's that?' It's cinnamon.*

**1 small carrot, sliced thinly along its length**

1 Bring the marinade ingredients to the boil, stirring to ensure the honey melts and doesn't stick on the bottom. (This is easily done before you add it to the mixture, putting a little sherry and soy into the bowl with the honey and heating it through in the microwave.) Set aside to cool.

2 Pour over the ribs to cover. This is best done in a wide glass or ce-ramic bowl, so that all the ribs get the treatment. The marinade is best left overnight but six hours is ade-quate as well. If you can, turn the top to the bottom, so all pieces get a good sight of the juice.

3 Heat oven to 200°C. Put a little water into a baking tray and, in-side it, or balanced on the edge, sit a grill or a cake rack, so you can repli-cate a barbecue in your oven. Of course you can do this on a real bar-becue, but only on hot coals, not on

a rich flame. All you will get from that is a carbonated mess.

4 Bake in the oven for about 30 minutes, turning the ribs after about 15 minutes. They should be tender and juicy, and a deal of fat and marinade will have fallen into the drink below.

5 Bring a cup of strained marinade to a fast boil and maintain it for a minute of so, running a wooden spoon through it. Pour over the ribs and eat furiously with a white bib wrapped around your neck.

6 Steamed rice, or baked potatoes (or pumpkin), fluffed up and tossed with chives, are beautiful partners for this dish.

WINE ✤ *Chinese tea or a traminer from Alsace. Too many Australian traminers have an 'oily' character I don't particularly like, but my favourites are from Delatite in Victoria and Flaxmans from Orlando.*

♥

## MICKY'S MARVELLOUS MARINATED PORK

Nothing makes my good friend Michael Gordon happier than a dirty apron, a wok, a bench loaded with spices, and a large crowd anticipat-ing a good feed from the Orient. Micky once did a Chinese cooking course which had the unexpected side-effect of turning his intimate dinner parties into banquets for twenty to thirty people. This is the Great Hall syndrome of Chinese cooking.

And so it was that we fronted a Gordon dinner party and couldn't find a park within 200 metres. The house was stacked when we arrived but Michael was remarkably cool as he bent before the oven and pulled out a steaming hot, brilliantly red slab of meat.

'What's that?' I said, full of doubt.

'That,' said a friend more used than I to Micky's grand style of catering, 'is Micky's world famous Chinese pork fillet.'

The chef himself sliced vigorously. The pork was perfectly pink throughout.

'Want to try some?' he said, a little nervously.

It was magnificent. I tried another and another. I dipped it into the fiery chilli sauce which accompanied it. It was, and still is, magnificent.

♥　♥　♥　♥　♥

### THE MARINADE

*This is enough for 10 fillets.*

¹/₂ cup soy sauce

¹/₂ cup sherry

180 g Hoi Sin sauce

3 garlic cloves, chopped roughly

¹/₄ cup water

3 pieces of ginger, chopped thickly

3 dessertspoons five spice powder (a combination of star anise, fennel, cinnamon, cloves and Szechuan pepper)

30 g brown sugar

¹/₄ cup sesame paste (tahini)

³/₄ cup olive oil

¹/₂–1 pork fillet per person
*Remove the sinew and any extra fat from the fillets.*

### THE DAY BEFORE

1 Combine all ingredients and beat loosely until it all comes together. Cover the pork, working the marinade into the fillets with your fingers. Marinate overnight in the refrigerator. You can leave them longer, but the longer the marinade works, the more intrusive its flavour becomes. We are not attempting to create a slab of meat which tastes like a marinade: the marinade is to tenderise the pork and to bring out its flavour. (If you do leave the pork in the marinade too long, it will need little cooking, and is best served cold, thinly sliced, as a sandwich filling.)

### ON THE DAY

2 Remove the pork fillets from the marinade, and leave at room temperature for about an hour before cooking.

3 Heat the oven to its maximum and roast the pork. It will take 10–15 minutes, depending on its thickness. When you think it is done, take it from the oven and slice a fillet half through. It should be warm to touch and pink in the middle. If you think it is right, feel it with your fingers and get to know the 'cooked feeling'.

4 Allow the pork to rest in a warm spot, perhaps the open door of your oven. The retained heat will maintain the cooking process for several minutes.

5 Serve as simply as that, or with a fiery chilli sauce; or tossed in a

little olive oil, garlic, bacon, and whatever vegetables you have; or tossed through a salad of old-fashioned vegetables in a thick garlic-flavoured dressing.

The richness of the pork is set off very well by the slightly acidic garlic dressing and the slightly sweet marinade. If you think it needs more sweetness, Michael's original recipe calls for the pork to be brushed with honey when cooked. If you are serving the pork cold, and perhaps on a buffet, you can really have people gasping by dressing it with some red food colouring as the Chinese like to do. I can't be bothered. If you want to try an excellent chilli sauce with the pork, see page 256.

♥

## VEAL AND PORK SAUSAGES

It never ceases to amaze me how much people love sausages. Why? Perhaps it is to do with the shape, or childhood memories; or the possibilities of the extreme flavour of a great sausage; or even how well a sausage melds with a classic tomato sauce.

My father used to look forward to his annual holidays in Daylesford as much for the 'Italian', garlic-laced sausages as the relaxation. People still make expeditions across town to buy sausages from particular makers, but the art of fine sausage making seems to be drifting away. Although a few excellent makers are clawing their way into the market, you wouldn't touch most commercial thick and thins with a barge pole, and butchers generally look on their sausages as profit makers. All leftovers are tossed into a machine and chopped almost to dust, before being squeezed into skins. The best

palate in the world would be unable to identify the components. One thing you can bet on — the fine grinding will ensure they taste dry, without any of the personality of their components.

I have tried dozens of ways with sausages over several years, but in the end two 'secret' ingredients were needed to make them, to my taste, as near to perfect as you could imagine. One was the fat from some delicious 'home-smoked' bacon. The other was more basic — we gave the easy machine away and chopped the meat more coarsely, forcing the farce into the skins by hand. Of course we used a stack of garlic! And don't forget one thing about snags: they need a lot of fat — it's almost better not to know how much really — to ensure they are moist within. There's a bit of work in making these little boys, but the results are well worth the effort.

Work out the amount you wish to make, then get together a mix of one-third good quality veal (shoulder or leg), one-third of pork (shoulder or leg) and a 50–50 mix of pork fat (from the back) and the best flavoured bacon fat you can find. These meats will make up two-thirds of the total mix.

♥   ♥   ♥   ♥   ♥

250 g veal from the shoulder or leg, sinews removed, chopped finely

250 g pork from the shoulder or leg

125 g pork fat from the back

125 g bacon fat

dried apricots, currants, sultanas

2 walnut-sized pieces of ginger, chopped roughly

4 cloves garlic, chopped roughly

*~ 1 4 5 ~*

2 onions, chopped roughly

parsley, tarragon, rosemary
(any or all)

2 chillies

salt and black pepper
(plenty of each)

garam masala

*This delicious Indian spice mix should be made regularly (see page 246), as it loses its punch about as quickly as coffee beans. If you buy it, make sure it comes from a friendly Indian spice seller.*

2 eggs

2 cups breadcrumbs

4 dessertspoons Dijon mustard

sausage skins

*Any decent butcher will sell you plenty of real pork intestines as casings for a song. Make sure you get the 'thick' ones. Better still, take your mix to the butcher and ask him to force the mince into skins. Ask him to use the most coarse blade on his blender.*

### THE 'TOPPING'

Dijon mustard

breadcrumbs

almonds, chopped finely (whatever nuts you have will do)

red peppers, chopped

parsley, chopped

butter

**1** Chop all the meats with the heaviest knife in your kitchen. If you have a mincer then put the lot through the medium grind. If not, just keep chopping. It's not as tough as it sounds, but you do need a rather heavy, very sharp knife.

**2** When you get the meats to a manageable consistency, add the other ingredients. Keep chopping and then work it all together with your hands. Check the seasoning by rolling off a little ball and baking it in the oven. Adjust seasoning if necessary. If you stop now, you have achieved a wonderful hamburger mix, or stuffing for pork or veal or chicken. If you're lazy, start cooking, if not, read on ...

**3** Use a strong piping bag to force the mix into the skins. It really is a much better use of your time if you get your butcher to do this for you. Get him to tie the sausages in lengths of about a metre. Allow them to rest in their skins at least overnight.

**4** Poach the sausages in simmering water until they just hold their own — they should be rare in the middle. Allow to cool and chop into usual sausage sizes — they will, of course, have 'square' ends.

**5** Remember all that work you put in to force the mixture into the skins. Well, now we undo all that labour by taking them out of the skins! Just slice the skin down the 'back' of the snag. You don't have to remove the skins, but I'm no fan of sausage skin, whether it comes from natural intestine or is artificial. It is no more than a casing. You can do much better than that. This method gives you a much more flavoursome sausage, some of it coming from the roasting process, some from the 'topping' on the sausage. The 'topping' is really a stuffing on the outside.

**6** Rub the cooked, skinned sausages with the mustard and sprinkle them with the breadcrumbs, almonds, parsley, red peppers and some nuts of butter, and roast in a flat-out oven for about 10 minutes — just to cook the sausages through. They should still be just cooked.

7 Obviously the naked sausages will be rather delicate, but it doesn't matter too much if they break up a little. The mustard, breadcrumbs etc., on top give you another 'fresh' flavour.

8 Ideally, you should serve the sausage with a simple warm salad of potato, bacon and beans, tossed in a light olive oil vinaigrette. Be naughty and stack your salad with garlic too! You're also allowed to serve them with your own tomato sauce, and stuff them into your own bread. The sausages can be frozen, but before the skins have been removed — it makes for easier storage.

WINE ✚ *I have to have red wine with garlic — so what makes a good snag wine? You need something with a touch of inky density. Reds from Clare have it, some from Margaret River and plenty from north-east Victoria.*

♥
## VEAL SHANKS, OR OSSO BUCO IN THE ORIENT

I delight in *osso buco* because I delight in veal, and the deliciously subtle flavour which comes from well-cooked veal bones is blissful. Put them together and you're in heaven. There are plenty of sound arguments why home cooks shouldn't bother to make stocks, the basis of the discussion being that stocks require too much work and

time to get to a result which can be approximated, compromised or ignored.

But cooking shanks, as in veal or lamb shanks, gives you the best of all worlds: you get some delicious slow-cooked meats, lovely impregnated vegetables and a stock which turns to jelly as soon as it cools down. Osso buco ends up as the savoury equivalent of having stewed apricots in the fridge. If it's the height of summer, and there's a stock on the stove, and stewed 'cots in the fridge, then you know you're going to eat well — soup, main course and dessert, with no added labour on the day.

♥   ♥   ♥   ♥   ♥

**6 veal shanks, sawn through into manageable pieces, depending on their size**

*It's worth trying shanks of all ages — from the tiny young vealers, through to those of several months.*

**2 cups white wine**

**1/2 ham hock, rind removed, sawn in half**

**water to cover**

**2 carrots; chopped roughly**

**2 parsnips, chopped roughly**

**2 cloves garlic, chopped roughly**

**2–3 chillies, chopped roughly**

**salt**

**bunch of coriander, chopped roughly**

**2 stems of lemon grass, sliced**

**1 piece of ginger, chopped roughly**
*If you can get galangal, use that.*

**zest of 1 orange**

2 red peppers, sliced in half and de-
seeded

juice of 1 juicy orange

black pepper

1 Keeping the veal shanks well separated in the pan, brown them in
a little oil and bake in the oven for
15 minutes.

2 Remove shanks and de-glaze the
cooking pan with half of the
wine until it cooks down, removing
all the sediment with a wooden
spoon.

3 Toss the shanks and the ham
hock into a stock pot, and cover
them with the juice from the de-
glazed pan, the rest of the wine,
some water, carrots, parsnips, garlic
and chillies. Simmer 100–110 minutes, adding salt after 20 minutes.
After an hour, add the coriander,
lemon grass, ginger and zest.

4 While the veal is bubbling away,
roast the red peppers in a 200°C
oven for about 20 minutes, until the
skins blister. Allow to cool and rub
away the skins. Taste a little, then
slice into strips and add to the simmering pot, once it has been cooking for about 90 minutes.

5 Just before the end of the cooking, add the orange juice and stir
until amalgamated. Test the seasoning and adjust if necessary.

6 Allow to cool and leave
overnight. Any fat will rise to the
top. There is so much gelatine in the
bones the stock will set tight. Remove any fat, and set aside.

7 If the veal is of the older variety,
serve on the bone, and turn your
eyes when your company sucks out
the marrow; if it's younger, on obviously smaller bones, remove the
meat when cold, and serve in deep
bowls with an array of the vegetables, a good pour of the stock and
plenty of bread for wiping up.

WINE ❖ *Italian Barbarescos are suddenly becoming expensive — basically
because Americans have discovered
them. They can be big, raw-boned
wines, but the best are delicious and perfect for this dish.*

♥

## ROAST VEAL FOR PICKY FEEDERS

There remain difficult people to please and to feed. I
have great sympathy for
these poorly guided folk. It was not
too many years ago that I was one
of them. Chops, sausages and
mashed potatoes. That was me.

So, whenever you are required to
cook for one of this unfortunate and
plentiful breed, give them something
they might not be too familiar with,
yet won't cause them to choke. Hare
is not recommended. Tender, subtle
veal certainly is.

♥    ♥    ♥    ♥    ♥

1 real fillet of veal per person

*The fillet is quite tiny, not much bigger
than a banana, with a wider section up
front. It is extraordinarily tender, mild
and non-aggressive in flavour, simple
and easy to cook, readily available, and
guaranteed to please even the most difficult eaters.*

a little flour

1 cup good quality white wine

150g butter, in chunks

salt

black pepper

juice of 1 lemon

**1** Trim the veal of any fat and sinew, and heat the oven to flat out.

**2** Heat a little oil in a pan which can go to the oven. Sprinkle the fillets with the flour and place them in the hot pan, ensuring that they are well separated and don't stick. Move them about and brown all over.

**3** Complete the cooking in the oven. The veal will be done when the fillet is firm, but gives to the touch — 5–8 minutes. Veal should be cooked until it gets a pinkish-white colour in the middle. It should not be rare. Test and decide.

**4** When the veal is done, remove from the pan and set aside in a warm place, covered. The cooking process should have browned the bottom of the pan. Herein lies the basis of the sauce.

**5** Add the wine to the hot pan, running a wooden spoon about to raise the sediment. Bring to the boil and keep cooking until the wine is all but evaporated. Remove from the heat and whisk in the butter piece by piece, until emulsified. Season with salt and black pepper.

**6** Whisk in the lemon juice and any juice which has come from the resting veal. Keep warm.

**7** Slice the veal, pour some sauce over, and serve with mashed pumpkin, and, when the season is right, Brussels sprouts, each given a touch of the butter sauce.

WINE ✤ *Veal is ambidextrous. It will take either red or white wine: a full-bodied chardonnay with 2 to 3 years bottle age or a 4- to 5-year-old, medium-bodied red.*

♥

## VEAL CHOPS

V eal chops seem to be perfect candidates for quick cooking on the grill, but all is not as it seems. The chops from a young vealer are often confused by fat and sinew and sheaths, hanging about. Remarkably, they are great when cooked slowly in stock or tomatoes. If you wish to cook them quickly, put in a bit of pre-preparation — tear them from the bones and remove all the extras. Then you'll be sure they are tender.

♥　　♥　　♥　　♥　　♥

**4 veal chops per person**

*Bone them and clean them of all fat and sinew, keeping the trimmings and bones for a stock. You will be left with rather tiny nuts of pink veal.*

**1** Tap lightly the cleaned meat with the flat edge of a heavy knife, in a criss-cross form on each side. The veal will flatten a little, without losing its shape. The grid will ensure perfect tenderness, even if the meat is not naturally tender.

**2** Heat a little oil in a heavy pan and slap the veal into the pan, making sure it does not stick. Move about gently until it is well browned. Cook for about a minute on one side, turn, and remove from the heat. The cooking will be completed in the hot pan.

**3** Make a sauce from the sediment in the pan, a little butter and lemon juice. Season and serve with some old-fashioned vegetables.

WINE ♣ *I like the idea of a buxom chardonnay with my veal chops. Len Evans calls them 'Dolly Parton styles'. Try the Chairman's Selection from Renmano or the Pinnacle or Mamre Brook from Saltrams.*

♥

## SOMETHING LIKE VEAL CORDON BLEU, WHATEVER THAT IS

Veal cordon bleu: is it real? Did anybody make it up? Or is it like an Hawaiian pizza, nothing more than the fertile imagination of an Australian pub cook, circa 1970. Remember? It was at about the same time as carpetbag steak, and ham steak, and sweet corn and onion salad, and baked potatoes and sour cream.

Anyway, whatever it is (it's not in Escoffier, nor Larousse) it can be marvellous, if you choose its components carefully and cook it gently and well.

My memories of the pub version of veal CB was a rather large, round, pear-shaped and pear-sized ball of meat, with a couple of tooth picks holding the thinly sliced veal (or more likely beef) around a mix of cheese and ham. The idea was that the veal would be very well cooked and the cheese would melt and ooze out. Whatever flavour the veal lacked, the cheese and ham would compensate.

I can't be bothered with that. What you should look for is a lovely, tender, pink slice of veal, mixed and matched with a first-class cut of ham, a sharp cheese, a stack of

herbs, plenty of butter and very quick service.

♥ ♥ ♥ ♥ ♥

**the back strap, or loin of veal, sliced away from the bone by your butcher**
*If you can't get that, go to a very good veal butcher and ask for a tender cut from the leg, flattened and tenderised à la veal schnitzel.*

**15 g butter per portion**

**all the fresh herbs you can find**

**the juice of 1 lime or lemon**

**the best ham you can find**

**a few slices of Provolone *piccante***
*This is a very sharp cheese from southern Italy, usually in the shape of a truncated cone and about 15 cm in diameter. You can use any melting cheese. Raclette would be marvellous, Gruyère great.*

**a little white wine**

1 Slice the strap almost through, then flatten it. Cut into individual portions and pound with the back of a heavy knife to tenderise.

2 Heat a little oil in a pan which can go to oven and slide in the veal, piece by piece. You will need to make sure the portions are well separated so they can fry, not stew. Heat oven to flat out.

3 Brown for about a minute on one side, then remove from heat. Gently squeeze the lime/lemon juice on top of the slices of veal, then sprinkle with plenty of herbs. Add one piece of butter to each slice, season with a little salt and plenty of black pepper, and cover with a slice of ham, then a slice of the cheese.

4 Return to heat and sizzle for about 30 seconds. Bake in the hot oven for about 6 minutes. The cheese should have just melted, and the butter should have poured out, joining with the veal and lime juices to provide a lovely sauce.

5 Optional: Set the veal aside and pour off the sauce into a sauce bowl. Return the pan to the heat, add the white wine, and, with a wooden spoon, gently remove any sediment. Remove from the heat again and whisk in the sauce set aside. Pour over the veal.

WINE ✤ *What makes great wines great is complexity of aroma and flavour. Orange juice is orange juice, but great red keeps giving you different signals as you waltz together through 750 ml. To my mind, Australia's three best cabernet-producing areas are Margaret River, the Yarra Valley and Coonawarra. All three regions would provide a delicious red for the veal CB.*

♥
## HAM HASH

E very year I fall into a ham for Christmas. And every year when I get the monster home I look at it and wonder what the hell am I going to do with it. It's a little easier with many mouths to feed, but it is always before Christmas that we start to look at other ways to ham it up.

I have searched every book in my library to find why we buy these monsters at Christmas time, and I couldn't find an answer anywhere. Not only no answers, but no references to a cultural tendency to buy whopping hams anywhere at Christmas. Is it purely an Australian/ British custom? I remember these

mountains of meat as part of my childhood — but in those days they were often gifts, and with a family bigger than a basketball team, with coach, they were always scraped to the bone. Never look a gift ham in the mouth.

There was no need to worry about leftovers in those days. In those days when life was about scrimping and saving, and a penny was about the same value as today's pound, it must have been a luxury to cop a Christmas ham.

These days I am more interested in ham as a flavourer of other things, rather than something to admire on its own. And of all the dishes that elevate ham, the simple, old-fashioned, very down-market American hash may well be the best.

♥　♥　♥　♥　♥

2 onions, sliced into rings

ham, from anywhere, cut into chunks

6 waxy potatoes, cut into walnut-sized pieces, cooked until tender, drained

1 hot chilli

2 cloves garlic, sliced finely

salt

black pepper

fresh herbs — tarragon, oregano, thyme, or parsley

25 g butter for garnish

1 Cook the onions in a little oil and butter until they soften, then brown. This takes no more than patience, and about 25 minutes. You might need to add a little water now and then. Set aside.

2 You will need a large, heavy-based pan so the ham and potatoes can have a free run. The secret to good hash is that the potatoes crisp and brown without burning. Heat some oil and toss in the ham and potatoes with the chilli, garlic, salt and several turns of black pepper. It helps if you have a strong wrist and can toss the lot regularly, so that all sides of the ham and the potatoes get a look at the pan.

3 When the potatoes have a good crust — about 10 minutes — and the ham has sizzled and browned, add the herbs, the onions and the butter. Serve as is. It makes great company with chicken.

WINE ✤ *You can serve a full-bodied dry white or a medium-bodied red here. As a wine maker mate of mine once said: 'White wine is what you drink while you wait for the red to be served.' I'm a red wine man.*

*McLaren Vale has gone through somewhat of a renaissance in the eighties as far as reds go — no more cow yard or leather smells, just rich fruit. Try the 'Traditional' from Ryecroft or Hardys Stoney Hill. Both would go down well here.*

# POULTRY, GAME AND OFFAL

I t's easy to sneer at chickens, especially if you've watched them at close quarters in the coop. They always make me laugh, and it would certainly be a five-setter between a chicken and a lamb in any intelligence championship.

We sneer, too, at their rather flat flavour these days — an insult to a bird which, in the good old days, had a delicious, individual taste about it. You can't blame the chooks for tasting a bit common; blame us. We used to rail at the prices we paid for chicken, prices which meant that for most Australians, chicken was the dish for special occasions like Christmas, or Easter, or 50th birthday parties.

So they invented chicken farms, and fed the chickens anything but what they really enjoy. And as their prices came down, so, too, their flavour faded away.

But even so, chicken plays an important part in our menus; even battery chicken tastes pretty good if you work on it hard enough — stuffing tarragon under its skin makes an excellent start, marinating its breasts in spicy yoghurt mixes or full-flavoured olive oil.

And even ordinary chicken makes for a worthy stock. So we can't complain too much. But the wheel is also turning, as it has with bread. Keen farmers are putting chickens back on diets which restore the pale yellow colour of skin and flesh, and the flavours of the old days. These chickens will cost you a bit more, naturally, but they are worth it, for special occasions.

An extra special occasion is one which has squab on the table. These young pigeons have a wonderful gamey flavour and provide deliciously tender flesh; they are far superior to quail in these matters. I have always found quail not quite worth the effort, especially as their price is rising inexorably to the luxury class.

Game requires not so much a special occasion, but a special need. The Europeans look forward with much anticipation to the winter and the sudden rush of game — deer, hare, wild pig, and all sorts of birds — to the market. Of all these, only hare is regularly available in this country, although venison and Northern Territory buffalo can be found at exclusive shops. Kangaroo is restricted in its distribution, with most States prohibiting its sale for consumption. Hare has a richness of flavour which is a test for those with tender palate. If you like its intense flavour, you will seek it to the ends of the earth.

## WHAT YOU'LL NEED

1 **A poultry trivet.** Chickens are best roasted if they can get a clean go at the heat of the oven. Poultry trivets are cheap and readily available, and make for a very good investment.

2 **A strong stomach is vital if you get into the offal department.** Remember, you're dealing here with the working parts of birds and animals, and, not surprisingly, the flavour and richness are commensurate with the duties of those parts. While you are fiddling with sweetbreads and kidneys and livers, you should consider yourself lucky that the days of swinging the axe in the backyard are long gone. I think this is one skill which needs to be acquired from a hardy parent, or uncle, or brother. I missed out, I am afraid.

## THE RECIPES

♥

## A THREE-TIME LOSER: A CHICKEN, STUFFED, ROASTED, THEN BOILED

I n the not-so-old days, chicken sat next to crayfish as the food of the fortunate. I remember seeing chicken once a year, at Christmas; although we did have it occasionally, as a 'casserole', in less celebratory times. Later I discovered foul play: the chicken in a casserole was more likely rabbit than chook.

Such deception seems impossible these days with foodie talk on everyone's lips, and chicken so readily available they just about give it away. The down side of that mass production is the remarkable loss of flavour. But here and there you'll find farmers sending the chickens back to the land, giving them select corn feed. The yellow colour of the skin and flesh and the subtle, yet individual, chicken flavour is returning. The extra cost is worth it.

♥ ♥ ♥ ♥ ♥

a little rosemary, parsley, tarragon

12 sage leaves

zest of 1 lemon

2 cloves garlic, peeled, chopped

1 chicken, preferably corn-fed, if you can find it, afford it

2 leeks, greens and roots removed, chopped roughly

a little olive oil

25 g butter for the leeks

2 cups breadcrumbs

1 hot chilli, chopped

juice of 1 lemon

2 dessertspoons peanut butter

25 g butter for the stuffing

1 egg

½ cup cream

salt

black pepper

1 Heat the oven to flat out. Make a mix of chopped parsley, rosemary, tarragon, a few sage leaves, some of the lemon zest and half the garlic, and grind it into a paste. Force the paste underneath the skin of the chicken about the breast. Rub the outer skin dry.

2 Make the stuffing. Cook the leeks and the rest of the sage gently in the oil and the 25 g butter until the leeks have softened and lost their white colour. Set aside half for the sauce. Mix the rest of the leeks–sage with the breadcrumbs, half the chilli, the juice of the lemon, the rest of the lemon zest, the rest of the garlic, the peanut butter and the 25 g butter, and whizz with the egg. Ram three-quarters of the mix into the chook's insides. Make potato-like blobs of the rest and spread them around the outside of the bird.

3 Set the chicken on a rack and roast in a hot oven for about 30 minutes, basting the skin after about 20 minutes. Remove and keep in a warm place. Reduce the oven temperature to 200°C.

4 Towards the end of the cooking, make a sauce with the leftover leeks, re-heated gently with the remaining chilli, a little more butter

and the cream until the cream bubbles. If you had some chicken stock, you could add it to the cream and cook a little longer, still waiting for the cream to thicken. Season with a little salt and plenty of black pepper. A tiny touch of garam masala or curry powder would be delicious, added late and stirred through.

5 The breasts will be ready before the legs. Slice the breasts from the chicken and return the rest of the chicken to the oven for another 10 minutes to cook the legs through to the bone; the now vulnerable bones will also get a little exposed roasting, giving them a little more flavour for tomorrow's stock.

6 Serve the breasts with the leek sauce and some of the stuffing from the cooking pan.

7 When the rest of the chicken is done, cut off the legs and wings and remove the now baked stuffing. Keep this lot for tomorrow's lunch.

8 The chicken will now look a little shabby and dishevelled. Throw it into a stock pot with some sliced aromatic vegetables (carrots, onions, celery), a chilli or two, some garlic, ginger, half a bottle of white wine, and cover with water, bring to the boil, and simmer gently for a couple of hours, skimming as you go. Leave overnight to allow any fat to rise.

9 Toss away the exhausted carcass, and you are left with a lovely chicken stock. Use what you need and freeze the rest for another day.

WINE ❖ *I generally prefer red with chook. A full-flavoured chardonnay will* *do the job, but I just like the red match. How about a rich, soft style like Wolf Blass Grey Label or Ryecroft Traditional (the 1988 if you can get it)?*

♥

## WARM CHICKEN SALAD

We went through a phase with warm salads. An entirely admirable one it was, too, and not to be dismissed now, even though it might be out of fashion.

Salads represent an apparently disparate group of ingredients drawn together by a sauce or a common flavour. They are the ultimate in freshness and honesty on the plate.

The best way to concoct tasty salad combinations is to look back at old sandwiches. It's the same process: teaching your palate the flavours which work together. Everybody, whether the best or worst cook in the world, knows what he or she likes in a sandwich. Which bread? Which cheese? Which meat? Hot or cold? Mayonnaise or mustard? An egg? Peanut butter? Beetroot or onion? And lately, avocado or smoked salmon?

The list is endless, look at the same list when you are creating a salad.

Perfection does not have to mean complexity; nor should it be a given that because you like twenty ingredients, the twenty together will make an appropriate salad. More likely they will make a mess. There are few salads better than washed and dried salad greens, preferably with a bit of zip in them, like watercress, touched along with salt, black pepper and olive oil — and a little vinegar only. Use it only as a highlighter.

Start from there. Experiment with several different greens; try different oils, vinegars; try cheese, nut, vegetables, garlic, herbs, bacon. Think about textures and flavours working together. This is real palate training. And remember, there are no recipes for salads, just suggestions which may or may not suit your palate; or your pocket.

♥　♥　♥　♥　♥

**1 chicken breast, skin on, per person**

**¹/₄ bunch of tarragon, leaves removed from stems (makes for ¹/₂ cup leaves)**

*Half of this is for the marinade, half for the chicken.*

### THE MARINADE

**1 cup virgin olive oil**

**1 hot chilli, chopped**

**a little brown sugar**

**30 g raisins**

**juice of 2 lemons**

### THE DRESSING

**vinegar, preferably balsamic**

**virgin olive oil**

**salt**

**black pepper**

**¹/₂ clove garlic, chopped finely**

### THE SALAD

**3 waxy potatoes, steamed or boiled in their skins until tender**

*Allow to cool and cut into cubes.*

**3 rashers bacon, fat removed, cut into squares, and cooked until crisp**

**¹/₂ punnet of cherry tomatoes, sliced in half**

**¹/₄ cup pine nuts or cashews**

**¹/₂ bunch of chives, chopped**

**a mix of salad greens**

*Try to use some watercress, or mustard cress, as well as some gently flavoured greens.*

**salt**

**black pepper**

### THE DAY BEFORE

1 Slide half the tarragon between the skin and the flesh, and mix the marinade ingredients with the chicken breasts. Refrigerate, covered, overnight.

### ON THE DAY

2 Make the dressing using one part of vinegar to 6 parts virgin olive oil. Season with salt and black pepper, and add the garlic.

3 Allow the chicken to drain, and cook the breasts in a hot oven for about 15 minutes. The chicken should give to the touch and be just cooked in the middle.

4 While the chicken is cooking, heat a little oil in the pan and add the potatoes slowly, giving each piece the space to brown and sizzle. The idea is not to cook them all the way through, just to give them a little crust, something like hash. Add the bacon to warm through, and towards the end, the cherry tomatoes and the pine nuts for 30 seconds. Sprinkle with chives.

5 Slice the chicken and toss through the greens with the dressing. Add the bacon and potatoes, mixing through gently. Season, serve a little, and replenish from the bowl.

WINE ❖ *Hunter Valley semillons are like the perfect marriage partner. When you first try them in their youth, you know there's something there but it's a bit ungiving. Then slowly, but surely, they get better and become stoic and stable in old age. My favourites are from Tyrrell's, Rothbury and Lindemans.*

♥

## HOT, HOT CHICKEN IN A FLASH

Let me present to you the world's most spectacularly successful, quick as a flash and wonderfully flavoured dish; a dish for cooks large and thin, old and young, keen and dull; for the flamboyant and the flat, for singles, doubles, triples and more.

It's a curry which takes the same time to cook as it does to uncover the takeaway menu you filed away in a safe place, and can never find when you desperately need it. It needs nothing more than a few chicken breasts, a little Thai curry paste and a tin of coconut milk. Any extras depend on your ingenuity.

I am almost embarrassed to put it down on paper, it is so simple … if you have a cache of Thai curry paste in your pantry. If you do, then you've probably made this dish, and hundreds like it already; if you don't, you should.

The pre-prepared paste is the key to the simplicity and pace of the dish. Curry pastes are the backbone of Thai cooking, providing all the heat and many of the nuances of this marvellous cuisine. These pastes are a little like Indian spice mixes — you can expect a different recipe from each of your neighbours, but the basics are much the same — chillies, chillies, chillies, chillies, lemon grass, shallots, garlic and spices. I have seven books on Thai cooking, including one in English and Thai, and each of them has a variation on the theme. The only one of these published in Thailand, *The Best of Thai Cuisine* by Sisamon Kongpan, is the only one which does not list curry paste as a separate item.

Ms Kongpan, a teacher at the Department of Home Economics in Bangkok, prefers to list the required spice mix for curries with the appropriate recipe.

This is her mix for a curry paste to go with chicken: 5 dried chillies, 10 cloves garlic, 1 teaspoon sliced galangal, 1 tablespoon sliced lemon grass, ½ teaspoon sliced kaffir lime zest, 1 teaspoon coriander root, 5 black peppercorns, 1 tablespoon roasted coriander seeds, 1 teaspoon roasted cumin seeds, 1 teaspoon salt, 1 teaspoon shrimp paste. Ms Kongpan isn't one to offer modern methods to get your mix into a paste. She says: 'Place chilli paste ingredients in a mortar and pound until ground and mixed thoroughly.' For people with grinders and whizzers, the way to go is to grind the dried ingredients in a special coffee grinder (spices only) until powdered, then add to the rest of the ingredients in the whizzer until a paste forms. Most of the other writers, including Charmaine Solomon (*Thai Cookbook*) and Mogens Bay Esbensen (*Thai Cuisine*), suggest at least a cup of shallots or onions as part of the paste. Chillies vary from five (Ms Kongpan) to 'twenty to thirty' (Mr Esbensen). Mr Esbensen must have a diamond palate. He also says you can add more chillies, without affecting the heat of the paste — if you remove the seeds. Apparently the chillies he used at Port Douglas were somewhat milder than the incendiaries available in Bangkok.

Even so, there's a lot of bad press about chillies. To me they are the greatest of flavour enhancers, and frivolous use of them for fire is folly.

All that detail is fine, but for most of us, making curry pastes is a little bit like making tomato sauce. We'll get around to it eventually. The good news is that pre-made curry pastes of very good quality and flavour are readily available at Asian stores and large supermarkets. I suggest you try them first before you get stuck into the fine detail of your own curry paste. They keep very well, and it's a rare household which will make more than one of these curries a week. And then, when you make your own, you'll know what you've got to beat.

♥　♥　♥　♥　♥

**1 chicken breast per person (this recipe is just as appropriate with fillets of firm fish)**

**1 dessertspoon red curry paste (that's hot!)**

**200 ml coconut milk**
*Note that coconut milk is at the top of ingredients not recommended for those who have cholesterol problems (it has a high level of saturated fat). If that's you, just swap the coconut milk for low-fat yoghurt. If you use yoghurt, it will curdle a little; that's fine. Note, too, it's a good idea to add a little sweetness to the yoghurt: that, to me, is what makes coconut milk such a wonder in these sorts of dishes. For sweetness, you can add, at the top of the list, a split vanilla bean; at the middle, a little honey; at the end, some sugar. Please yourself, and your budget.*

**1 stem of lemon grass, chopped**
*Even though this is included in the paste, fresh lemon grass really does enhance the final product.*

**¹/₂ clove garlic, sliced finely**
*If you make Ms Kongpan's paste, you will have no need for the garlic.*

**¹/₂ cup fresh herbs, chopped or picked from the leaves**
*Thyme is excellent in this dish, as are tarragon, basil, and the most commonly used Thai herb, coriander.*

**1 onion, chopped finely**

1 Remove the skin from the chicken and pull away the underfillets for another day. Slash the chicken breasts several times three-quarters of the way through the breasts.

2 Whizz the curry paste and coconut milk/yoghurt together quickly, and add the sliced lemon grass, sliced garlic and herbs. Pour the mix over the chicken breasts, and leave for a couple of hours, turning the breasts here and there.

3 Heat the oven to 200°C. Cook the onion gently in a little oil, until softened, about 10 minutes. (You can leave this out, but the crunch and sweetness of the onion is a winner.)

4 Pour the sauce/marinade into the onion pan, add the chicken breasts, and gently bring to a boil. Boil for a minute, stirring to ensure there is no burning or sticking, and then place in the oven.

5 Cook for about 10 minutes, or until the chicken is just done and the sauce has thickened.

6 Serve the chicken with enough sauce to hold the breast. This

dish is delicious in the traditional way, with steamed rice; extra delicious in the Aussie way — with baked potatoes, steamed spinach, and cauliflower and white sauce, tinted with nutmeg. Try the latter, and see.

WINE ❖ *Depending how carried away you get with the chilli, you can swing from water to tea to a good New Zealand sauvignon blanc.*

♥

## TANDOORI CHICKEN, ALMOST

You're not ever likely to have a tandoor oven in the kitchen, never likely to have access to the brilliant dry heat of these marvellous Indian vats of cooking, but with a bit of trickery and a touch of magic, you can produce some of the flavours of the tandoor, simply.

♥　♥　♥　♥　♥

6 chicken breasts — 1 per person

### THE MARINADE

1 red pepper, roasted and peeled

1 onion, chopped finely

1 clove garlic, chopped roughly

1 similar-sized piece of ginger, skinned and chopped

salt

2 cups plain yoghurt, no sugar added

### THE PASTE

1 clove garlic, chopped

1 similar-sized piece of ginger, skinned and chopped

1 chilli, chopped

2 dessertspoons paprika

1 dessertspoon chilli powder

juice of 2 lemons

black pepper

### THE NIGHT BEFORE

1 The chicken needs to be marinated overnight, a bit like tired feet after a long march. Mix the red pepper, onion, garlic, ginger and a little salt with the yoghurt.

2 Make the paste: whizz the garlic, ginger, chilli, paprika, chilli powder and lemon juice together.

3 Remove the skin from the breasts and rub the paste all over them. They will have the bright orange-red colour of an auctioneer at the fall of the hammer.

4 Prick the chicken breasts all over with a fork and cover with the yoghurt marinade. Leave overnight.

### ON THE DAY

5 Heat the oven to flat out.

6 Cook the chicken on a tray until it is done, just giving to the touch. Turn the pepper mill over the top.

7 Serve with a dressed salad, with crisp bacon tossed through it; or a little of the marinade, brought to a boil, reduced and strained.

WINE ❖ *Big, full-flavoured fumé blanc or sauvignon blanc will suit this dish. Try Taltarni's or Tim Knappstein's. Another I like is De Bortoli, Windy Peak.*

♥
## A CHICKEN'S INNER SECRET

There is a most underestimated treasure lurking in poultry parlours and butcher shops across town. You might well have to search diligently for these little wonders, and perhaps even argue with your butcher as to your rights to them.

They are difficult to find because most of us wouldn't even think to look for them. Stuck on the underside of a chicken breast (or pheasant or squab or any flier), is the underfillet, attached to the breast by a few threads of sinew and fibre. This is the treasure.

It took me ages to wake up to the extra meal on every couple of chicken breasts. This is the ultra premium cut of the chook, needing a minimum of cooking — no more than a quick sear on each side in a very hot pan.

There's more to this salutary tale. The same lovely tender underfillet is part of every lamb. If you think well about your buying patterns, and grab an entire loin, bones and the works attached, you will see a deliciously pink and tender fillet clinging on like grim death (excuse me) to the edge of the fillet. This too, is pure tender pleasure.

It's very unlikely you'll be able to buy these things. Butchers and poulterers leave the chicken underfillet attached. You must pull it away and freeze it until you have enough for a meal. You will need at least two per person for a substantial feed. But think of it this way: it's free. The slightly smaller portion on a usual chicken breast meal will have no effect on anybody. If you are keen on chicken, it won't take long to gather enough underfillets for a substantial meal.

♥  ♥  ♥  ♥  ♥

**¹/₂ cup soy sauce**

**¹/₄ cup first-grade sherry**
*You should have a bottle of sherry handy for all occasions, including resuscitation when the pressures get you down. Even the best is cheap.*

**¹/₂ cup chicken stock, or water if you have none**

**1 hot chilli, chopped**

**1 heaped teaspoon brown sugar**

**sprig of rosemary**

**several sprigs of tarragon**

**2 tomatoes, skinned and chopped**

**8 underfillets of chicken (2 per person)**
*Next time you buy a chicken breast, have a look underneath. The spear-shaped piece, hanging by threads, is what we're talking about here.*

1 Mix together the soy, sherry, stock/water, chilli, sugar, herbs and tomatoes, and bring to the boil. Then simmer on a very low heat, just keeping everything at a bubble. The tomatoes will soften, then disintegrate, adding their body and flavour to the mix. Taste for seasoning.

2 Add a little oil to a pan and heat until very hot. Sear the chicken for about 45 seconds on one side, then turn and do the same on the other side. Remove from the heat and add the chicken to the simmering sauce. Turn off the heat and leave in a warm spot. The cooking of the chicken will be completed in the hot sauce.

3 Serve with simple noodles, the sauce tossed through, and the chicken pieces here and there.
Note: The chicken fillets love a simple marinade of equal parts of soy sauce and sherry, flavoured with a dessertspoon of honey per cup of marinade. Heat the lot through with chilli, garlic and ginger, until the honey has dissolved. Bring to the boil, allow to cool, then cover the fillets. Allow to sit for a few hours, then cook the chicken quickly in a hot pan. Serve with some hot marinade.

WINE ❖ *Full-bodied dry white, like a chardonnay, or medium-bodied red, are equally welcome — it depends what you feel like. If it's a chardonnay, don't chill it too much — the colder it is the less flavour it will give. Any old publican will tell you that if you chill the guts out of a crook white wine, no one will complain.*

♥

## GOPAL'S STUFFED CHICKEN BREAST

Gopal Kulkarni has a CV which would get him a job in just about any restaurant or hotel in the world. In fact it did, from Paul Bocuse's famed restaurant out of Lyon, to several huge hotels in England, India, Nigeria, and more, until finally he came to Australia to make his mark and his fortune. He finished in a place as far from the great hotels as imaginable — a tiny takeaway in Melbourne's eastern suburbs. The environment means nothing. The food he is cooking is as good as that from any five-star restaurant. I asked Gopal Kulkarni for the recipe for a delicious chicken dish, cooked quickly, and simply, in a spicy cream sauce. Here it is.

♥ ♥ ♥ ♥ ♥

4 chicken breasts, skin kept on

salt

black pepper

THE STUFFING

½ cup slivered almonds

paste of cashew nuts, made from ½ cup cashew nuts, whizzed

½ teaspoon mace

½ teaspoon nutmeg

salt

black pepper

½ dozen dried dates, chopped roughly

¼ cup basil leaves

a little onion paste: the paste from cooked onions

juice of 1 lemon

1 onion, chopped finely

touch of garlic, sliced finely

chicken stock or water

THE SAUCE

2 onions, chopped finely

2 cloves garlic, chopped finely

a little ginger, chopped finely

1 tablespoon sultanas

2 tablespoons fine broken cashews

salt

black pepper

a little sweet fenugreek

½ teaspoon garam masala*

pinch of chilli powder

1 cup cream

1 Season the chicken breasts well with salt and black pepper, slit the

breast quite deeply on the side closest to the bone, and leave for an hour.

2 Make the stuffing. Mix together the almonds, cashew paste, mace, nutmeg, salt, black pepper, dates, basil leaves, onion paste, lemon juice, onion and garlic, and force one tablespoon of stuffing inside the breast. Press the sides to enclose the stuffing, and flour the breast lightly.

3 Fry very lightly in a little oil. There is no need to fry them hard, just enough to change the texture, slightly.

4 Arrange the breasts in a pan to go to the oven, and sit them in a little chicken stock, made from no more than a carcass and water, simmered for a couple of hours. Cook at 200°C for 25–30 minutes, testing on the way. They should be firm but give slightly to the touch.

5 Allow the breasts to cool in the stock. This can be done several hours before serving.

6 Make the sauce. Cook the onions and garlic in a little oil until softened and then add the cream, spices, nuts and fruit, until the cream thickens — about 5 minutes.

7 Re-heat the chicken breast in the microwave — about 3 minutes on high. It should be warmed through, not cooked further.

8 Remove the cream from the heat, and add the chicken, spooning the sauce over the top. Leave for a couple of minutes. Then serve.

*Gopal's garam masala
1 teaspoon cloves, 1 teaspoon cinnamon, 5 teaspoons cumin, 2 teaspoons black peppercorns, 1 teaspoon cardamom pods, 5 teaspoons coriander seeds, 1 teaspoon star anise, 1 teaspoon fennel seeds, 1 teaspoon mace, ½ teaspoon nutmeg, 1 teaspoon dried bay leaves, 1 teaspoon kabab chini (like juniper berries — if not available, ½ teaspoon juniper berries).

Place the lot on a baking tray and put in a 150°C oven for about 20 minutes, just enough to remove any extra moisture. Then whizz. The best tool for this is a coffee grinder. Gopal says this mixture has been developed over many years and suits his palate. To me garam masala (warm spice mix) is a mix of whatever spices you have, try together, and like.

WINE ❖ *A wood-matured dry white (chardonnay or semillon) or medium-bodied shiraz with some 'black pepper' spice character is what you need. For both styles, try something from Eden Valley in South Australia.*

♥
## ROASTED SQUAB
Please read this after breakfast.

T he question is this: would we all be vegetarians if we had to kill before we cooked? I pose this curler after coming not from a kill, but from a clean.

I had dragged home a couple of squab — necks, heads, beaks and feet attached, feathers removed. Do you have the picture? I approached the job with a brave face, but there was a lump in the throat when the cleaver went through the bird's neck. Believe me, it is tough going, and it is something I much prefer to leave to somebody else. The first one was okay, a routine chop at the neck and feet, guts torn out, a bit of a wash, and it was ready for the pan.

Across the bench, the mother of our children said plaintively: 'They look so much like babies.' I gulped and soldiered on.

About then things started to go terribly wrong. I put the heavy knife through the little fellow's neck and, there was its last meal, a handful of dried peas. Now look here, you are saying to yourself, why is this mug putting such things down on paper for perpetuity? Simple, I want to elicit in you the sort of feelings that came through me. This was revulsion at its highest level. Even now as I write I wonder how I kept going. On your behalf, I suppose.

But is it not true? If we had to kill our own, would we not all be eating salads, rather than saveloys? Certainly not squab.

But, take note. If you treat squab just like any other bird or beast, it is truly a food of wonder. Deeply flavoured, on the way to gamey; rich, red, tender, lovely. Like most richly flavoured dishes, it needs little to improve its flavour. If you serve it in a salad, use a sweet vinegar to cut through the bird's richness — perhaps raspberry vinegar, or balsamic vinegar with a simple oil. There is nothing wrong with a strongly flavoured stock-based sauce, but it seems a waste of time to me.

Get your butcher to clean your squab. Wipe it inside and out, getting the skin as dry as you can. One bird will serve two people, easily.

1 Roast the squab in a hot oven for about 15 minutes. Remove from the heat, but leave in the same hot pan for another 10 minutes while you get the rest of the show organised. Squab is best served on the rare side of medium, but not dripping with blood. Cook it more, if your prefer. The breasts will be most tender when on the bottom side of medium, but still tender enough when dry and well done.

2 Cover the breasts with silver foil towards the end, or even better, slice the breasts free to leave the legs a little longer to cook.

3 The carcasses make for a delicious, rich, gamey stock — a wonderful base for a winter soup, laced with beans, carrots and pasta; or, at its simplest, tossed through rice or cooked into risotto.

4 You can slice the breasts and legs clear, and cook them quickly in the pan, or on the grill or barbecue. The breasts will take only a few minutes, at most. Serve with the breasts sliced very finely — about a dozen slices to the breast — and serve tossed through freshly made pasta, lightly touched with tomato and thyme; or simply through a rich virgin olive oil; or even more simply, allowed to cool and served as a squab sandwich on thin, homemade white bread, with stacks of black pepper.

WINE ✤ *Squab. On the way to gamey — like the hunter who came into a clearing to find a beautiful, naked woman. He slinked up and said, 'Are you game?' 'Yes,' she husked. So he shot her.*

*Penfold's style of red is the go here — Bin 389, Magill Estate or Bin 707, preferably one with six or more years bottle age.*

## ♥
## OX TONGUE, SIMPLY

It was while my little daughter was sliding her umpteenth slice of ox tongue down her tiny throat, like sardines into a pelican's gob, that I started to wonder what it is in the pickle that helps preserve the tongues, and then makes them go pink when you cook them.

Would she turn pinker if she kept up the intake? What else might be hidden in these gross appendages?

I asked about this at a couple of butcher's shops, and the reply was they used a pre-prepared pickling mix to pickle the tongues. It was also surprising to hear that the market for ox tongues was dwindling. Only old-time Australians, it seems, enjoy tongue any more. I rang the supplier and was told there was nothing to fear from the pickle. There was no saltpetre (potassium nitrate, one of the components of gunpowder), no sodium nitrate, and only a tiny (acceptable) amount of sodium nitrite, a simple salt which has been linked here and there to the development of carcinogens.

What you get in ox tongue is pretty much the same as you get in ham and bacon and salami and all those things we eat so much of we don't even think about what is used to cure them. I suppose we look at tongue with such distaste because of where it comes from, what it does when it's still at work, what it looks like, and how it feels.

It was suggested that children should probably eat fewer cured products than adults do, because of their smaller body mass. But maybe that rule applies more to ham than to tongue. Even I, who love tongue dearly, would serve it but a few times a year. So I think the little ones will survive on the salt, sodium nitrite (125 parts per million), spices and sodium erythorbate. (This is an extract of ascorbic acid or vitamin C, which is used to stop the meat from discolouring. It is the ingredient which stops hams going grey once they have been cut.)

So slip a tongue into your menus. There is no better way to enjoy it than sliced and sluiced with an intense beef stock, mashed potatoes on side; tongue and salad is a wonderful mix, much better than ham; and of course, why not warm, just from the pot, sliced, daubed with hot mustard and stuck between slices of crusty bread?

There is nothing to the cooking. Buy the tongue from a butcher you know and trust: there is nothing worse than buying a licker and discovering that it hasn't been pickled correctly, and there are rivers of grey and pink running through it when it is cooked.

1 Toss the tongue into a large pot of water and bring to the boil, then reduce to a simmer. The tongue will take at least 2 hours to cook, and that's that. All that has to be done during all this is to change the water in the pot once or twice to reduce any extra salt content. Remove any scum which could come to the surface.

2 After 90 minutes, and after the water has been changed, throw in some old-fashioned vegies — potatoes, carrots, parsnips, leeks, turnips — and herbs. The tongue is done when the tip gives to a gentle squeeze.

3 If you are going to use it straight away, peel away the tough, hairy

section — it comes off like the peel of a mandarin — and you will be left with a luscious, tender, subtly flavoured pink mass of loveliness.

4 Tongue keeps wonderfully well, and is just as good re-heated gently the next day, or the day after, or the day after that. It is far better hot, than it is cold.

How to use it:
♥ Serve with beef stock, mashed potatoes, and shelled peas tossed with finely chopped bacon in a gentle vinaigrette.
♥ Make a dressing of hot mustard, a little mild vinegar, a lot of full-flavoured olive oil, salt, black pepper, a sharp cheese and fresh herbs, especially parsley, and toss the warm tongue through the dressing. Serve the sliced warm tongue on top of the best mix of greens you can find, tossed with a walnut dressing, some cubes of a sharp cheese, and half a dozen chopped walnuts. It might sound a little strange, but I ran into a salad like this in a tiny hotel called Ma Clocher, in a tiny non-designer ski resort in France, le Mont Doré. This salad was based on cubes of delicious ham, but warm tongue is better.
♥ Cover one slice of thick, crusty white bread with rich butter and the other slice with a thin layer of hot English mustard. Slap a slice of warm tongue in the middle. Munch away.

WINE ✤ *Depending what accompaniments you serve with it, tongue will go with just about anything. Stay on the lighter side with the reds; the whites need something with a firm acid structure. I like the idea of an Eden Valley or Clare Rhine riesling with lots of fruit and acid structure.*

♥
## DIARY OF A DISASTER

I want to tell you about a disaster. It was pheasant season, and the call had come from my butcher. He had a beautiful brace of birds and he promised to keep them hanging in his cool-room until they were ripe, pluck them, gut them, and present them to me to turn into something special for special friends.

The time came, the birds were presented, and the man explained what a damned nuisance the pheasants had been to pluck. 'Their skin is so delicate,' he said. 'You have to be so careful with them.' Of course we don't ever think of such things. This is the society in which everything is done for us. I often hanker for the past, but I must say that pheasant-plucking is not a part of that hankering. Streets without cars, trains that run regularly and reliably, bakers on every corner, yes — but plucking pheasants, no.

You think I'm joking. Well I'm not. Let me quote you a few lines on plucking from one of my favourite books, *The Woman's Mirror* recipe book, publication date about 1930, target audience: housewives of Australia.

'Selection, preparation, and cooking of poultry. Seasonable hints by *Mirror* cooks. When a fowl is to be killed, starve it for 12 hours. The crop will then be empty and cleansing made easier. Dislocate the neck and pluck the bird while still warm. Remove the biggest feathers first, holding the bird by the legs, head down. If the fowl is cold, plunge it into hot water before plucking, then pluck quickly.'

See, you didn't believe me. That book is the equivalent of today's 'Women's Whatever Cook Book'. Haven't we got it easy these days?

Anyway, I tied up the breasts with whole sprigs of coriander, covered them with water and olive oil, sprinkled some chopped chilli over the top, and put the lot in the oven.

After 10 minutes, I checked them out, and all seemed well. The water was very hot, but not bubbling, and the breasts were well away from cooked through. Then the phone rang. It was my mother. We nattered away for a few minutes and the birds went out of my head, and then she started on a story and I remembered the birds but I couldn't draw myself to interrupt, and then she finished, and I said goodbye and rushed out, and the love of my life was at the oven door, looking in with hope and doubt in her eyes, and she said 'I didn't know what you wanted me to do,' and I said with hope and doubt in my voice that all would be well, while looking at the pheasants sitting in the hot stock shrivelling up, and she added that she hadn't cooked the pasta to go with the pheasants, and I swore and blamed her, and she said 'Well you should have told me,' and I swore again and blamed my mother, and our friends laughed, and we sat down and ate tough, overcooked pheasant, and got drunk.

Much later, I took pheasant at Stephanie's, the delicious Melbourne restaurant. It was so tender, so delightful. I asked Stephanie for the trick.

'You roast it very quickly,' she said, 'in a very, very hot oven.' 'Quickly' means about 9 minutes. 'Then,' she said, 'remove the bird, slice the breasts free and keep them in a *bain-marie* of stock, walnut oil, (and truffle juice) until the gentle heat of the stock has completed the cooking.' I can vouch for it. It was a ripper.

WINE ✤ *Well at least I can recommend something to get drunk with — only kidding! French Burgundy can do things to you, when consumed with pheasant, which rival Mozart or Beethoven on a good day. Unfortunately there is good and bad burgundy, and if you want a good one be prepared to part with seventy-odd dollars or more. The Aussie pinots nearly hit the high notes but just aren't quite there.*

♥

## DROWNED RABBIT

Rabbits have never been something to make the mouth water, but they are cheap, readily available, and have a firm place in Australian folklore. For all those reasons, rabbit is something you should have at the table several times a year. There's another reason for that: the longer you cook rabbit, the better you cook it. Don't ask me why; perhaps it's the subtle flavour which needs a bit of added personality. Perhaps it's like all slow-cooked dishes. The more you cook this way, the more you get to know about happy partners, about timing, about ideal presentation.

Don't be put off by the wildness of the rabbit. Despite the fact they hop about in the wild, they have none of that tongue-biting gamey taste, and they are the dickens to cook to tenderness. Even the loin is prone to dryness, no matter how gently you cook it. It has nothing at all in common with its much larger partner in the wild, the rich red hare.

You can try all sorts of marinades for the loin, you can wrap it in bacon fat, baste it, but it always seems to be on the edge of dryness. Never the melting tenderness of the loin of lamb or veal. These hoppers just don't have enough fat running through them, which, ironically, is a good reason for getting to know them better.

Usually I am into letting flavours speak for themselves, but with rabbit those flavours are so subtle you wouldn't hear them. But this makes them ideal candidates for slow cooking, and that's pretty much always been the way. I have vague memories of rabbit in milk, rabbit in a simple stock laced with carrots and potatoes. More recently, I have enjoyed rabbit cooked slowly, then shredded with bacon and served with tomatoes, olives and herbs.

♥ ♥ ♥ ♥ ♥

**2 rabbits, the lungs, kidneys and liver removed**
*Chop the rabbit into 5 segments: 2 front legs, saddle, 2 back legs. If you're into the richness of offal, you can make a tiny entrée with noodles or rice. Pan-fry the kidneys and liver briefly with a little garlic and toss with buttered noodles/rice and fresh herbs.*

**20 Roma tomatoes, skinned; or 500g tin of tomatoes, no added sugar, no added salt**
*Whichever you use, put them through the whizzer.*

**2 large carrots, sliced**

**2 large parsnips, sliced**

**2 hot chillies, sliced finely**

**2 cloves garlic, peeled, sliced finely**

**salt**

**fresh herbs: rosemary, thyme, or basil**

**black pepper**

**1 eggplant, sliced into circles**

**juice of 1 lemon**

#### THE DAY BEFORE

**1** Brown the rabbit pieces all over in a little oil, removing each from the pan as you go, to ensure consistent browning all over.

**2** Return all the rabbit pieces to a heavy-based pot and cover with the tomatoes, carrots, parsnips, chillies and garlic. The rabbit must be covered. If not, add a little water. Season with a couple of teaspoons of salt.

**3** Bring to the boil, then reduce the heat, and cook gently on a low heat for about 20 minutes, keeping your eye on the pot to make sure the rabbit is covered, and there is no chance of burning on the bottom. Pre-heat the oven to 200°C.

**4** Put the pot in the oven, and cook for another hour, removing the saddle after 45 minutes. The stock should have thickened and the rabbit should come easily from the bone. Add the herbs. The dish is best prepared several hours in advance and allowed to cool, so the flavours can be drawn out and come together.

#### ON THE DAY

**5** Re-heat the rabbit gently in its sauce.

**6** Put the eggplant slices, separated, on a flat, round plate. Cover with wrap and cook in the microwave for about 3 minutes until tender. Sprinkle with lemon juice and a touch of salt.

7 Place several eggplant slices on each plate, pour some tomato sauce and sprinkle some pepper over the slices. Serve the rabbit on top, surrounded by the vegetables from the pot.

8 If there are any leftovers, remove the meat from the bones, taking care of any tiny bones. Mix through the sauce and heat through gently. Serve with pasta, olives and herbs.

WINE ❖ *I remember last Christmas having a bunny that Jacques Reymond cooked and a glass of Mildara 1988 Coonawarra Cabernet Sauvignon. I can still remember the flavour of both. A good 'juicy' year from Coonawarra, like 1988 or 1986, is the go here.*

♥
## HARE, ON THE NOSE

F ine scents and quality foods don't necessarily marry. Think of the aroma of some of your favourite cheeses. Hardly alluring are they?

Game is the same. The best game looks like something left over from a Rambo movie, all blood and guts, and smells like an untended underarm, wiped clean with a pair of old socks. Whenever you are offered fair dinkum game in a restaurant it will just about always come with a *caveat emptor*. I have even seen a menu with this addendum to a hare dish:

'Beware: the only similarity between hares and rabbits is that they both hop. Don't believe they taste the same. Please ask our staff for further advice.'

You wouldn't find the same warning on a menu anywhere in Europe. Across the continent, the game season is anticipated with much relish. I will never forget the game stall at the Florence market. There were pheasants by the dozen, their necks still dripping from the slash of a butcher's knife; a deer hanging by its hooves from the roof; hare everywhere. Across the table lay a wild boar, disbelief still etched across its almost twitching snout.

Behind the counter stood the proprietor, a cigarette rammed between his teeth. He, too, had a gamey look about him. His apron was spattered with very old blood, and the boar, even in its rather advanced state of *rigor mortis*, had a better set of teeth.

Back home, hare is the only real thing in the game department. The only hare which gets to market comes from wizened old men who take to the bush and shoot the pests. I know this for sure as, one time in the restaurant days, a customer sent back a note with a very cleanly wiped plate, which, a few minutes earlier, had featured a fillet of hare. At the side of the plate were three little black balls, which I took, at first glance, to be peppercorns. I read the note:

'My compliments to the chef. The hare was delicious, and clearly gathered under authentic conditions. I suggest you give these pellets a good clean, and perhaps your hunter can use them again.'

For those of you who have not tasted hare, it might be wise to ask your game seller for a hare that has not long been shot. If they have been hanging around in their skins for a few weeks, as is the way for hare freaks, they get richer and richer, both on the nose and on the palate.

First triers might not be able to manage a hare which has spent a fortnight in heaven. But if you start your run at game with a freshly killed specimen, you should manage adequately, understand the strength of flavour, and go on to bolder tries. The longer the hare has been hung, the more tender it becomes. And when you cook it, don't fiddle with it. It needs a little something on the side to assist through the richness, like mashed potatoes or baby carrots, but certainly not a rich sauce, or a marinade.

♥    ♥    ♥    ♥    ♥

**1 fillet of hare, sinew and sheath removed**
*One fillet should serve 2 people, it is so rich. Trim away the thin end pieces, which run into the neck, so your fillet is of equal thickness through its length. Keep the smaller pieces for another quick meal.*

**¹/₂ cup good quality port**

**salt**

**black pepper**

1 Set the oven to its maximum temperature a few minutes before you start cooking.

2 Heat a little oil in a pan which can go in the oven. Place the hare fillet in the oil, moving it around so it does not stick. Brown all over and leave to cook on top of the stove for about a minute.

3 Place in the oven and cook for about 5–6 minutes longer, depending on the thickness of the fillet. Test by pressing the flesh with your forefinger. The hare should be served rare to ensure its tenderness and maximum flavour.

4 Set the hare aside on a warm, covered plate and scrape any sediment from the pan with the port. Reduce heavily over high heat, adding a little salt and some black pepper. Some people like to add a little sweet jelly to this sort of sauce. During the reduction, add any juice which may have run from the hare on to the plate.

5 Slice the hare thinly and serve with a little of the port reduction.

♥

## HARE, SLOW-COOKED

♥    ♥    ♥    ♥    ♥

**1 hare, jointed, fillets removed and kept separate**
*Trim the fillets as described in the previous recipe.*

**2 cups red wine**

**4 waxy potatoes, sliced into quarters**

**3 carrots, sliced roughly**

**1 celery stick, sliced roughly**

**1 clove garlic, sliced finely**

**1 hot chilli, sliced roughly**

**1 walnut-sized piece of ginger, sliced finely**

**water to cover**

**250g tin of tomatoes**

**3 teaspoons salt**

**pasta shapes**

**bunch of chives, chopped**

**salt**

**black pepper**

1 Brown the joints of the hare in a little oil. Remove and de-glaze with half the wine.

2 Put the lot into a stock pot —
the potatoes, carrots, celery, garlic, chilli, ginger and the rest of the
red wine, and cover with the water.
Add salt.

3 Bring to the boil, then turn down
to a mere bubble.

4 Cook for about 2 hours until the
hare is tender, and the carrots
and potatoes are just done.

5 Allow to cool. Drain the stock,
remove the hare joints, and pull
the meat from the bones. Discard
the bones. Set aside the vegetables.

6 Cook the tomatoes with a little
salt, in the microwave, until
thick.

7 Add the tomatoes to one cup of
the hare stock and cook rapidly
until it all comes together.

8 Add the hare and the vegetables
to the tomato sauce and cook
gently until all have heated through.

9 While the meat and vegetables
are warming through, roast the
hare fillets in a hot oven for 5–6
minutes, as above. They should be
served rare, or they will be tough.

10 At the same time, cook the
pasta.

11 Slice the hare fillets and add
them to the tomato-based
sauce with the rest of the vegetables
and hare. Toss through the pasta
and serve, well sprinkled with chives
and black pepper.

WINE ✤ *They certainly get great big
hares in Coonawarra. Maybe it has got*
*something to do with eating vines. As a
regional treat, Coonawarra hare and red
is hard to match. The longer you hang
it, the bigger and richer you will need the
red wine. The best hare catcher in Coonawarra is Demetry Zema. His 1988
Shiraz would slip down here very nicely
indeed.*

♥

## DUCK LIVERS WITH A CRISPY SKIN

The French, you will know
well, rave about the livers
of birds, notably that of
the goose, but also that of the duck.
Duck livers, too, are really the sort
of food which you really have to
love to like. There is no middle
ground. But to eat them rare is not
so much a matter of love, but ado-
ration. That's how I found them
at the restaurant Girardet near Lausanne in Switzerland. This is one
of the great restaurants of the world,
and the crispy-skinned duck livers
is one of the dishes most spoken
about.

Fredy Girardet has the knack of
serving the skin as crisp as a potato
chip, the middle as soft and tender
as butter. I tried many ways to find
the secret. What follows is the closest and the best I could do. Even if
you don't achieve ultimate glory
with the cooking, the combination
of livers, raspberry vinegar, apples
and tamarillos is a ripper.

♥   ♥   ♥   ♥   ♥

4 teaspoons vegetable oil or mild
olive oil

2 teaspoons raspberry vinegar

salt

black pepper

**2 livers per person; 3 would make for a substantial meal**

*Trim the livers of any excess fat and cut out any dubious green sludge.*

**a little of your favourite lettuce, washed and dried**

*Cos is a good choice.*

**1 sharp apple, peeled, cored, chopped into matchsticks and tossed in lemon juice**

**2 tamarillos, peeled**

*Tamarillos are often called tree tomatoes. They are sharp to the tongue, with a mild taste of tomato, but in truth they have a sweet–sour taste all their own. They are ideal for taking away the richness of game and liver.*

**small bunch of chives, chopped finely**

1 Whisk the oil into the vinegar until it becomes a little fluffy, and is emulsified. Season with salt and black pepper. It should have a strong taste of raspberry. The fruit in the salad and the dressing are not there for show, but to ease the liver's richness. The apple not only does that but adds much needed crunch to the dish.

2 Set the oven to its lowest mark.

3 Pat the livers as dry as possible with a tea-towel, and then paper towels. Leave for an hour on a wire rack, then dry again.

4 Place them, well separated, on a rack, and put them at the bottom of the oven for a few minutes. Turn them and leave for a few minutes longer.

5 You will need a very hot, heavy-bottomed pan, or a non-stick pan. When the pan is very hot, hit the livers very hard in the pan, using no oil. Work them around with a wooden spoon for about a minute, then turn them and do the same to the other side for about 30 seconds.

6 Leave them in the pan off the heat for about a minute, then remove. Slice one almost through to check its progress. It should be pink and juicy, not rare.

7 Toss the salad leaves and apple sticks with a little dressing. Slice the livers halfway through and toss through the dressing, so the dressing can enter the cuts. Spray the tamarillos all about. Sprinkle with chives and serve.

WINE ✤ *Liver does not suffer fools when it comes to wine — there's something about the richness and iodine flavour that knocks many wines for six. Try a good pinot noir with four to five years bottle age or a cool-area shiraz.*

♥

## BRAINS, FOR THOSE WHO NEED THEM, LOVE THEM

B rains used to be the real food of the masses; or more exactly, lambs' brains and bacon served with a beer at the counter of your local pub. Not these days: all these old-fashioned cuts have become very old-fashioned. The new man, the new woman, have no place in their lives for brains and livers and sweetbreads and tongue.

Some of that has to do with the remarkable concentrations of cholesterol in some of them, most of it to do with a lack of familiarity. Mum just doesn't serve these things any more it seems.

But if you put any of these dishes on a restaurant menu, you will find wonderful enthusiasm for them from the afficianados; a trusted restaurant is just about the only place they can get them now.

The few things to remember about cooking brains are:

(i) don't overcook them and send them mushy;

(ii) serve them with a heavily flavoured accompaniment — thus the bacon of the old days;

(iii) because of their soft, delicate texture, serve them with something crunchy and nutty to balance that texture.

The method described here is quite unusual, but the results are wonderful. If you like brains, you will love them cooked like this.

♥　♥　♥　♥　♥

### FOR THE TOPPING/TEXTURE CHANGE

a couple of rashers of bacon, cooked, fat removed and then chopped finely

50g almonds, finely chopped

small bunch of parsley, chopped somewhere between fine and rough

1/2 red pepper, skinned, seeded and finely chopped

a little salt

black pepper

enough clarified butter to cover the brains

*You can use ghee if you haven't the time to clarify the butter yourself.*

2 brains per person for a main course portion

*Be sure of your butcher when you buy brains. They have a short life after death. Soak the brains in several changes of cool water, removing any blood hanging*

about. *Remember if you have diet problems and love brains: they are almost pure cholesterol.*

a mild-flavoured mustard

1 Combine the bacon, almonds, parsley, red pepper, salt and black pepper until well mixed.

2 Heat the clarified butter until just warm to the touch and add the brains. The butter should be just warm to start, or the brains will fall apart.

3 Bring the butter just to the boil, then reduce to a bare simmer. The brains will take about 20 minutes to cook. It is rather difficult to describe how you will know the brains are cooked. They don't feel like brains cooked just right. In fact they don't really obey any of the usual rules of cooking. They look as though they are severely undercooked. They are not. The first time you try them, take a slice, a deep breath and eat.

4 When the brains are cooked, they will still retain their curious shape and softness. Smear the top with the mustard, and sprinkle with the bacon, red pepper and parsley mixture.

5 Serve with a little butter and lemon juice; or a chunky tomato sauce. Brains also need a few crunchy vegetables, like broccoli or beans, to assist.

WINE ✚ *In Geoff's restaurant days, I was accused of being the entrée bore — I went for the brains nine times out of ten. They have quite a lovely texture which lends itself to méthode champenoise, fine, structured chardonnay or elegant red. Try French Chablis with some*

bottle age for a treat — or, if I do say so
myself, Murrindindi Chardonnay with
at least three years on it.

♥

## A ROSE BY ANY OTHER
## NAME

I always believed 'sweetbreads' was a modern moniker, a name doubtlessly dubbed by a smart butcher who couldn't get rid of the not-so-little bloody blobs known more correctly as the thymus glands of vealers and lambs. Sex on the cover of a novel is said to guarantee sales, so sexy names to move non-sellers. Not so. According to the *Shorter Oxford*, the term has been hanging around in English since the sixteenth century. Mr Oxford has no idea why, although it seems that 'brede' can mean roast meat. The Latins were not so prim, calling it as they saw it — *glandium vitulinum* (veal glands).

Australians generally couldn't care less what you call these glands. Despite a notation in an old Australian cook book I picked up for $2 at a book sale (marked up from 50 cents!) that sweetbreads are 'considered a great delicacy, much used for entrées, and a good dish for invalids', I have seen them only once or twice in a butcher shop. I can guarantee that my mother never put them to table. Not even as a substitute for scallops, the closest thing in texture and flavour.

Their absence from the meat-sellers' shops is simple to explain. Sweetbreads apparently greatly assist our balance of payments. They are ripped out, stuffed into plastic bags, snap-frozen and sent to more appreciative places far and wide in 27-kilo lots. Even whole vealers come to the butcher minus their sweets. Nobody seems to complain.

The way to cook them is to hardly cook them at all. Soak them for a couple of hours to get rid of any nasty blood. Toss them into some boiling water for a minute or so to firm them up, and to assist you to remove the membranes and plumbing devices. Break them into their fairly small components, removing any membrane and pipes as you go — they will end up about the size of walnuts. Keep them covered in a little stock if you have some, or water if you don't.

1 Heat a little oil in a very hot pan. Throw in the sweetbreads. If you are adept with your wrist, toss them around for no more than a minute. If you have a limp wrist, use a wooden spoon. Coat them with walnut oil and spoon the sweetbreads onto some heavily buttered toast. Sprinkle some lemon juice and black pepper over the top. It could be the start of a beautiful friendship.

2 Sweetbreads are brilliant in salads, tossed in a nutty oil like walnut oil, especially with nuts, avocado, generous lacings of lemon and orange zest and — a real clincher — roasted and peeled red peppers.

WINE ✤ *If you are putting them on toast on a cold Sunday afternoon, why not serve a not-so-small glass of amontillado sherry? Don't put it in one of the terrible little shot glasses that you got sherry served to you in at bush weddings. Put it in a decent wine glass and swirl it around — something you can stick your nose in.*

# SWEETS: FROM BREAKFAST TO SUPPER

The best dessert ever made starts with a punnet of perfectly ripe raspberries, fresh from the vine, picked at summer's dusk; warmed through until the berries give just a little of their juice. The lot is then poured over vanilla bean ice cream, fresh from the churn.

But if you stop there, you stopped watching cricket when Bradman retired; gave up tennis when Laver departed; and found no time for golf, post-Thomson.

There's a modern train of thought which says that the perfect meal ends with perfect, seasonal fruit, and plenty of it. There's much to be said for that school, but it neglects two fundamentals: making delicious desserts is without question the most satisfying plank in the cook's platform; and a classic dessert is guaranteed to lead to a standing ovation. Will a bowl of the best raspberries, a tropical passionfruit, a mango from the Philippines, a rollinia from Queensland, or the first Jonathan of the season do that?

Desserts are the greatest diet busters imaginable. I am surprised, in fact, that Adam lost his way with a mere apple (certain to have been a Jonathan). I reckon he would have fallen earlier if Eve had concocted an early version of Girardet's passionfruit soufflé; or if she had cooked the apples, ground them to a purée, and covered them with a crumble; or if she'd sat next to him at table, taken a chocolate mousse with her fingers, and licked the bowl clean, a gleam in her eye. Who could resist such overtures?

I can't. Never could, never will. Desserts were always important to our growing family. I think my mother recognised early on that main courses were treated as fuel, and desserts as the main event. Choruses of 'Thanks for dinner, mum,' always followed one of her classic puddings or pies; mumbles after roast lamb and a bowl of fruit.

Desserts are paradise for a creative cook. The foundations have been set by generations, and now we can fine-tune, bring forward lost flavours, fiddle endlessly, and create something uniquely ours. There will be failures along the way; but there is no fun without a fumble.

## WHAT YOU'LL NEED

**1** A battery of bowls, for mixing, cooking, storing.

**2** A rubber spatula to draw up the absolute last piece of foam, or batter, or sauce from the bowl.

**3** A large balloon whisk to make your whisking so much easier, and several wooden spoons for beating.

**4** A quality pastry brush, to get your pastries shining. Pay a little more: you don't want the brush to leave its bristles on the pastry.

**5** A Kenwood or Kitchen-Aid mixer, or equivalent. For some reason or other, these marvels drifted out of favour with the introduction of the food processor. Don't fall for that. There is a place for each in the world. How else can you cream butter or eggs easily? Keep your eyes peeled for a bargain in the trading papers.

**6** A vigorous food processor. Don't believe they are all the same. The absolute champion for me is an early domestic version produced by Robot, the makers of the big commercial models, and later the Magimix. My whizzer is called a Robot Chef, and I bought it in 1979. It served five years in a restaurant kitchen, before the bowl collapsed. I fluked a hardly used version from a trading paper, and it fills me with joy when I use it. This was a case of the first model being the best. If you ever see one, snap it up. Whatever you buy, make sure it has a powerful motor, no less than 500 watts.

**7** A large bench. I couldn't do without a big bench. Where else to put all the bowls, and the elbows of the 'helping' children? If it's marble, you're lucky, but don't go out and buy marble unless you make heaps of pastry.

**8** A fair dinkum ice cream machine is the ultimate luxury. Not only does home-made ice cream lift any meal from the ordinary to the extraordinary, it is also a whizz for cocktails, especially those based on champagne. This is another thing which turns up in trading papers: well-meaning husbands buy them for wives who can't be bothered making ice cream. I know; that's how I got mine.

**9** A microwave is indispensable for stewing fruit perfectly, and making the quickest, easiest and best jams and jellies. If all a microwave could do was this, it would make me happy.

**10** Vanilla beans by the truckload. I used to think vanilla beans were expensive until I discovered the labour involved in growth, harvest and marketing the little dears. Try these for size: the vanilla plant (*vanilla planifolia*) is a member of the orchid family, which climbs and creeps and can grow as long as 110 metres! Grown commercially, it is allowed growth of 1.5 metres; its favourite growing places are the wetlands of Africa; Madagascar produces 50 per cent of the world's natural vanilla; vanilla flowers are hand-pollinated for several months; the green pods are scent-free, and undergo a five-month process of baking, sweating, wrapping in woollen blankets and baking in the sun, before they are exported in metal boxes lined with grease-proof paper.

No wonder they are so expensive. We shouldn't really quibble with the cost anyway — they provide ecstasy to creams and cakes. Pay; damn the cost.

**11** Fancy moulds, to turn the ordinary into the extraordinary.

**12** Your grandmother's recipe book; where else will you find perfect, time-worked puddings, that work all the time? Don't let these wonderful concoctions disappear. If they are all stuck inside her head, ply her with sherry and get them written down. You owe them to your children too.

**13** A sugar thermometer is a perfect tool to let you know just how far you can go when cooking custard. You won't need it after a while — your eye will do the job — but it will set you on the path to desserts glory.

## THE RECIPES

♥
## CUSTARD, THE KEY TO THE DOOR; TO ICE CREAM AND MORE

C ustard is one of those things we should mark down as an early and vital lesson in learning to cook, leading as it does to so many wonders at the end of the meal. What would a Christmas pudding be without a custard sauce? How would you sink into profiteroles without pastry cream? And ice cream just ain't ice cream without custard as its base.

Not so many years ago, when I was an ankle-biter and the big sisters were learning how to cook, I took part in an ice cream tasting. This was ice cream made without custard, held together with gelatine and frozen in the ice-block trays so important to the new electric fridge. The ice cream was icy, filled with bubbles of gelatine which had set awry, and tasted like nothing at all. I, who then and now would eat ice cream in a blizzard, would not even touch it.

It was not because of the trays. It was the base — no custard, no ice cream. I know now you can make pretty good ice cream in ice-block trays if you use common sense. Decide early that it's not going to be as good as that from a churn, and it will still have its place at table. The secret is that you make it for consumption not only for use on the same day, but almost within the hour — well before the mix is frozen solid. For example, if you want to show people how smart you are at 10.00 p.m., throw your mix into the freezer at 7.30 p.m. It won't be per-

fect, but the flavour will be wonderful, and the mix left melted on the plate will be just the same as melted perfect ice cream.

♥   ♥   ♥   ♥   ♥

## A BASIC CUSTARD

2 cups milk (or one each of milk and cream for a richer custard)

1 vanilla bean

75 g caster sugar

4 egg yolks

1 Pour the milk-cream into a heavy-based saucepan. Split the vanilla bean down its length and scrape the fine seeds into the milk, with the pod as well. Add half the sugar and bring to the boil, stirring so all the sugar dissolves cleanly.

2 The next step is best done with an electric whisk or a Kenwood, but it is not so daunting that you wouldn't do it with a hand whisk. Whisk the rest of the sugar through the egg yolks, until the sugar has dissolved and the mix is light, white and forms a ribbon.

3 Pour a little of the flavoured warm milk into the egg-sugar mix, whisking, so that the mixture can be easily poured. Pour egg-milk-sugar mix back into the rest of the vanilla-flavoured milk.

4 Bring back to a low heat and cook, stirring constantly with a wooden spoon until the mix registers 85°C on a sugar thermometer. If you don't have one, keep stirring until the mix noticeably thickens and forms a clean pair of lines when

you rub your finger across the back of your mixing spoon.

5 When the temperature is right, you must stop cooking quickly. The best way is to pour the mix through a fine sieve into a cool bowl, whisking vigorously as you go.

For an infused custard, add mint, vanilla beans, chocolate, etc. during cooking; for a flavoured custard, add muscat, brandy, and so on after cooking.

### ICE CREAM

**2 cups milk**

**2 cups cream**

**1 vanilla bean**

**150g caster sugar**

**4 egg yolks**

1 Follow the previous steps 1–5, adding the cream with the milk. Allow the mix to cool, then refrigerate until very cold. Despite the fact that ice cream is obviously frozen, take it as a rule to cook everything before you go to the churning stage. If you have an ice cream churn, it's just a matter of churning until just about set, then spooning into an ice-cold container. If you don't have a churn, don't despair, try the following method, but make sure you serve it the day it is made.

2 Pour the cold mix into flat trays in the freezer. After about an hour, remove and whisk furiously with a heavy fork, taking care not to spill any.

3 Do the same again, more gently, after another hour, then, again after another hour. Just before you serve it, take a strong spoon and fold the mix on itself, rather than beat it. Serve it just under fully set. It won't be creamy ice cream, but it will be the next best thing.

♥
### CARAMEL ICE CREAM

You must make the caramel first. Add a little water to 150g sugar, and gradually bring the mix to the boil. Keep cooking on a gentle heat until the mixture bubbles and then turns to a caramel. It should reach 160°C. Set aside in a warm place and then follow the routine for making ice cream, whisking 25g of sugar with the 4 egg yolks. Heat the milk and cream with the vanilla bean, exactly as described in the basic ice cream recipe. Add the milk-cream slowly to the caramel, taking care it does not spurt. Bring to the boil again.

Continue as for vanilla ice cream.

Caramel ice cream is particularly delicious when churned with praline — almonds set in caramel — and then broken into tiny pieces.

To do this, cook some sugar to a caramel. Add 100 g chopped almonds and mix through. Pour the caramel-almond mix onto greased metal tray. Allow to cool. Break up and chop or whizz into small pieces. Store in an airtight container.

♥
### CHOCOLATE ICE CREAM

Make the basic custard, adding 100 g rich, dark chocolate in small chunks when the custard has reached the correct temperature. Whisk the chocolate through the warm custard, until it melts and the mix has turned a rich brown colour. Churn in the usual way.

♥
## BAVAROIS

Add 6 leaves of leaf gelatine (don't use the grains — you can taste them) and your flavouring after step 5 of the basic custard recipe, and while the mixture is still warm. Allow to cool until almost set. Fold in 2 cups of whipped cream — whipped to achieve the same consistency as the almost set custard — when the gelatine has almost done its job. The custard (with the gelatine added) and the cream should have the same consistency. Mould and refrigerate. Unmould, to present in triumph.

♥
## PASTRY CREAM

Follow the basic custard recipe, adding 40 g sifted flour after step 2. And instead of stopping the cooking when the mix reaches 85°C, bring to the boil, stirring furiously for a minute. Don't let it stick and don't be a wimp about stirring. When cooked, force through a sieve and allow to cool. If you wish to make a chocolate custard, add your chocolate when you take the pan off the heat, and beat it into the mixture.

♥
## FRUIT SOUP

There's another, very simple dessert to put together with custard. You just make the custard, whizz a fruit purée through the custard, and serve

it very cold with another type of stewed fruit.

1 Put a bowl of very cold custard and a similar amount of stewed apricot purée into the processor, and purée quickly. It doesn't matter if there are streaks of this and that. Place in the coldest part of the refrigerator for several hours.

2 Place some stewed blood plums, syrup strained, in a cold bowl and pour the custard over the top. Drizzle with the syrup kept aside from the plums.

WINE ✤ *One day, try some good old Rutherglen muscat with ice cream. Even better, put it in the fridge for a few days, then use it as topping — it will be gluggy and rich and wonderful.*

♥
## CREME BRULEE FROM NEW YORK'S LE CIRQUE

Crème brûlée is one of the simplest of desserts, and a triumph to serve — if you have the equipment to do the job. I fiddled and failed several times with this dessert all over the place — at home, in the restaurant, all ways — but couldn't get that glassy caramel on top of the silky smooth custard. I had given it away until a visit to Le Cirque, the New York restaurant.

This is one of those typical swank Manhattan Italo-French eating houses, with tables close enough together to allow you to cuddle the person sitting next to you, a person who may or may not be a close friend. It is one of old Ronnie Reagan's favourites, which may or may not be an advantage. The waiters have just the right mix of arrogance and twinkling eyes. We had praised the food universally, an event which caused the gruffly spoken Italo-American to mutter, smile: 'Of course. It is as good as the service.'

The five of us hopped into the crème brûlée. So good is this version that Paul Bocuse, the great French chef, has included it on his menu, calling it *'crème brûlée Sirio'* after Le Cirque's proprietor, Sirio Maccione. The dish was a triumph. A richly flavoured, smooth-as-smooth custard, exploding with vanilla seeds, all topped with a crunchy, glassy caramel. Perfect.

I asked Daniel Boulud, Le Cirque's chef, for the recipe. Certainly, he said. 'It is very simple.' Then he smiled, and screwed up his face a little. 'As long as you don't cook the custard too long, and you don't put too much sugar on top.'

He might have added another rider. For perfect crème brûlée, you need a blow torch or a red-hot sala-mander (griller) to achieve perfect glassy crackle-crackle caramel. But even if you haven't either of these, the dish is worth trying. Even 80 per cent right, it's still a winner — and then you'll give the dish greater re-spect when you come across a per-fect version in a restaurant. Even without the sugar on top, it is a de-licious moulded custard.

♥　♥　♥　♥　♥

1 vanilla bean

500 ml cream

65 g caster sugar

3 egg yolks

brown sugar for the top

**1** The recipe is simple, as the chef said, but there are plenty of ifs, buts, twists, turns and maybes, as we shall see. Heat the oven to 160°C. Scrape the seeds from the vanilla bean into the cream, and warm the cream with the vanilla pod and seeds until it just starts to bubble and has thinned. Set aside.

**2** Whisk the caster sugar with the egg yolks until the yolks have thickened and whitened.

**3** Remove the vanilla pod and whisk the cream slowly into the egg yolk mix. (Dry the pod and put it into your sugar jar. It will infuse the sugar with its deli-cious aroma.)

**4** Pour the flavoured, enriched cream into flat gratin dishes, or flat ceramic pie moulds. Single-serve soufflé moulds are too big. This dish should be offered in small serves, else it is too rich.

**5** Warm about 2 cm of water in a flat pan, or a baking dish. It should be no more than warm to the touch, but well away from boiling. Gently place your moulds in the pan, and put the lot into the oven. Daniel Boulud says it takes about 30 minutes to cook. I reckon it takes more like 45 minutes. Remember, this custard does not have to set rock-solid. It should thicken and firm up, but it will never be like the custards and crème caramels you buy in coffee shops.

**6** You'll need to keep an eye on it as it cooks. It needs only to be firm enough to hold a thin layer of sugar. Don't panic if it takes longer than 45 minutes; some of this depends on your oven. If the custard gets too hot, it will curdle.

7 Remove gently from the oven, making sure no water splashes into the custard. Allow to cool, then refrigerate, covered with a plastic wrap. Half an hour before you are ready to cook the caramel 'glass', heat the grill flat out.

8 Sift the brown sugar over a bowl, then sift it again over the custard, spreading it thinly over the top. It should be no thicker than the cover of a paperback book.

9 Place the sugar-covered cream under the grill, about 5 cm from the flame. Watch it closely. It should take about 90 seconds. This is the sort of recipe which teaches as you try. You have to know how hot your grill is and how well it works. Trial and error. (Boulud's recipe, by the way, says 12 seconds! They must have a white-hot salamander at Le Cirque. Most restaurants prefer to use a blow torch, so don't be alarmed if you peek through a kitchen door and see a chef brandishing a fearsome flame. He or she is not about to attack the kitchen-hand.)

10 Remove it gently, as the top will be very hot and probably bubbling. Leave for a few seconds and don't be tempted to feel the top to check its firmness. The temperature of the caramelised sugar is more than 150°C, and touching it will give you an instant, painful blister.

11 You might not succeed at the first time, or second, or third, but keep trying. The result might never be as perfect as that at Le Cirque, but even a silver medal is still worth winning.

WINE ✤ *Rutherglen tokay, like muscat, is a unique style of wine and one of which Australians can be enormously proud. Try Baileys, Bullers, Chambers, or Morris's. Any of them will be perfect with this.*

♥
## CHILDHOOD MEMORIES: A KREEM-B-TWEEN

T he concept of the Kreem-b-tween was a triumph for Peters Ice Cream. You know the company — it went by the swinging slogan 'The Health Food of a Nation'. The health freaks of the nineties might dispute that ice cream is a health food, stuffed, as it should be, with eggs, sugar, milk and cream! I love it with a passion.

The Kreem-b-tween worked because it combined the simplicity of the best vanilla ice cream with the crunch of delicate biscuits. As a commercial product it was superbly conceived. You could eat it on the run, and it tasted better than most mass-produced ice creams. I thought that if it worked so well with the inadequacies of commercially made ice cream, and often stale biscuits, what if it was made it with perfect ice cream and crunchy, flavoursome, yet delicate biscuits? It worked beautifully. It tastes great, looks great; on its own, or lying in a fruity sauce, with lots of fruit splashed around. You could make it with any ice cream flavour, but to me, ice cream made with vanilla beans is the best. Vanilla ice cream enhances just about any dessert, the only possible exception being chocolate cake.

With that, the rich chocolate needs a fruity sorbet.

♥　♥　♥　♥　♥

## THE ICE CREAM

2 cups milk

2 cups cream

1 vanilla bean

150g sugar

4 egg yolks

## THE WAFERS

110g butter

130g sugar

2–3 egg whites

zest of 1 lemon

130–140g plain flour, sifted

1 Make the ice cream (see page 182) and spoon it into a square mould. You must have a churn to make this ice cream. It must be perfect, yet much firmer than the usual serving consistency. A square bread tin is ideal. The tin should be tall enough to make two Kreem-b-tweens when a slice is cut in half. In case you've forgotten, each Kreem-b-tween will be about 10cm x 5cm x 2cm.

2 You will need a good solid baking tray and a food processor. Heat the oven to 200°C. Cut out some cardboard templates in the shape of rectangles — about 5 cm x 10 cm is a good shape. The butter should be quite soft. In the blender, cream the butter, sugar, lemon zest and egg whites until smooth. Add the flour gradually. The mix will finish like softened butter.

3 Using a spatula or wide knife, wipe the mix on to a baking tray. The mix should be no thicker than the hard cover of a book. Bake briefly — no more than a few minutes — until golden colour.

4 This paste can be moulded to just about any shape you like while it is still warm. You can cut it into squares and slip over a tea-cup — and you've got a pastry cup. Use it any way you like. For our purposes cut out rectangles — using the template on the baking tray — and put the completed biscuits in a stack. Allow to cool. The biscuits will still be malleable. As they cool, they will become firm and crisp, yet delicate. They will keep very well in an airtight jar.

5 Prepare the ice cream. Ten minutes before unmoulding, put a cold tray in the freezer. Unmould the ice cream onto the tray. This is best done by dipping the base of the tray into warm water. Put the ice cream back into the freezer, until it is very firm.

6 Slice the ice cream with a warm knife into slices about 2 cm thick. The ice cream should be sliced about half an hour before it is served. Don't do it much earlier as it could gather some ice from the freezer. Unlike most ice cream, this dish is best if served quite firm. Not so hard that you need a laser to cut through it, but solid enough to hold its form in the biscuits, and solid enough so you will need to bite it first, then let it fade away.

7 Put the ice cream onto a wafer and put another wafer on top. Sprinkle the top of the top wafer with icing sugar. Sit one 'Kreem-b-tween' on a fruity sauce (a purée of mangoes with orange juice and a

sprinkling of passionfruit is terrific), and place another — at right angles — on top. Eat it with your fingers and you will feel like a kid again!

WINE ❖ *With the fruity sauce for the Kreem-b-tweens I'd go for a botrytis style of white wine. In Australia, these are generally produced from Rhine riesling or semillon. They are expensive because they are very costly to make.*

♥

## PEACH MELBA THE WAY IT USED TO BE, SHOULD BE

S ometimes we forget the most simple things. Which is why there has been such a trend in smart restaurants to serve up the old dishes that have been forgotten or so mistreated by years of sloppy cooking that they have been discredited. Thus lamb shanks, fish 'n' chips, pesto, bread and butter pudding, a dozen others ... and peach Melba.

My first peach Melba was a dessert in one of the old Coles cafeterias. Here we had sliced cling peaches from a tin, vanilla ice cream, and sickly raspberry sauce, the same desperately sweet concoction used in milk shakes. It was all a far cry from the turn-of-the-century dish created by Georges Auguste Escoffier for Dame Nellie Melba during one of her sojourns at London's Savoy. Singing must have been a fair little earner in those days. Melba stayed at the Savoy for a year during one of her seasons in London.

The legendary Frenchman seemed to have been pretty much at the top of his form when he created this favourite, presenting the poached peaches and vanilla bean ice cream in a swan cut from ice. It was served in a lightly sweetened raspberry sauce.

But now this brilliantly simple dish has been complicated and reduced to ridicule. If you put together the original ingredients the way they were meant to be, you will have something to sing about.

♥  ♥  ♥  ♥  ♥

### THE RASPBERRY SAUCE

**1 cup best quality muscat, if you have it**

*It will add a wonderful richness to the raspberry sauce, but if you haven't got it, don't go out and buy it. A perfect raspberry purée, sweetened a little, is marvellous anyway.*

**20 g caster sugar, depending on the natural sweetness of the raspberries**

**2 punnets of raspberries, most of them for the sauce, several for the plate**

### THE PEACHES

**sugar to taste**

*Aim for about 100 g sugar per litre of water.*

**water to cover**

**2 medium peaches per person**

1 Bring the muscat and sugar to a simmer while stirring, and cook gently for a couple of minutes, until all the sugar has dissolved. Allow to cool a little, then add the raspberries, and bring to a simmer again, mixing the raspberries through the muscat-sugar mix. Cook for a couple of minutes more on a gentle heat. When the raspberries have softened, purée in a food machine, and sift the seeds from the sauce. Taste, adding more sugar if you need it — I doubt it, but you never know. Set aside to cool, then refrigerate.

2 Escoffier, and almost everybody else, suggests you halve and skin the peaches. I prefer to cook them as they are, in a very gentle syrup, then rub the skin from them and serve them whole. If you cook them in their skins and leave them that way overnight, the pigment in the skin will colour them deliciously, and they look marvellous on the plate. There's only one difficulty. You have to impale them with a fork to eat them. It's worth it — after all, we never complain about eating corn that way, do we?

So, make a syrup with the sugar and the water, bringing the solution to a gentle boil. If you have plenty of money, simmer with a vanilla bean, split through the middle. Return to a simmer and poach the peaches gently in an open pot until tender — 10–15 minutes, depending how many peaches you have in the pot. Once cooked, refrigerate them overnight in the syrup. Remove and discard the mottled skins, then re-turn the peaches to the syrup. They must be very cold.

3 Make your own vanilla bean ice cream (see page 182). It's the only way. You will then have brought together three of the greatest of ingredients in cooking: vanilla bean, peaches, raspberries, and a pretty fair singer as well.

4 Serve two very cold peaches per person, with a little syrup still clinging; a large scoop of the ice cream; and the raspberry sauce poured over the ice cream with a lit-tle on the peaches. Scatter some fresh raspberries all about.

WINE ✣ *Botrytis is a mould that in-fects grapes late in their ripening and concentrates their sugar levels. It's some-times called Noble Rot. The great sweet wines of Bordeau (Sauternes and Barsac) and Germany are made from grapes thus affected. Australia is pro-ducing some wonderful botrytis styles. My favourites are De Bortoli's, some of Wolf Blass' and Lindemans.*

♥
## PEPPERMINT ICE CREAM WITH CHOCOLATE CHIPS

The best ice cream is vanilla bean ice cream, the best dessert is vanilla ice cream with just-warmed-through raspber-ries, but …

… you have to vary the routine occasionally, or else you'll be sick of it before you know it. I made my way down this course when the pep-permint bush started to grow and grow and grow just outside the back door.

Flavouring ice cream is simple — as long as the flavouring to be used is potent. Thus most fruits don't make for great ice creams, no matter how ag-gressive their flavour when you bite into their flesh.

Save fruits for sorbets. Sorbets are pretty much the simplest form of ice — just a mix of juice and purée, and occasionally zest — mixed or whizzed with a similar volume of sugar syrup. The proportions of the syrup are rather important — 800 g sugar and a litre of water brought to the boil and bubbled rapidly until the solution forms large bubbles. The fruit content depends on the fruit and the season. But generally, I have found that the add and taste method is best.

With ice cream, it's best to go for flavourings that are powerful and you know work and taste attractive at all levels of the palate — don't just choose a flavour to be different. So go for cinnamon, but forget asparagus; be happy with peppermint, but dismiss rose petals; try lemon verbena and decide; and when in doubt you know you can always rely on vanilla beans.

The best ice creams and sorbets come from the best churns. If you're keen to make ice cream regularly, then invest in a real churn. And if you really want to taste ice cream at the peak of its glory — take it straight from the churn.

♥   ♥   ♥   ♥   ♥

2 cups milk

2 cups cream

150 g caster sugar

bunch of peppermint

½ vanilla bean, split along its length

4 egg yolks

30 g your favourite chocolate, in bite-size chips, or grated

1 Mix the milk and cream with half the sugar. Toss in the peppermint and the vanilla bean, the seeds scraped from the pod into the cream.

2 Bring the mixture to the boil, stirring to dissolve the sugar. Remove from the heat.

3 Whisk the egg yolks with the rest of the sugar, until blended, and keep whisking until the mixture whitens and forms ribbons.

4 Pour a little of the flavoured milk-cream into the egg-sugar mix, and then pour back into the saucepan off the heat.

5 On a low heat, stirring all the while, heat the flavoured cream-eggs mixture until it thickens (85°C). Remove, force through a sieve to remove the peppermint and vanilla bean, and plunge the saucepan base into cold water to stop the cooking, whisking to assist the reduction in temperature.

6 When cool, place in the fridge, covered with plastic wrap until cold; then churn, tossing in the chocolate chips. (If you prefer, leave the peppermint flavour to itself, and grate the chocolate over the top at the table.) Put your mould in the freezer while the mix is churning.

7 When churned, spoon into the very cold bowl. Make sure you remove from the freezer and put into the fridge at least 20 minutes before serving. Solid ice cream is most off-putting.

Note: If you like moulded ice cream for a dessert, the peppermint makes a terrific partner for chocolate ice cream. Just put into a teacup shaped mould, large or small, individual or for a party, and leave a hole for some chocolate ice cream. Make the chocolate ice cream (see page 182) and spoon it into the hole. Freeze and serve, sliced. This version is marvellous in the old 'bombe' moulds.

WINE ✤ *As a rule, wine and chocolate don't mix. As a second rule, peppermint and wine don't mix. Rutherglen muscat's about the only thing I have found to match chocolate-based desserts.*

♥

## RHUBARB PARFAIT, WITH A DIFFERENCE

I first ran into this type of dessert in a little hotel in the middle of France. We were all bemused to see on the menu 'soufflé glacé'. Something wrong here, I thought. How can you have an iced soufflé? 'Simple,' said the *maître d'*, 'It's just a parfait, frozen inside a mould extended by some cardboard tied around the edge to extend its height, so, when the cardboard is removed it looks like a soufflé.' Touché.

I tried it when we came back, but was always disappointed that because the mix had not been churned, it was always a little icy. Then I changed tack. Why not the best of both worlds? — a hard, icy exterior, surrounding a cold, but still soft centre. Just like a true soufflé, only cold.

♥   ♥   ♥   ♥   ♥

4 stems of rhubarb, sliced, leaves removed

a little sugar for the rhubarb

4 eggs, separated

2 cups cream for the custard

60 g caster sugar

1 cup cream for whipping

40 g caster sugar for whipping the egg whites

1 The day ahead if you like, cook the rhubarb with a little sugar until the rhubarb has softened. Allow to cool, then purée. You will need a little more than a cup of purée. Refrigerate. Any over makes for a delicious breakfast.

2 Make a thick custard with the egg yolks, the 2 cups cream and the 60 g sugar. Refrigerate.

3 Whip the rest of the cream until it holds firm peaks. Refrigerate.

4 Whisk the egg whites in a ridiculously clean bowl, using a ridiculously clean whisk, until just firm. Add the 40 g sugar and whisk until a firm snow. Set aside and refrigerate.

5 The idea is to fold together the cream, rhubarb and egg whites, and to do this they all need to be of the same consistency and temperature. The cream and the whites are pretty much the same, but the rhubarb will need to be 'thinned down' with the custard. Whisk the custard into the rhubarb until it is the same consistency as the other components.

6 Gently fold the three together and pour into the smallest individual moulds you have. The moulds have to be small because the dish is very rich, and remember, the soufflé extends over the rim of the bowl. Make collars with cardboard and fill to the rim. Freeze.

7 This dish must go to the freezer no more than 3 hours before it is to be served. It must not be allowed to freeze through more than a centimetre all round — top, sides and bottom. It is a dish that succeeds because of the surprising change of texture — hard top, soft and cuddly in the middle. Obviously it is served in the moulds, so choose your flashest.

## ♥
## MY MUM'S CHRISTMAS PUDDING

There is only one recipe for Christmas pudding. It belongs to your mother, who picked it up from your grandmother, who learnt it from her neighbour, who once was lover to the cook to Queen Victoria, who got it from her mother ...

For all generations before us, it was mum, or her mum, or her grandmum, who did all the work in preparation for Christmas Day. For this is an ancient dish, drifting back through time as a mix of meat broth and spices, with lucky charms and rings and coins tossed in to ward away evil spirits. I am loath to admit it, but much of my initial joy at Christmas pudding came from the coins picked clean and piled high on the plate beside me. It was rather nice to end Christmas lunch with a pile of two bobs to last through the holidays. But decimal currency came, and that form of greed was replaced by others, the coins no longer suitable for the pud. I think we can all survive without them; but not without mum's recipe.

Whenever I think about Christmas pudding, I can recall on my palate the richness of flavour, the moistness, the surprises — a raisin here, an almond there — all brought together superbly with the most delicious custard. But most of all it was the tradition — to end the meal with a communal feast. It wouldn't be Christmas without it.

♥  ♥  ♥  ♥  ♥

400 g suet, cleaned and stripped
*That will come down to about 200 g*

cleaned. *If you don't want to use suet, try 250 g butter or margarine.*

1 cup self-raising flour, or 1 cup plain flour with 2 teaspoons baking powder

5 cups soft white breadcrumbs

1 cup brown sugar

1 teaspoon freshly ground allspice

1 teaspoon freshly grated nutmeg

1 teaspoon ground cinnamon

*If possible, whizz the spices just before you use them.*

250 g almonds, chopped roughly

zest of 2 lemons and 2 oranges

1 kg (total) raisins and sultanas (and dates and prunes if you wish)

8 eggs

1 ½ cups good quality muscat

1 teaspoon bicarbonate soda, dissolved in a little water

¾ cup good brandy

1 It takes a while to clean the suet. There are so many membranes, inner and outer skins, pockets of meat and fat. Just persevere. Then whizz it until it is as soft and smooth as butter. Suet is really only there for its tradition. You are just as well to use butter or margarine.

2 Mix the flour with the breadcrumbs, sugar, spices, almonds, zests and dried fruits.

3 Mix through the whizzed suet (or the butter), working it with your hands until it is well and truly amalgamated. Don't look for anything complicated with this recipe. Basically it is a matter of mixing it up, throwing it into bowls, and being patient.

4 Beat the eggs and add the muscat. Mix this and the sodium bicarbonate into the mix of dry goods and suet/butter. Add the brandy. The pudding mixture should be quite moist, certainly not liquid, but pourable, perhaps like lava in a good sci-fi movie. If it's not of that consistency, add more muscat.

5 Leave the mix overnight to allow the flavours to mingle. You should have enough for a couple of large puddings. Cook the puddings in a well-greased, old-fashioned pudding bowl, well protected against any intruding water (use aluminium foil or pudding cloth), for about 6 hours, making sure the water is maintained at the boil. This is the only time you really need to take much care — to ensure the water doesn't boil over or run dry.

6 I have never had the patience to keep the puddings for more than a day. To keep, they really need to be kept in muslin and allowed to dry out in a place with little humidity. Serve them doused with warm brandy, flamed.

WINE ✤ *I serve Rutherglen muscat with Christmas pud. Good Australian 'Show' brandy is also delicious. Try Renmano, Hardys or Mildara and expect to pay thirty-odd dollars.*

♥

## A SIMPLE APPLE FLAN, OR KIDS IN THE KITCHEN

How do you teach your children to not only cook, but to enjoy cooking, to use the kitchen creatively? Do you leave it to interaction: all in together 'helping' to chop and whisk and smash eggs etc? Or to osmosis: smells, and tastes, and admiring great results? Or do you leave them to it, handing over the sharp knife to cut the vegetables and fruit and tiny fingers?

There are no books on the topic, so I've gone with a touch of the lot. They love helping, especially when the machines are running; they love tasting, especially when sugar is prominent; and they love chopping.

So I got them chopping apples and pears to be stewed with a little sugar, and hit on a winner. Even a baboon can cook an apple and/or pear, and make it something flash (I know, because that's where I started learning) which makes it a perfect starting point for teaching the kids some tricks in the kitchen. It's a lot like tossing a handful of radish seeds into the garden and watching the almost instant results. From little radish seed tossers do big gardeners grow.

So we peeled, and cored, and sliced, and tossed, and came up with something which works hot as a dessert, cold as a snack, and best of all, as a vital component of play lunch. 'Dad,' said the chip off the old block. 'It's beautiful.'

♥　♥　♥　♥　♥

### THE PASTRY

200 g plain flour

25 g sugar

pinch of salt

125 g butter, not hard, not soft

1 egg, whisked lightly

enough cold water to bind

THE APPLES

75 g sugar

juice of 1 lemon

1 kg tart apples (Granny Smiths, or Jonathans in season), peeled, cored, and quartered

1 teaspoon ground cinnamon

*This is optional. If you want a brown flan with a spicy flavour, use the cinnamon. If you want a lemony, sharp, whitish flan, leave it out.*

1 Mix the flour, sugar and salt, then work the butter with your fingers into the flour until it forms large 'crumbs'.

2 Work in the egg, using a fork, until it breaks up, then add the water little by little until the mixture forms a solid mass. If it's too sticky, mix in a little more flour.

3 Flatten, rather than leave as a ball, and refrigerate, lightly flouring the pastry top and bottom.

4 Work the sugar, lemon juice and fruit together, and cook, covered, in the microwave for about 15 minutes on medium (high in a 500 watt machine) until the fruit is quite soft and has given out a deal of moisture. This can easily be done on top of the stove, but it's easier in the microwave — you don't have to watch it.

5 Purée in a whizzer, adding the cinnamon through the spout.

The mix should be light-brown and firm although still liquid, as lava is liquid.

6 Put back in the microwave and cook for another 5 minutes. Again, this can be done on top of the stove — the idea is to remove a little of the excess moisture. Set aside to cool.

7 Roll out the pastry and fill a flan dish (27 cm x 20 cm), with a removable edge. Refrigerate again for 30 minutes.

8 Prick the pastry all over to stop it bubbling and bake 'blind', pastry covered with aluminium foil, for 20 minutes, at 190°C. Remove the foil and bake for another 5 minutes.

9 Remove and spoon in the apple mix, smoothing it to the edges.

10 Bake for another 15 minutes and serve warm with cream or ice cream; or let cool and refrigerate for a dish of another sort.

11 When it's cold, the apple purée will set well enough to allow you to cut it into bite-size pieces. Serve with tea, sprinkled with a little icing sugar, just for style.

12 You can make exactly the same dish of apples and pears 50–50; or quinces all on their own.

WINE ❖ *Apple flan has the delicacy to go with most dessert wines. If you can find it, or afford it, look for a German Auslese with about six years bottle age. If not, there is a lot of good Australian riesling auslese styles. Try Orlando, Wolf Blass or Mitchelton.*

♥

## AN APPLE AND BERRY PUFF PASTRY TART

I owe a lot to Anne Willan's excellent work *La Varenne Cooking Course*. Not that the work provided any instant recipes, but it did more than any other book to teach me the basics of cooking. It is simply written, full of lovely anecdotes, beautifully illustrated, and clearly pronounces the do's and don'ts of the kitchen. And, although not in as many words, it declares: 'Stay cool don't panic.' More than any other work it demystifies the soufflé. And, once a hack has beaten the soufflé, I guess he/she is halfway to cooking for the King. It was in Willan's book that I first came across a simple and delicious recipe for a puff pastry jam tart. The French call it a '*jalousie*', which paints a quaint picture of the final result — *une jalousie* is a venetian blind. I cooked this tart in the restaurant for months. Later, when we were looking for another version of an apple pie, my mind went back to this dish for inspiration. We retained the original concept, kept a little of the raspberry jam, added lots of berries, some cubed apples, and a richly flavoured caramel and Calvados sauce (see page 254). Delicious.

♥  ♥  ♥  ♥  ♥

**500 g puff pastry (see page 240)**

**a little raspberry jam**
*If you don't have it, use something you like which works with apples. Any berry jam, or apricot jam, or home-made marmalade, would be great.*

**2–3 Granny Smith apples**
*If you are making this tart in January or February, the apples can be peeled,* cored and cut into cubes. They will have that lovely tartness of new apples. If it's spring and you are using cold-store apples, you will need to douse the cubed apples in lemon juice for about 30 minutes.

**1 punnet of raspberries**
*You can use frozen raspberries.*

**a mix of any other berries in season: blackberries, strawberries, blueberries, blackcurrants etc**

1 Roll out the puff pastry as thinly as possible. When you think it is thin enough, have another roll. Be gentle but firm.

2 Cut out a template from some cardboard. The tarts will be rectangular, about 13 cm x 7 cm. Cut out the pastry to the required size. You will need two pieces per tart, one for the top, one for the bottom. The top piece will be slightly larger than the bottom, as it has to envelop the filling.

3 Lightly oil or butter a baking tray and put the bottoms on this tray. Put them in the refrigerator.

4 Put the roller lightly over the tops, then fold gently in the middle, joining the long sides. Cut through the fold about a centimetre apart, all along its length and unfold. Place the pastry in the refrigerator to allow it to relax; if you're busy you can do this quickly in the freezer.

5 Take the pastry bottoms from the refrigerator and lightly spread some raspberry jam over them, leaving an edge of about a centimetre. Pile on the cubed apples and the berries. Moisten the edges with a little water.

**6** Cover the apple-berry mound with the latticed top, and press top and bottom together. Refrigerate. Heat the oven to 200°C.

**7** Brush a little egg wash (a mix of egg yolk and milk) over the pastry and bake for 25 minutes. It's important to make sure the pastry is well cooked. It is very tempting to believe that puff pastry is cooked after 10 or 12 minutes. It certainly has puffed up and looks cooked, but in fact, my experience is that it takes at least 25 minutes, probably 30 minutes, at 200°C to ensure the pastry is cooked to that flaky perfection that separates flaky pastry from all others. A good test is that your heart beats a little faster when you take the tart from the oven — you think that it has burnt. If that's the way you feel then it is probably just right. If you haven't time to make your own pastry, and you can't buy some from your favourite patisserie, then you shouldn't attempt this tart. Certainly you can replace the base with a different type of pastry, but never the top. Once you've successfully made your own puff pastry, you'll know what I mean.

**8** The pastries will be golden brown, firm on the bottom, and very flaky to the bite. Some juice and jam could ooze out during the baking, but if the pastries have not been overfilled, and the edges are securely joined, there should not be too much of that. You can cook and re-heat on the same day.

**9** Pour some caramel sauce (see page 254) or cream onto the plate. Place the pie in the middle. Serve with a few berries, a little cubed apple and cream or ice cream.

**WINE** ❧ *Once again, you can't go past a botrytis Rhine riesling (auslese style) — but why not try a glass of* méthode champenoise? *You will find the acid in the bubbly matches the tartness of the apples beautifully.*

♥

## APPLES IN CARAMEL

I am particularly fond of this version of apple pie, as it came together with much lateral thinking. It is a combination of the cooking technique of two French delicacies: tarte Tatin, the famous upside-down caramel and apple pie, and clafoutis, cherry pie in a pancake batter.

♥   ♥   ♥   ♥   ♥

### THE BATTER

3 eggs

125 ml milk

40 g flour

60 g sugar

zest of 2 lemons

1 teaspoon baking powder

60 g melted butter

### THE FILLING

5 apples, preferably Granny Smiths

a little sugar for the apple purée

juice of ½ lemon

60 g sugar

a little water

½ cup almonds, chopped roughly

**1** Whisk all the batter ingredients together and allow to rest for at least half an hour.

**2** The pie includes apple three ways: puréed, cubed and sliced.

Chop 3 apples and cook with a little sugar until soft, then purée. Chop 1 apple into little cubes and another into fine slices, allowing them to soak in a little lemon juice

3 Make some caramel by gently cooking the 60g sugar with a little water. Keep the heat low and keep working the sugar with a wooden spoon. Once the sugar melts and caramelises, keep swirling the saucepan until it reaches the flavour you like. This is much easier in the microwave. Once you have it to your liking, set it aside and keep it warm.

4 Pour the caramel into the base of a large heavily buttered pie dish (or several small ones if you have them). Add the batter, then the purée, sliced apples, chopped apples and almonds. The collection should reach to just under the top of the mould.

5 Bake in a 220°C oven until cooked, between 20 and 30 minutes. It should be firm, but yielding to the touch.

6 Unmould onto a plate, so the bottom is the top! The unmoulding takes a little work. You might need to prise the bottom away from the mould with a spatula, but if the pie is still hot from the oven, it should come away easily. If you intend to serve it cold, unmould while the pie is still hot.

7 You could also use pears or rhubarb or apricots with this dish, but if you're as happy with apples as I am then why bother? The dish really does look great on the plate, and the variations in texture

and flavour through each layer make it a real winner. Be careful not to have a heavy hand with the sugar when cooking the apples, as the caramel provides plenty of sweetness on its own. One of the beauties of this pie is that it can be made well in advance and loses absolutely nothing in re-heating.

WINE ✤ *Try a youngish botrytis Rhine riesling — something that has some acid backbone to cut through the caramel.*

♥

# A SHORT CUT TO AN APPLE PIE

We don't always have the time for pastry, although it is one of the more pleasant tasks for a relaxed kitchen. But when you're tired, and it's late, and you still must have a pie for dessert, then there is another way. Just use a well-flavoured bread, sliced and soaked in a liqueur or spirit, bake until the bread has dried out, and invert, in the style of a tarte Tatin.

♥   ♥   ♥   ♥   ♥

8 of the freshest Granny Smith apples, or Jonathans

4 pears

juice of 2 lemons

80g caster sugar

1/2 cup water

1 lemon, sliced very finely

juice of 2 oranges

2 walnut-sized pieces of unsalted butter

a punnet of raspberries

20 raisins (a handful)

thin slices of strongly flavoured
white bread

¹/₂ cup good sherry or muscat

**1** If you have an apple or pear corer then good luck to you. Use it wisely. If not, like most of us, peel the apples and pears, and chop them roughly into walnut-sized pieces, cutting out the cores as you go. Toss the pieces in the lemon juice and half the sugar.

**2** Make the caramel. In a heavy saucepan, gently heat the rest of the sugar and water until it bubbles, and add the lemon slices. Keep moving it around until you see it changing colour. It will gradually darken. Keep cooking until the mixture goes through several bubbling changes and caramelises. All this is easily done in a microwave. Warm the orange juice and add it slowly, taking care it does not spurt. Keep it in a warm spot.

**3** Heat the oven to 200°C.

**4** In a heavy, low-sided pan, toss in the butter, apples, pears, raspberries and raisins, and pour the caramel-orange juice mix over the top. Heat quickly over a high flame for about a minute.

**5** Remove from the heat, cover the apples-pears-etc. with the bread, and sprinkle the bread with the sherry or muscat. The bread should not be soaked, just given a light shower.

**6** Place the pan in the oven and cook on the bottom shelf for about 40 minutes. Remove and test

with a knife. It should pierce the apples like butter. The bread should have dried out and be on the way to crisp.

**7** Remove from the oven. Cover with a strong plate and invert the pan over the plate. Be careful. It's very hot. Lift the pan away gently, and there it is, a self-saucing, easy-as-you-like apple pie.

WINE ✤ *There are some lovely Australian botrytis wines made from semillon. These tend to be richer, more powerful styles than their riesling cousins. De Bortoli makes the most famous (labelled Sauternes), Wolf Blass makes a ripper at Clare (labelled Noble Gold), and Morris at Rutherglen occasionally releases one.*

♥

## QUINCE AND PEAR SOUFFLE

**T**he quinces and pomegranates of autumn teach you a salutary lesson: never judge a fruit by its beauty, or lack of it. Quinces are a bit as they sound: round and heavily dimpled, and hard as rocks. Nothing, in short, to write home about. Pomegranates, on the other hand, are Hollywood stars. Alluring, expensive, a gorgeous colour, but totally lacking heart or flavour. The pair make for a good comparison, coming into season.

Fortunately quinces take on a new life when you cook them. But nothing can save pomegranates. Cut them in half and you are faced with a mass of seeds stuck in a red pulp. Once you get through them, an endless job, they are not worth the

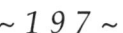

trouble. They are a waste of time, an absolute bore.

There are those who like the look of the quince, but they are usually old and grey, wearing thick glasses and filled with memories or dreams of the time they pinched them from the neighbour's trees fifty years ago. My dear old mother is in this school.

'We used to pinch them on the way to school,' she said (I tried not to listen — my mother a thief!) 'and eat them before getting to class, and the teacher would smell them — they have such a powerful aroma — and rush around shouting: "Who's been eating quinces?"'

She told me that story after I had been fiddling with this forgotten fruit. All praise to her for trying the forbidden fruit, but the teacher should have handed them all a medal for managing to eat them raw. It's not easy. I mention this tale because I had been slavishly following a recipe for cooking quinces, one of a dozen references to quinces I had consulted. Each claims the fruit is only decent when it is cooked for ages, and so it is, but ... why don't any of them say: 'Taste it and see'?

I had cut up three quinces before I thought of tasting. It's something of a shock: hugely acid palate, with a final sweetness. Something like a sweet'n'sour lolly: only with the quince it's a case of sour, sourer, sourest and, oh yeah, sweet.

And it's that final sweetness which separates quinces from rocks to throw at avowed enemies. They are great slow cookers and mixers. And, fortunately for us, quinces love the microwave.

Before the microwave I wouldn't have touched quinces with a goal post. Quinces in the preserving pan were testament to patience, patience and more patience. These days there are few enough of us with patience for anything, much less standing and stirring. Although the oldies and the goldies are still content to do it. One told me that preserving days were days of quiet reflection, days of stirring with a good book, page wedged open at the side of the stove, or times for good old-fashioned radio. Never TV.

So to the microwave, and all the possibilities with quinces: purées, chutneys, jellies, compotes, paste, anything. And the remarkable thing is that when you cook them in the microwave, they stay their original golden colour. None of this delicious pink/orange/magenta, but gorgeous golden.

I have rarely been entirely content with pear soufflés, although they are big deals in restaurants; nor apple, nor quince. But if you put the three blood brothers together, cook them down a little to intensify their individuality yet commonality of flavour and texture, then you are in for one of the great soufflés. And so simple too.

♥   ♥   ♥   ♥   ♥

**2 quinces, peeled, cored, cut into slices and sprinkled with lemon juice to keep the colour**
*Try a slice before you sprinkle on the juice. Sour, hey?*

**60 g caster sugar for the quinces**

**3 pears**
*William pears are great, prepared as above.*

**5 egg whites**

**20–30 g caster sugar for the soufflé**

1 Sprinkle the quinces with the 60 g sugar and cook on high in the microwave (covered) for about 10 minutes, or until tender. Test with a knife. They should be tender as butter and have given out a deal of juice.

2 Cook the pears in the microwave. Pears in season have no need for sugar and should take half the time that the quinces take. If it's winter and they're from the cool-room, add a little sugar and they will take a little more cooking.

3 Mix the two fruits together and whizz until they form a thick purée.

4 Put the purée back into the microwave again, uncovered, and cook for between 5 and 10 minutes, depending on the power of your machine. You don't want it to be solid, as in quince paste, but thick enough to hold its own on a spoon. This is a double whammy episode:
(i) to intensify the flavours by reducing any extra water;
(ii) to provide a firm base for the soufflé.
The purée should have a thickness something like stewed rhubarb in purée.
Note: At this point you could easily turn the mixture into a jelly, by adding several leaves of gelatine while warm, or mixing a little whipped cream through and adding gelatine to form a sort of bavarois.

5 Taste and see. What you have is the flavour base for the soufflé. This, and the sweetened, mounted egg whites, will make the soufflé. No more, no less. So taste it now. Is it sweet enough? Too sweet? Your answer to these questions will decide how much sugar to add to the egg whites. Allow the purée to cool.

6 Now to the egg whites. The secret to perfectly mounted whites is scrupulously clean everything: whisk and bowls. Wash everything twice. You can't be too careful. Whisk to your heart's content, adding about a dessertspoon of sugar, gradually, after the egg white loses some of its thickness and starts to lighten. Whisk and whisk, left hand, right hand, until the whites hold their own and form soft peaks.

7 Toss a quarter of the whites into the fruit mix, folding gently. Then add the rest in quarters, folding, folding, lifting the mix in the air as you go. That's it. There ain't no more folks. Taste it. The final product will be no more than a warm version of what you have now: the flavours will be much tighter when the mix is cooked, so if it tastes great now, the best is yet to come.

8 Fill a soufflé bowl or oven-safe bowl (don't worry if it doesn't come to the rim) and bake at 200°C for about 20–25 minutes. The soufflé is done when it is well risen and just brown on top. It should be just warm in the middle — definitely not firm.
Note: What you've done here is form the basis of most fruit soufflés — full-flavoured fruit purée, reduced to intensify, mixed with mounted egg whites and baked until just done. Try it with raspberries, apples, pears … anything.

WINE ✤ *What couldn't you serve with this? It's delicate enough to put on a full-flavoured champagne and yet a sweet white wine would go just as well.*

♥
## SHEER JOY: A QUINCE AND PEAR CRUMBLE

I f heaven doesn't include apple crumble, or raspberry crumble, or quince and pear crumble, served, of course with vanilla bean ice cream, then we have been fed a lot of ordinary lines for a long time.

This crumble provides all the textural and flavour variation of a crusty pastry, with none of the effort of preparation, and none of the heavy after-effects. And it is so simple to prepare, it should be written in indelible ink on all fridge doors.

♥   ♥   ♥   ♥   ♥

### THE FILLING

**3 quinces, peeled, seeded, cut into smallish pieces and tossed in lemon juice**

**4 pears, peeled etc as for quinces**

**30–40 g white sugar**

*Taste as you go. You could need more sugar depending on the sweetness of the pears. Don't use brown, as it colours the purée.*

### THE CRUMBLE

**1 cup self-raising flour, sifted**

**½ cup brown sugar**

*Demerara sugar makes for outstanding results for this dish. It seems to provide just that extra bit of crunch that turns a crumble into seventh heaven.*

**about 100 g cold butter, cut into cubes**

1 Put the fruit and sugar into a flattish bowl which can go into a microwave. Cover with plastic wrap and cook on high (500 watt) for 20–25 minutes until the fruit is butter-tender and has given off a deal of juice.

2 Toss the lot into a whizzer and process to a fine purée. Taste again. Set aside to cool.

3 Mix the flour and the sugar, and work in the butter piece by piece until the mixture has the consistency and appearance of breadcrumbs. Set aside. You might like to make double, for another crumble the day after you demolish this one.

4 Spread the fruit mix over the bottom of a pie dish, and sprinkle the flour-sugar-butter mix over the top, to a depth of about a centimetre. You can do this if the purée is still hot.

5 Bake in a 200°C oven for 25–30 minutes, until the crumble has browned and has cooked through. Usually the purée will be starting to bubble a little at this point. Don't let it get too aggressive, lest it bursts through the crumble.

6 Serve with vanilla bean ice cream. You can serve with cream, but for a very hot crumble, straight from the oven, you can't beat the temperature variation and texture that come from perfect ice cream.

Any combination of quinces and apples and pears; or apples and pears; or rhubarb; or raspberries, blackcurrants or gooseberries in season work well in this crumble.

WINE ❖ *German wines must wonder what they did to the world in the seventies when they were all the rage. Now, ask any retailer of good wine. They are hard work to sell. For this crumble, lash out and get a good auslese from the Moselle or the Rhine and enjoy.*

♥

## PEARS IN CARAMEL, EFFORTLESSLY

Pears are the sort of raw ingredient that should be handed out as a confidence booster to anybody who claims an inability to cook. Not eggs or bacon, not spuds, not steak. Pears, especially at the peak of their season.

Think about it for a moment. Those who claim a lack of interest, understanding or care about cooking often put out news bulletins claiming: 'All I can cook is bacon and eggs.' I'd lay odds on that.

The truth is that of all the so-called simple dishes, bacon and eggs may well be the most difficult, marginally ahead of steak. If you don't know what you are doing, how can you be sure the yolk of the egg is perfect, still in its runny state, but firm and warm, while the white — in all its forms — is set but not rubbery? And while you are making sure about the egg, what about the bacon? Crisp or not crisp, fat attached or not, oil drained or left to rumble about in your tummy?

Scrambled eggs you say? With curds, or smooth and creamy? An omelette, then. Okay, hard in the middle, or soft and gooey? Cooking eggs is a bit like practising a bad backhand. If you don't know how to do it in the beginning, all the practice/usage in the world just perfects an imperfection.

But pears? Any mug can cook them if you remember one key point. Taste them when they are perfectly ripe (the best place for this is in a warm bath), and don't alter that gorgeous, natural, juicy, soft, sweet flavour. Just warm that through; or cook tough, cold store pears until they attain that same delicious texture.

But even if you slaughter pears and leave them in a mushy mess, you can whizz them up with a little sugar and end up with a delicious sauce, or, if you have the equipment, a sorbet.

♥　♥　♥　♥　♥

**1 pear per person**
*William pears are great, but choose the variety which is at its best, and at the best value.*

**juice of 1 lemon**

**50 g sugar**

**½ cup best muscat (this much for two people)**

1 Core and peel the pears, halve them, and toss the pieces in the lemon juice to stop them discolouring.

2 Gently melt the sugar in half of the muscat, stirring all the while with a wooden spoon. Once the sugar has melted, allow the mix to cook vigorously, still stirring, on a medium flame, until the bubbles are large and the mix is full of life.

3 Remove from heat and add the rest of the muscat — gently, because it could spurt. Repeat as above, until the large bubbles appear again. Keep cooking for a minute or so, and then pour over, and then spoon over, the pears.

4 Heat the oven to flat out.

5 Place the pears core-side down in a pan which can go into the oven and pour over half the muscat syrup again. (You should use a pan only slightly larger than all the pears.) Heat gently on top of the stove until the syrup boils, then put in the oven for 5 minutes.

6 Remove and spoon some of the syrup from the pan — now enriched by some of the pear juice — and then add the rest of the muscat syrup. Put back into the oven for another five minute burst.

7 That's it. Simple as poaching an egg. Serve simply, simply, in the middle of a white plate, sauce spooned over and about, and with some rich cream somewhere handy.

8 It's likely there will be some sticky syrup left in the pan. Wipe it up with your fingers.

If you cook the pears similarly, and place the cooked and soused version on a slice of puff pastry, or puff pastry cut into the shape of a pear, it will make for a brilliantly simple, yet stunning dessert. If you make this dish, it is usual to sit the pear in a little pastry cream, flavoured (in paradise) by *eau de vie de poire*; in a less than perfect world, flavour it with vanilla beans, or muscat, or port. Brush the pastry with a mix of milk and egg yolk, and bake it in a 200°C oven for 25–30 minutes. You can also pre-bake the pastry, slice it in two, and serve the pears, sliced, in between two layers of the baked pastry, like a pastry sandwich.

Remember, too, that pears in season are ideal partners for a dry cheese like Parmigiano Reggiano.

WINE ♣ *This one is easy: just a glass of the best Rutherglen muscat you can find.*

♥

## A FRUIT SPONGE OR COBBLER

My mother loved cooking desserts, probably, I guess, because she received so many standing ovations. The earlier courses were just food for fuel, but desserts were a different matter. And the most consistent winner was probably the simplest — stewed fruit, usually apples, or blackcurrants during Christmas, topped by a butter cake. She called it a sponge, the Americans call it a cobbler. Delicious firm cake on top, bursting through to a bubbling, richly flavoured chunky fruit purée underneath. Doused with cream or ice cream, it made for a wonderful finale. Not surprisingly, in a big family, there was never any left for tomorrow. My favourite of all would be blackcurrants, but they have such a short and glorious season. Blackcurrants are particularly appropriate for this sort of pudding without a base. When cooked in a pastry case, they (gooseberries too) give out a tremendous amount of juice, affecting the crispness of the pastry.

This recipe makes enough for eight. Why make less? It lasts well for days, if you can hold the children off. Use whatever stewed fruit you like in a pie. Apples, or pears, or rhubarb, or quinces, or plums or apricots, or blackcurrants, or gooseberries, or raspberries, separately or together, are my favourites. Take eight apples or a punnet of the berries as a guide for quantities for the rest. Stone the apricots and remove any loose stems from the blackcurrants and gooseberries.

♥   ♥   ♥   ♥   ♥

8 apples

60–100 g sugar for the purée

180 g unsalted butter, at room temperature

200 g caster sugar for the sponge

1 vanilla bean

4 eggs (at room temperature), lightly beaten

zest of 1 lemon

250 g sifted self-raising flour, or plain flour with 2 teaspoons of baking powder

1 cup milk, out of the fridge for an hour or so

1 Using whichever method you prefer, stew the fruit with the sugar until it softens. This is best done in the microwave, covered. You might like a purée, or a mix of purée and chunks of fruit, or entirely chunky. Whatever, keep it warm, or gently warm it through when you have finished making the batter.

2 Cream the butter with the sugar, scraping the seeds from the vanilla bean into the mix. Do it by hand for the first time. It takes time, but it is good for the spirit, and gives you the feeling in your hands forever. You never need do it again this way, but you must know how the mix feels as it goes through its various stages. The butter should be chopped into quarters and then care-

fully softened in your hands. Work the mix with a strong wooden spoon, adding the sugar bit by bit. It is tough work, believe me. Beat and beat and beat until the sugar is incorporated, and the mix lightens and whitens and expands. The end result will be a very light, white, fluffy mix, something like whipped cream.

3 Toss away the spoon and go with a whisk. It's time for the eggs. The eggs must be added very gently and slowly. The idea is to maintain the aeration from the beating of the butter. Let the eggs drip into the butter, whisking them firmly as you go. The mixture will remain light and fluffy. If it separates, you can get it back together in a whizzer. Add the zest.

4 Now for the spatula. This is something like surgery. Keep thinking light as you fold in the flour, gently, little by little, alternating with the milk. You will end up with a very light, but thick, yellow-white batter, not quite at pouring consistency, but just thick enough to spread on its own.

5 That all takes about half an hour by hand, but a food processor or Kenwood (with K-beater) will do it in about 5 minutes. Do it that way next time.

6 Spread the batter over the warm stewed fruit (it must be warm), and bake in a 200°C oven for about an hour, or until the kitchen is filled with sweet smells, and a knife poked into the sponge comes out clean. Serve hot with cream, ice cream, custard, or some very cold low-fat yoghurt.

WINE ❖ *It will depend on what fruit filling you use. Botrytis white wines would be nice or even an aged spaetlese riesling style.*

♥

## AN APRICOT PIE, SERVED FROM THE PAN

Before the apricot season departs, and the 'cots are ripe and rich in sugar, try them one more way to keep you anxious for the next summer. Try the apricots in something like a tarte Tatin, that wonderful French upside-down version of the apple pie. This is not really an upside-down pie, but it takes on all its characteristics.

♥   ♥   ♥   ♥   ♥

12–15 apricots, seeds removed, cut in half

1 cup caster sugar

2 Granny Smith apples, peeled, cored, chopped into walnut-sized pieces, and tossed in a little lemon juice to prevent discolouring

juice of 1 lemon

1 dessertspoon Calvados, if you have some

*If not, forget it. It's too expensive to buy just for this dish. Try whatever appropriate liqueur, fortified wine, or spirit you believe will suit this dish.*

puff pastry (see page 240) or short pastry (see page 247)

egg yolk and a little milk

1 Toss the apricots with the sugar into a pan which can go into the oven later, and cook them gently for a few minutes, until the apricots have taken up the sugar, softened a little at the edges, and started to give some juice to the pan. Add the apples and toss around until the apples start to soften — a few more minutes. Add the lemon juice and Calvados, and toss through. Set fruit and pan aside to cool.

2 Heat oven to 200°C. Cover the apricot-apple mix with pastry, so that the pastry adheres to the sides of the pan. Refrigerate again for 20 minutes, then brush the pastry with a little egg yolk-milk mix. Bake for 35 minutes, or until the top is well browned.

3 Serve from the pan. (You can turn it over like a tarte Tatin if you wish, but the main reason for cooking like this is to allow the juices to run freely. If you wish to unmould so the pastry is on the bottom, just run a knife about the edge and turn it over onto a plate.)

4 Serving straight from the pan makes this an appropriate method for cooking juicy fruits like blackcurrants or gooseberries.

WINE ❖ *A lot of good botrytis whites develop an apricot-like aroma and flavour. This is a lovely match. De Bortoli's Semillon Sauternes is great or try Mitchelton's Botrytis Rhine Riesling or Tim Knappstein's Auslese.*

## ♥
## A BLACK AND WHITE BAVAROIS

I worked on the perfect bavarois for months — probably 18 months if the truth be known. There always seemed to be two insurmountable difficulties. The dish was always too rich, and always unattractive. I tried variations on cream content, cut down on eggs, piped different colours into the middle, served it sliced in half, in dozens of different moulds. Nothing seemed to work. Then one day the answer hit me on the head. Two birds with the one stone. Why not go for alternating layers of jelly and bavarois — the jelly cuts down on the richness, adds a different texture, and because it has no cream content, it allows for brilliant, clean, natural colours. Black and white was obvious. Blackberries provide a terrific jelly, and Calvados the most marvellously flavoured bavarois, and the combination of Calvados and blackberries is a proven winner. The striped dessert was a natural, served with berries and apples strewn about, in a lovely blackberry sauce, garnished with berries, apples and a swirl of cream. It had colour (even though the black of the berries changes to purple when cooked), flavour and texture. It needed nothing else.

♥   ♥   ♥   ♥   ♥

### THE GARNISH

punnet of blackberries, or a mix of berries in season

1 Granny Smith apple

Calvados

lemon juice

sugar to taste

### THE SAUCE

500 g blackberries, fresh or frozen

about 100 ml water

sugar to taste

a little thin cream for embellishment

### THE BAVAROIS

6 sheets of leaf gelatine

*Don't use the powdered variety. You can taste the difference. Certainly the leaves cost a little more, but the dish is not worth doing if you don't use them.*

4 egg yolks

100 g caster sugar

1 vanilla bean

2 cups milk

Calvados to taste

*Calvados is liquid gold. If you can't afford it, be content with vanilla flavour. Leave out the Calvados and add another vanilla bean.*

500 ml cream for whipping

### THE JELLY

7 sheets gelatine

500 g blackberries, preferably fresh, but this dish will not suffer with frozen fruit

sugar to taste

about 300 ml of water

*The amount depends on the amount of liquid coming from the berries.*

1 Several hours before, prepare the garnish. Core the apple. Cut into slices about 0.25 cm in thickness. Douse the apple slices in a bowl of lemon juice mixed with Calvados. Cut the slices into matchsticks, so there is a little of the green skin on each end. Throw back into the

lemon juice-Calvados mix, toss around, and allow to sit. The amount of lemon juice depends on the acidity of the apples. If you are making this dish at the height of the apple season — January to March — the lemon juice component can be minimised, and if you really want to be fancy, try several different types of apples. These apple matchsticks can be a dish on their own with berries, and cream (and) or ice cream.

2 Bring some water to the boil in a pot with a narrow diameter. Fit a stainless steel bowl on the rim of the pot to 'steam' the berries in the metal bowl. Throw in the berries to be kept for the plate and add a couple of teaspoons of sugar. When the berries start to give off their juice, grab the bowl (with a towel) and work the berries around. As soon as they have just softened and given off a little more of their juice, remove from heat. Allow to cool. (Served with ice cream while warm, all berries taste marvellous prepared like this, even those picked straight from the bush.)

3 Make the sauce, cooking gently to soften the blackberries in the water. Add the sugar carefully, tasting all the while. Stop when you are happy, but the sugar should be just enough to take away the natural sharpness of the berries. Too much will give you a jammy result. When cooked, force the sauce through a sieve. If using fresh berries, you might prefer to retain the seeds. If using frozen fruit, definitely discard the seeds. Set aside to cool. The sauce will be served cold.

4 The bavarois is merely a flavoured custard, lightened and made more rich with added cream, and given substance with gelatine. Soften the gelatine in warm water.

5 Make a custard ( see page 181) with the egg yolks, sugar, vanilla bean and milk.

6 Squeeze any moisture from the gelatine and add the leaves to the custard while it is still warm. When the mix is cool, add Calvados to your taste. Leave the mix at room temperature and allow to thicken. If the room is too warm, put the mix in the fridge. You can actually hasten this process by putting the mix in the fridge anyway, but it can be a little tricky, as the setting process accelerates near the end and the cream could set while you attend to an unexpected phone call. If this does happen, don't worry too much. Gently, very gently, warm the mix, and then allow it to cool and thicken again.

7 Whip the cream until thick enough to hold its own, but it should still be pourable — just.

8 Remove the flavoured custard from the fridge. It should be starting to thicken. You must act before the custard is firm. The two creams should be of the same density. Fold the two creams together to form a homogenous mix. The mix should be quite thick but not yet beginning to set. Place in a warm spot to retard the setting process until you have prepared the jelly.

9 Whenever you make a fresh fruit jelly, you wonder why companies like McLintock's did so well selling jellies in packets. Soften the gelatine in a little warm water.

**10** Cook the berries gently with the sugar and water as for the sauce. Sieve to remove the seeds. You will need 600 ml juice. Squeeze the gelatine and add to the warm mix. Allow to cool.

**11** The recipe is for ten portions. Metal moulds of about 200 ml capacity are best, but if you have none, even a tea-cup will do.

**12** Pour some of the blackcurrant jelly into the moulds. It should be about 0.5 cm deep/thick. Place in fridge to set.

**13** Pour a similar amount of custard mix on top of the jelly. Place in fridge, where they will set very quickly.

**14** Repeat until the moulds are filled. Refrigerate until set. The only trick is to keep the mixtures short of setting before they are added to the mould. They should be kept in a warmish environment. You can tell easily when the mould is set. It is firm to the touch on top.

**15** This dish looks best on white plates. Pour some sauce onto a plate and wiggle the plate until the sauce spreads almost to the edges. Make a little mound of berries and some of the apple 'matchsticks'. Run a little cream through the sauce and then, with the end of a spoon, run a 'slalom course' through the cream to create a white pattern on the blackberry sauce.

**16** Run a little warm water around the bavarois moulds,

and with the palm of your hand on the bottom, shake the mould to break the vacuum. You should hear and feel the bavarois come free. Make sure the water is not too hot, or there could be a little running of the colours. If the colours do run, the streaks can be rubbed away fairly effectively.

**17** Allow the bavarois to fall free onto your flattened fingers, and gently place the dessert against the fruit nest, and next to the swirl of cream. The presentation is simple, as most of the work can be done several minutes before serving.

WINE ❖ *This is a rich dish. Why not try a small glass of Calvados with it? In summer, take it straight from the fridge.*

♥
## CHOCOLATE SOUFFLE

I t seems if you mention the word 'chocolate', combined with 'recipe', most ears in the room prick up, and pens and paper are quickly gathered and put to work. To make triply sure of an audience, toss in the word 'soufflé', and you'll find you're as popular as Bob Dylan.

No matter what the health revolution is telling us, people are not turning away from chocolate, no matter how rich it is, no matter how filled with fat it is. They take it, lick the bowl and announce they are returning to their health kick the next morning.

Soufflés are a natural with chocolate. There's an illusion of lightening the load, but it's only an illusion. You end up eating stacks of chocolate, and a couple of egg yolks, and some cream to help it down, and sugar, and, oh hell, if you're going to love it, love it. Don't feel guilty.

♥     ♥     ♥     ♥     ♥

### 100 g dark chocolate
*Cadbury's Energy and Small's Club are fine.*

### 60 g caster sugar

### a little milk to help mix sugar and chocolate

### 4 egg whites

### 20 g sugar to assist whisking

### 2–3 egg yolks

### 10 hazelnuts, peeled and chopped roughly
*The nuts aren't necessary, but I like a little surprise in my soufflés. Any nuts you like with chocolate will be fine.*

1 Melt the chocolate with the 60 g of sugar in the milk in the microwave. Cook on high for about a minute, then mix together with a wooden spoon. Return for a minute until the chocolate has melted. Beat for 20 seconds, until it has all come together. It should be liquid, as lava is liquid. Set aside to cool for 5 minutes or so.

2 With a perfectly clean whisk in a perfectly clean bowl, whisk the egg whites through the rest of the sugar until they form firm, snowy peaks. Leave for a minute.

3 Test the chocolate mix with your finger. It should be hardly warm. Beat in the egg yolks until well blended.

4 Using a spatula, fold half the egg whites into the chocolate mix.

Take care to maintain the air in the whites as much as possible. Toss in the chopped nuts. Heat the oven to 200°C.

5 Fold in the rest of the egg snow, lifting and folding to maintain ultimate lightness.

6 Butter your soufflé dishes and pour the mix in until it reaches the top.

7 Bake in the oven for 15–20 minutes, until the top has fluffed up, but is still clearly undercooked. Serve with cream or ice cream.

8 You will note that the spoon meets little or no resistance. I like soufflés to be what they are named to be: breaths of air, rather than heavy winds. If you cook the soufflé longer, it will firm up, and take on the texture of a very light pudding — that's the egg yolks doing their job, I guess. It tastes richer, but it's not my soufflé.

WINE ✦ *Have you ever tried a big, full-flavoured méthode champenoise like Seppelt Sallinger, Yellowglen Vintage or Croser with a chocolate soufflé? If you want something sweeter, try a good Rutherglen tokay.*

♥

## A LIGHT AND FLUFFY CHOCOLATE PUDDING

I think this would have to be the most satisfying dish I have put together. I cannot believe there could be a lighter, more flavoursome, more consistently perfect chocolate pudding than this. It is so light, you can feel the air bubbles bursting in your mouth. Yet it is nothing like a soufflé. It is certainly substantial, so much so that during my time in the restaurant we had to take it from the menu every now and again, because those puddings we did not sell were adding too much to everybody's waistline, especially mine. We used to eat the leftovers from the night before for breakfast with ice-cream and cream. Hardly the ideal way to start a long day's night! The recipe evolved, as is the way with these things. We made an extraordinarily light spicy pudding from a French food magazine, *La Bonne Cuisine.* So I thought, what if we used a similar method, but replaced all the spices and dried fruits and such with chocolate: would the pudding retain the lightness? Would it ever! It was a triumph.

♥　♥　♥　♥　♥

(For ten individual 200 ml moulds)

75 g butter

75 g caster sugar

6 eggs (55 g size), separated, at room temperature

30 g plain flour

15 g cornflour

250 g chocolate

*Use Small's Club, Cadbury's Energy, or equivalent.*

10 g milk chocolate for grating

1 Cream the butter with half the sugar. The best way is to soften the butter in your hands, then whisk in the sugar until the butter is white and light and the sugar is finely incorporated. This is a cinch if you have a Kenwood with a K-beater.

2 Beat the egg yolks one by one through the butter, keeping the mix as light as you can.

3 Sift the flour and the cornflour, and fold it into the mix, making sure there are no lumps. Melt the chocolate gently in a stainless steel bowl over boiling water. It should be quite fluid. Allow it to cool a little, then pour into butter, flour and egg mixture.

4 In a perfectly clean bowl, with a perfectly clean whisk, whisk the egg whites with the rest of the sugar until firm.

5 Fold the egg whites into the chocolate, flour, butter etc. mix, again keeping the mixture as light as possible. The best way to do this is to mix a quarter of the whites loosely into the mix, then fold in the rest. At the end of it all the mix should be light and easily pourable.

6 Pre-heat the oven to 200°C. This dish is best served in individual moulds with a capacity of between 200 ml and 250 ml. If you haven't any of this size, small soufflé dishes would be ideal.

7 Butter your moulds amply and dust with caster sugar. Pour in the mix to about three-quarter capacity and cover each mould with silver foil.

8 Prepare a *bain-marie*: pour some boiling water into a baking tray, so the water will come halfway up the sides of the moulds.

9 Cook for at least an hour at 200°C. The puddings should have 'filled' the silver foil and will be firm to touch. The best way to check if they are done is to unmould one of them. Better to be sure.

**10** If you are entertaining, you can have the puddings ready at least an hour before you wish to serve them. Just leave them in their moulds in the *bain-marie* on top of the stove. When you are ready for dessert just bring the water to the boil and let it simmer away until the puddings are re-heated. They will not be quite as light as when taken directly from the oven, but never fear, the margin is very fine. Only the afficianados will know.

**11** When cooked, unmould gently onto a white, pretty plate. Serve with a simple raspberry sauce, at room temperature, underneath. Sprinkle the grated milk chocolate on the top.

**12** Serve with the best ice cream you can make or buy, and/or some lovely rich cream.

**13** If there are any puddings over, never mind. They last for ages in the refrigerator, and it is a great wonder to me that even several days later they will re-heat successfully, not quite attaining their initial fluffiness, but still puffing up enough to melt in the mouth. If you can't be bothered heating them through, just eat them cold, for breakfast.

WINE ✤ *As per chocolate soufflé.*

♥

### A RICH AND FLOURLESS CHOCOLATE CAKE

I came across Mark Armstrong's 'flourless' chocolate cake in an issue of *Vogue Wine and Food*

*Cookbook* of about 1984. I tried it and it worked perfectly. It was held together by chocolate and eggs, and was full of cream to boot. Then I tried the recipe without the liqueurs the original called for. Then I found the best result was obtained when the very best chocolate was *not* used. For some reason, it appeared to be less rich, easier to eat, and just as full of chocolate flavour. Even then, it was still so rich that it needed several props to make it easier to eat and enjoy. I used a strongly flavoured raspberry and muscat sauce, cut the cake thinly, and served it with whipped cream, some berries, orange segments and the like. In the restaurant days, I added an orange sorbet on side. It looked stunning and tasted wonderful. Much later, I tasted Armstrong's original at his lovely Paddington eating house, Pegrum's, since passed on to other hands, and it was, in fact quite different. It was certainly much richer, but then he didn't use as many props. I am forever grateful for the inspiration.

♥ ♥ ♥ ♥ ♥

**8 whole eggs**

**¹/₂ cup brown sugar (or caster sugar)**

**675 g chocolate, melted**
*Use Small's Club, or Cadbury's Energy, or something dark and rich.*

**250 ml cream, whipped until just firm**

*Any baking tin will do, but make sure the sides and bottom are heavily buttered and lightly floured to allow the cake to be removed easily. Use greaseproof paper if you, like me, always have trouble with cakes sticking.*

**1** Whisk the eggs and sugar in a bowl over gentle heat until the sugar is melted and the mix is thick and mousse-like. Slowly incorporate the melted chocolate, then leave to cool a little.

**2** Fold into the whipped cream, until all ingredients are as one.

**3** Pour the mix into the prepared tin and cover with aluminium foil.

**4** Pre-heat the oven to 200°C. The cake is baked in a tray of just-boiling water. Allow the water to come halfway up the sides of the cake tin. Cook the cake in the bottom of the oven. It will take at least 2 hours and, when done, will resist your touch throughout. It will not be wobbly in the middle. Allow to cool thoroughly and leave in the tin in the refrigerator overnight.

**5** Unmould by placing the base of the tin in a little warm water for about 60 seconds. It should come out easily.

**6** Slice with a warm knife and serve with a fruit sauce — raspberry is perfect, but you could make a sauce of orange or strawberries — and, if you really want to make a display of it, make an orange sorbet and serve at the side, along with all sorts of berries. Whipped cream is probably taking it all a bit too far.

WINE ✤ *One of my favourites to eat, not to match with wine. It's so rich and intense that it demands to be eaten on its own; maybe with a short, black coffee. This cake is a beauty to find in the fridge the next morning and hop into before anyone else gets up.*

♥
## CHOCOLATE MOUSSE

C hocolate mousse has become a bit like avocado vinaigrette. Once upon a time you could bet that a hollowed-out avocado doused with a dressing of a little vinegar, a very good olive oil, and a handful of chives would take us through the first course of a flash dinner party, and the chocolate air would be a finale of triumph. Then, heavens above, we would discover that Mrs Kerphoops was serving chocolate mousse, and that it was no longer appearing on restaurant menus, and how could we offer it again?

The first chocolate mousse all of us took would have been as firm as an old time jelly. Rubbery even. Probably at a pub, probably in a cocktail glass (we thought they were champagne glasses in those days). So much so that I have been in many arguments about the firmness, or lack of it, of a true chocolate mousse. It should be as light as a feather in the mouth, filled with bubbles, and inclined to wobble if you turn it on its edge. The other (pub) mousse is more like a chocolate Bavarian cream — a mousse, with gelatine and cream added.

What is beyond argument is the fact that chocolate mousse is one of *the* great desserts, never to be underestimated, always well received. Just because it's old, it doesn't mean it should be discarded.

Oh, one other thing. If you have a cholesterol problem, or think you have or might have, or even could have, forget it.

♥   ♥   ♥   ♥   ♥

**150g good-quality chocolate, broken into chunks**

*The best readily available for this are those marketed as 'dark' chocolate.*

**¼ cup strong coffee**

**4 egg yolks**

**50g brown sugar for the egg yolks**

**6 egg whites**

**20g caster sugar for the egg whites**

**100ml cream**

**1 teaspoon freshly ground coffee for decoration, texture**

1 Melt the chocolate very gently with the coffee. This can be done over steam, or, watched closely, in the microwave. The chocolate should finish up fluid, but not hot. Leave it aside to cool a little.

2 Whisk the egg yolks with the brown sugar over steam, until they have lightened, and tripled in volume. Whisk in the melted chocolate-coffee mix and keep the dish in a warm place.

3 Whisk the egg whites in a scrupulously clean bowl, until they stiffen, adding the caster sugar on the way.

4 Whip the cream until it has tripled in volume.

5 Add the cream to the chocolate-coffee-egg yolk-sugar mix, folding it through so as to maintain its volume. Add a third of the whites similarly and gently fold in the rest. Keep folding the mix into itself until it is homogenous. You do not wish to have white streaks through the chocolate mix.

6 Put the mix in the fridge, covered, and leave overnight. It will be as light as a feather, a chocolate snowflake.

7 Sprinkle the freshly ground coffee over the top. You don't need much, just enough to enter every mouthful. To lighten the eating load, serve with/over some very cold stewed fruit.

This mousse is quite a deal lighter, and less firm, than the mousse which results from the more usual method of adding raw yolks to the melted chocolate. Please yourself whether you prefer to cook the egg yolks.
  Try not to eat too much.

WINE ✤ *I would have to go back to a Rutherglen tokay or muscat. They have the intensity and balance to match chocolate.*

♥

## CHOCOLATE FUDGE CAKE

Not all chocolate recipes have to be mind-blowing in their effects on your body. I discovered this marvellous joy in a terrific American cooking magazine called *Eating Well*. This is not one of these New Age products which scolds and berates like an old Irish cleric breathing fire and brimstone from the pulpit. This is a magazine which recognises that we are weak, fragile, when it comes to controlling what we eat.
  We know we shouldn't, but we do, don't we? And of all the unmentionables we eat, chocolate is probably the worst. But here was a health magazine with the richest chocolate dessert you have seen on the cover. Inside I discovered that

chocolate freaks with health problems can get the same sort of a kick by using cocoa. Almost all cocoa powder we use has a fat content of between 10 and 20 per cent. Unsweetened chocolate is about 52–56 per cent fat; and semi-sweet chocolate about 36 per cent fat. It was just the motivation I needed to start experimenting with cocoa.

♥ ♥ ♥ ♥ ♥

3 eggs

150g caster sugar

50g cocoa powder

¾ cup vegetable oil, or 1 cup melted butter or margarine

½ cup strong coffee, best made with a plunger or machine

80g double-sifted plain flour

50g almond meal

2 teaspoons baking powder

1 In a mixer, whisk the eggs with the sugar until the mix is very light, very fluffy. You cannot overbeat the mixture.

2 While the eggs are beating, stir the cocoa into the oil and coffee, whisking gently to bring it all together.

3 Reduce the speed of the beater and drip the chocolate mix into the eggs, slowly, gently, making sure you do not lose that wonderful fluffiness.

4 Stop the beating and fold in the flour with the baking powder and the almond meal, gently, gently, maintaining the lightness of the mix.

5 Grease well a flat tin, like a lamington tin, and put some greaseproof paper on the bottom. Pour in the chocolate batter and bake at 200°C for about 20 minutes, checking all the while. If you bake the mix in a narrower, deeper tin, it will take longer.

WINE ✤ *Take with a cup of great coffee or well-brewed tea.*

♥

## SUMMER PUDDING AS A JELLY

J elly is one of the most underestimated dishes, at both ends of the menu. The jelly which comes together after nicely cooked veal bones, and pig's trotters, and chicken feet, and vegetables, is one of the cheapest and best of additions to any meal; and fruit juices, held together with the best leaf gelatine make for a terrific finale.

It's the texture that gets you first, then the flavour: a roll around the mouth, then fade away feeling, so different from the usual run-of-the-mill tucker. Unfortunately, most of the sweet jelly we have taken in our time has been from packets. Consistency is fine, ease of preparation, fine, but the flavour is not for me. Always too much sugar, and the colours are impossibly artificial.

If you think of jelly as rich in natural flavour, and, through its moulding ability, pretty good to look at, it makes for a wonderful stand-alone ooh and aah finale to a feed. I realised this during yet another summer of sneering at old-fashioned summer pudding, that

English standby of gently compressed seasonal berries held together with bread, soaked with the juices of the berries. They always look attractive, but always let me down because the soaked bread always tastes like ... soaked bread.

But the berries, the berries. I couldn't dismiss it altogether, so I put it in a jelly. Firm but wobbly, all the colours and flavours of a summer pudding, with more guts. You can tell it's a ripper when you see the jelly — pale, slightly washed out. It couldn't have been made from a packet.

♥    ♥    ♥    ♥    ♥

#### 500 ml orange juice
*You must produce the juice yourself, either through a juicer, or by hand. It is a no-no with bottled or packaged juice. You may as well use packaged jelly.*

#### 75 g caster sugar

#### 5 leaves gelatine
*Don't use the grain gelatine if you can help it. It tastes like something I can't put my tongue on — in more ways than one. You can use fewer leaves if you don't intend unmoulding the jelly, but that does seem rather pointless. One of the delights of this dish is the effect it has on good eaters when you present it to them.*

#### 3 punnets of the best quality berries
*When in season, you must use raspberries, and even strawberries — banished from the real summer pudding — are great in the jelly.*

1 Bring the juice and the sugar to the boil. Simmer for a few minutes, removing any impurities which might rise to the top.

2 Soften the gelatine in cold water, squeeze out any excess moisture,

and add the softened gelatine to the warm juice.

3 Pack the berries in a mould — preferably metal, so it can be unmoulded easily. If you must use a porcelain mould, run a sharp knife about the edge before unmoulding.

4 Pour the juice (gelatine added) over the berries and refrigerate for a couple of hours. Unmould and serve with a little cream, ice cream, or cold custard.

WINE ✤ *Frontignan or frontignac is an intensely flavoured white grape that makes lovely, raisiny, sweet white wines. In Australia, good styles are made by Brown Brothers, Wolf Blass (Green Label), Krondorf and Orlando.*

♥
# A VARIATION ON FREDY GIRARDET'S PASSIONFRUIT SOUFFLE

Souffles are so simple I am forever astonished at the oohs and aahs they elicit even in the world's great restaurants. Fredy Girardet's renowned passionfruit soufflé is served at Girardet's knockout eatery just out of Lausanne in Switzerland with all the pomp and ceremony usually reserved for royalty. In fact, it wouldn't be surprising if M. Girardet's staff did their training at royal weddings. All that is missing as the soufflé arrives is the trumpet fanfare, and the adoring customers make up for that with their gushing.

The bearers present the little A-Bomb gently to the table, step back with a flourish, and, as you bow towards the heavenly dessert, the forever flamboyant *maître d'* wheels in with a flourish, rips the top away with a pair of spoons, and carves the air up before you. They finish the little show with a mellifluous 'Bon appetit'. A curl of the eyebrows, and the cast of thousands is gone. They could do it in their sleep, so many soufflés do they sell.

The show's the thing at Girardet, but I prefer the pleasure of breaking the dome myself, drawing the foam through some syrup at the base, and letting it all melt away on the tongue. Forget the foreplay — it's more fun doing it yourself.

Girardet's soufflé is so light because it is basically air, held together by sugar, egg yolks and whites, and intensely flavoured by passionfruit juice. The intensity is increased *chez* Girardet by the pouring of a passionfruit sauce around the excavated soufflé on your plate. The trick Fredy would like you to play out is to draw your spoon through the sauce, into the foam, and into the gob. Guaranteed passionfruit purity. (Every chef has these little eating 'rules' for his/her favourite dishes, but few customers adhere to them. You can but hope.)

Something went wrong between the serving of the soufflé and the writing of Girardet's excellent work *Cuisine Spontanée*. Girardet's written recipe requires six tablespoons of sugar for one egg. It cannot be. I tried it, and the result was akin to those vile Coolers which are spreading through the world — unbearably sweet. There are people, I suppose, who prefer that sort of soufflé. It is guaranteed to retain its dome long after the lights have gone down and the milk bottles have been put out. Too sweet for me, and Girardet's *in situ* is not like that. I tried his recipe with one-sixth the sugar, and won an award for

desserts from the French Chamber of Commerce.

The incredible thing is that after years of providing pure joy in the restaurant, I went without making this soufflé for some time. But you always come back to the things you love. (Sigh.) And so there I was, sieving passionfruit pulp methodically, cleaning whisks and bowls with a scrubbing brush, whisking egg whites with a fury. And, as soon as the kids had achieved Noddy-land, there we were, fighting each other for puffs of passionfruit flavoured air. Fighting is not too strong a term for it. When it was over, we looked at each other, and wondered aloud: why had we left it so long?

Selfishly, we had dismissed the children, because we know only too well how keen they are on this particular creation. Nasty aren't we? I will never forget the first time we tried M.Girardet's signature tune. Our little boy, then six months, now seven years, had accompanied us on the very fast, very wonderful, train from Paris to Lausanne on the French/Swiss border, to take lunch at the famous restaurant. Being the good child he was/is, he fell fast asleep as soon as we arrived at our table. We tucked him underneath, surrounding him with the overhanging table-cloths. You would not have known he was there.

He did not move, until the soufflé arrived at table. Then he came from his resting place like a lion, attacking the soufflé and its accompanying ice cream and sauce with the sort of relish he has not yet lost, and I suspect never will. The soufflé has that sort of effect on you.

You can make this soufflé for a pair, but it is far easier, especially for the inexperienced, to make it for at least four, preferably more. This recipe is for six.

♥  ♥  ♥  ♥  ♥

**10 eggs, separated**

*You will need 6 yolks and all the whites. With the leftover yolks you can make a custard. You may not need all the whites, but better to have too much air, than not enough, and that applies to any soufflé.*

**100 g caster sugar**

**enough passionfruit to provide a cup of juice**

*There is no easy way to eliminate the seeds. It does help to warm the seeds and pulp gently, before you sieve them, but even then you have to push and shove the juice and pulp for ages. The rest of it is so, so easy. No harm going through a little hard labour.*

1 Make sure your whisks and bowls are perfectly clean. The most certain reason for egg whites failing to mount is the presence of dust or grime in bowl or on whisk. Clean everything twice, and you won't miss.

2 Whisk the yolks furiously with half the sugar, added bit by bit, until the mix thickens, then becomes light and fluffy and extra white. Incorporate as much air as you can into the yolks. You will work up quite a sweat, but more is to come.

3 Now to the whites. Ten egg whites is a rather hefty job for a new comer to whisking, but you must do it by hand first, so you can get the feel of the egg whites mounting. Next time, you can do it in a machine. Lift the whisk (if it's the same as you used with the yolks, clean it again, more thoroughly this time) through the mix, adding sugar as you go, as if you were turning the soil in the vegetable garden. Try it with left and right hand. Once it gets going it will get easier, and the whites should mount rather quickly. They are ready when they are firm, forming soft peaks against the whisk.

4 Lightly butter some soufflé bowls. It is best that each person has his/her own individual bowl, as the soufflé cooks more quickly, and better, in smaller bowls. But the result in family-size bowls is rather attractive anyway, although I find it sets a little at the edges. Set aside a little over half a cup of juice to mix with the yolks and whites, and dribble a millimetre of passionfruit juice into the bottom of each of the bowls.

5 Add a little juice at a time to the egg yolk mix, whisking it in as you go. The idea is to maintain, as best you can, the foaminess of the yolks, so they can be folded into whites of a similar consistency. Start folding, adding a quarter of the whites at the beginning, then the rest bit by bit, folding gently, trying as best you can to maintain the lightness of the mix. Keep drizzling the juice into the mix as you fold. Taste it, to make sure there is a strong taste of passionfruit. You can't have too much passion.

6 Fill each bowl to the top, and bake in a pre-heated, 220°C oven for somewhere around 18 minutes. You can open the door to see how it's going. Be brave, take it out and have a look. Poke it. Put it back.

It should be just firm, with a little spring to the touch. If you have done the job properly, the soufflé will be firm on the outside, soft and creamy and just warm in the middle. Serve with the best ice cream you can make, or buy.

WINE ✤ *You can serve good bubbly with this or a fine, botrytis white — nothing too heavy or overpowering.*

♥

## JAMIE FORD'S LEMON TART

There are only a few desserts I have come across which have caused me to wish, instantly, for the recipe. Girardet's passionfruit soufflé was one; Sirio Maccione's crème brûlée at New York's Le Cirque was another; Gay Bilson's Sussex Pond pudding — an old-fashioned pudding soaked with the flavour of lemon — from Sydney's Berowra Waters; and Stephanie Alexander's raspberry crumble at Stephanie's.

Then came Jamie Ford's lemon tart. Ford has been cooking terrific tarts in a tiny lunch bar in Melbourne for several years. If he was cooking in New York, he would have been a neighbourhood celebrity, but such is rarely the case in this country. People had told me about his lemon tart, but I had never bothered to try it — I had been disappointed too often by too many versions of lemon tart in too many places across the globe. But at last I tasted a slice, then another slice, then another, until there was no more.

It can stand with any of those desserts above. It is the only lemon tart I have eaten which does not leave a lingering taste of egg on the palate. This is a tart impregnated with lemon, as light as the lightest soufflé. It is truly brilliant. I wish I'd thought of it.

♥  ♥  ♥  ♥  ♥

### THE PASTRY
300 g plain flour, sifted

100 g caster sugar

200 g unsalted butter, in cubes

3 egg yolks

### THE LEMON FILLING
3 eggs (55 gm)

$^1/_2$ cup caster sugar

juice of 1 large lemon, strained, zest removed and retained

$^1/_3$ cup almond meal

120 g unsalted butter, melted so it is just warmer than tepid

1 Mix the flour and sugar together, and then the butter, rubbing through with your fingers until crumby and blended.

2 Mix in the egg yolks with a spatula until a pastry block is formed. Break up into the size you need, roll out flat and put straight into the shell, making sure the pastry is not too thick in the corners.

3 Put in the freezer for a few minutes.

4 Bake blind in a 200°C oven, the pastry covered with aluminium foil, until the edges brown.

5 Remove from the oven, take out the foil, and return until the pastry is well browned and looks like biscuit. Beware: if you don't

bake it enough the pastry will stick to the pan.

6 The filling sets best if the pastry shells are warm from the oven; but it will still set well if they're not.

7 Cream the eggs with the sugar. This is best done in a Kenwood, with the whisk attachment, in order to get the maximum amount of air into the mixture. You cannot over-beat the mix.

8 Turn down the pace of the beat-er and add the lemon juice, bit by bit; add most of the zest, keeping a little aside.

9 Then add the almond meal. The beaters should be kept running. The end result will be very, very fluffy.

10 Take out a couple of scoops of the batter and whisk in the warm butter, bit by bit. Then whisk in the new butter–batter mix, slow-ly but surely. It is vital to maintain the airiness of the mixture.

11 Pour the mixture into the shells gently. You will think it is filled but then it will take some more. Leave it for a minute, then add some more. Fill almost to the edge. Sprinkle some zest on top.

12 Bake in a 180°C oven, on the bottom shelf, with an empty dish on the shelf on top. It can be tricky to bake. It will be done when it is set, not wobbly, and the lemon mixture will be brown on top. Test after 15 minutes. It will take about 20 minutes.

13 Remove and allow to cool, then refrigerate until quite cold. It is impossible to cut when warm.

14 Serve with icing sugar sifted over the top. The tart will keep easily for several days, if it sur-vives sticky fingers.

WINE ❖ *I'd suggest a Rhine riesling that is not overly sweet. Look for some-thing from Eden Valley with some rich-ness coming from bottle age. Orlando, Krondorf and Yalumba all make superb styles — they will keep developing for ten years or more in the bottle.*

♥

### SLATTERY'S SUMMER SOUFFLE, CHRISTMAS 1990 AND FOREVER MORE

The perfect Christmas pre-sent from a cook has to be something fantastic, yet simple to make, something surpris-ing, yet so obvious when you make it; full of colour without gratuity; and something you'd want to make again and again and again. And it has to be seasonal, of summer exclu-sively, so it will be longed for at this time next year and forever. I finally found it after a lot of tasting and test-ing: a soufflé of apricot, raspberries and blueberries, served, of course, with vanilla bean ice cream.

It sounds, I know, a monument to the worst excesses of smart-arse cooking. Put as many flash ingredi-ents as you can into a bowl, whoosh them all around, make clever noises at the end, and you'll be sure to fin-ish up with a load of old rubbish.

Not here. What I wanted to do was create a vehicle which would see the berries just cooked, just barely warmed through, so they would be at the point of giving off their juices, without getting even close to the fall apart stage. I included blueberries in the recipe because I wanted to find some use for them after years of searching, and I was certain they were at their best when just warmed through. Anyway, I've got an eye for the US market: they go bananas over blueberries. Raspberries, I knew, are at the height of the glory when warm and running with juice.

I tossed in the apricots because I wanted to create the perfect berry soufflé without using berries as a base, because if you whizz berries and fold them with egg whites they lose a lot of their ooomph, react with the sugar to get jammy, and lose that delicious, intense colour. Not so apricots.

So, it became a soufflé of stewed apricots, with raspberries and blueberries in suspension. It's my Christmas present to me, every Christmas, and to you too. I hope you love it as much as I do.

♥　♥　♥　♥　♥

**10–12 best quality, slightly sharp apricots**

**1–2 dessertspoons sugar for stewing the apricots**

**4 egg whites**

**2 dessertspoons sugar for whisking the whites**

**dozen perfect raspberries**

**dozen perfect blueberries**

*You could also use blackberries, or blackcurrants, but not strawberries: they don't handle cooking.*

**1** Cook the apricots with just enough sugar (probably about

1 ½ dessertspoons) to maintain their delicious flavour without getting sweet. You can do this in the microwave or on top of the stove. They should be cooked until soft enough to purée with the back of a fork and a sieve. Or do it in the whizzer. Allow to cool.

**2** Prepare your whisk and bowl so they are absolutely clean. Now whisk the egg whites with the 2 dessertspoons of sugar until they form peaks and are firm enough to hold their own. Be patient: about 5 minutes of effort.

**3** Lightly grease a soufflé mould, or moulds. You can also use a flat, low-sided baking dish.

**4** Fold half the egg whites through the apricot purée, folding and folding to maintain the lightness of the show. Add the rest of the whites and incorporate all the apricot purée. Taste to ensure there remains a ripping apricot flavour, with just a touch of sweetness.

**5** Put a layer of raspberries and blueberries at the bottom of the bowl, then some soufflé, followed by a layer of raspberries gently, then some mix, then blueberries, then raspberries, etc., until you get to the top of the bowl. Make sure the top of the last row of berries is covered by mixture. You should get maybe two rows of raspberries and one of blueberries, depending on the size of the bowl.

**6** Bake in a 200°C oven for about 18–20 minutes until the soufflé has cleared the top of the bowl and is standing up as happy as a new Christmas tree.

7 Dust the top with a little icing sugar for real style. Serve with your best ice cream. And a Happy Christmas to you all.

WINE ✤ *When it's 100°F in a water bag on Christmas Day, this makes a lot more sense than the traditional pud. You can serve it with an icy-cold glass of sweet white wine — then retire for coffee and brandy in the next room.*

♥

## RHUBARB SOUFFLE, FROM THE BOOT

Now that you have conquered the soufflé, it's time to get arrogant. This is the sort of soufflé you can prepare at home, toss in the boot of a car, and cook it at a friend's place. And it's impossibly simple.

This one's made with rhubarb, but any fruit that produces a thick richly flavoured purée will do the job.

♥　♥　♥　♥　♥

4 stems of rich red rhubarb (green rhubarb is fine for flavour, not so good for colour)

50 g sugar for stewing the rhubarb

6 egg whites

30 g sugar for whisking the whites

a few berries for a surprise in the middle of the soufflé

1 Cook the rhubarb with the sugar to take away the tartness. Purée and sieve once the rhubarb has softened. You should have about three cups of lovely pink purée.

2 Allow to cool, then whisk the whites with the sugar.

3 Keep aside a half a cup of purée. Fold the rest of it with the egg whites, starting with half the egg whites, then the rest. Make sure that the mix remains reasonably firm and very airy, and that it still has a powerful rhubarb taste. Add some more rhubarb if you are not perfectly happy. It won't be a grand success unless it is richly flavoured.

4 Butter the moulds well and pour a centimetre of rhubarb purée into each mould, and put a couple of berries on top of the purée.

5 Spoon the soufflé mix into the bowls. Put the lot in the fridge until you are ready to cook. You could even do it the day before; just make sure you fold the mix together again. When the time is ripe, sneak away from the dinner table, bake the soufflés in a 200°C oven for 18–20 minutes, and return triumphant.

WINE ✤ *As you return to the table triumphantly, why not pop a bottle of top-class bubbly. It's a delicate soufflé and could be overpowered by a wine too sweet.*

♥

## COLD RHUBARB SOUFFLE, CREAM AND AIR

I was cooking for my daughter's first birthday, and wanted to provide something the mature three- and four-year-olds could go ooh and aah over and then stick their fingers in, causing parents to scold; something that would have them lining up for seconds. I went for a cold rhubarb soufflé, light as a feather, held together by egg whites, whipped cream and just enough gelatine to keep it bouncing about on the plate like a ... well, you know what I mean.

♥   ♥   ♥   ♥   ♥

**8 stalks of rich red rhubarb, cut into 10-cm sticks**

**60 g sugar**

**6 leaves gelatine (for a litre of soufflé)**
*Do not under any circumstances use powdered gelatine. You can taste the gelatine.*

**4 egg whites**

**30 g caster sugar for the egg whites**

**1 cup whipping cream, whipped until just holding its own**

1 Cook the rhubarb, the sugar stirred through, until soft. Those of us who are lazy do this in the microwave. Cover and cook for about 8 minutes, or until soft. Whizz until smooth and allow to cool in a wide, flat bowl. Ideally this step is carried out ahead.

2 Soften the gelatine in a bowl of warm water.

3 Whip the egg whites in a perfectly clean bowl, with a perfectly clean whisk, adding the sugar every now and then, until the mix is light, white and holding soft peaks.

4 Heat a little of the rhubarb, wring out the gelatine and mix it through the warmed rhubarb, then mix this back into the rest of the rhubarb.

5 It's downhill from here. Fold the cream through the rhubarb,

keeping the mix as light as you can, then do the same with the egg snow, adding a third at first, then the rest. Keep folding until the mix is light and pink, with no white streaks.

6 Gently pour into a mould and refrigerate for at least an hour, probably two. It is ready when it is just firm. You will know it's right when the bowl is very cold.

7 Unmould onto a white plate, and keep the kids at bay until you have set aside a slice for yourself. This amount of gelatine just holds the mix together. It does not need to stand on its head. It should hold its own, but be as soft as a soufflé. In fact, if you unmould it when it is just cold, the centre will still be very soft, like a real soufflé.

WINE ✤ *It would be easy to overpower this with a very sticky, sweet wine. It's a fine-structured dessert and needs a fine-structured wine. I'd go for a good bubbly.*

♥

## A CAKE OF RHUBARB

Rhubarb, you might have noticed, is one of my favourite fruits. Well, it's not really a fruit, but a stalk, but that's for botanists. If you eat it like a fruit, then to me it's a fruit, which makes a tomato a vegetable, although it's a fruit, and who cares anyway?

Whatever it is, I have always loved rhubarb. Perhaps because it's always been so versatile, so cheap, so plentiful, and it grows so prolifically outside most back doors. Most back doors, that is, except mine. I have tried growing rhubarb in just about every location under the sun, and some not under the sun, to no avail. I have starved it, drowned it, fertilised it, choked it. All it does is form a small stem, and then fades away. One day it will work, along with my lemon tree, and cumquat tree, and lime tree. One day. At least it's cheap while I'm waiting.

♥  ♥  ♥  ♥  ♥

5 eggs

200g caster sugar

200g almond meal

25g peeled almonds, roughly chopped

2 cups rhubarb purée: the purée of well-cooked rhubarb and a little sugar

2 teaspoons baking powder

1 Whisk the eggs with the caster sugar until fluffy and thick. This is best done in a set-and-forget mixer.

2 Mix the baking powder with the almond meal and fold through, gently, with the chopped almonds.

3 Fold in rhubarb purée. You will have a very light, very airy mixture, almost filling the bowl of a Kenwood mixer.

4 Pour the mix into a well-greased pan, the bottom covered with grease-proof paper.

5 Bake in a 200°C oven for about 35 minutes, until the top is browned and gives to the knife. If you allow it to cook longer, it will get firmer and drier. If you prefer it that way, watch it for burning.

6 Allow to rest for a time, then unmould.

7 Allow to cool and serve dredged with icing sugar. It is also lovely served warm.

WINE ✤ *How about a cup of your finest tea — in a pot with the full ceremony? Otherwise, try a tawny port — Seppelt O.P. 90, Mildara Cavendish, Hardys Show are some of my favourites.*

♥
## MUESLI WITH STRAWBERRIES, BANANAS AND COCONUT MILK

Once I started to think seriously about breakfast, questions started popping up here there and everywhere.

Should we eat breakfast at all? Contradictions galore here from a stream of experts. When I was young I was sure the first meal of the day should be considered a visit to the fuel pump. Fill 'er up. This is my children's solution. Stacks of food first thing, and not much for the rest of the day.

Then, as is the way with such things, came another medical breakthrough. Have nothing for breakfast, and use the midday meal as a stoker. Problem here. Aren't we at work, or school, or asleep, at noon?

The only constant seems to be that you don't eat too much for dinner, as it rocks and rolls around in the tummy all night. I speak for this theory, but ignore its wisdom. Dinner is pretty much the only time, in our culture, when we have a chance to eat together as a family, and/or socialise, so, as with most things to do with good medical advice, if it doesn't suit, I roll on regardless. Which, in the end, is why I always eat breakfast: always have, always will.

So, if we all ignore the medics, and all eat breakfast, why do we treat it with such disdain, preferring coffee, toast and packaged cereal (now that we are scared off eggs) day in, day out? No argument here. We are too lazy, and prefer the extra half hour in the cot.

No more. I decided to make my own version of what the Swiss call muesli, the Americans crunchy granola. Now it is part of my life's work to wean my daughters off Weet-Bix and on to crunchy granola.

I don't think it will succeed. Even my trump card — replacing plain milk with a strawberry and banana thick shake was, excuse me, fruitless. 'I can't like that yukky milk,' they both proclaimed, simultaneously. Well, I can. So there.

♥   ♥   ♥   ♥   ♥

### THE 'ICE' CUBES

1 cup coconut milk

1 cup milk

¹/₂ cantaloup or a banana

### THE CRUNCH

1 cup oats

¹/₂ cup sesame seeds

³/₄ cup whizzed oats

1 cup whizzed pecan nuts

¹/₄ cup desiccated coconut

³/₄ cup raisins

¹/₂ cup flaked almonds

¹/₂ cup honey

¹/₂ cup walnut oil

¹/₂ cup water

### THE FROTHY MILK

a little milk

whatever soft fruit you have available, but strawberries are a must

*Other likely lads are bananas, cantaloup, raspberries, and if the pocket is okay, some pawpaw, papaya, or mango.*

### THE DAY BEFORE

1 Whizz up the coconut milk, milk and cantaloup/banana, and freeze in a cube tray. This is not absolutely vital, but as near as. The milk mix at breakfast must be ice-cold.

2 Mix all the grains, raisins, etc. There are plenty of other options — grains and dried fruits (check the larder), but I wouldn't do without the oats, or sesame seeds. Warm through the honey, walnut oil (extravagant this: vegetable oil will do, but you should at least try walnut oil — it is delicious with salads, anyway) and water, until the honey melts and mixes through the grains until all are touched by the honey-oil. Spread out on tray(s).

3 Heat the oven to 200°C and put in the grains. When the aroma is quite strong, remove and stir so that none of the grains stick. If you want your breakfast really roasted and crunchy, put back in the oven until they are quite tanned, but be careful, lest they burn. Otherwise remove when they separate easily. Allow to cool, and put in jars.

**BREAKFAST TIME (OR LUNCH TIME, OR AFTERNOON SNACK TIME!)**

4 Make the frothy milk. Combine the milk with the soft fruit and a couple of coconut–banana–milk ice cubes. Whizz until fluffy and pour over your crunchy business. At the right time of the year, serve with raspberries and mango slices.

# BAKING: NO SHORT CUTS

aking is not one of my strengths. For one simple reason. The best baker is one who methodically follows routines and directions. That's not me. The best baker is one who bakes constantly; who has taken the routines into the soul and can reproduce them this way and that at will; that's not me either. I can't imagine having the time and discipline to define and refine and perfect; and finally, the best baker is inclined to be, shall we say, corpulent. That would be me, and my family, if I were a baker. We share a marvellous lack of discipline when it comes to cakes and tarts and buns and puddings.

Bread is a different matter. I need bread. I need it for breakfast, lunch and dinner. I use it in ways which drive my wife crazy. Still she cannot understand that a potato sandwich is one of the world's great delights, still she cannot understand that the lamb which took her ages to prepare tastes doubly wonderful on top of a piece of crusty bread, still she cannot understand that such theatrics are my ultimate compliment; and now that our children are doing it too, she cannot see that as a reasonable maintenance of close family bonds.

We got lazy with bread making, somewhere in the sixties. It was too easy to buy what appeared to be attractive and flavoursome; we got busy, and didn't put aside the time to make our own. Soon enough, the flour we needed for bread making was no longer easily available. A skill which once came naturally, was too hard for the person with two cars, a PC, a dishwasher, a fan-forced oven, a microwave and a whizzo mixer.

What I enjoy about baking bread is its lack of discipline. When you're making a special cake, or a delicate scone, or a mighty muffin, you need to measure to the line. With bread, the more flamboyant you are, the more fun the end result is. And it doesn't make you fat.

## WHAT YOU'LL NEED

1 **You must have so-called 'strong' flour for making any sort of bread.** 'Strong' means ripping with protein, or gluten. This is the muscle of the flour, the organiser of the strands of molecules and such, which will keep the mass together when the dough is expanding. If your flour does not have the gluten strength, your best endeavours will get you nowhere. Buy bread flour in large quantities — it's cheaper and it encourages you to make it, and make it, and make it.

2 **Make sure you have a supply of dried yeast as a permanent fixture in your pantry or freezer.** Yeast works perfectly well straight from the freezer, although I have never felt the need for such preservation. Yeast does not hang around if you use it every day.

3 **An old-fashioned mixer, with all the beating attachments.** These machines drifted out of fashion when the modern food processor arrived on the scene. Whizzers are marvellous, but unless you have a commercial version, they are neither powerful enough to work dough, nor large enough to produce a batch to feed the family. The Kenwood mixer is just the thing for terrific bread making. But don't be discouraged if you haven't got one: the first loaf was put together with shoulders and forearms and strong hands. Instead of going to aerobics, make your own bread.

## THE RECIPES

♥
## BREAD, FOR STARTERS

F unny thing about making bread. If you succeed, people look at you as if you have just taken a set off Steffi Graf. But the great irony here is that cave dwellers were making bread before they discovered there was more to communicating than grunting and pointing, and screaming and hitting people over the head with clubs. Which probably means that John McEnroe is a pretty hot baker.

Five thousand years on: the fast world, and nobody makes bread. Sad, isn't it? The pace of life has made it more convenient to buy the staff of life in plastic bags, and the need to earn an even bigger quid has turned professional bread makers into merchants of air and strange, sliced, flavourless rubbish.

I have a vague memory of the introduction of sliced bread. I remember kicking and yelling and screaming at my mother — which probably explains why I like John McEnroe — that my sandwiches had to be made with sliced bread since all the other kids had sliced bread and why shouldn't I? For much of the sixties, seventies and early eighties it seemed that sliced bread was all you could get — thus the now *passé* saying: 'The best thing since sliced bread.'

But somewhere through those times, a few hankerers for old times started making old-style bread, and people liked it, and supported them, and now it seems that here and there sliced bread is fading away. Such are the twists and turns of progress.

But still there are very few of us who make bread at home. Most of that is to do with time, or the lack of it; but not to be under-rated is the difficulty in buying flour with enough protein (gluten) to allow for the dough to come together happily and then flex its muscles. Complicated thing flour, for what looks like no more than an inert white powder. Not so.

Whenever I bring together flour and yeast and liquid and salt into a dough, I can't help but think of that marvellous 'sperm scene' in Woody Allen's *Everything You Ever Wanted To Know About Sex ...* The sperm are hanging around waiting for action, and suddenly it's all go, go, go ... (Please, if you haven't seen the movie, use your imagination for the climax, etc.)

Bread making is pretty much the same. Add yeast and water to flour, flavour it with a little salt, add a little muscle, and suddenly all these molecules start working up to a frenzy — creating powerful bonds, then a silky smoothness, and finally a slow expansion as the yeast produces carbon dioxide. We then have the first stage of a loaf.

The variations are up to you. Start with the right ingredients, follow the basics, then enlarge your repertoire as you gain confidence. Persist, fail, examine, persist, succeed. The only rule I concern myself with is this: the final size of the loaf depends on the amount of liquid you start with. Lots of liquid, plenty big loaf. A little liquid, itsy-bitsy roll. So start in a haphazard way, pour some liquid into a bowl, add some yeast, and then make it into a ball with some flour and salt and sugar, and see what happens. When you get really serious, buy a book like *The Italian Baker* by Carol Field, and try as many of its recipes as you can.

♥ ♥ ♥ ♥ ♥

**2 teaspoons sugar**

**2 teaspoons yeast**

*Use the dried version. It keeps well and works well.*

**1 cup water at room temperature**

**enough flour to bring the mixture into a firm ball**

*It will be somewhere about 2 cups. Remember it must be 'strong' flour, meaning flour with at least 12 per cent gluten. It is usually marked 'bread flour,' often available only at health food shops. (If you are making a wholemeal loaf, mix the wholemeal flour with a high percentage of unbleached white flour. This is where the muscles come from.)*

**2 teaspoons salt**

**1 dessertspoon caraway seeds or poppy seeds**

**egg yolk and a little milk, mixed together for the glaze**

**You don't need an electric machine to make bread, but it helps**

*Make it by hand the first time, mixing and kneading by hand, then leave it to the machine next time.*

1 Mix the sugar and yeast with the water, and add the flour, salt and caraway seeds.

2 Turn on the machine, with the dough hook in place, and mix until it shapes into a ball, or something like it. Feel the dough with your finger. It should be smooth and a little glossy, and have come away from the sides of the bowl. If it feels wet and sticky, add a little more flour and mix again. The more you make, the more experienced you will

be with the feel. (If you are doing this by hand, mix first with a spoon until it comes together, then by hand, on a well-floured bench, kneading until it is glossy and smooth.)

3 Leave to prove in a warmish place. The best temperature is 27°C, but cooler is okay and warmer is not too bad. It should double in size in about 2 hours.

4 When it has doubled, punch it back and knead it briefly. (You can tell when it has had enough — if you press it with your finger, the indentation will hold its shape. When the yeast is still working, you will see it push back.)

5 Now that it's back to its starting size, shape it and place it in a well-oiled tin. Allow to rise until doubled again — this takes about half the time the first rising took. Paint the top with the egg yolk and milk mixture. Sprinkle some caraway or poppy seeds (or sesame seeds) on top.

6 Bake in a 200°C oven for about 20 minutes, then remove the loaf from the tin. Return to the oven, and continue baking for another 5–10 minutes.

♥

## SOURDOUGH, FROM THE BEGINNING

When you have made sourdough bread you have returned to the dark ages, when bread makers were feeling their way, and strange things happened to the pile of dough in the corner of the cave; the only machines were their arms, and the bread tasted different every time it came out of the coals.

It's very easy to lose sight of the fact that bread is nothing more than a liquid (usually water), flour, salt, and yeast (and there is plenty of this wild micro-organism hanging around in the air we breath). Sourdough bread relies on its environment, the air that it breathes, for its flavour and structure. You can give it a kick-start on its journey, but once you start, you're there for the long haul. Treat it like a pet, and you'll get to love it.

Don't think of it as time-consuming. Treat it as a hobby. No matter how busy you are, once you get into the routine, you should be able to mix your dough in the morning, allow it to rise all through the day, shape it in the evening, allow it to prove as you sleep, and bake it while you shower the next morning. And so it goes.

♥   ♥   ♥   ♥   ♥

## SATURDAY MORNING

### THE STARTER

½ teaspoon dried yeast

½ cup water, at room temperature

enough unbleached white flour to bring the above to a sticky mess

*If the end result is too solid, add a little more water. You will need about a cup of flour.*

**1** Mix the yeast into the water, and add the flour, stirring, beating with a wooden spoon until it has come together smoothly. In the beginning, flour and water were left to their own devices to create yeast, but it does take more time than we have

got. My mother talks about making yeast with potatoes during the war. That is going a bit far these days. Set aside, covered, in a warm place, for the rest of the day and night.

## SUNDAY MORNING, AFTER THE MORNING STRETCHES

**2** The starter should be smelling strongly of yeast, should have a spongy, creamy, cratered look. Taste it. It will have a certain sourness. Set aside half for tomorrow, 'feeding' it with a little more flour and water until the new is as smooth as was the old. This will be the next day's 'starter'.

1 cup water, at room temperature

1 teaspoon salt

enough flour to bring the starter, the water and the salt to a firm yet sticky, not dry, not wet dough

**3** You can do all this in a mixer, but I prefer to do things by hand until I can do them backwards. So add the water to the remaining starter, stirring until it is well broken up. Add the salt and toss in the flour.

**4** Mix it all together in a bowl until it gathers into a ball. Be tough with it — all you have to concern yourself with is its consistency. It must be firm, but not dry; sticky, but not wet. You'll get to know exactly the right consistency, and then it will be like riding a bike.

**5** Now knead it any way you like. With your palm, your elbows, your nose, your feet. Just knead it until it really feels strong. You are working in pockets of air by the process of compressing and folding and bringing the gluten into orderly lines, untangling the inner mess that occurs when the water meets the flour. The gluten is happy when the dough gets stiff, is harder to work, and takes on a smooth, almost glistening surface, something like a baby's botty. Work it into a ball.

6 Rising time. Leave the dough covered, in a warm place, to rise. It will take most of the day. For this dough, the longer the rise the better.

### SUNDAY EVENING/NIGHT

7 The dough should have doubled, filled with carbon dioxide, and produced lovely yeasty smells, some time around darkness. If you leave it too long, never fear, just punch it down and start again. You can re-knead at any time. If all is well, punch it down, knead it briefly (it will be easier this time), shape it, and put it in the tin in which you will bake. Again it will be smooth, glistening. Place in a warmish spot, uncovered (a flavoursome crust is formed), and leave overnight to rise.

### MONDAY MORNING

8 Heat the oven to 210°C as soon as you wake. Toss the bread in and bake for about 30 minutes. The bread is done when it sounds hollow to the tap.

9 Before you shower, start the process again with the starter you kept aside (from step 2 above). Don't be tense. You won't be late for work. On the way to the office, think of the smells you experienced, the potential creativity you have in your hands, and think of your starter as a friend of mine does. 'It's like the cat,' he once said. 'You can't help caring for it, wondering whether it's happy, has had enough to eat and drink, and whether it's growing.'

♥

## FOCACCIA, PIZZA, OR WHATEVER

D on't be fooled by all the terrific press about focaccia. It's just a flash name for flat bread. You make it just the same way as bread, treat it the same way as bread, love it just the same way.

If you make it yourself, or buy it (usually at an exorbitant price), it makes for a terrific way to overcome the dreadful pizzas at the corner takeaway. Just slice the focaccia in half (vertically, not horizontally) and cut out a lid, leaving raised edges. Fill the exposed base with puréed tomatoes and olive oil and red peppers and all the things you like in a pizza, bake it, and you've got the best of all worlds, without a trip into the night.

A filled focaccia takes this particular bread right back to its beginnings. Focaccia comes from the Latin *focus* (meaning hearth), and it was here at the hearth the flattened bread had its humble beginnings. Smart bakers used to poke the dough on the way to the oven to provide little pools in the top for lovelies like oil, or herbs, or salt, or spices, or all of the above.

Naturally, there is nothing to making it. Just get hold of some strong flour and pour a liquid into a bowl, starting with water, then perhaps milk, or some olive oil. Add some yeast, salt, sugar, some herbs maybe, then enough flour to make into a dough. Then start kneading. Or, better still, get a machine to do it.

♥    ♥    ♥    ♥    ♥

3 teaspoons dried yeast

2 cups just warm water, or a mix of milk and water (makes about 1 kg of dough)

2 teaspoons sugar

enough strong flour to bring it all together

*For this dough you can use a mix of strong flour and plain flour.*

2 teaspoons salt

a handful of fresh herbs, or a teaspoon of spices

a good pour of the best flavoured olive oil

1 Mix the yeast through the liquid until it has dissolved, and then add the sugar, flour, salt, spices and herbs, slowly, to allow them all to come together with the liquid.

2 Knead by hand or with a machine until the dough glistens and feels slightly cool. Form into a ball, cover with a dampish cloth and allow to rise in a warm place. It will take a couple of hours.

3 When the dough has doubled in volume, or thereabouts, go at it with a gusto, punching out the carbon dioxide which has built it up. Roll it out flat, and put it onto the oiled tray on which it will be baked. You should have enough to make two focaccia or a pair of pizzas. Focaccia can be as thick or as thin as you like. I prefer it to be reasonably

thick. Leave it to rise, covered again. After half an hour, you can press some dimples into the dough. Leave it to rise for another half hour.

4 Brush the top with some olive oil or milk and water, and spray some rock salt, or sesame seeds, or caraway seeds about. Bake in a pre-heated 210°C oven for about 20–25 minutes. The aroma will tell you when it is done. If you like, you can scatter some finely sliced garlic over the top after about 15 minutes baking. When it is done, turn it over for a few minutes to give the bottom a bit of free hot air.

5 Serve as you wish — as is, or torn in the rustic style, for sandwiches. Or freeze it for the day when you really can't do without a pizza.

Now, how to turn a flat focaccia into a whizzo pizza.

♥    ♥    ♥    ♥    ♥

6 ripe plum tomatoes, peeled, or a small tin of tomatoes

salt

1 bunch of basil

1 focaccia (will make two good-sized pizzas)

best virgin olive oil

dozen olives, seeded and chopped (or preserved artichokes, or mushrooms, or salami, or ham or whatever is hanging about)

black pepper

12 slices melting cheese

*I love Raclette, the Swiss melter, or Gruyère, or Provolone, or even cheddar.*

1 Cook the tomatoes, with a little salt, in the microwave, for 25–30

minutes, until they have broken down and the resulting sauce is rather thick. (You can add chilli here, if you like it.) Break up with a fork, add the basil leaves, and set aside to cool.

**2** Cut the focaccia in half and make a slit halfway through the top crust, 2 cm from the edge, all the way around each half. Gently remove the lid and any loose crumbs, until halfway through. You should be left with something like a pie crust, with four high edges.

**3** Heat the oven to 200°C and place the case inside for about 10 minutes, until the bread base is firm and crisp, but not brown.

**4** Remove from the oven, and drizzle olive oil across the base. Spoon the tomato mix on the base, to the edges. Sprinkle the olives (or whatever) about, make several turns of the pepper mill, and cover with the sliced cheese.

**5** Return to the oven, and cook again until the cheese melts — about 10 minutes. Serve in wedges.

♥

## A LITTLE LIKE PIZZA, OR BRUSCHETTA; AN OILY LOAF

**Y**ou can have the perfect pizza at home, one that can be put together in the same time it takes to venture into the night to visit the local licence-to-print-money. And you don't have to make the dough. You don't even need focaccia.

All you need is a white cottage loaf — the sort with a circular base and a semi-spherical top — the best olive oil, garlic, tomatoes, salt, a few vegetables, a well-flavoured melting cheese, whatever else is about, and a little lateral thinking.

Although this dish represents the ultimate in simplicity, it is important that the ingredients be first class. The best breads are the crunchy white Italian loaves, or a similar local version from your favourite baker. If you make it yourself, all the better.

You must have plenty of the best, richly flavoured virgin olive oil. The origins of this dish are worth noting. It comes from the olive-growing regions of Italy during harvest. Large slices of bread are toasted, rubbed with garlic and covered with oil, still warm from the press. It is known as *fettunta* (oily slice) in Tuscany, and *bruschetta* about Rome.

♥   ♥   ♥   ♥   ♥

**a loaf of bread**
*Slice the bread parallel to the base, about 2 cm thick. You should end up with 5 slices of varying diameters.*

**1–2 red peppers, roughly chopped**

**4 tomatoes, skins removed by making an X on the base and dunking them for about 20 seconds in boiling water**
*If they're out of season, use tinned tomatoes, no salt or sugar added.*

**pinch of salt**

**1 cup full-flavoured virgin olive oil**

**2 garlic cloves, chopped finely**

**100g hot salami, skinned and sliced to whatever thickness you like**

**100g melting cheese**
*Try Raclette, or Parmesan, or Gruyère, or cheddar.*

black pepper

bunch of chives, chopped

1 Heat the oven to 200°C. Put slices of bread on a baking tray and place in the oven until the tops dry out. Turn until bases are crisp. This should take about 15 minutes. You are not about making toast, just drying out the surface to make it firm and crisp.

2 Allow the dried bread to cool.

3 Steam the peppers until soft. Set aside. Peppers taste much better when roasted and skinned, but that takes time. If you're thinking ahead, take the time and effort, and skin them.

4 With the back of a fork, or a potato masher, or best of all, a hand-held whizzer, mash the tomatoes with a pinch of salt and three-quarters of the olive oil, added gradually. Mix in most of the chopped garlic. The rest of the garlic should be mixed with the remaining olive oil. Depending on your machine, you will end up with anything from a tomato pulp to a tomato purée.

5 With a pastry brush, paint the dried-out bread with the olive oil–garlic mix.

6 Spoon the tomato–olive oil mix thickly on the base, cover with the salami and peppers. (Marinated mushrooms, available in quality food shops, work superbly in this combination, as do artichoke hearts marinated in olive oil.) Sprinkle with the cheese.

7 Bake in a 220°C oven until the cheese has melted and the tomato mix has been heated through, about 10 minutes. Keep an eye on the show to make sure the cheese does not burn.

8 Just before serving, sprinkle the pizza with a good dose of olive oil, black pepper and the chives. The pizza will be dripping with olive oil and have a delicious aroma. Serve in tiny slices.

The dried and oiled bases make for marvellous platforms for purées of olives, or raw tomatoes, warmed through — use your imagination — and they are great for openers at a dinner party, when the guests are standing around, not quite knowing what to do, or where to go.

♥

## HOT CROSS BUNS

I had always believed that hot cross buns had come from our English, Christian roots, and that may be so as far as Australia is concerned, but in the big, wide, wonderful world, 'twas not always so.

In the very old days, it was common to mark a cross on bread or bun dough, not as a cross might be considered in these Christian times, but as a mark of the four quarters of the moon — thus honouring various gods and goddesses. The mark of the cross could well have been intended to ward off evil spirits that could stop the bread from rising.

Hell on earth. It seems like a good idea for those of us who have been befuddled with non-rising loaves.

One thing's for sure. Hot cross buns these days have as much to do with Good Friday as they do with the first Tuesday in November. They now are no more than the tradition left over from old truly Christian times, multiplied a thousandfold by the need for bakers to make a quid. You can also mark down the recipe for any time of the year. Buns made at home are worth a million of those from the shops. This recipe makes twenty.

♥   ♥   ♥   ♥   ♥

**1 cup sultanas, or currants, or both**
*Don't use chopped peel, unless it's your own.*

**750 g unbleached plain bread flour**
*You will need strong flour for this.*

**4 teaspoons ground cinnamon**

**2 teaspoons ground cloves**

**1 teaspoon ground allspice**

**a little salt**

**100 g brown sugar**

**100 g unsalted butter, not soft, not firm**

**2 cups tepid water**

**1 egg yolk**

**3 teaspoons dried yeast**

**THE CROSS**

**some caster sugar**

**a little water**

**a little plain flour**

**1 egg yolk, beaten, and a little milk, mixed together**

1 Mix the sultanas through the flour and then work through the cinnamon, cloves, allspice, salt and sugar.

2 Rub the butter through the flour, as you would if making a crumble, or some pastry. It should blend in easily.

3 Mix the water, egg yolk and yeast in the bowl of a mixer, and add the flour.

4 Using the dough hook on the mixer, mix rapidly until it all comes together, forming a ball. This can be done by hand, of course, but it is a million times easier with the machine. Mix it for a few minutes, until it is well worked, and the sultanas start to pop through the dough. Leave, covered, to rise until double in size — about 2–3 hours, depending on the warmth of the day.

5 Once doubled, punch down and knead by hand for a couple of minutes. The mix will be smooth and glossy.

6 Cut in half and freeze half for another day. Half of the dough will make ten buns.

7 Divide the dough into pieces about as large as a squash ball. Rub them in your palms until they form rough balls, and place into a greased baking dish, about 2 cm apart. Leave to rise for about an hour, until doubled. The individual buns should have expanded to meet one another.

8 While the dough is rising, mix the sugar, water and plain flour into a paste, and paint the top of the buns with a cross. This can also be done with a very rough pastry.

9 Paint the tops with the beaten egg yolk–milk mix and bake in a

200°C oven for about 25 minutes. Remove from the tray and return to the oven for another 5–10 minutes.

10 Serve buttered, with your best coffee and best goodwill.

♥

## MICHELE DAY'S FRUIT CAKE

It was during the fête season, and I was, as usual, picking through the jams and chutneys and cakes, when I picked up a cake labelled 'wholemeal boiled fruit cake'. It felt heavy, looked full of fruit, and, despite its weight, I felt sure it would be moist. But things aren't always as they look. I bought it, took it home, and ate it in one day. It was indeed what it seemed to be, and full of flavour as well.

I wrote glowingly about the cake, started a network to find its maker and the recipe, and, before you could could knock off a block of chocolate, there was the maker at the end of the phone.

'How did you do it?' I said, a little nervously to Michele Day, mother of two sets of twins.

'I went out with a boy when I was about 18,' she said, and I fumbled with the phone a little more nervously, 'and this was pretty much the recipe of his mother.' That was it, nothing more. She was not, she said, any great cook.

'It was a fluke,' she said.

'And why the bicarbonate of soda at the boiling stage?' I asked.

'I don't know,' she said. 'It has been trial and error. I just adjusted the recipe to suit my tastes — replacing white sugar with raw, white flour with wholemeal, varying the spices, and this was it.'

I had the recipe in my hand and started cooking. It all seemed so easy. It couldn't be true. Ten minutes preparation, an hour's cooling off, 90 minutes cooking, and there it was: light, moist, blackened at the edges. Just like the one at the fete. I had the wonder in my hands, for now and forever.

I made it again and took it to a party. Rave reviews. Naturally I took all the credit. Now, it was mine. That's the beauty of sharing recipes. Now it's yours too.

♥　♥　♥　♥　♥

2 cups raisins

2 cups sultanas

1 cup currants

300 g unsalted butter

2 short cups raw sugar

2 teaspoons bicarbonate soda

2 cups water

2 teaspoons nutmeg

2 teaspoons cinnamon

dash powdered cloves

4 well-beaten eggs

2 cups wholemeal plain flour

1 Put the raisins, sultanas, currants, butter, sugar, bicarbonate soda and water in a large saucepan, and boil for about 5 minutes, stirring until the sugar has dissolved. Keep a close watch on affairs or the violent reaction of the bicarbonate of soda will cause the lot to go over the top. Set aside to cool — about an hour.

2 Add the nutmeg, cinnamon, cloves and eggs, folding through the mixture. Then fold in the flour,

bit by bit, until it is well blended. The mix will be quite fluid. Perhaps this is the secret to the lightness: a minimum of flour to a lot of fruit makes for a very light mix. It tastes very much like a perfect Christmas pudding.

3 I greased a tin the first time, and the bottom stuck. Second up I used grease-proof paper, and it worked like a dream. Cook for about 90 minutes at 170°C, or until a knife tests clean.

♥

## SCONES, SLOW AND EASY

I always wondered why the old and doddery (mums, grans, etc.) always made better scones than I did. Then I started to get older and almost doddery and slower and wiser (the accumulated drip of experience) and started applying those fragments of age to making scones.

Guess what. Now I make scones like the old and etc. Why?

Only one answer to that. I'm doing it more slowly. Start thinking back through those accumulated drips. When you're at your peak, taking screamers, hitting the golfball 220 metres, cutting square off middle stump, life is hardly slow. You're flamboyant, cocky, your eyes dart, you're impatient, seeking, trying on, looking for quick gratification.

Then the ageing begins. You play from in front, looking for frees, you approach the par fours as par fives, and you play back to the bowler when it's on the stumps. So it is with scones. Do it slowly, do it methodi-

cally, do it gently, and you'll be amazed at the lightness of the heart, the crispness of the crust. They say, as well, that good scone makers are good in bed. I wonder …

You can make double this mix. Scones freeze beautifully, and I always reckon one load of washing up makes up triply for the slightly increased labour. And, with frozen scones in the freezer, you can toss one into the microwave at any time of day and night, and you will have steaming scones in 20 seconds flat. This batch will make about 2 dozen small, wimpy scones, and about 15 tough guys.

♥　♥　♥　♥　♥

1/2 teaspoon baking powder (for security)

1/2 teaspoon salt

300 g self-raising flour, sifted

plenty of sultanas, or currants, or raisins

150 g cold butter, cut into cubes

1 cup (and a bit) milk

sugar, if you wish

1 egg yolk, beaten, and a little milk, mixed together

1 Mix the baking power and salt into the flour, and add the sultanas etc.

2 With your fingers, work the butter into the flour. It should be slightly on the crumby side, a bit like the result you would get on the way to a crumble.

3 Work in the milk gently, bit by bit, mixing it through with a

fork. The mixture will gradually form into a dough, but will still be quite sticky. When it has come together well enough to work into a mass, stop adding the milk, and pat it with a bit more flour on your hands.

4 Flour a bench and remove the dough from the bowl. Cut the dough into two, and work each gently into a long thick sausage, pushing gently into shape rather than kneading. Flatten so the dough is about 5 cm thick. Make sure it is at least this thick. The last thing you want is wimpy scones. Give them size, and guts. Heat the oven to 200°C.

5 Slice into scones, and place gently on a greased baking tray. Brush the tops with the egg–milk wash and bake for 20 minutes, or until the kitchen takes on the tell-tale aroma of generations. Serve any way you like. Who needs to be told how to eat scones?

♥

## PASSIONFRUIT MUFFINS, GIVEN AN EXTRA ZING WITH RASPBERRIES

Whenever passionfruit are plentiful and cheap, don't miss any opportunity to try them any way you can or like, or think you like or think you can. Their flavour is so powerful they can even make a pavlova work, and that is saying something.

I was going through this stage of trying passionfruit with all my favourites, and it was natural to try them in muffins. In the end I felt like a passionfruit and looked like a hippopotamus. My boy had three for breakfast and then 'blued' when his sister nicked the fourth. They have that effect on you.

♥　♥　♥　♥　♥

**200 g plain flour**

**100 g white sugar**
*You can use brown, but you will get brown muffins.*

**2 teaspoons baking powder**

**3–4 passionfruit, including seeds and every last touch of juice and flesh**

**20 raspberries**
*Of course you don't need raspberries in this dish, but to deny them is to be happy with the same nine-to-five job all your life.*

**zest of 1 lemon**

**1 egg, beaten**

**100 g melted butter, or margarine**

**1 cup milk**

1 In a large bowl, combine the flour, sugar, baking powder, passionfruit, raspberries and lemon zest gently with a fork until they are well mixed. Make sure you do not overwork the mixture at any stage. If you can keep all the flesh adhering to the pips of the passionfruit, and the raspberries pretty much intact, you'll enjoy the end result even more.

2 Whisk the egg lightly and add it to the mixture, working it through gently. Add the butter, again working it through gently. You should have something of a batter, although it will still be quite firm.

3 Now the milk. The amount of milk you need depends a little on the moisture in the air, but if you

add a cup you'll never go wrong. Add it by halves, and you'll feel the mix lighten and easily leave the end of a spoon. It's ready to go.

4 Ease, rather than pour, into well-oiled muffin tins. For added security, I use roughly cut out grease-proof paper at the bottom of the moulds. Bake in a 200°C oven for about 30 minutes, until the muffins are well risen, the air is filled with lovely baking aromas, and the kids are lining up at the oven door.

♥

## MUFFINS WITH PEARS AND SULTANAS

200 g plain flour, sifted

100 g brown sugar

2 teaspoons baking powder

1 pear, peeled, cored, cut into cubes, and tossed in lemon juice

zest of 1 lemon

25 g sultanas

100 g just melted margarine, or butter

1 egg, well beaten

1 cup milk

1 Do all this by hand, in a large bowl. It comes together very quickly, works very well, and there is absolutely no need for a whizzer. Mix flour, sugar and baking powder together, making sure the sugar and flour are well mixed. Mix through the chopped pear, lemon zest and sultanas (or anything else you like).

2 Make a well in the flour, and mix in the butter and egg with a fork. There will be plenty of flour still unincorporated.

3 Add the milk, slowly, turning the mix into a homogenous, thick batter. You will need just short of a cup of milk. The mixture should not be pourable, but will need a pair of spoons to drop it into the muffin tray.

4 Grease the moulds or muffin cups and bake for 30 minutes at 200°C. Serve warm, as is, with coffee, or as a dessert.

♥

## BANANA CAKE SPLASHED WITH PASSIONFRUIT SYRUP

One of the first dishes I made successfully when I left home was a banana cake. I had no idea what I was doing, but those were the days when you tossed everything into the whizzer, pressed the button, and presto, there was the batter for a cake.

Nothing had come near to that cake over the years (from Tess Mallos' *Summit All Colour Cookbook*), but I'd been fiddling here and there with possible challengers, and finally, I managed a cake which has all the moistness of a brilliant cake and all the flavour of fresh bananas. The late addition of passionfruit came from the old restaurant days, when we used to put passionfruit syrup at the bottom of soufflé bowls. Passionfruit and banana are such perfect partners, the syrup seemed like a natural for this dish. It was.

♥   ♥   ♥   ♥   ♥

4 eggs at room temperature

125 g caster sugar

²/₃ cup buttermilk

*If you can't get buttermilk, whisk together some milk and yoghurt.*

zest of 1 lemon

3 egg whites

2 cups plain flour, double-sifted

2 teaspoons baking powder, mixed into the flour

150g butter, melted gently and allowed to cool

2 bananas, sliced finely, tossed in a little flour

6 passionfruit, seeded, 2 kept aside for the batter

2 teaspoons caster sugar for the passionfruit

1 You really do need a powerful mixer to ensure this dish's final lightness. Whisk the eggs and sugar with the whisk attachment until the mixture is very fluffy, and three or four times its starting volume. You cannot overbeat it.

2 With the beaters a little slower, allow the buttermilk to drip into the fluffy egg until well blended. Add the zest.

3 While the eggs are beating, whisk the egg whites until they have mounted and formed firm peaks.

4 Still whisking furiously with the machine, add the flour bit by bit, again making sure you maintain the lightness. Add the 2 passionfruit.

5 Remove a few ladles of batter into a separate bowl and whisk in the melted butter, slowly but surely. Then whisk the resulting butter–batter mixture into the main bowl, again slowly but surely. You're almost there.

6 Fold the egg whites through the mixture, half first, then the rest, keeping it as light as you possibly can.

7 Fold through the bananas and pour the mixture (it will be pourable and rather light) into a well-greased cake tin. Bake in a 200°C oven for 55–60 minutes.

8 While the cake is baking, cook the pulp and juice from the 4 remaining passionfruit for a couple of minutes (in the microwave or on top of the stove), making sure it does not cook too fast. Scrape the seeds, pulp and juice on a fine sieve over a bowl, retaining only the juice. This can be quite tedious, but is well worth the effort. Add the 2 teaspoons of sugar, and cook on a high heat, stirring, for about a minute. Set aside.

9 Test the cake, and when done, unmould.

10 While the cake is still hot, paint the bottom with the passionfruit syrup, allowing it to seep through. Served warm is ideal, but it's pretty good in the lunch box.

♥

## PUFF PASTRY AND FOOTBALL

There is one sure sign that you have made it as a cook. You not only announce to the world that you are about to make puff pastry, you actually succeed in your attempt. Not that it's any big deal making the revered mix of butter and flour; all you have to do is bring together all the key points of fine cooking —

care, concentration, commitment and common sense — and there'll be a spectacular crowd pleaser at the end. And, as with soufflés, there are volumes of sad stories about failed attempts at puff pastry. All the more satisfying to succeed.

Puff pastry making is an ideal Sunday afternoon exploit, especially in winter, not only because it is beautifully relaxing, but because you will need an afternoon to succeed. Making puff pastry is to me what gardening is to those with sturdy backs, and golf to those with fluid joints. The rolling pin is the six-iron of the kitchen.

If you are one of those people who decides at a moment's notice that you are going to attempt something dramatic, then this one's for you. A few words of caution. You will need plenty of room, the more the better; for clumsy types (like me), the deck of an aircraft carrier is just about right. Those of you with housekeepers and gardeners will probably want to rush out and buy a marble slab for your pastry. I wouldn't bother. Just wipe the breakfast crumbs from the kitchen table. If the temperature of the kitchen and/or the table is ever a worry (as in too hot) you won't be inside making pastry anyway — you'll be out making the most of the sunshine.

Remember, always make plenty more than you need. Puff pastry freezes perfectly, and you won't often have the time to devote to making it.

♥ ♥ ♥ ♥ ♥

1 kg flour

400 ml water

100 g melted butter

900 g butter

**1** In a large bowl, mix together gently the flour, water and melted butter, and then form the mix into a ball. Allow to rest for about 30 minutes in the refrigerator. There are several resting periods to allow the gluten in the flour to stop flexing its muscles. (That's the beauty of making puff pastry. You can justify a lazy day by pointing triumphantly to the completed mound of pastry. In fact, you can clock on at midday and off at five o'clock, do about 15 minutes real work, and crash exhausted at the end. Perhaps Sunday afternoon football was invented for puff pastry makers. The breaks fall perfectly in line with the resting periods! )

**2** Unwind yourself from the couch, and cut an 'X' into the ball, to about three-quarters of its depth. Pull down the flaps formed by the cut and roll them out quite firmly. You will have a square in the middle, and four flaps, each flap being a quarter the thickness of the square.

**3** Now to the solid butter. The butter is about to be placed primly on the centre of the pastry square, but first it should be bashed into the same shape as the square. Work it so that it will sit securely in place. The butter and the pastry should be at the same temperature: cool, but not cold.

**4** With the butter in place, fold the flaps over and join the edges with a little water to hold them firmly in place. The mound may need a few light taps with the rolling pin at the start to get it to a manageable thickness for rolling. Roll out gently, firmly and carefully into a rectangular shape. You should be able to *feel* the pastry through the rolling pin.

5 Now we are at the first climax, and that, in this case, is no tautology. I have heard people say that success with puff pastry is one of *the* great feelings. You are about to find out.

6 Roll to a rectangle with a length that is *four* times the width. This is the danger area. It takes some trial and error before you get to feel the ideal density and temperature of the dough–butter. If the butter is too hard it could crack through the dough. If the dough is too soft the butter could ooze through. Have plenty of flour on hand to flour both bench and dough. Keep rolling, gently but firmly, working the pin at each end of the rectangle. You must be careful not to force a great tidal wave of butter to one end of the rectangle. If that does happen, you can cut your losses by slicing away the extruding butter. When you are satisfied you have reached the required length, 'square' off the ends.

7 The best way to picture the next step is to do it with paper. Cut out a piece of paper 30 cm x 11 cm (a piece of foolscap cut down the middle). This ratio of width to length (3:1) is sufficient for paper, but for the more unwieldy pastry you will need a ratio of about 4:1. All the folds are done with the long side — the short side will still be 11 cm at the end of the folding. On the long side, from the left, measure 10 cm, then 15 cm, and finally 5 cm, marking each

area A, B and C. Fold A over B and C over B so that the edges of areas A and C touch. You will now have an area 15 cm x 11 cm.

8 Make a line through the middle of the area leaving 7.5 cm on either side; fold the left half over itself to touch the middle line, and do the same with the right side. You will now have an open, long, but narrow 'book'. Close the book. The final 'book' will be about 11 cm x 4 cm. What you have done with the paper, you must do with the pastry.

9 With your sheet of paper at your side, follow exactly the same routine with the pastry. Once you have a long, narrow, and quite thick piece of pastry, you again roll it out until it is four times as long as it is wide. After that mammoth exercise of both mind and body you must be in need of a rest. So is the pastry. Leave it for at least a half an hour in the refrigerator, then once more roll it firmly, but gently, so it is four times as long as it is wide.

10 Again you must feel the pastry working beneath your roller. Be strong, be gentle. When you have achieved the length required, the dough will be smooth and sleek. Fold it over itself as before and leave it to rest for about an hour. If you feel content at this stage, the job is nearly done. One more rolling and folding will give you a superbly flaky pastry, two more and it will be explosive. If you have made an absolute mess don't worry too much. Just roll your mess into a ball and call it rough puff. It will still make a delicious and buttery pastry.

11 If, however, you have been successful, you should now have enough pastry to make about thirty pretty flash variations of pastry dishes, so cut the pastry into four blocks, and freeze three of them for other days.

12 To get the taste of the pastry, make a quick apple tart. Peel and slice some apples roughly, and cook them gently with some lemon juice, some lemon zest and a handful of sugar, until the apples are soft and mushy. Force the mix through a sieve to remove the pips and set aside.

13 Meanwhile cut away a small block of your pride and joy and roll it as thinly as you can, no more than 2 mm thick. Heat the oven to 200°C. Cut the pastry into the shape of a diamond, score some lines lightly on top, and place it in the refrigerator for about 10 minutes. Remove and brush the top with a mix of egg yolk and milk. Bake the pastry for at least 25 minutes, until the top is golden brown. Warm the apple purée. When the pastry is cooked, slice it in half, spoon some purée onto the base, and put the lid on top. Wolf it down with stacks of cream.

14 Make a toast to your amazing cooking prowess. There is simply nothing you cannot do.

# ODDS AND ENDS

On the way through a work like this you come across little odds and ends that, by themselves, might be insufficient to form a recipe, or a tale, but can often lead to little surprises within a dish, on a buffet, or at a barbecue — or these days, as part of a flash antipasto.

Then there are the basics, the assumptions you make when you're about to make a sauce, or a sandwich. Remember, not all the things you do in the kitchen need discipline and routine. What you do in the kitchen might be the only opportunity you have in your life to entertain, to be flamboyant, to make people happy, to be a star. Take it on with a relish. Take a bow. Be Pavarotti.

♥

## PARMIGIANO REGGIANO

This is the very best of all the Italian cheeses, created under a strict regimen at Parma in the region of Emilia-Romagna. This is not the Parmesan that frequents dull plastic packets in supermarkets. This is one of the great cheeses of the world, full of flavour and style, with a marvellous tradition behind each wheel. It is magnificent when grated over or tossed through pasta, sensational when sliced finely and worked through a simple spinach salad with black pepper and virgin olive oil, superb when eaten with a fresh peach or a poached pear, stands alone just as it is. There are some places which will sell this great cheese at different stages of maturity; the rule is, the older the better, but it is still a great joy to try a young (ish) 18-month-old cheese. It is, as is the way with such things, rather expensive. Parmigiano Reggiano has its name stamped on the rind, so there can be no mistake. Do try some; even if you buy it just once, the memory will be worth the price.

♥

## GRANO PADANO

This is the usual Parmesan sold in most delicatessens. If you had never tasted its superior rival, Parmigiano Reggiano, you might well be saying this is one of the great cheeses of the world. It is, but it misses out when you compare the pair head to head. The 'Grana' in the title refers to the grain of the cheese, a hard grating variety, which shares all the attributes of Parmigiano Reggiano, except for that wonderful middle flavour. It is, however, the cheese most on my table, because of its affordability.

♥
## PROVOLONE

This is a very Italian cheese, richly flavoured when it gets old, delicious and subtle when young. I much prefer the older version, which has a much sharper flavour — thus the addendum *piccante*. It makes a terrific top to a pizza.

♥
## OLIVE OIL

I'm sure you can't operate a decent kitchen without a large cache of olive oil. In fact, and this is close to heresy, I think I'd prefer a well-stocked cellar of olive oil than a well-stocked cellar of red wine. The Italians reckon there is no other ingredient more important to the flavour of Italian cooking; I reckon that rule applies to all cooking. You can add it to soup, highlight a salad, cook in it and with it, rub your hands with it. I am sure of this: if you have a very good olive oil, which usually means a virgin olive oil (oil crushed by mechanical means, rather than with chemical or heat treatment, brilliantly flavoured, with a minimum of oleic acid — no more than 1%) your cooking will march ahead. Go to a very good deli, and ask the people behind the jump for a taste and see; pick a brand you like and stick with it, and then develop your palate through the more expensive and difficult to

find varieties. And put your favourite olive oil on your list of Christmas and birthday presents: for giving and receiving.

♥
## YEAST

I always use dried yeast because it is always there, always ready to go, and you never have to toss it out when you buy too much. It also can be used directly from the freezer.

♥
## GARAM MARSALA

This is no more than warm spice mix. Every Indian home has a different recipe; my view is you should try all sorts of mixes, starting with what you've got in the cupboard, until you hit on one you really like. There are a few musts: cumin seeds, coriander seeds, cinnamon, dried chilli, cloves, black peppercorns, star anise, fennel and nutmeg. Use seeds, whizz them in a spare coffee grinder, and keep them for all sorts of flamboyant flavour hits. Try this in your next cheese sandwich. Grate a carrot and sprinkle it over the slices of cheese, then hit the lot with a couple of teaspoons of garam masala. It gives a tired old sandwich a real how do you do.

♥
## PIGS' TROTTERS

Don't attempt to bone and cook a pig's trotter at home. Seek out a special restaurant which has this classic on the menu, take it, and savour it.

## ♥ SHORT PASTRY

I t always used to drive me nuts making pastry until I came across this mixture. It's easy, it holds together, and it rolls out easily and well. You can rely on it.

♥   ♥   ♥   ♥   ♥

1 ½ cups flour

125 g butter, softened

pinch of salt

1 egg

¼ - ½ cup water

Work the butter and salt into the flour with your fingertips until it gets something of a crumby feel. Stir in the egg. Add the water gradually until the dough has been worked into a ball. The amount of water depends on the moisture in the air, and in the flour. Mix it all together gently, then put into the fridge until you're ready to roll it out.

## ♥ CHESTNUTS

T hese lovely orbs were very much part of my childhood holidays in Daylesford, my mother's and grandmother's home town. They made for very social evenings about the fire roasting, peeling and munching. When you cook chestnuts just right they have a delicious texture and sweet flavour, so different from most nuts. Fortunately for all us chestnut lovers and fast livers, modern technology has given us the glorious roasted flavour in seconds, without the need for the roaring fire. Just prick the shell with a sharp knife and put the nut in the microwave for about 20 seconds. The shell will split and the chestnut will be cooked, and delicious, and easy to peel.

## ♥ RASPBERRIES WITH GOAT'S CHEESE

F or those of you who think you have tried raspberries every possible way, try this one. Serve them as an accompaniment to a creamy goat's cheese: i.e. goat's cheese with raspberries, not raspberries with goat's cheese. You'll be amazed at how happy they are together.

## ♥ SPINACH

D on't underestimate spinach. I think Popeye has much to answer for. The bulging bicepped one certainly put me off it as a young 'un, and I'm not sure why. Maybe it was that appearance of sludge that did it for me. Lately I have taken young spinach leaves straight from the garden, tossed them with a little vinegar and a good run of olive oil, and loved them. Older greens I've steamed and used as part of a stuffing; or to kick along a ravioli; or as part of a sauce in a richly spiced Indian curry; or, if steamed until well softened, chopped with nuts as a vegetable. There are thousands of other ways. Keep trying.

Come to think of it, young spinach and a good dose of Popeye's girl-friend Olive Oil, and you could probably survive most plagues and pestilence. I think I would probably have a cache of black pepper, and some chillies, just to be safe.

♥
## SILVER BEET WITH PEANUT BUTTER

I have no idea what made us attempt this apparently bizarre combination, but it sure as hell works. Clean and cook the silver beet as usual (it works as well with spinach), steaming it in a little, little water. When the silver beet is cooked, work in a little butter, some black pepper, some chopped (hot) chilli and the barest teaspoon of peanut butter. Work it all around, and serve on its own, with some pasta or rice, or smeared on some bread and butter.

♥
## BROCCOLI

Whatever you do, don't pay crazy prices for winter peas and beans; go for broccoli. Buy enough broccoli only for the meal of the day, as it deteriorates very quickly once cut from the plant. Cut the heads into their individual flower pieces, and serve them tossed through pasta, with a small amount of fried bacon. Cook the bacon until crisp in a pan, drain off the fat, and de-glaze with a little cream and white wine. Add extra bacon to provide further bacon flavour to the cream, and season with salt, black pepper and fresh herbs. Toss the pasta through the cream and add the broccoli pieces.

♥
## BROAD BEANS

Don't miss out on broad beans as they ease their way into the market. The gorgeous green-ness of the cooked beans makes for one of the more alluring of vegetables. You can cook them in their inner pods, or squeeze them free, and toss them through a sauce, or pasta, or rice, allowing the heat of the sauce or pasta or rice to warm them through. And when they get old, cook them gently for an hour in some well-flavoured beef or lamb stock, and serve them with the stock as sauce.

♥
## BEER AND RADISH

I have discovered the perfect food combination for cold beer, and it isn't greasy pizza. Try your pre-dinner beer with freshly pulled radish. And if you don't have any fresh radishes then plant some out today, you'll have plenty in a couple of weeks. The rich crunch of radish, followed by its peppery after-palate, makes a wonderful partner for beer. I couldn't believe it the first time. So I tried another beer, and another radish, and did it again, and again. It works.

♥
## LEMONS, LEMONS

A little lemon tip from one of my favourite cooking books, *The Fruit and Nut Book* by Helena Radecka. Ms Radecka explains why all the golden oldies I know reckon a hot lemon drink is the way to go when you're feeling a little off. 'For a sore throat,' she writes, 'squeeze the juice of a lemon, or chop it roughly and simmer it in water for about 20 minutes to make a lemony liquid. When mixed with honey, hot water and whisky or vodka, it makes a soothing toddy that helps fight infection.' Heh, heh, heh.

♥

## AND NOW, SOME RHUBARB

Helen Radecka has written some quite wonderful nonsense about rhubarb too. 'Rhubarb Hair Lightener: simmer 3 tablespoons rhubarb root and 550 ml of water in a stainless steel pan for 30 minutes. Leave to cool and steep for 6–8 hours, then strain. Use as a rinse after shampooing and leave the hair to dry naturally. You could use white wine instead of water which would be more expensive, but also good for the hair.'

I offer that recipe for you without having tested it myself. I have run out of use for such things.

♥

## CHERRIES

This is one of the few fruits which seem to be available only in season. I've never seen them imported from here there and everywhere, and I'm sure we're better for it. The first bite of the first cherry of the season is an absolute joy, year in, year out. But to my surprise, Australia's largest cherry-growing region is Young in central New South Wales. I had always thought the Dandenongs were the only place to go if you wanted a decent cherry, but no. They've been growing in Young for more than 100 years. This is one fruit which

does not need complicated recipes, despite the famous French tart, the clafoutis. Forget all that, just eat 'em, and eat 'em, and eat 'em …

If you want to read a marvellous essay on cherries, have a look at *Jane Grigson's Fruit Book*. 'In the Middle Ages,' she begins, 'and until recently in some parts — the cherry fair was a great festival. People wandered about the orchards; the fruit was picked and sold; there was dancing, drinking and making love …'

♥

## ORANGES IN WINTER

This is how stupid I am. While I was playing football and cricket all those years ago, I could never work out why oranges tasted so wonderful at three-quarter time in June, but so unsatisfying at drinks in January. It never occurred to me that the season for oranges could be winter. How could something so sparkling be around when the weather is so cold?

Here's a recipe for those of us relying only on our memories. When you finally manage to hop out of the cot on a freezing winter morning, put in your old mouth guard before you make it to the kitchen. Slice a navel orange into four, toss it into the dirtiest old ice cream container you can find, and go stand in the middle of the back lawn. Stick the mouth guard into your pyjama pants, and attack the orange quarters with a tough look on your face. As soon as you have taken the last ounce of juice from each quarter, toss them on the ground, run on the spot, and yell to the world: Carn the (Hawks, Dogs, Cats, etc.; fill in whoever you used play for). Dash around the back yard, slide in the mud, and run inside to a cold shower.

## ♥
## TROPICAL PASSIONFRUIT

I had thought it impossible there could be something with more flavour per cubic millimetre than the common, purple-brown, home-grown passionfruit; then I ran into its tropical cousin. I had never seen a passionfruit like it: firm of skin, about twice as large, mottled pale yellow/brown in colour. I sliced it in half, saw the slightly larger seeds, surrounded by slightly brighter pulp, in slightly more juice than you might expect. These are to passionfruit what a Rolls is to a Saab. This fruit had all the tanginess of our better known varieties, but there was more, much more. A final flavour like the perfect fruit punch. I will never forget it

## ♥
## CUSTARD APPLES

These strange, heavy, heart-shaped tropical fruits which arrive in late autumn/early winter are beautifully named: they are laced with natural sugar, and have a texture and look like the best custard. They should be eaten when soft, in the same style as avocados, and are generally sold when firm. Allow them to ripen at room temperature, slice them, and take them straight from the skin, especially for breakfast.

## ♥
## NASHIS

I have been convinced and lost and convinced and lost with this fruit which looks like an apple, and at its best has the texture of an apple, the juice and sugar of a pear, and the surprise of a little passionfruit around the core. At its best, it is brilliant. But no matter how popular nashis become, they are never going to be cheap, and the question you must always ask yourselves when you are handing out several coins for each fruit is: are they better than Jonathans, or William pears? And if the answer is no, then is that enough reason? And is this a question which could decide your philosophy, my philosophy and the good or otherwise of mankind? It may well do.

## ♥
## QUINCE JELLY

I took a long time to fall in love with the jelly which comes from quinces; mainly because I had had so many versions which were intolerably sweet. Then I decided to make some myself. It's much easier than the old cook books say. Wipe the quinces clean, chop them haphazardly, cover them with water, and cook gently, covered, for several hours until the quinces are soft as warm butter. Remove the quinces, measure the remaining liquid, and add half the weight of sugar to the volume of the mix. Put the mixture into the microwave, and cook on high for about 20 minutes, until the mix is bubbling furiously and is well reduced. It should have taken on a brilliant pinkish hue, and set quickly on a cold plate.

♥
## CUMQUAT MARMALADE, A DREAM

Pick up a cumquat. Bite into it. That's it. Now again, with gusto. Bitter? Sour? Both? Think about it for a few minutes. As those original flavours dissipate, what comes through as well. A perfume? An underlying sweetness? What you have done is to work out the sort of flavours you want, and those you don't, when you make the raw fruit into marmalade.

This is the basis of all cooking. Taste it first. Don't just wade blindly through the fog of yet another recipe. Don't believe what you read: try it first and make up your own mind.

Sometimes you get to first base after tasting the end result first, which is what happened to me with cumquats. I had been led to believe that they were just another ornamental citrus, not worth a cracker for anything but making the patio look sharp.

Then I happened across a jar of cumquat marmalade, and now I'm hooked. It's that after-sweetness that does it. And look again at that fruit you have chewed into: note the ultra thin skin, where all the bitter flavours and some of the sweet, are housed; note the thinness of the membrane surrounding the inner segments; note the number of pips in each fruit. This is not likely to be a chunky marmalade, laden with tough membrane — but it is going to take one hell of a time to get rid of all those damned pips.

Once you've picked out those accursed seeds — why have seeds been bred out of certain grapes and mandarins, but not cumquats? — the rest is a cakewalk. Just whizz up your fruit with some sugar, toss the lot into the microwave, and relax.

Don't attempt to make huge quantities. Make a reasonable amount, and do it two or three times through the season. This way, you'll always come back, and not be marmaladed out. The presumption here, of course, is that you don't have a laden tree. If you do, make plenty of jam, and give it away. Or better, make a little, and give the rest of the fruit away in the expectation of some jam in return.

If you don't have a tree, the best way to get some fruit is from a lazy friend who has a prolific tree. Offer to make the jam for a jar. For every two kilos of fruit, offer a jar in return. If your fruiterer hasn't got any, ask him/her to get some from the market. Most fruiterers don't keep cumquats on spec — most prefer to take orders and be sure of selling. If you are picking them yourself, snip them from the tree, stem and all. If you rip them off, they don't keep well at all.

♥    ♥    ♥    ♥    ♥

**1 kg cumquats, the weight after the stems and seeds have been removed**

**750 g sugar**
*Take it as a rule: 75 per cent by weight of sugar to fruit.*

1 Remove any stems from the fruit as you remove the seeds. Do this

job over a bowl to catch all the juice which runs free. Don't worry if you are rough with the fruit. Things will only get rougher. Set aside the seeds. Be patient. Removing the seeds is time-consuming, and tedious. Think of what's to come.

2 Whizz the fruit with half the sugar for about 45 seconds, then mix the whizzed up fruit and sugar with the rest of the sugar.

3 Tie up the seeds in a muslin cloth or clean dish-washing cloth like Chux.

4 Put the lot into an open bowl which can go into the microwave, and start cooking. Set the machine on high and cook the pants out of the fruit. My machine is cheap and nasty (500 watts) and it takes about 50 minutes for this much fruit to reach a nice jammy firmness. When I first made it, I got distracted, of course, and the fruit cooked about 20 minutes longer than it needed. The result was a most pleasant surprise. The eventual marmalade was about as thick as paste, but as spreadable as butter, with a delicious sweet and sour flavour. I liked it better than the result I was aiming for, but please yourself. Cooking jam like this in a microwave is a breeze: no stirring, no dreadful observation, minimal risk of burning. The only negative for the ultra fastidious is that the final product does not shine like those marmalades that are continually watched for any impurities rising to the top. I am prepared to cop that: relaxation is far more important than a shiny jam.

♥
## APRICOT JAM

A pricots make the most glorious jam, but only rarely do they set sufficiently, or last all that long. The microwave fixes that, and eliminates all the agony of stirring and watching and waiting, and getting bored, and seeing all your preparation burnt away.

♥    ♥    ♥    ♥    ♥

1 kg (with seeds removed) of cleaned apricots, preferably those from the early season, with a little acid

750 g caster sugar

1 cup orange juice

1 sharp apple, skinned, cored, and chopped into little pieces, and tossed in a little lemon juice

1 lemon, washed, sliced very finely

a little whisky

1 After removing the seeds, cut most of the apricots into pieces (do this in the food processor), keeping several as halves, and cover the lot with the sugar and orange juice. Mix well with a wooden spoon and add the chopped apple and the sliced lemon.

2 Cook in the microwave for about 50 minutes, depending on its power, until the apricots have softened and the mixture has thickened noticeably and sets on a cold plate. Take a look see every now and then, removing any impurities which have risen to the surface.

3 Ladle the mixture carefully (use a glove to hold the jars) into warm, sterilised jars, filling to just under the brim. Top each jar with a little whisky (optional). Seal immediately. If you're using metal seals, invert until cooled.

♥

## LEMONADE FROM LOADED LEMON TREES

I have a complex about lemons. No matter where I live I am surrounded by lemon trees abundant with fruit, while my feeble, ever optimistic attempts to grow the trees turn into spindly, barren jokes. Every day, summer, winter, spring, I make the long trek to the back of the yard — yes, the tree is facing north — to see if it has grown, or paled. Nothing changes, day in day out. I have even taken to inspections late at night to watch and assist the twinkling of the stars under the lemon tree. Still nothing.

Meanwhile, these superior neighbours, presumably with trees sitting on the same soil, with similar aspects, flaunt their fruit at me.

The funny thing about owners of loaded lemon trees: they moan about as much as I do. It seems they never know what to do with the damned things. It makes you wonder: when it comes to lemons, is anybody happy?

♥ ♥ ♥ ♥ ♥

enough lemons to provide 250 ml of sieved juice
*Depending on size, that should be somewhere between 4 and 6*

zest of 3 large lemons
*Here's a tip: do it with a potato peeler.*

*The zest comes off like a shot, as clean as a whistle.*

250 g white sugar
250 ml water
the tips of fresh peppermint or mint

1 Bring the sugar and water and zest to the boil, stirring until the sugar dissolves. Allow to boil until it starts to roll — about 30 seconds.

2 Leave to cool with the zest, then add the lemon juice, and return to the boil. Add the peppermint and leave to cool. Strain and bottle.

3 Use the cordial sparingly with ice-cold water. Try it with gin. You'll want more.

♥

## RASPBERRY JAM, OR GOOSEBERRY JAM, FROM FRESH OR FROZEN BERRIES

Taking frozen berries for jam displays as sensible a use of the brain as I could imagine. The fruit freezes perfectly, provided you are going to cook it, or use it as a sauce, and with the wonderful microwave, you have a brilliant, shiny jam within an hour — even in the depths of winter, when such things as raspberries are but a dream. Frozen berries are great for sorbets, and terrific for crumbles as well, and give you that lovely sneak preview of summer.

♥ ♥ ♥ ♥ ♥

500 g frozen raspberries or gooseberries, defrosted or not
*Any frozen berries are fine, and of course the same applies to fresh berries. Gooseberries cooked this way make for the most fantastic jam you can imagine.*

350 g caster sugar (400 g for gooseberries)

½ washed lemon, sliced very finely

1 In a large, open bowl, toss the berries with the caster sugar and add the slices of lemon.

2 Cook on high in the microwave for somewhere around half an hour (depending on the power of your machine), removing in 20 minutes or so to remove any impurities which have risen to the surface. The berries will have thickened, reduced in volume, and darkened in colour. The jam should be the right consistency after about 30 minutes.

3 Test on a cold plate to ensure it sets. If it hasn't set, keep cooking. The thing about the microwave is that there is hardly an ounce of danger of the jam burning. It can get too thick, but even that's no disaster. Just keep watching after about 25 minutes until it sets to the test. When done, pour into sterilised jars. This amount of berries should make about half a litre of jam. Once it's cool it should be set well enough to hold its own.

♥

## HOT CHOCOLATE, WITH OR WITHOUT WHISKY

We all know that hot chocolate is a mix of Ovaltine or Milo and boiled milk and sugar, don't we? Such is the way we have developed that the beauties of long ago have been cut about and replaced with packets and pacy preparations.

Look again, and go back to the roots of hot chocolate. Give yourself

a treat, every now and again, or whenever you've got some very special chocolate and some very expensive vanilla beans. Give them a run together.

♥ ♥ ♥ ♥ ♥

3 cups milk

25 g best dark chocolate

2 dessertspoons honey

1 leftover vanilla bean, any seeds scraped into the milk

Heat the milk with the seeds gently on a low heat, add the chocolate and honey until they all meld, and then gradually allow the heat to increase. Whisk furiously if you are doing this on top of the stove, putting as much air as you can into the milk. As the mixture gets close to the boil, remove from the heat, and whisk as if your life depended upon it.

You can save some muscle if you have either a wand-processor of the Bamix style, or a home cappuccino machine.

Hot chocolate has to be fluffy, or it just ain't hot chocolate.

♥

## A CARAMEL AND CALVADOS SAUCE

These unlikely partners came together through not unusual means. I was wiping a plate clean of caramel sauce with one hand, and hanging on to a glass of Calvados with the other. As soon as the two met on the palate, I knew it was the start of something beautiful. Calvados is the subtle flavour of apples in a Normandy fire-water;

and I don't offer that assessment in any critical way. It may be subtle in flavour, once you get through the alcohol, but it has a marvellous ability to add flavour to custards and creams. Not surprisingly, it's a perfect marinade for apples.

♥　♥　♥　♥　♥

2 vanilla beans

100 g caster sugar

½ cup cream

4 egg yolks

1 ½ cups milk

Calvados to taste

*Calvados, the apple brandy from Normandy, is very expensive. So don't go out and buy a bottle just for the sauce — unless you like drinking the stuff, or you intend to make plenty of this sauce. If you taste it once, and can afford it, you'll always have a bottle in the cupboard. Once you've tasted this sauce, you'll keep a bottle just for it.*

1 Split the beans and place in the pot with the sugar, making sure you run the seeds into the sugar. Cook to a caramel over a gentle heat, stirring and working until the required caramel is reached. You can do this in the microwave — it makes for a brilliant, easy caramel.

2 Once you have the caramel, carefully and slowly add the cream, keeping the heat low. Be careful, as it could spurt from the pan. The low heat is necessary or else the cream could set the caramel.

3 Make a custard. Whisk the yolks until white and creamy. Boil the milk and whisk furiously into the creamed yolks.

4 Pour the custard onto the caramel-flavoured cream and cook, stirring in a figure-eight pattern, until the mixture thickens slightly. If you rub your finger along the spoon it should leave a firm line. (The mix should register 85°C on a sugar thermometer.)

5 Pour through a sieve and whisk until the sauce cools. Add Calvados until the taste is in ideal balance. For a half litre of caramel custard you will probably need about 50 ml Calvados. Serve warm or cold.

♥

## RASPBERRY AND MUSCAT SAUCE

This is one of the great dessert sauces, a must with any chocolate, or any ice cream. The muscat must be of the best quality, from north-east Victoria.

♥　♥　♥　♥　♥

500 g raspberries, fresh or frozen

200 ml good quality muscat

*The better the quality, as ever, the better the flavour of the sauce*

50 – 60 g sugar, or to taste

*If the raspberries are very sweet, this amount could be halved.*

Cook gently to soften the raspberries. Add the sugar along with the muscat, and cook until the raspberries soften and separate. The sugar is not to sweeten, but to take away the natural sharpness of the raspberries. Too much sugar makes the sauce go 'jammy'. When cooked, force the sauce through a sieve to eliminate seeds. If the berries are fresh you can leave in the seeds, but if using frozen berries, the seeds must go.

♥

## 'INSTANT' CHILLI SAUCE

This sauce is best when tomatoes are in season, and the best tomatoes for any sauce are the Roma variety. Chop about six tomatoes roughly, and throw them into the microwave. Give the tomatoes a good sprinkle with your best olive oil. When the mix has started to bubble, add a few pinches of salt and a pour of good soy sauce. Slice some onions and toss them in. Chop as many chillies as you fancy. The more chillies you eat, the more you can stand. Add a branch of rosemary. Cook gently over a low heat until the tomatoes have all but disintegrated and the onions have softened. Towards the end of cooking add some slices of ginger. Remove, strain and whizz. This sauce goes particularly well with pork. Use it quickly, or put some in the freezer. You can use it to add flavour to a wimpish soup.

♥

## OLD-FASHIONED TOMATO SAUCE

We probably eat tomato sauce more than anything else in the world; yet so few of us bother to make it ourselves. For something so simple, such lack of interest is remarkable. And now that the microwave is so much part of our lives, you can put it together more quickly, more simply and with just as much flavour.

♥   ♥   ♥   ♥   ♥

**2 large onions, peeled and sliced**

**1 carrot, peeled and chopped roughly**

**200 ml cheap white vinegar**
*The vinegar should be there not for its flavour, but for its preserving qualities.*

**100 g brown sugar**

**2 kg Roma tomatoes, skinned; or the equivalent from a tin**

**1 dessertspoon salt**

**2 dessertspoons black pepper, crushed**

**2 bunches of basil, leaves removed from the stalks**
*Keep the basil in a muslin bag or wrapped in kitchen cloth.*

**a little balsamic vinegar**
*This is definitely optional. I like adding a little to each jar after the cooking, just for fun.*

**3 chillies (optional)**

1 Cook the onions in oil until they have softened. Set aside.

2 Steam the carrots in some water or stock until they give to the knife.

3 Add the cheap vinegar and the sugar to the tomatoes, then the cooked carrots and onions, salt, black pepper and basil.

4 Put the lot into the microwave and cook on high for 20–30 minutes, stirring occasionally. (This can be done on top of the stove; you just need to watch it more closely.) The sauce is done when thick and with all the flavours well blended.

5 Remove the basil and discard. Purée and bottle in sterilised jars, adding a few drops of balsamic vinegar to each jar if you wish.

♥

## SCALLOPS

A little silliness. This comes from one of my absolutely favourite reference books, the *Woman's Mirror Cookbook*, circa 1930. Take in the words, ignore the recipe, and you'll know why some forms of cooking lost their way in the old days.

'Scallops,' it says, 'those bivalves with fan-shaped fluted shells often left lying by fishermen on southern beaches, are well worth cooking. Boil them for a few minutes in seawater [so far so good], then open the shells, pick out all the white meat, place it in a saucepan, with grated potato, milk, butter, and a little dried parsley, and simmer gently for half an hour. [Aaaaaaaaaagh!] A very fine soup results.'

# LISTS

*I love lists — lists of top videos, TV shows,
cricketers, salary earners, etc.; they take me straight
to the heart of the way we live and dream.*

## MY TOP TEN

Here is a list of my favourite dishes from this book. Not necessarily those I cook most — in fact I have this strange need to set aside the things I love, to know they are there and to call on them in times of need — but those dishes which have served me well for a long time, and will continue to do so.

1 The loin of lamb with garlic (see page 135). All the lamb dishes in my life will stand beside this dish in judgement. There is nothing complicated about it, no big deal about its creation — and the power the garlic gives to the lamb makes it forever mouth-watering. It was a constant on the restaurant menu, and it never let us down. Since then, it has never failed me, at any dinner party, no matter what the company.

2 A variation of Fredy Girardet's passionfruit soufflé (see page 214). I first heard of this wonderful dish from Iain Hewitson. Hewitson told me we must take the passionfruit soufflé, no matter what else we had. We did, and we took the feel and flavour home with us, changed the sweetness level, and served it for what seemed forever. There is no better soufflé. Thanks, Fredy.

3 *Osso buco* (see page 147). This was a dish created in an environment of great fun. Sally and I went head to head cooking two versions of this traditional Italian veal dish. In the end, we each declared ourselves winners, and ate more *osso buco* in one week than any other two mortals might in a lifetime. It thus represents a hidden attribute of great cooking: memories.

4 A Kreem-b-tween (see page 185). This dish proves that commercial thinking is just as much a source of pleasure in the kitchen as are more traditional sources. We just took the idea from Peter's, used classic vanilla bean ice cream, and delicious crisp wafers, and served it with lots of tropical fruit in a mango and

passionfruit sauce. During the restaurant days, I probably had one a day — and that for four years.

5 Risotto, any way you like (see page 43). I came to love risotto pretty late in my life, after trying it many times in the restaurant and being discouraged by a lack of interest from the customers. Now it's a certainty, several times a week, in our diet. Delicious, filling, ripping with all sorts of flavours and textures, every bit as good today as tomorrow, racing back through generations, and yet as cheap as dirt.

6 Crab, in the eastern way (see page 58). Another marvellous memory, buoyed in this case by the brilliant texture and flavour of the giant crab. Those of you who know and love Woody Allen's great movie *Annie Hall* as I do, will recall the two great scenes surrounding the crayfish cook-off. In the first case it was fun and games and wonderful love and joy; in the second it all back-fired — no communication, no flippancy, no rule-breaking, no love. Now every time I cook crays or crabs, I think of *Annie Hall*.

7 Scallops in the open shell (see page 91). Scallops are the essence of the sea, rich in saltiness, deep in flavour, marvellous of texture. When you mix all this with a little soy, tomato and chives, you have pure simplicity, but a marvel of flavour.

8 Any perfectly fresh fish, cooked to the second. What you do with it belongs entirely in your imagination. Butter, or olive oil, or cream, or coconut milk, or just lemon juice and black pepper. It's up to you, but I'm starting to love fish with coconut in the Thai style.

9 A simple salad, of mustard cress, watercress, and spinach, with Parmigiano Reggiano, black pepper, virgin olive oil, tiny just-preserved olives and balsamic vinegar. Clean as a whistle, brilliantly flavoured, oily enough to drip down your chin. A tribute to freshness and ingenuity.

10 A wiggly pasta, with a rich, hot, tomato sauce; or a thick, crusty pizza made with your own hands (see page 231). These two are the essence of Italian cooking, I suppose. A thick, rich sauce, clinging to hot shapes of pasta or bread dough. Full of wit, full of flavour, simple, cheap, traditional and — here's the key — always available.

## TWENTY IDEAS FOR PICNICS

1 Chicken breasts, marinated in coconut milk, a little red curry paste, ginger and garlic, cooked, cooled and served in a salad of spinach and sesame seeds.

2 Australian smoked salmon, with creamy goat's cheese, dill, hot mustard cress, olive oil, lime juice and black pepper.

3 Roast some garlic (do this in the microwave for a minute, allow to cool, then peel) and whizz it with some creamy goat's cheese, a pour of virgin olive oil, some fresh herbs and black pepper. Pack it into a ramekin, and serve with crusty French bread, and olives.

4 Lambs' brains, cooked gently, cooled, sliced thinly, marinated

in a little soy, sprinkled with chopped walnuts and served on a slice of sourdough.

5 Guacamole: the wonderful Mexican mix of crushed avocado, cubes of tomato, chilli, onion and coriander.

6 Onion tarts like Fredy Girardet makes. I took this appetiser during my one and only meal there and can still remember it. It's a delicious pastry, covered with some almost-caramelised onions and a good pour of spicy custard, and baked in a slow, slow oven for about 25–30 minutes.

7 Cold goat's cheese and spinach ravioli, impregnated with pesto, and extra Parmesan.

8 A wedge of a young Parmesan, with young spinach leaves, nashis, pears, apples and walnut oil.

9 Young leeks, cooked gently with lamb shanks in a lamb stock and allowed to set into the lamb jelly, served with sandwiches made with meat pulled from the shanks.

10 Finely sliced tuna, cooked gently, allowed to cool, tossed with lemon juice, chilli, virgin olive oil and chervil, served on black pumpernickel with rich butter.

11 Mussels steamed, shelled and crammed into a black casserole dish, mixed with seeded Ligurian olives, chopped tomatoes, basil, chilli and chives.

12 Radishes, pulled fresh from the garden, chomped with bubbly, malty beer.

13 Older, large, end-of-season broad beans slow-cooked with ox tail, sliced potatoes, carrots, parsnips and all the usual slow-cooking suspects. Keep the broad beans in a muslin cloth while cooking, then remove and serve them in the stock. If you take out the ox tail, and remove the meat by hand, it makes for the most stupendous sandwich.

14 A bowl of shredded carrots, mixed with crushed black pepper and hazelnuts, and well-soaked in virgin olive oil.

15 Here's a sandwich for toffs. The breast of turkey or chicken, sliced finely, and placed in a poppy seed bagel on a solid smear of Gippsland Blue cheese (no butter).

16 A bowl of well-marinated, peeled, fresh, seasonal tomatoes. Peel the tomatoes, slice them roughly, and cover them with a good amount of salt, black pepper, virgin olive oil, chives, chunky parsley, sliced olives and a few drops of balsamic vinegar. Allow them to marinate overnight, turning them just before bed and just after rising.

17 Aged Parmesan, broken into walnut-sized chunks, and tossed through a salad of young spinach and watercress, with a good sprinkle of crushed black peppers, a pour of virgin olive oil and a couple of teaspoons of balsamic vinegar.

18 Core some pears, cover them with lemon juice, briefly, and cook in red wine and cinnamon. Serve floating in large bowl on top of crushed ice, skewers on the side to spear the pears.

**19** Pithiviers. This is one of the great French pastries, a puff pastry tart filled with almond meal and pastry cream. Best served just warm, and must be served on the day it is made.

**20** Raspberries, blueberries and blackcurrants are at their best when gently warmed in a little caster sugar until they give their juice to the bowl. If your picnic is at home, pour a little of the juice over some ice cream and return it to the freezer. Serve the berries warm with the ice cream.

## TEN PERFECT PRESENTS

The best gift is something of yourself. So when Christmas comes, or Mother's Day, or a special birthday, roll up your sleeves and make something special. Here's a few ideas:

**1** A jar of pesto, particularly appropriate for Mother's Day. Make sure it's done the old-fashioned way, by hand.

**2** Cumquat marmalade, easy to make in the microwave, if you can get rid of those &*%$#@*! pips. It's old-fashioned, and if it's for your mum, she'll goo.

**3** Muesli. Find a recipe you like, and fill a 5-litre jar with a rib-tickler.

**4** Make a dozen jars of tomato sauce. If you can't get fresh tomatoes, make some with the tinned variety.

**5** Make a jar of baba ghanoush (eggplant dip) and one of hum-mus (chick pea dip) for a real taste of the Middle East.

**6** Make your favourite curry powder or curry paste.

**7** If you are a cooking illiterate, get a cook book; it's not quite the same as making something, but the thought is there. Don't buy any old book —get hold of some of the great influences on cooking:
*Microwave Gourmet* by Barbara Kafka
*On Food and Cooking* by Harold McGee
*Jane Grigson's Fruit Book*
*Jane Grigson's Vegetable Book*
Any of the Time-Life *Good Cook* series of books. If you're a big spender, get the lot.
*The Italian Baker* or *Celebrating Italy* by Carol Field

**8** If he/she can't cook, and wants to, seek out a special cooking school, and enrol him/her. Be delicate with this one.

**9** Get hold of a side of Tasmanian smoked salmon or trout.

**10** Get together a selection of the best Australian cheeses.

## HERBS EVERY HOME GARDEN SHOULD HAVE

**1** Rosemary. You can see the beautifully tender tips of this perennial poking through fences right across town, and the aroma of its oil is wonderful. Add rosemary to any style of sauce you like and you'll be on a winner: with beef stock — 10/10; with lamb stock — 10/10, with cream, 10/10; with a Chinese soy base — 10/10; with butter 10/10. It's always there, but it's at its best in spring.

2 Thyme just won't go away. When the garden is bare, and the cupboard is drab, you've always got thyme. It's particularly wonderful with mushrooms, and also with liver.

3 Oregano is fundamental to all gardens. It's vigorous, loves tomatoes, and is always there when most of them have wimped out. Sprinkle it furiously into any stock, late.

4 Basil for all the reasons everybody in the world with space grows it every spring. Don't be the odd person out.

5 Tarragon is a wonderful perennial. No chicken should be cooked without it; any risotto is enhanced by it; all salads love it. And every year it pops up, when you've forgotten all about it.

6 Parsley is supremely under-rated. Don't chop it, just pick it and use it generously.

## WHAT YOU NEED IN YOUR PANTRY AND YOUR FREEZER

These two places might well be the most important places in your house. Each is the reservoir of special things which can assist any ingredient on its path to heaven. These odds and ends don't have to be expensive, just well thought through.

1 A small jar of the best quality virgin olive oil, for special occa-

sions, supported by a 5-litre tin of not-so-perfect-but-still-pretty-good virgin olive oil. This means you can turn anything new, old, or indifferent into something extra special, in a flash, in a swirl. Like this: toss a clove of garlic into the microwave, cook for a minute, peel, and squash on oiled, crisp toast, and you're in heaven.

2 A bottle of cheapish balsamic vinegar. Combine olive oil with balsamic vinegar, salt, black pepper and any salad green and you're on the path to being a three-star chef. Remember: the oil is for holding the leaves, the vinegar is for a hint of flavour for the middle palate, a sharpener, a surprise. Treat it sparingly and make sure your greens are clean and dry. Balsamic vinegar is the classic vinegar from Modena, made with the same style and dutiful dedication as the best wine. Treat it wisely, gently, and well.

3 Two frozen focaccias, the Italian flat bread, made for ripping apart at table, but perfect for quickly made, extra super duper pizzas. Make sure you have two, so you'll always have one, if you know what I mean.

4 Several tins of tomatoes, making sure they have no added sugar or salt. These are the only tinned products I heartily endorse: they are just like the tomatoes you bottle yourself, without the agony of the labour. To open one in winter is to recall the heights of summer. You don't use them for anything but sauces or flavour enhancers or thickeners for stocks and soups and stews: add to an iffy stew and you've got style; put into the microwave with some chilli

and salt and you've got a pasta meal in a flash; or cook down with some carrots and co., and you're on the way to a special soup

5 Parmigiano Reggiano or Grana Padano; never start the day without checking to see you have some.

6 Pears are always cheap, and, because of the cool-store, always available. Naturally they are best when fresh and tender, but when they are hard and tough they still make for brilliant quick desserts, all year around.

7 Two tins of chick peas, presoaked. Add to a dodgy soup and you've got a surprise, whizz them with tahini and garlic and cumin and lemon juice, and you've got hummus.

8 A packet of cones for that dreadful moment when all inter-familial negotiation fails and the only way you can restore sanity is through bribery — i.e. ice cream.

9 Rice from all over the world: Arborio rice for risotto, Basmati for a taste of India, and Thai fragrant for a fling at the Far East.

10 Twirls of dried pasta, for fun and games with the kids' meals, perfect for the quick tomato sauce above.

11 A couple of jars of tahini — for hummus and baba ghanoush, and as a surprise lifter for a thin soup.

12 A secret cache of black peppercorns, which nobody else but you knows about. I die when we run out of pepper. Only vanilla ice cream can save me. Make sure you have invested in a quality pepper grinder, which really works, and gives you the grind of pepper you want. If your grinder doesn't work efficiently, it can be as infuriating as a car that keeps stalling. Invest a bit, and be content.

13 As many vanilla beans as you can afford. If you buy them in bulk they are usually much fresher and sweeter, tight packaging keeping all of them moist. They are expensive, but no dessert I know is not improved by the addition of vanilla beans. Once they have been used they should be wiped clean, chopped into little pieces and put in a jar of sugar. The leftover bean(s) will flavour the sugar. Make sure, when you buy, that they are moist and supple.

14 A vat of gluten-enriched flour and plenty of dried yeast. There is nothing in the world like home-made bread, and no cook is a cook unless he/she makes his/her own as often as time permits.

15 Brown sugar, caster sugar, plain flour, baking powder, and all such things required to make muffins, scones and cakes; and whenever you go to an oriental grocer, be sure to come away with a packet of a different spice, always in seeds, never ground. You never know when you'll need one or t'other.

# INFLUENCES

These are the books I have perused over many years, for inspiration, motivation, or pure joy. When you start cooking as a kitchen illiterate, you need all the props you can find. I found mine in the works of all sorts of cooks: from marvellous professionals, geniuses even, through to mere hard workers, compilers of tradition and detail. Those here are not listed in any particular order.

**The Great Chefs of France**, *Anthony Blake, Quentin Crewe* (Artists House/Mitchell Beazley)
This book hit me between the eyes with the power of a sledge-hammer, its marvellous journalism allowing for a rare insight into the way great kitchens operate.

**Cuisine Spontanée, The Cuisine of Fredy Girardet**, *Fredy Girardet* (William Morrow)
We went to Girardet's place just outside Lausanne in Switzerland and discovered all the PR was right: this is one of the greatest restaurants in the whole world. I loved it because the chef was a man of the people, willing to converse in detail, to admit 'possible' error, to be generous, and loyal to his customers. After lunch there, I told him I thought one of his dishes was overcooked, and he zoomed to the kitchen to provide a personally cooked replacement. He then not only signed my French copy of this book, but gave me the English translation. The two signed copies sit proudly at the top of my collection.

**Lenôtre's Ice Creams and Candies, and Lenôtre's Desserts and Pastries**, *Gaston Lenôtre* (Flammarion, Barron's)
These were the books that developed my love for desserts, that taught me some of the detail, that showed me the way to display and organise recipes.

**Roger Vergé's Cuisine of the Sun**, *Roger Vergé* (Robert Laffont, Papermac)
Vergé was one of the heroes of the new way of cooking. The simplicity of his book is marvellous, holding dearly as it does the traditions of the home and the hearth. Much later, I had the misfortune to write a scathing attack on a Vergé meal during a promotional visit by him to Melbourne. I met him and put my concern to him. It was one of my bravest moments in journalism. He was charming.

**Michel Guérard's Cuisine Gourmande**, *Michel Guérard* (Robert Laffont, Papermac)
For Vergé, read Guérard. Guérard's book has the most wonderful explanation of the background and basics of cooking: stocks, roasting, sauces and the like. I'd like to read it weekly.

**Chef Paul Prudhomme's Louisiana Kitchen,** *Paul Prudhomme* (William Morrow)
We pinched Prudhomme's signature dish, the blackened spice mix, and made it a restaurant constant.

**The Food Lover's Guide to Paris** (and the follow-up, **The Food Lover's Guide to France**), *Patricia Wells* (Methuen, Workman)
Wells is something of an oddity — a female, and a foreigner, writing about food and restaurants for a Paris newspaper. No wonder they took her on with such gusto. I can't afford France these days, but a few hours with these books are next best.

**The French Kitchen,** *Di Holuigue* (Methuen)
This is where all cooking started for me. We went along when we decided to start a restaurant, having no previous experience, or, in my case, knowledge of food or cooking. The restaurant idea came after a flamboyant trip to France, an eating extravaganza, a marvellous time of bright-eyed love. We came back sure we could do anything, as long as it was together. A restaurant seemed the obvious choice. What we learnt during a brief session at the French Kitchen was not so much a technical appreciation of cooking, but an understanding that organisation and coolness have more to do with good cooking than just about anything else.

**New Classic Cuisine,** *The Roux Brothers* (Macdonald)
I flicked through this book thousands of times during our restaurant days, picking an idea here, taking in a technique there, re-interpreting, pinching. This is one of the most careful, most detailed, most professional cook books there is. Entirely relevant then, remaining so today.

**Microwave Gourmet,** *Barbara Kafka* (William Morrow)
The microwave meant nothing to me until I picked up this book. Suddenly we had a truly professional, comprehensive assessment of the microwave. Kafka went into it with an extraordinary amount of detail and perserverence, opening floodgates for me and millions of others. All at once, the microwave was another hand in the kitchen, something to work miracles.

**The Chez Panisse Menu Cookbook** (and other books emanating from this famous restaurant of California), *Alice Waters* (Random House)
I reckon every professional cook in Australia had a copy of this book when it arrived in the early eighties. It offers an intense appraisal of food at its simplest level, and an insight into the complexity involved in running one of the great restaurants of the United States.

**The Simple Art of Perfect Baking,** *Flo Braker* (William Morrow)
This book examines baking from all conceivable angles, suggesting a person of all-consuming passion. For some reason, it has never been available in Australia. Lord knows why.

**The Taste of France,** *Robert Freson* (Webb & Bower, Exeter)
This was/is a constant source of inspiration, not so much for recipes, but for faces. Take up this book and look at the faces of the people of France, the people who cook as though their lives depend upon it; and they do, of course. This is a book which draws on the tradition of fine cooking through generations.

**The Foods of Italy,** *Guilano Bugialli* (Stewart, Taboori and Chang)
Bugialli is a passionate proponent of the Italian way with cooking, and this book puts flesh and bones on to that passion.

**The Good Cook,** (Time-Life Books) edited by *Richard Olney*
There are more than twenty of these, twenty books which started on stream in the late seventies and are still dribbling into the market. I cannot look at these without shaking my head in wonder at

them — the concept development, the photography, the simplicity of instruction, the flawlessness of the detail. These are the ultimate in home education, still unbeaten; perhaps unbeatable.

**The Italian Baker, and Celebrating Italy,** Carol Field (William Morrow)
The first book is all any baker would need, forever; and the second may well be one of the great 'travel' books I have read, given that travel writing should be, must be, the incorporation of culture into words. Praise be to Ms Field.

**La Cuisine Italienne Réinventée,** Gualtiero Marchesi (Robert Laffont)
Marchesi is the man who reached the top of the Michelin Guide re-interpreting Italian cooking. The traditionalists have been inclined to scorn the philosophy, but I'm one who loves the concept of enhancing traditional cooking through new thinking and detail and presentation. I can't wait to hoe into Marchesi's food, in situ.

**Japanese Cooking: A Simple Art,** Shizuo Tsuji (Kondasha International)
Japanese cooking is about the exultation of the ingredients, and few books exult on that basis as well as this work. It examines scrupulously and heartily the background and layered detail of the cuisine of this great nation.

**Stephanie's Menus for Food Lovers,** Stephanie Alexander (Methuen Haynes)
Cooking is Stephanie Alexander's art and passion and love. Her writings on food have been inspirational to me over a long period — her essential Australianism rushes through; her joy in her country is plain for all to see. May she live forever.

**Jane Grigson's Fruit Book** (and **Jane Grigson's Vegetable Book**), Jane Grigson (Michael Joseph, Penguin).
The joy of food and writing is most evident in these superb collections of historical detail, anecdote and recipe. If there is anything you wish to know about any fruit or vegetable, these are the books you turn to.

**Mastering the Art of French Cooking** (volumes 1 and 2), Simone Beck, Louisette Bertholle, Julia Child (Penguin)
The incredible thing about the first volume is that it was written in 1961. It was fifty years ahead of its time, so if you, like me, have a well-worn, stained copy, with pages starting to yellow — it's still got twenty years in the tank. This was the book I went to the first time I attempted to cook for show, and tried on the beef Wellington. I had no idea what I was doing, but it worked perfectly. To this day there has not been a book with better detail in the writing of the recipes.

**Beard on Food,** James Beard (Alfred Knopf)
This is my greatest bargain. I picked it up at a library disposal sale for 20 cents. It is an ideal reference book, written by a man who has influenced generations of cooks. When you want to know something, you go to the index and hope that Beard has written about it. Chances are he has.

**On Fasting and Feasting,** Alan Davidson (Macdonald Orbis)
Towards the end of 1990, I was starting to wonder whether my slightly left of centre, intensely personal, and passionate style of food writing was the way to go. Then I read this book, a collection of writings from all over the world, from all over time, and I was reassured.

**Marcella's Kitchen,** Marcella Hazan (Macmillan)
This is a wonderful appraisal of Italian cooking from its best source, the home and the hearth. Hazan puts down recipes that take you from the toe to the top of Italy, drinking in its smells and style. All with no apologies or compromise.

**White Heat,** Marco Pierre White (Pyramid)
All young chefs in the world love this book, because it helps them to challenge authority and the old ways.

**La Varenne Cooking Course,** *Anne Willan* (William Morrow)
I paid a fortune for this back in 1982. I remember as if it were yesterday: $48. Years later, I saw it in a remainder shop for $12. I nearly bought the lot to save the author from the ignominy of an appearance in that deathly environment. This is a wonderful work, taking a technical, yet friendly look at all aspects of cooking. It does what all classic books should do: it demystifies, then motivates.

**The Fruit and Nut Book,** *Helen Radecka* (Sphere)
A lovely book, filled to the brim with great recipes, marvellous information and some terrific (nonsenical) home remedies which have been tried with all sorts of fruit in all sorts of times and cultures. I love the rhubarb hair lightener, the pear hand or foot bath, and plenty more.

**The Food of Italy,** *Waverley Root* (Vintage)
Want to know anything about anything to do with food in Italy? This is your book. I can't imagine the research which went into this massive tome.

**The Woman's Mirror Cookbook** (The *Bulletin*)
This book keeps me well in touch with the roots and traditions of Australian cooking. It is a collection of recipes published in this indubitably useful journal for women, circa 1930. This is one of those books which you pick up in op shops, hoping that something will jump from its pages. This one achieved that and more. It's even better than a pristine original, coming as it does with pen and ink notes scribbled here and there by the original owner.

**On Food and Cooking,** *Harold McGee* (Scribners)
The more you cook, the more you wonder why. Harold McGee provides the answers to all the questions you have ever posed. What's happening when yeast and water and flour get together? Why does meat become more tender when allowed to age? What holds sauces together? How seeds germinate ...

**Desserts,** *Christian Teubner, Sybil Grafin Schonfeldt* (Rigby)
A grand assault on grand desserts. Every professional cook has a well-worked copy of this book, not so much for the recipes, but for the marvellous examples of presentation, taken from great restaurants across the globe.

**Eating Well** is a cooking magazine from the United States which has been published specifically for me. It's a mag which lets you know well and good that a sensible, balanced diet is vital for a long, happy life. That's the bad news; the good news is that it does it with wonderful common sense, providing food with all the flavour of 'bad' food, with all the sense of an intelligent diet. It's worth getting hold of. It's published by Telemedia Eating Well Inc. If you want to phone about subscriptions, call US(800) 344–3350. Subscriptions are $US30, and inquiries should be directed to *Eating Well*, Ferry Road, Charlotte, VT 05445.

# INDEX

# Index